3—

TO THE CAFETERIA...
FOR JUSTICE!

A COLLECTION OF THE PS238 COMIC BOOK, VOLUME II • ISSUES #6 THROUGH #10
BY AARON WILLIAMS

PUBLISHED BY HENCHMAN PUBLISHING,
DISTRIBUTED BY DORK STORM PRESS

E-mail: aaron@ps238.com
Marketing & Advertising: sales@dorkstorm.com

HENCHMAN
PUBLISHING

PRINTED IN CHINA • FIRST PRINTING, APRIL 2005 • ISBN 1-933288-10-8

INTRODUCTION

by Scott Kurtz

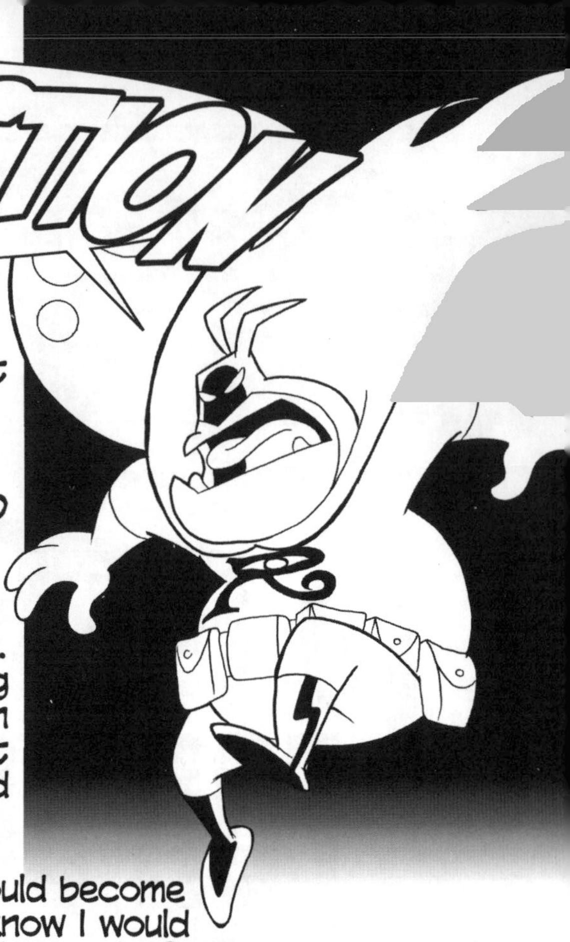

I want to talk to you a little bit about Aaron Williams. Mostly because Aaron refuses to talk about himself and, as a fan of his work, you deserve to know him better.

I met Aaron in October of 2000 in a restaurant in St. Louis. Over lunch we plotted out my joining Dork Storm Press; a company which Aaron (at the time) was part owner. He spent the meeting quietly taking notes on an outdated Apple Newton which, he proudly pointed out, cost him MUCH less than a new PDA and worked JUST as well.

I didn't know then that Aaron would become one of my closest friends. I didn't know I would visit his home, take bets on when he would finally propose to his girlfriend, attend his wedding, share his hardships, seek his council, collaborate on projects, drive eight and a half hours just to visit him and feel a genuine sadness whenever it was time to leave.

Aaron spends every waking hour working on his comic books. When he's not working on HIS comic books, he's working on OTHER people's comic books. If you have laughed out loud at my work, then there's a good chance that Aaron had a hand in writing it. He's the perfect soundboard. You send an idea at him and it returns to you funnier. Aaron is happy to do it and although he's probably not happy remaining uncredited, he does so quietly.

Aaron's studio is a collection of items he bought at either a comic book shop, a gaming con or an estate sale in the Kansas City area. It's cozy, cluttered, and filled with the sound of whirring computer fans and national public radio. It has a wall papered with old CD boxes (remember those?), a stuffed dragon hanging from the ceiling by fishing line and a fish aquarium, full of bubbling water, but no fish. The hardwood floor creaks as you walk across it towards one of the most comfortable office chairs I've ever had the pleasure of sinking my rear into. Aaron's working environment is just like his work; warm and inviting.

Aaron loves to talk and he never stops. He can not answer a question without making a joke, which doesn't go over well when you're really serious about getting the answer. He clearly doesn't feel comfortable around kids or small animals, but I've never seen him be anything but great with both.

The most honorable thing about Aaron is also the most frustrating: he refuses to promote himself. In both personal and professional circles, Aaron is happy to let others do the talking and he avoids the spotlight if he can. He never seems comfortable to hear a compliment and he's always shocked to have received it. His self-deprecating humor is something I discourage because I know Aaron to be brilliant and I wish he would demand that the world take notice. If only he would, I believe the world WOULD take notice. But Aaron, despite not being content with his current level of success, just can't bring himself to say anything positive about his own work.

You can imagine what a foreign concept that is for me, a man with an ego so big, it has its own zip code. I can't imagine passing up an opportunity to toot my own horn. But that's Aaron and, ultimately, I guess that's why we love him so much.

PS238 began after we encouraged Aaron to double his workload and self-publish a SECOND bimonthly comic book that had a more mainstream appeal. His existing comic book, fit tightly into a niche audience and we all wanted Aaron to have a second avenue to take advantage of.

The concept of PS238 is so simple and pure that it's amazing nobody thought of it sooner. It's an idea so good that Disney has stolen it twice. Not even the Mouse will be able to replicate what Aaron has done with this concept and these characters.

The book you hold in your hands is the second what I'm sure will be many volumes of PS238. I thank you for buying it and I guarantee that when you finish, there will be a quiet smile on your face.

If you really want to support Aaron, and repay him for his work, take this book and give it to a friend when you finish it. Then go out and buy yourself another copy for your shelf.

Your friend will thank you for it... and so will I.

Scott R. Kurtz
Little Elm, TX
March 2005

When not writing introductions to comic collections, Scott Kurtz draws the world-famous and amazingly funny comic strip, "PvP!" You can read it in Scott's monthly Image comic as well as at his website, www.pvponline.com. He lives in Texas with his lovely wife Angie, his cats Tiffany and Scratch, and his Basset Hound, Kirby. Together, they fight crime...

School lunches stick to the wall.

Patrick, age 10

It makes my mommy happy if I keep my mouth closed when I chew my sandwich.

Preston, age 4

I've learned that goldfish don't like Jell-O.

Julie Ann, age 9

Quotes excerpted from "Wit & Wisdom" by H. Jackson Brown, Jr.

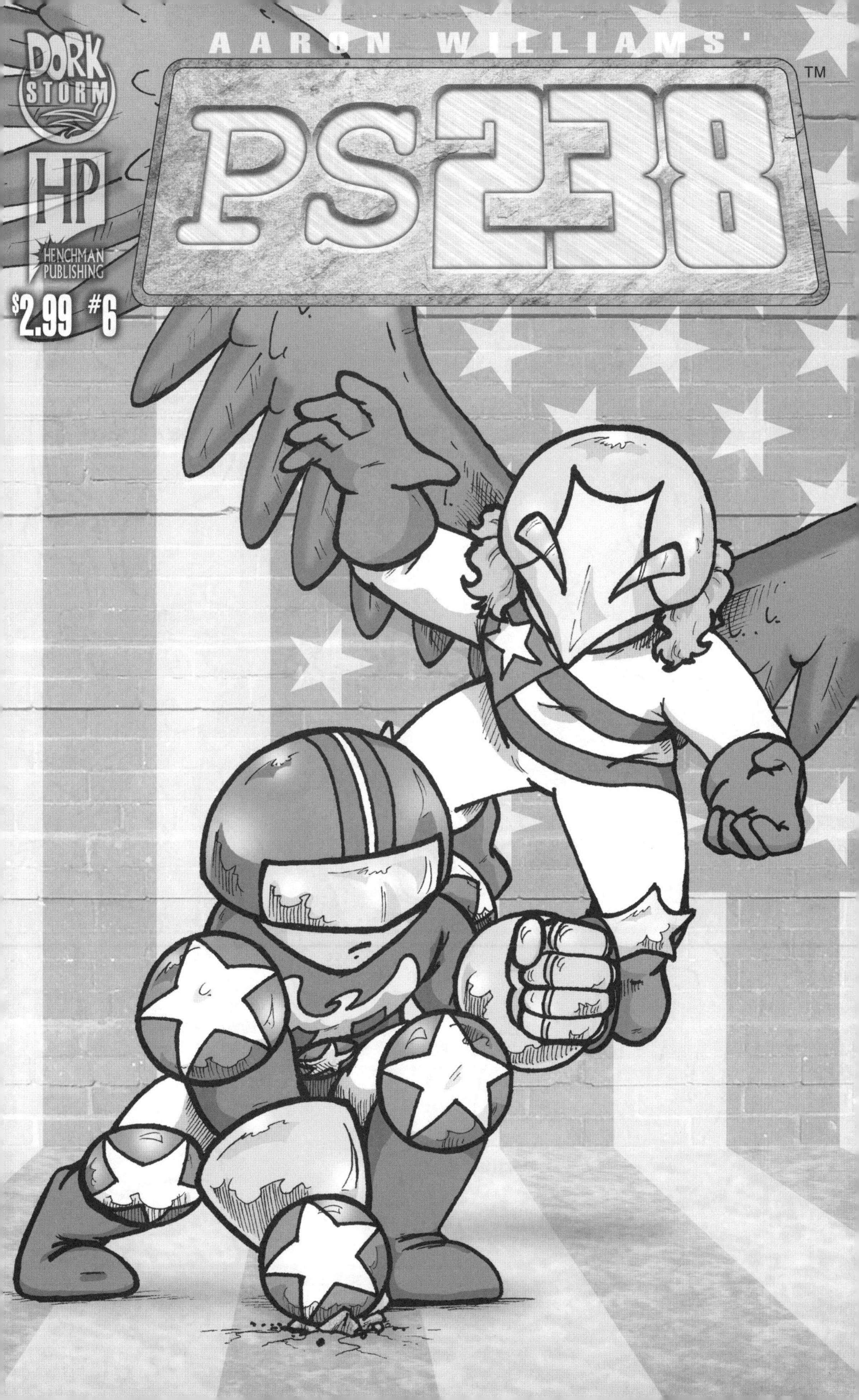
DORK STORM
AARON WILLIAMS'
PS238
TM
HP
HENCHMAN PUBLISHING
$2.99 #6

PS238 #6 by Aaron Williams, March 2004. Distributed by Dork Storm Press, published by Henchman Publishing, 5545 Holmes St, Kansas City, MO 64110. Fax: (608)255-1342. E-mail: aaron@ps238.com. Story and art ©2004 Aaron Williams. "The Revenant" is ©2004 Michael Stackpole. All rights reserved. No portion of this publication save for brief review excerpts may be reproduced without the express consent of the copyright holder. This is a work of fiction: any similarities to any actual persons or metahumans save for the purpose of satire is purely coincidental. ADVERTISING: sales@DorkStorm.com. SUBSCRIPTIONS: $26 per year. Please contact adventureretail2@qwest.net, or call (651)-488-2433 details. All letters to PS238 assumed intended for publication unless otherwise stated, and become the property of the copyright holder. *Democracy: It's your vote that counts. Feudalism: It's your Count that votes.* FIRST PRINTING, December 2004. PRINTED IN CANADA

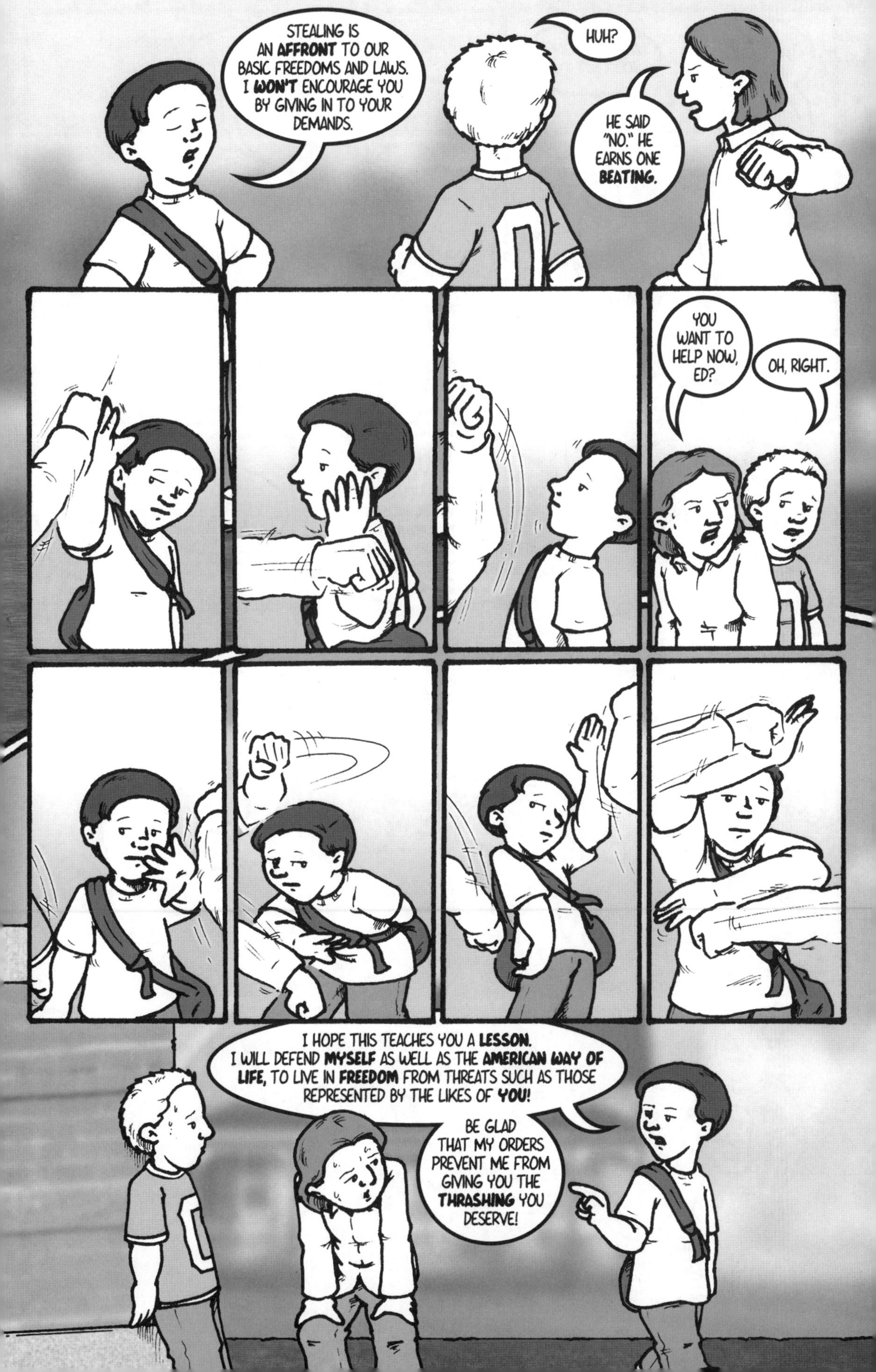
STEALING IS AN **AFFRONT** TO OUR BASIC FREEDOMS AND LAWS. I **WON'T** ENCOURAGE YOU BY GIVING IN TO YOUR DEMANDS.
HUH?
HE SAID "NO." HE EARNS ONE **BEATING.**
YOU WANT TO HELP NOW, ED?
OH, RIGHT.
I HOPE THIS TEACHES YOU A **LESSON.** I WILL DEFEND **MYSELF** AS WELL AS THE **AMERICAN WAY OF LIFE,** TO LIVE IN **FREEDOM** FROM THREATS SUCH AS THOSE REPRESENTED BY THE LIKES OF **YOU!**
BE GLAD THAT MY ORDERS PREVENT ME FROM GIVING YOU THE **THRASHING** YOU DESERVE!

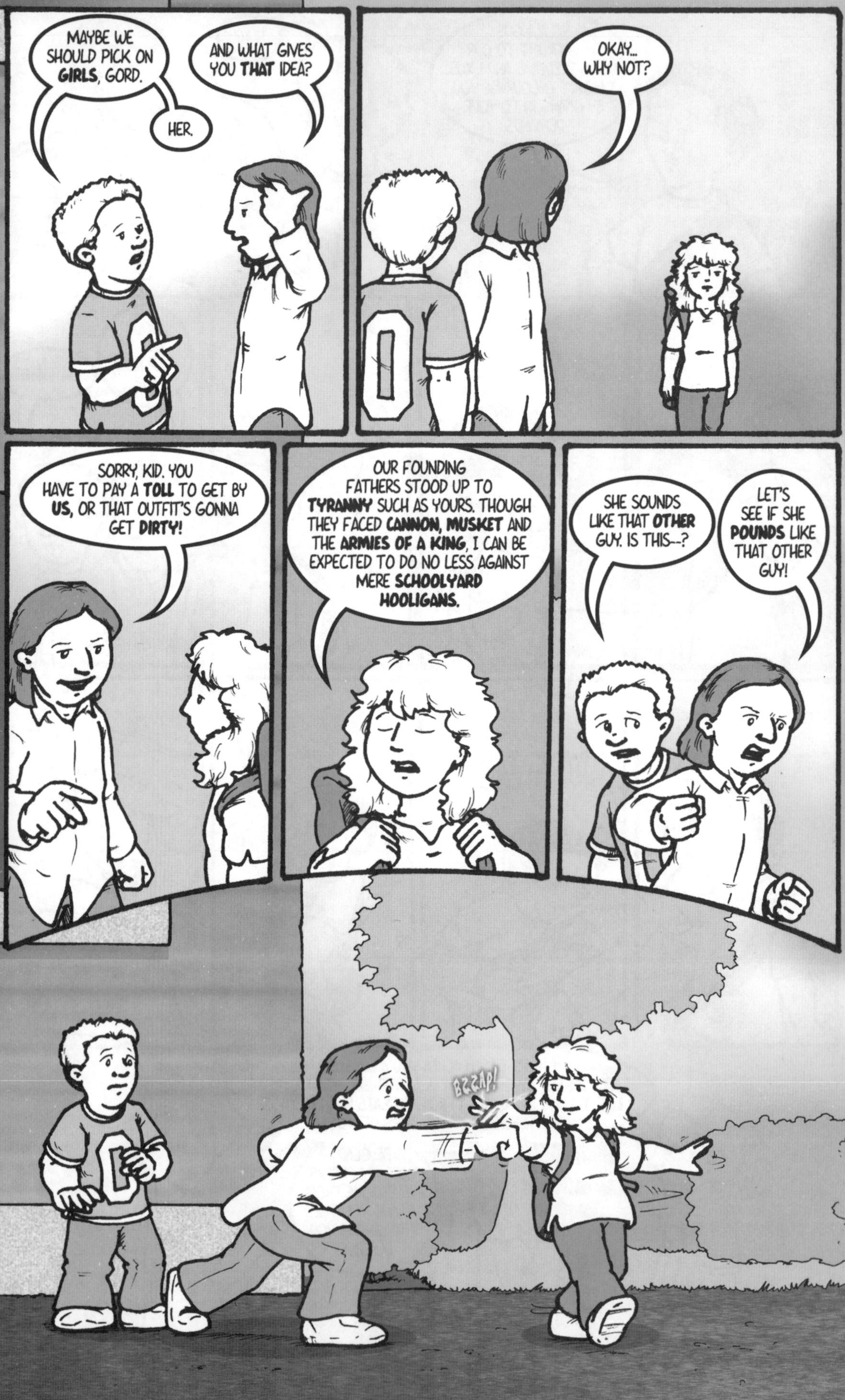
MAYBE WE SHOULD PICK ON GIRLS, GORD.
AND WHAT GIVES YOU THAT IDEA?
HER.
OKAY... WHY NOT?
SORRY, KID. YOU HAVE TO PAY A TOLL TO GET BY US, OR THAT OUTFIT'S GONNA GET DIRTY!
OUR FOUNDING FATHERS STOOD UP TO TYRANNY SUCH AS YOURS. THOUGH THEY FACED CANNON, MUSKET AND THE ARMIES OF A KING, I CAN BE EXPECTED TO DO NO LESS AGAINST MERE SCHOOLYARD HOOLIGANS.
SHE SOUNDS LIKE THAT OTHER GUY. IS THIS--?
LET'S SEE IF SHE POUNDS LIKE THAT OTHER GUY!
BZZAP!

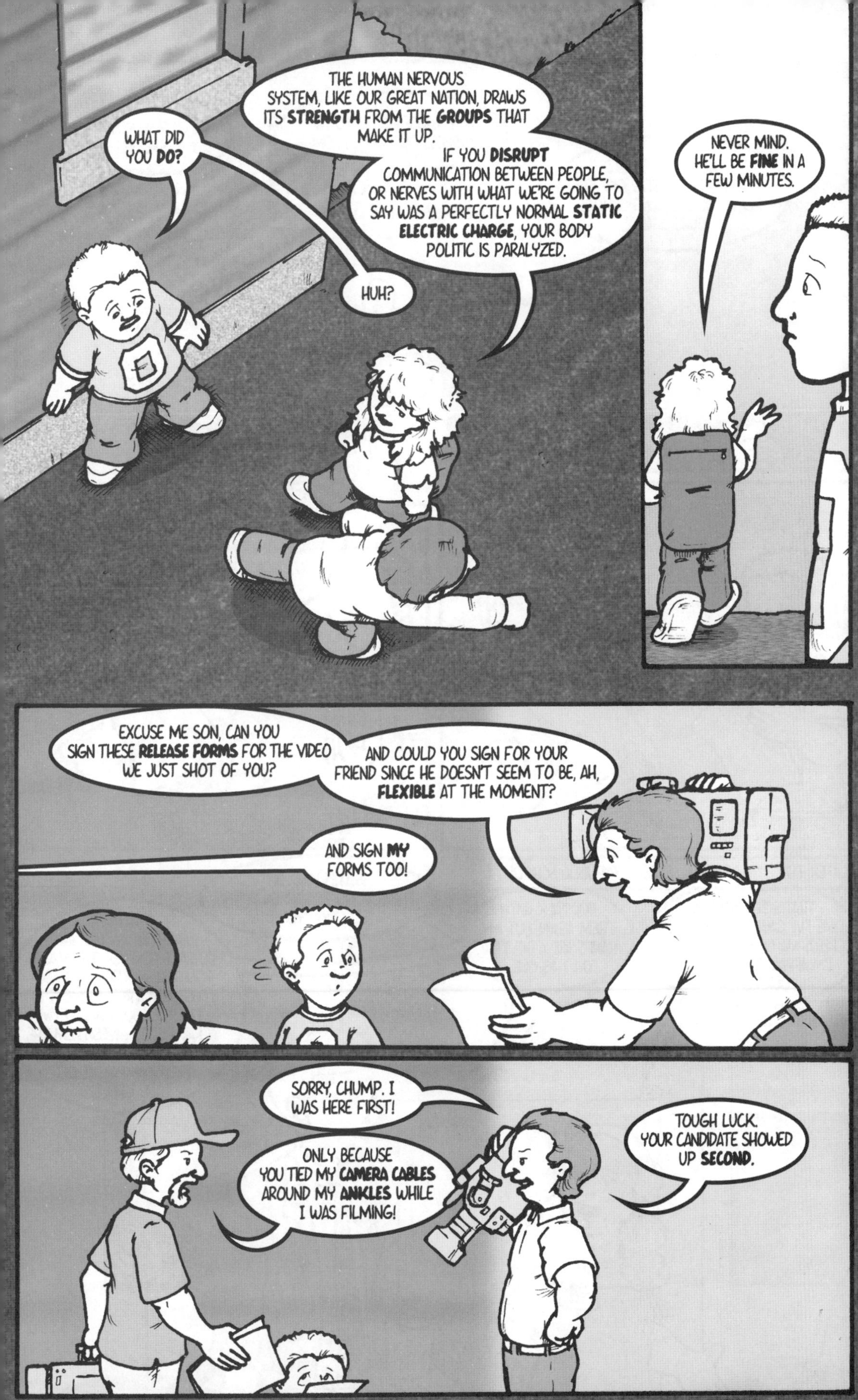

WHAT DID YOU DO?
THE HUMAN NERVOUS SYSTEM, LIKE OUR GREAT NATION, DRAWS ITS STRENGTH FROM THE GROUPS THAT MAKE IT UP.
IF YOU DISRUPT COMMUNICATION BETWEEN PEOPLE, OR NERVES WITH WHAT WE'RE GOING TO SAY WAS A PERFECTLY NORMAL STATIC ELECTRIC CHARGE, YOUR BODY POLITIC IS PARALYZED.
HUH?
NEVER MIND. HE'LL BE FINE IN A FEW MINUTES.
EXCUSE ME SON, CAN YOU SIGN THESE RELEASE FORMS FOR THE VIDEO WE JUST SHOT OF YOU?
AND COULD YOU SIGN FOR YOUR FRIEND SINCE HE DOESN'T SEEM TO BE, AH, FLEXIBLE AT THE MOMENT?
AND SIGN MY FORMS TOO!
SORRY, CHUMP. I WAS HERE FIRST!
ONLY BECAUSE YOU TIED MY CAMERA CABLES AROUND MY ANKLES WHILE I WAS FILMING!
TOUGH LUCK. YOUR CANDIDATE SHOWED UP SECOND.

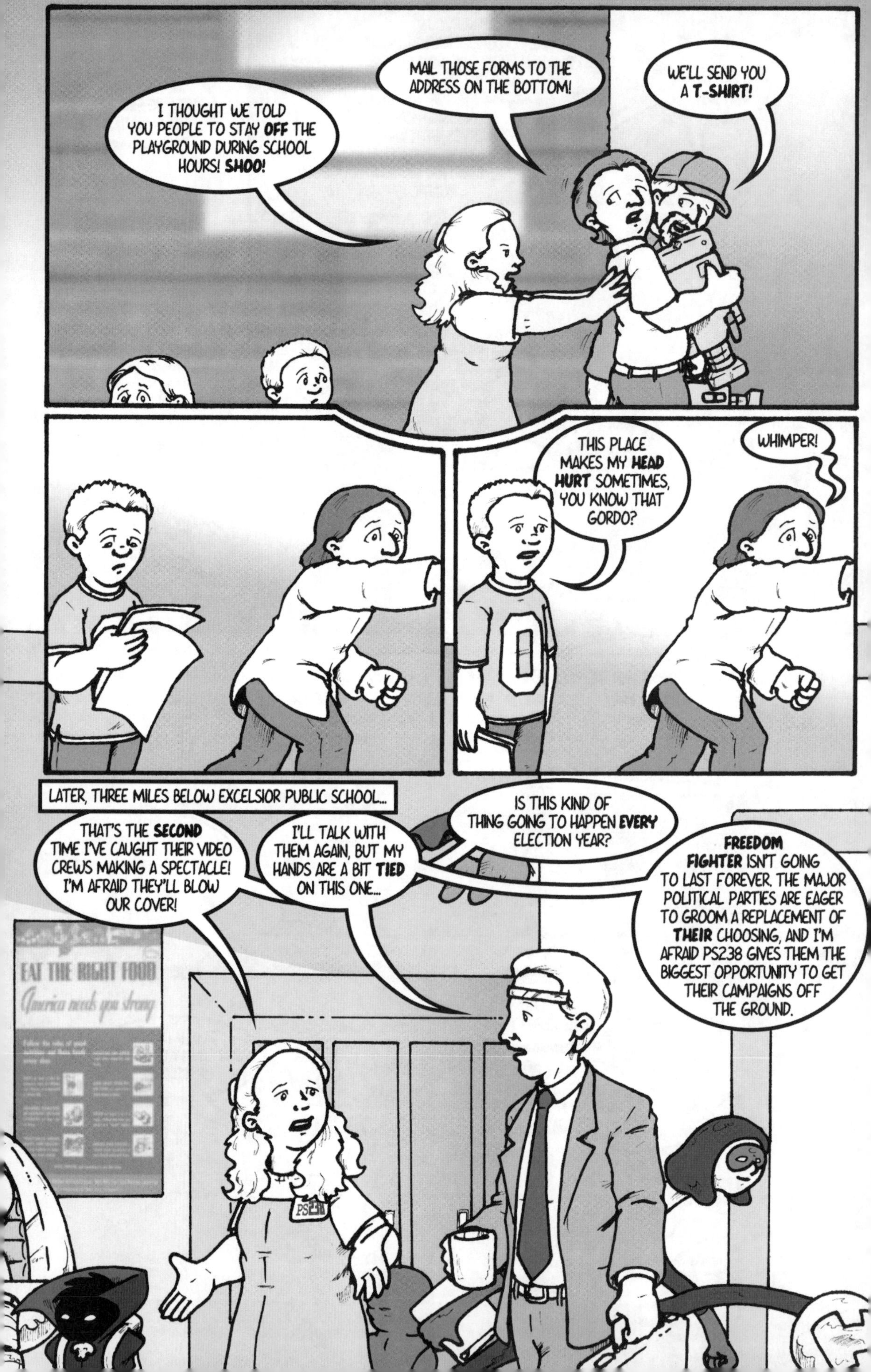
I THOUGHT WE TOLD YOU PEOPLE TO STAY **OFF** THE PLAYGROUND DURING SCHOOL HOURS! **SHOO!**
MAIL THOSE FORMS TO THE ADDRESS ON THE BOTTOM!
WE'LL SEND YOU A **T-SHIRT!**
THIS PLACE MAKES MY **HEAD HURT** SOMETIMES, YOU KNOW THAT GORDO?
WHIMPER!
LATER, THREE MILES BELOW EXCELSIOR PUBLIC SCHOOL...
THAT'S THE **SECOND** TIME I'VE CAUGHT THEIR VIDEO CREWS MAKING A SPECTACLE! I'M AFRAID THEY'LL BLOW OUR COVER!
I'LL TALK WITH THEM AGAIN, BUT MY HANDS ARE A BIT **TIED** ON THIS ONE...
IS THIS KIND OF THING GOING TO HAPPEN **EVERY** ELECTION YEAR?
FREEDOM FIGHTER ISN'T GOING TO LAST FOREVER. THE MAJOR POLITICAL PARTIES ARE EAGER TO GROOM A REPLACEMENT OF **THEIR** CHOOSING, AND I'M AFRAID PS238 GIVES THEM THE BIGGEST OPPORTUNITY TO GET THEIR CAMPAIGNS OFF THE GROUND.
EAT THE RIGHT FOOD
America needs you strong
PS238

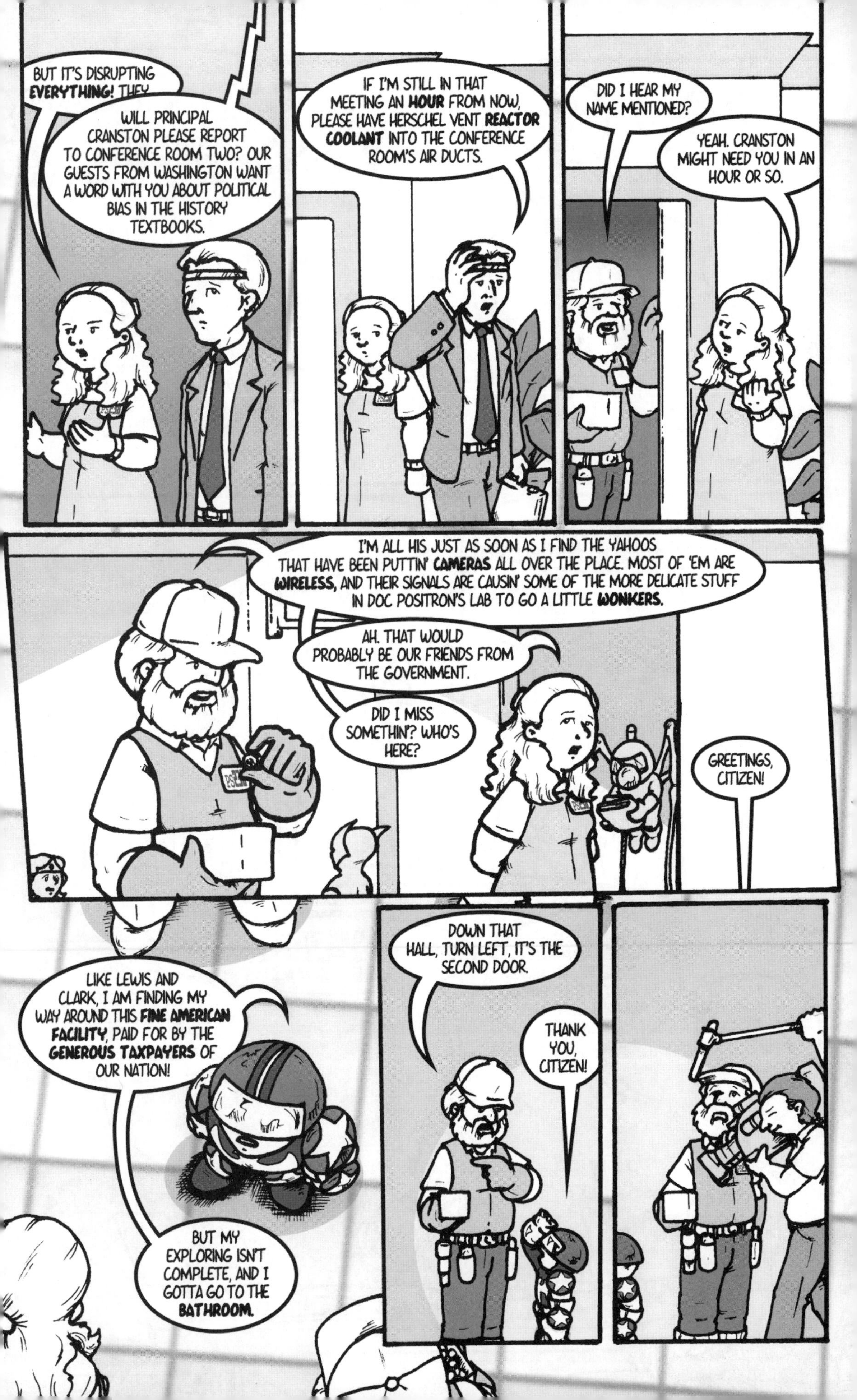
BUT IT'S DISRUPTING **EVERYTHING!** THEY
WILL PRINCIPAL CRANSTON PLEASE REPORT TO CONFERENCE ROOM TWO? OUR GUESTS FROM WASHINGTON WANT A WORD WITH YOU ABOUT POLITICAL BIAS IN THE HISTORY TEXTBOOKS.
IF I'M STILL IN THAT MEETING AN **HOUR** FROM NOW, PLEASE HAVE HERSCHEL VENT **REACTOR COOLANT** INTO THE CONFERENCE ROOM'S AIR DUCTS.
DID I HEAR MY NAME MENTIONED?
YEAH. CRANSTON MIGHT NEED YOU IN AN HOUR OR SO.
I'M ALL HIS JUST AS SOON AS I FIND THE YAHOOS THAT HAVE BEEN PUTTIN' **CAMERAS** ALL OVER THE PLACE. MOST OF 'EM ARE **WIRELESS,** AND THEIR SIGNALS ARE CAUSIN' SOME OF THE MORE DELICATE STUFF IN DOC POSITRON'S LAB TO GO A LITTLE **WONKERS.**
AH. THAT WOULD PROBABLY BE OUR FRIENDS FROM THE GOVERNMENT.
DID I MISS SOMETHIN'? WHO'S HERE?
GREETINGS, CITIZEN!
LIKE LEWIS AND CLARK, I AM FINDING MY WAY AROUND THIS **FINE AMERICAN FACILITY**, PAID FOR BY THE **GENEROUS TAXPAYERS** OF OUR NATION!
BUT MY EXPLORING ISN'T COMPLETE, AND I GOTTA GO TO THE **BATHROOM.**
DOWN THAT HALL, TURN LEFT, IT'S THE SECOND DOOR.
THANK YOU, CITIZEN!

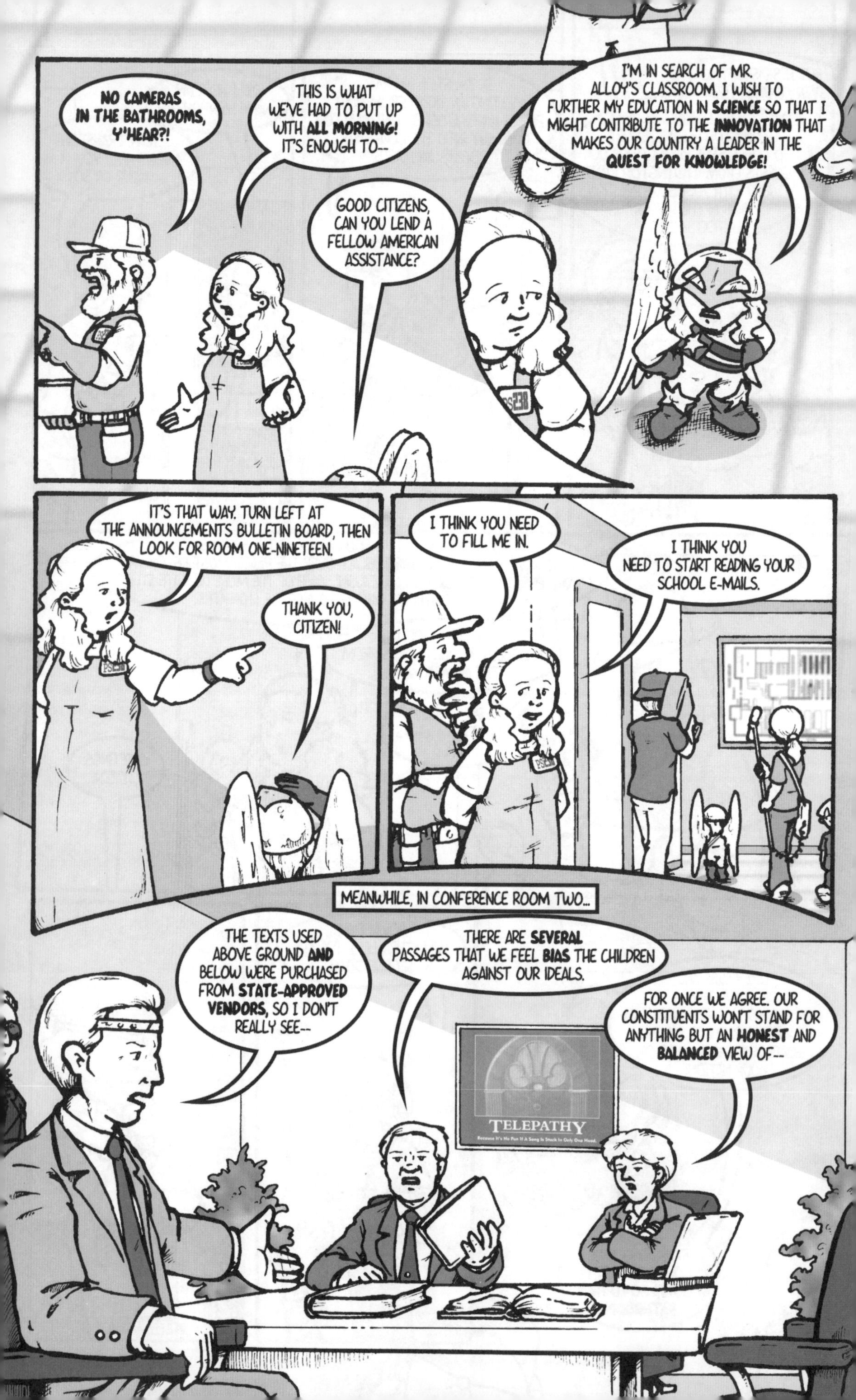
NO CAMERAS IN THE BATHROOMS, Y'HEAR?!
THIS IS WHAT WE'VE HAD TO PUT UP WITH ALL MORNING! IT'S ENOUGH TO--
GOOD CITIZENS, CAN YOU LEND A FELLOW AMERICAN ASSISTANCE?
I'M IN SEARCH OF MR. ALLOY'S CLASSROOM. I WISH TO FURTHER MY EDUCATION IN SCIENCE SO THAT I MIGHT CONTRIBUTE TO THE INNOVATION THAT MAKES OUR COUNTRY A LEADER IN THE QUEST FOR KNOWLEDGE!
IT'S THAT WAY. TURN LEFT AT THE ANNOUNCEMENTS BULLETIN BOARD, THEN LOOK FOR ROOM ONE-NINETEEN.
THANK YOU, CITIZEN!
I THINK YOU NEED TO FILL ME IN.
I THINK YOU NEED TO START READING YOUR SCHOOL E-MAILS.
MEANWHILE, IN CONFERENCE ROOM TWO...
THE TEXTS USED ABOVE GROUND AND BELOW WERE PURCHASED FROM STATE-APPROVED VENDORS, SO I DON'T REALLY SEE--
THERE ARE SEVERAL PASSAGES THAT WE FEEL BIAS THE CHILDREN AGAINST OUR IDEALS.
FOR ONCE WE AGREE. OUR CONSTITUENTS WON'T STAND FOR ANYTHING BUT AN HONEST AND BALANCED VIEW OF--
TELEPATHY

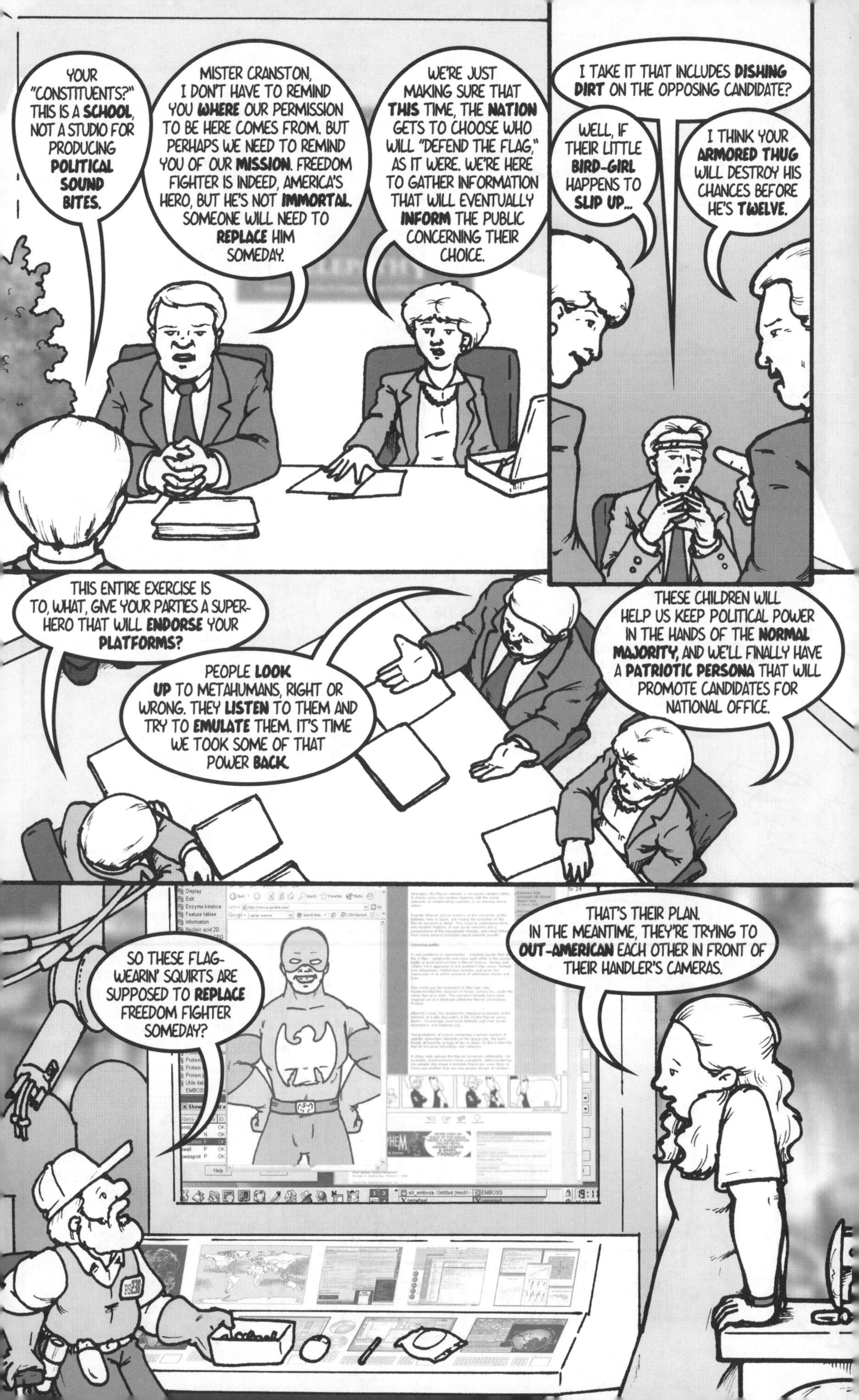
YOUR "CONSTITUENTS?" THIS IS A SCHOOL, NOT A STUDIO FOR PRODUCING POLITICAL SOUND BITES.
MISTER CRANSTON, I DON'T HAVE TO REMIND YOU WHERE OUR PERMISSION TO BE HERE COMES FROM. BUT PERHAPS WE NEED TO REMIND YOU OF OUR MISSION. FREEDOM FIGHTER IS INDEED, AMERICA'S HERO, BUT HE'S NOT IMMORTAL. SOMEONE WILL NEED TO REPLACE HIM SOMEDAY.
WE'RE JUST MAKING SURE THAT THIS TIME, THE NATION GETS TO CHOOSE WHO WILL "DEFEND THE FLAG," AS IT WERE. WE'RE HERE TO GATHER INFORMATION THAT WILL EVENTUALLY INFORM THE PUBLIC CONCERNING THEIR CHOICE.
I TAKE IT THAT INCLUDES DISHING DIRT ON THE OPPOSING CANDIDATE?
WELL, IF THEIR LITTLE BIRD-GIRL HAPPENS TO SLIP UP...
I THINK YOUR ARMORED THUG WILL DESTROY HIS CHANCES BEFORE HE'S TWELVE.
THIS ENTIRE EXERCISE IS TO, WHAT, GIVE YOUR PARTIES A SUPER-HERO THAT WILL ENDORSE YOUR PLATFORMS?
PEOPLE LOOK UP TO METAHUMANS, RIGHT OR WRONG. THEY LISTEN TO THEM AND TRY TO EMULATE THEM. IT'S TIME WE TOOK SOME OF THAT POWER BACK.
THESE CHILDREN WILL HELP US KEEP POLITICAL POWER IN THE HANDS OF THE NORMAL MAJORITY, AND WE'LL FINALLY HAVE A PATRIOTIC PERSONA THAT WILL PROMOTE CANDIDATES FOR NATIONAL OFFICE.
SO THESE FLAG-WEARIN' SQUIRTS ARE SUPPOSED TO REPLACE FREEDOM FIGHTER SOMEDAY?
THAT'S THEIR PLAN. IN THE MEANTIME, THEY'RE TRYING TO OUT-AMERICAN EACH OTHER IN FRONT OF THEIR HANDLER'S CAMERAS.

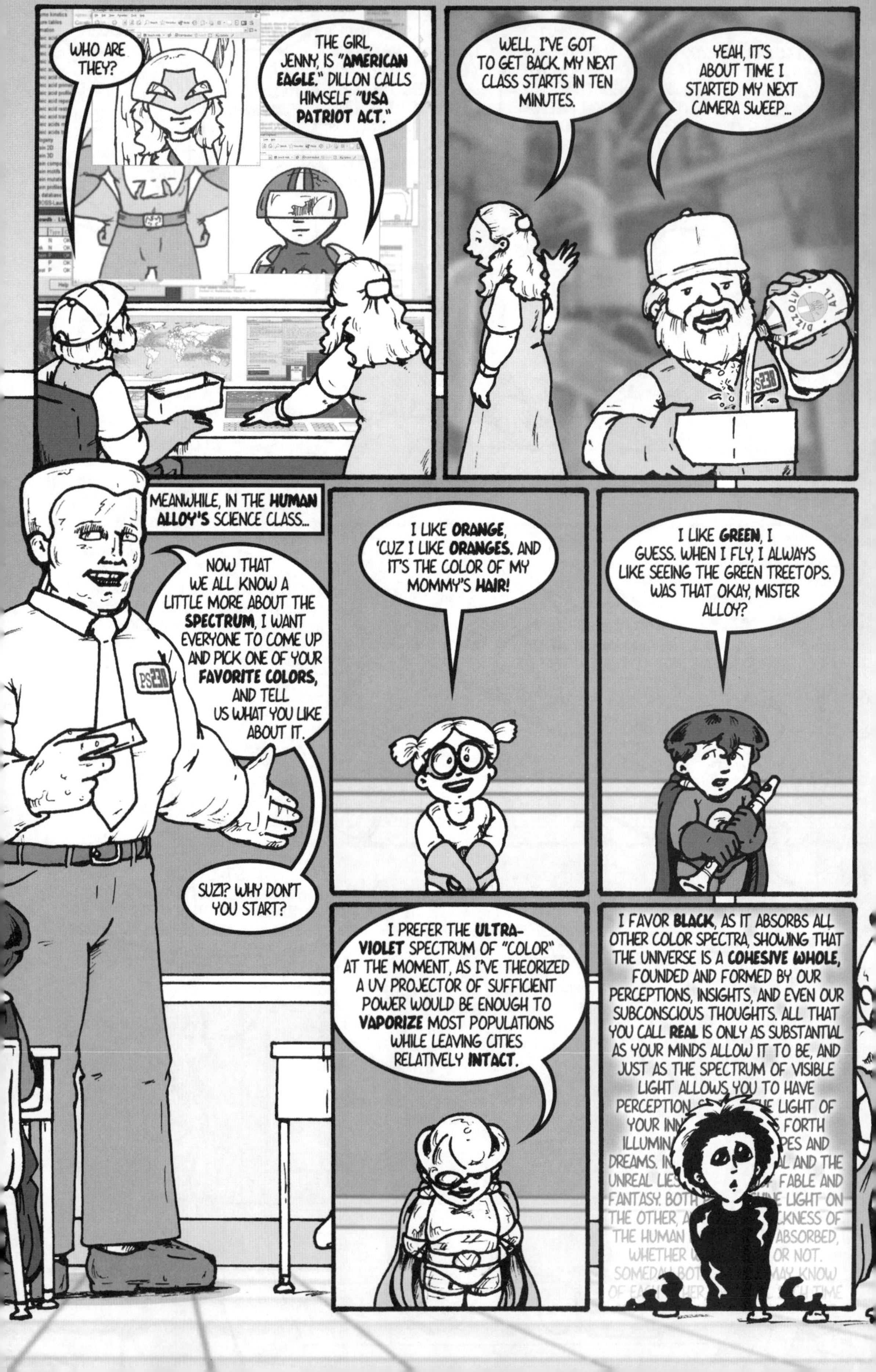
WHO ARE THEY?
THE GIRL, JENNY, IS "AMERICAN EAGLE." DILLON CALLS HIMSELF "USA PATRIOT ACT."
WELL, I'VE GOT TO GET BACK. MY NEXT CLASS STARTS IN TEN MINUTES.
YEAH, IT'S ABOUT TIME I STARTED MY NEXT CAMERA SWEEP...
MEANWHILE, IN THE HUMAN ALLOY'S SCIENCE CLASS...
NOW THAT WE ALL KNOW A LITTLE MORE ABOUT THE SPECTRUM, I WANT EVERYONE TO COME UP AND PICK ONE OF YOUR FAVORITE COLORS, AND TELL US WHAT YOU LIKE ABOUT IT.
SUZI? WHY DON'T YOU START?
I LIKE ORANGE, 'CUZ I LIKE ORANGES. AND IT'S THE COLOR OF MY MOMMY'S HAIR!
I LIKE GREEN, I GUESS. WHEN I FLY, I ALWAYS LIKE SEEING THE GREEN TREETOPS. WAS THAT OKAY, MISTER ALLOY?
I PREFER THE ULTRA-VIOLET SPECTRUM OF "COLOR" AT THE MOMENT, AS I'VE THEORIZED A UV PROJECTOR OF SUFFICIENT POWER WOULD BE ENOUGH TO VAPORIZE MOST POPULATIONS WHILE LEAVING CITIES RELATIVELY INTACT.
I FAVOR BLACK, AS IT ABSORBS ALL OTHER COLOR SPECTRA, SHOWING THAT THE UNIVERSE IS A COHESIVE WHOLE, FOUNDED AND FORMED BY OUR PERCEPTIONS, INSIGHTS, AND EVEN OUR SUBCONSCIOUS THOUGHTS. ALL THAT YOU CALL REAL IS ONLY AS SUBSTANTIAL AS YOUR MINDS ALLOW IT TO BE, AND JUST AS THE SPECTRUM OF VISIBLE LIGHT ALLOWS YOU TO HAVE PERCEPTION ... LIGHT OF YOUR ... FORTH ... PES AND DREAMS. ... AND THE UNREAL ... FABLE AND FANTASY. ... LIGHT ON THE OTHER, ... OF THE HUMAN ... ABSORBED, WHETHER ... OR NOT.

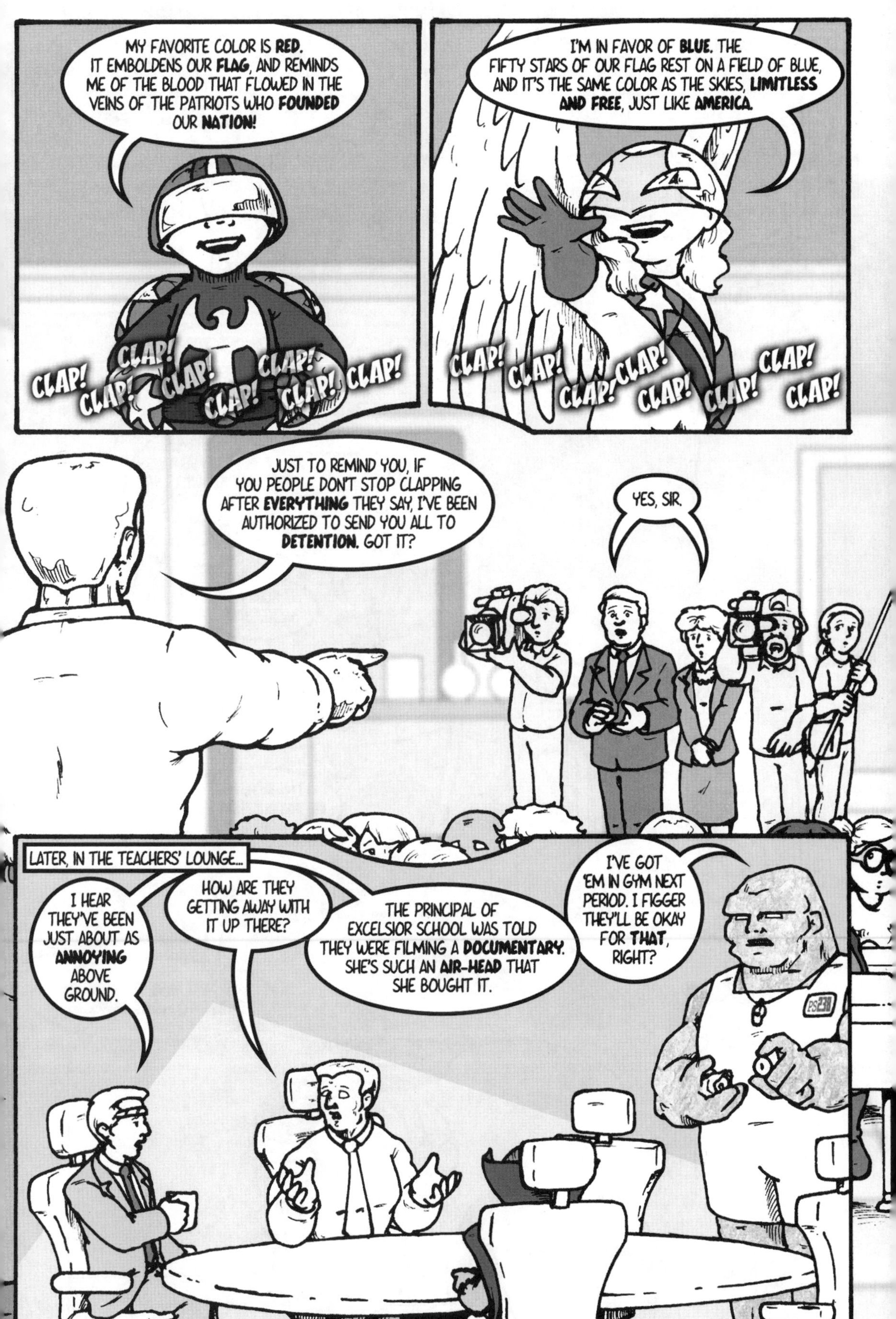
MY FAVORITE COLOR IS RED. IT EMBOLDENS OUR FLAG, AND REMINDS ME OF THE BLOOD THAT FLOWED IN THE VEINS OF THE PATRIOTS WHO FOUNDED OUR NATION!
CLAP! CLAP! CLAP! CLAP! CLAP! CLAP! CLAP! CLAP!
I'M IN FAVOR OF BLUE. THE FIFTY STARS OF OUR FLAG REST ON A FIELD OF BLUE, AND IT'S THE SAME COLOR AS THE SKIES, LIMITLESS AND FREE, JUST LIKE AMERICA.
CLAP! CLAP! CLAP! CLAP! CLAP! CLAP! CLAP! CLAP!
JUST TO REMIND YOU, IF YOU PEOPLE DON'T STOP CLAPPING AFTER EVERYTHING THEY SAY, I'VE BEEN AUTHORIZED TO SEND YOU ALL TO DETENTION. GOT IT?
YES, SIR.
LATER, IN THE TEACHERS' LOUNGE...
I HEAR THEY'VE BEEN JUST ABOUT AS ANNOYING ABOVE GROUND.
HOW ARE THEY GETTING AWAY WITH IT UP THERE?
THE PRINCIPAL OF EXCELSIOR SCHOOL WAS TOLD THEY WERE FILMING A DOCUMENTARY. SHE'S SUCH AN AIR-HEAD THAT SHE BOUGHT IT.
I'VE GOT 'EM IN GYM NEXT PERIOD. I FIGGER THEY'LL BE OKAY FOR THAT, RIGHT?
PS238

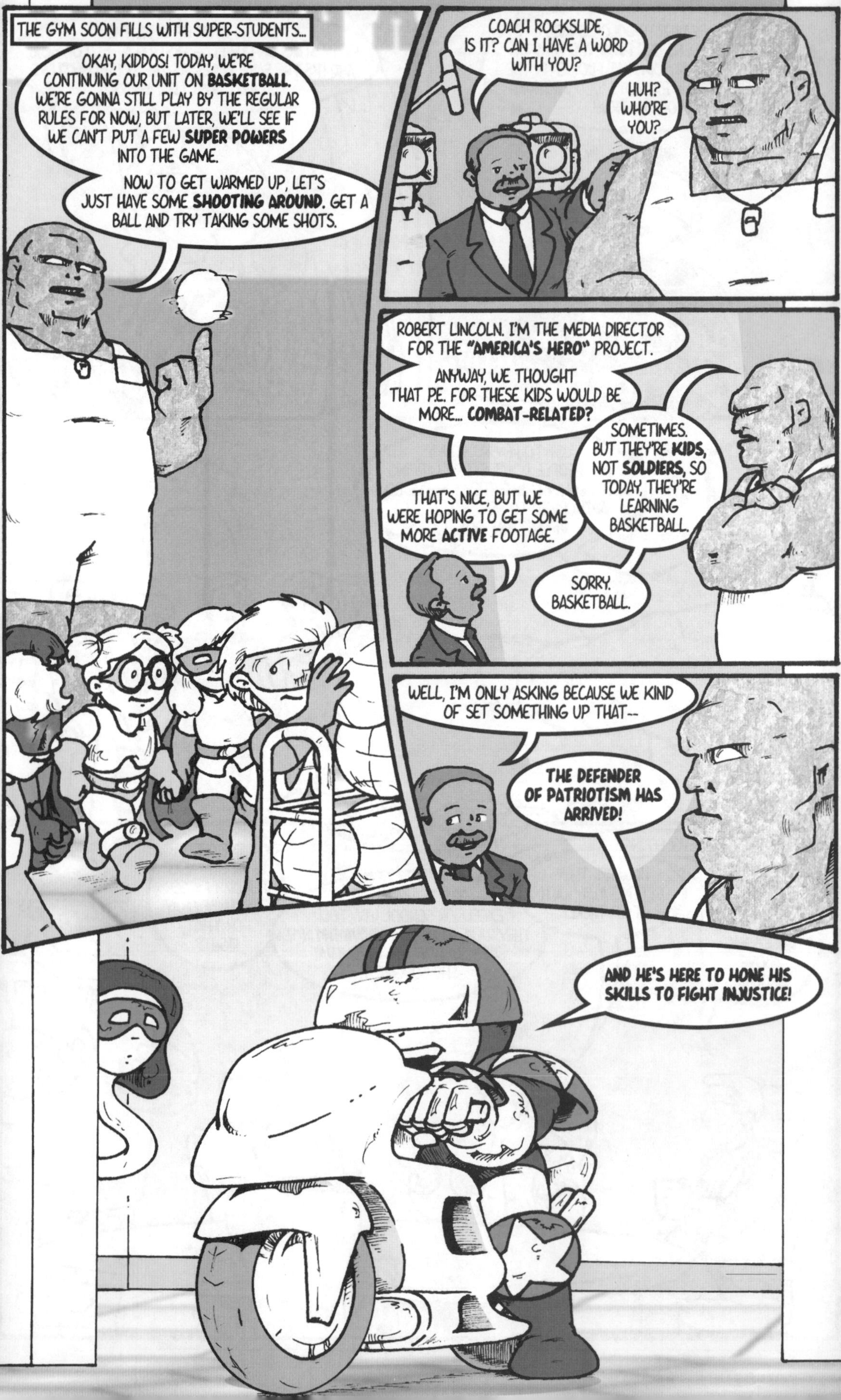
THE GYM SOON FILLS WITH SUPER-STUDENTS...
OKAY, KIDDOS! TODAY, WE'RE CONTINUING OUR UNIT ON BASKETBALL. WE'RE GONNA STILL PLAY BY THE REGULAR RULES FOR NOW, BUT LATER, WE'LL SEE IF WE CAN'T PUT A FEW SUPER POWERS INTO THE GAME.
NOW TO GET WARMED UP, LET'S JUST HAVE SOME SHOOTING AROUND. GET A BALL AND TRY TAKING SOME SHOTS.
COACH ROCKSLIDE, IS IT? CAN I HAVE A WORD WITH YOU?
HUH? WHO'RE YOU?
ROBERT LINCOLN. I'M THE MEDIA DIRECTOR FOR THE "AMERICA'S HERO" PROJECT.
ANYWAY, WE THOUGHT THAT P.E. FOR THESE KIDS WOULD BE MORE... COMBAT-RELATED?
SOMETIMES. BUT THEY'RE KIDS, NOT SOLDIERS, SO TODAY, THEY'RE LEARNING BASKETBALL.
THAT'S NICE, BUT WE WERE HOPING TO GET SOME MORE ACTIVE FOOTAGE.
SORRY. BASKETBALL.
WELL, I'M ONLY ASKING BECAUSE WE KIND OF SET SOMETHING UP THAT--
THE DEFENDER OF PATRIOTISM HAS ARRIVED!
AND HE'S HERE TO HONE HIS SKILLS TO FIGHT INJUSTICE!

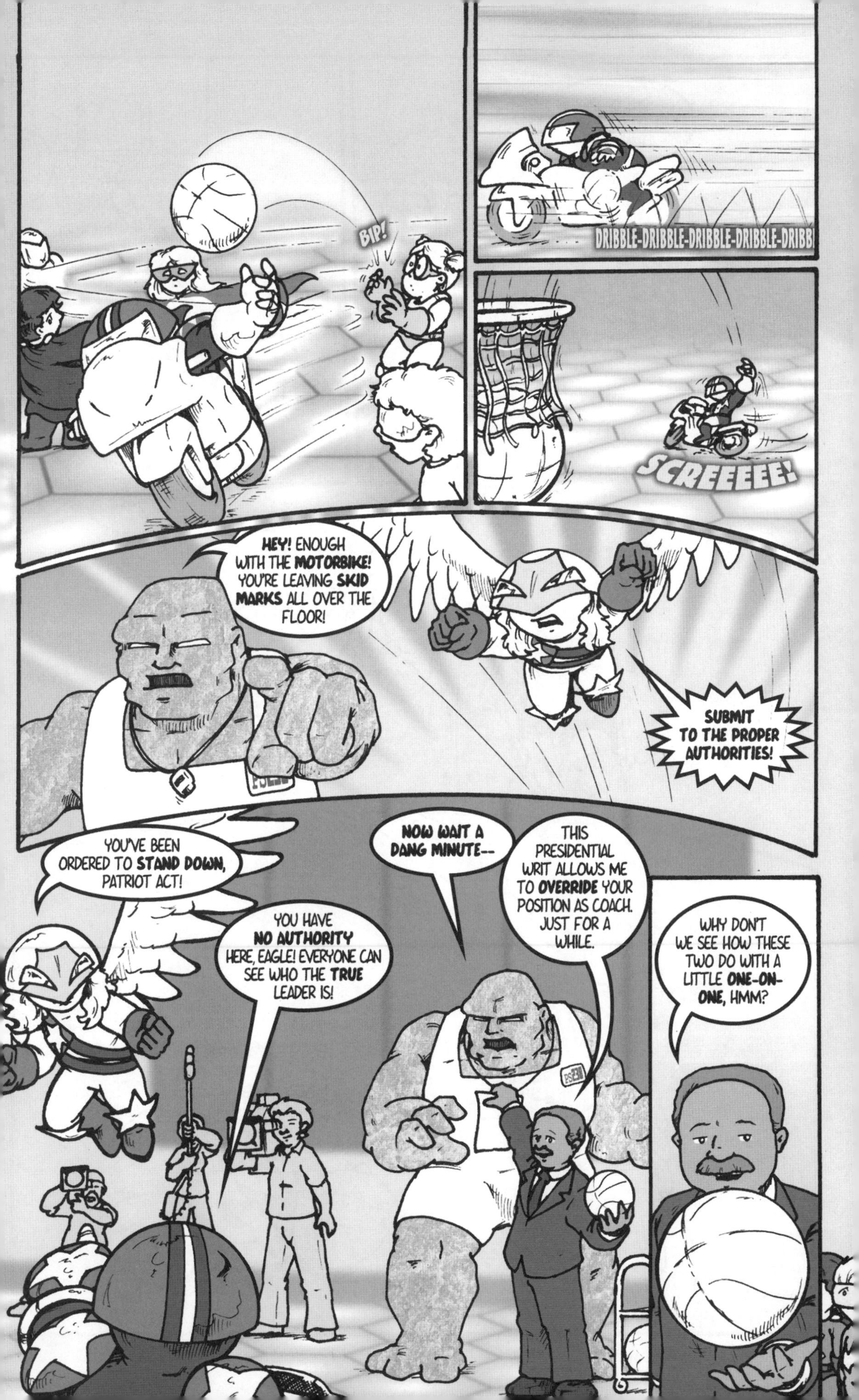

BIP!
DRIBBLE-DRIBBLE-DRIBBLE-DRIBBLE-DRIBB
SCREEEEEE!
HEY! ENOUGH WITH THE MOTORBIKE! YOU'RE LEAVING SKID MARKS ALL OVER THE FLOOR!
SUBMIT TO THE PROPER AUTHORITIES!
YOU'VE BEEN ORDERED TO STAND DOWN, PATRIOT ACT!
YOU HAVE NO AUTHORITY HERE, EAGLE! EVERYONE CAN SEE WHO THE TRUE LEADER IS!
NOW WAIT A DANG MINUTE--
THIS PRESIDENTIAL WRIT ALLOWS ME TO OVERRIDE YOUR POSITION AS COACH. JUST FOR A WHILE.
WHY DON'T WE SEE HOW THESE TWO DO WITH A LITTLE ONE-ON-ONE, HMM?

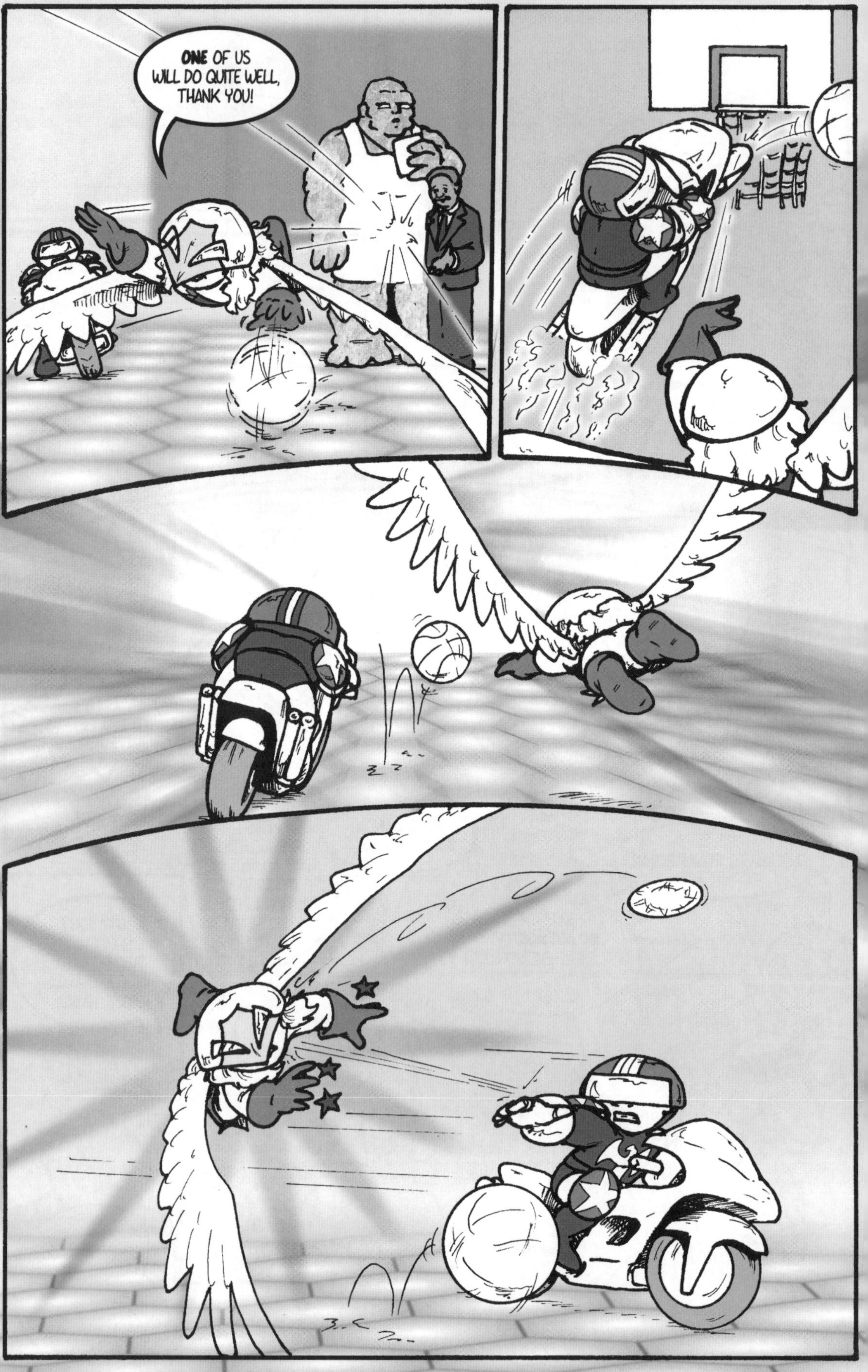
ONE OF US WILL DO QUITE WELL, THANK YOU!

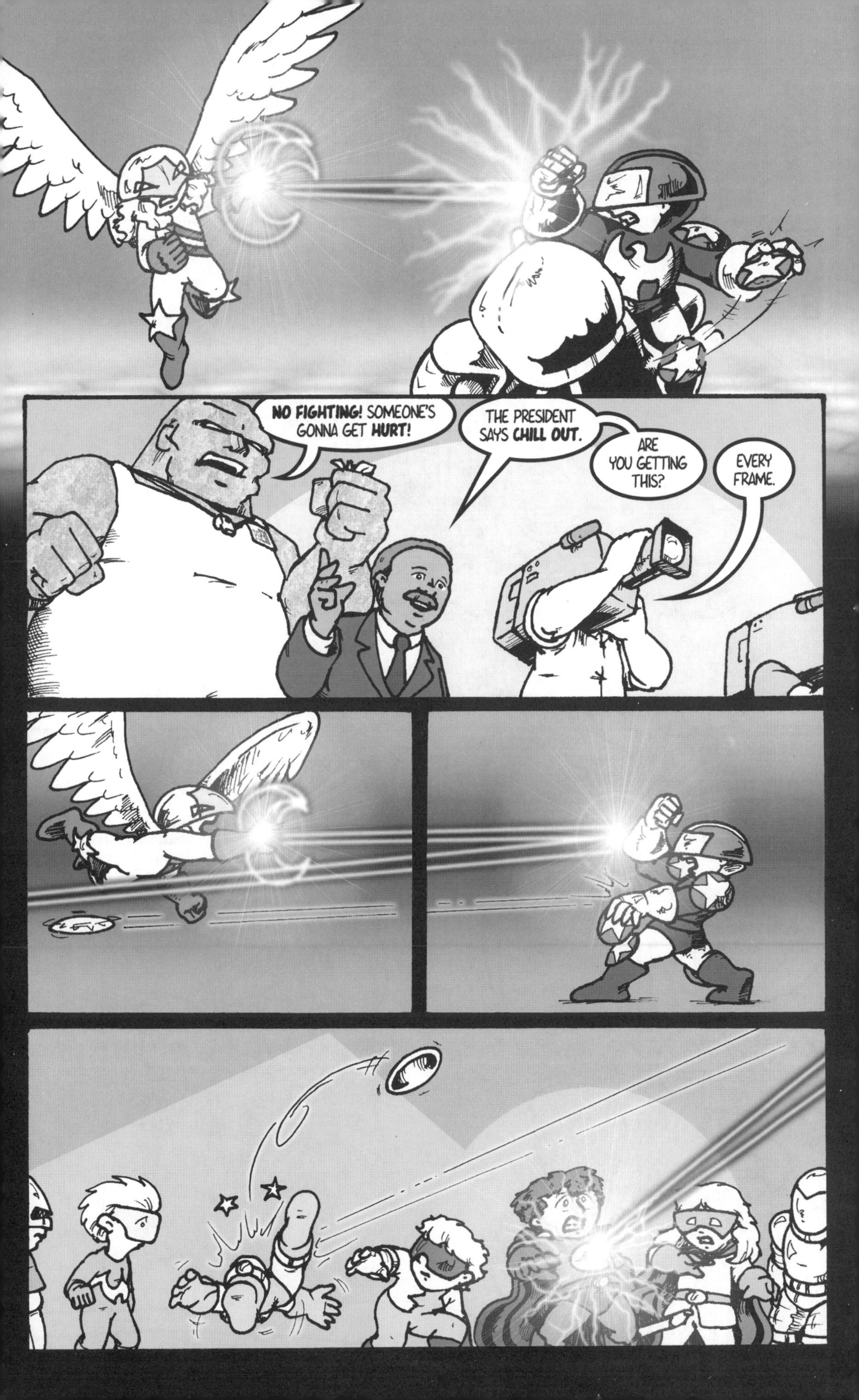

NO FIGHTING! SOMEONE'S GONNA GET **HURT!**
THE PRESIDENT SAYS **CHILL OUT**.
ARE YOU GETTING THIS?
EVERY FRAME.

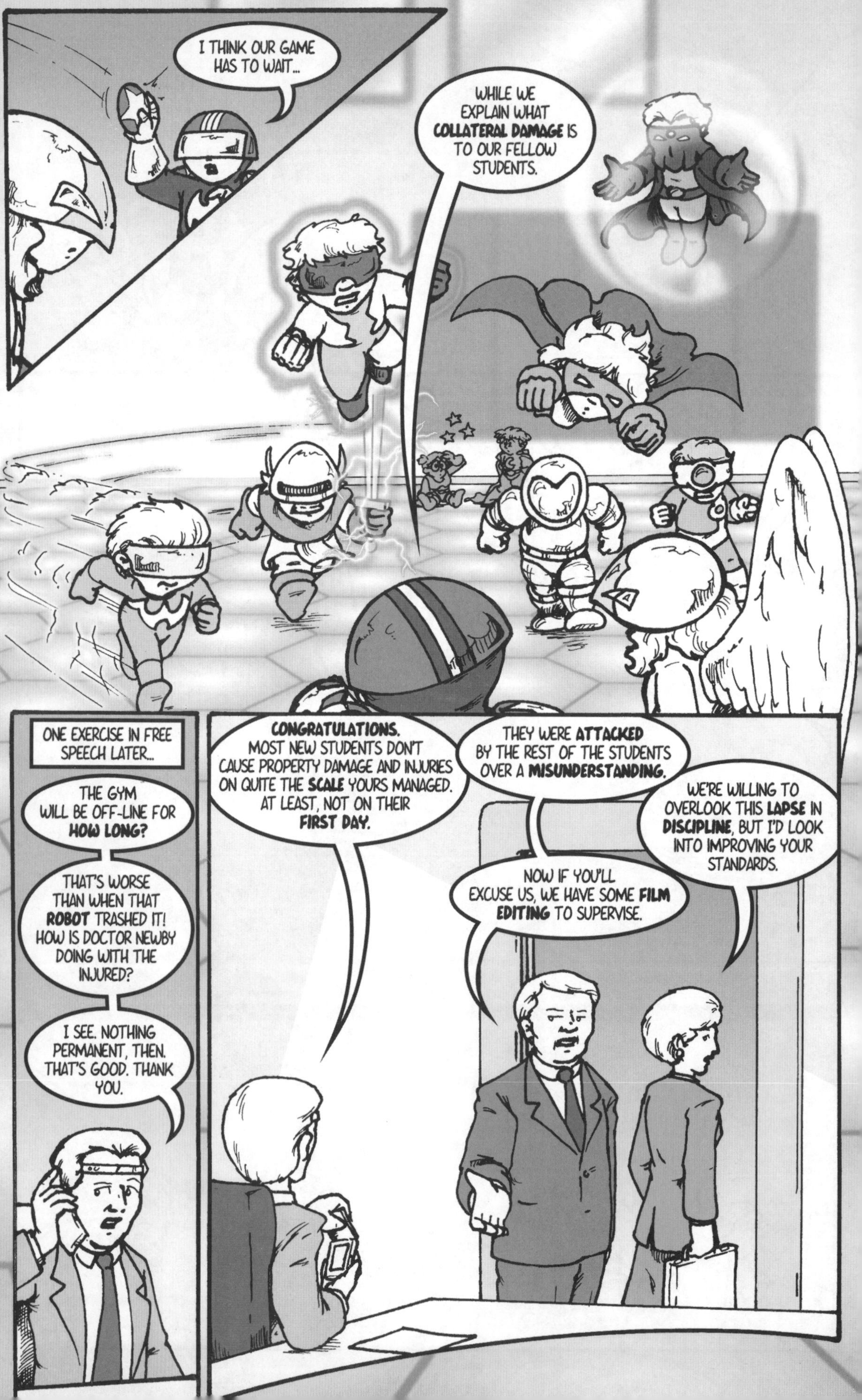
I THINK OUR GAME HAS TO WAIT...
WHILE WE EXPLAIN WHAT **COLLATERAL DAMAGE** IS TO OUR FELLOW STUDENTS.
ONE EXERCISE IN FREE SPEECH LATER...
THE GYM WILL BE OFF-LINE FOR **HOW LONG?**
THAT'S WORSE THAN WHEN THAT **ROBOT** TRASHED IT! HOW IS DOCTOR NEWBY DOING WITH THE INJURED?
I SEE. NOTHING PERMANENT, THEN. THAT'S GOOD. THANK YOU.
CONGRATULATIONS. MOST NEW STUDENTS DON'T CAUSE PROPERTY DAMAGE AND INJURIES ON QUITE THE **SCALE** YOURS MANAGED. AT LEAST, NOT ON THEIR **FIRST DAY.**
THEY WERE **ATTACKED** BY THE REST OF THE STUDENTS OVER A **MISUNDERSTANDING.**
WE'RE WILLING TO OVERLOOK THIS **LAPSE** IN **DISCIPLINE**, BUT I'D LOOK INTO IMPROVING YOUR STANDARDS.
NOW IF YOU'LL EXCUSE US, WE HAVE SOME **FILM EDITING** TO SUPERVISE.

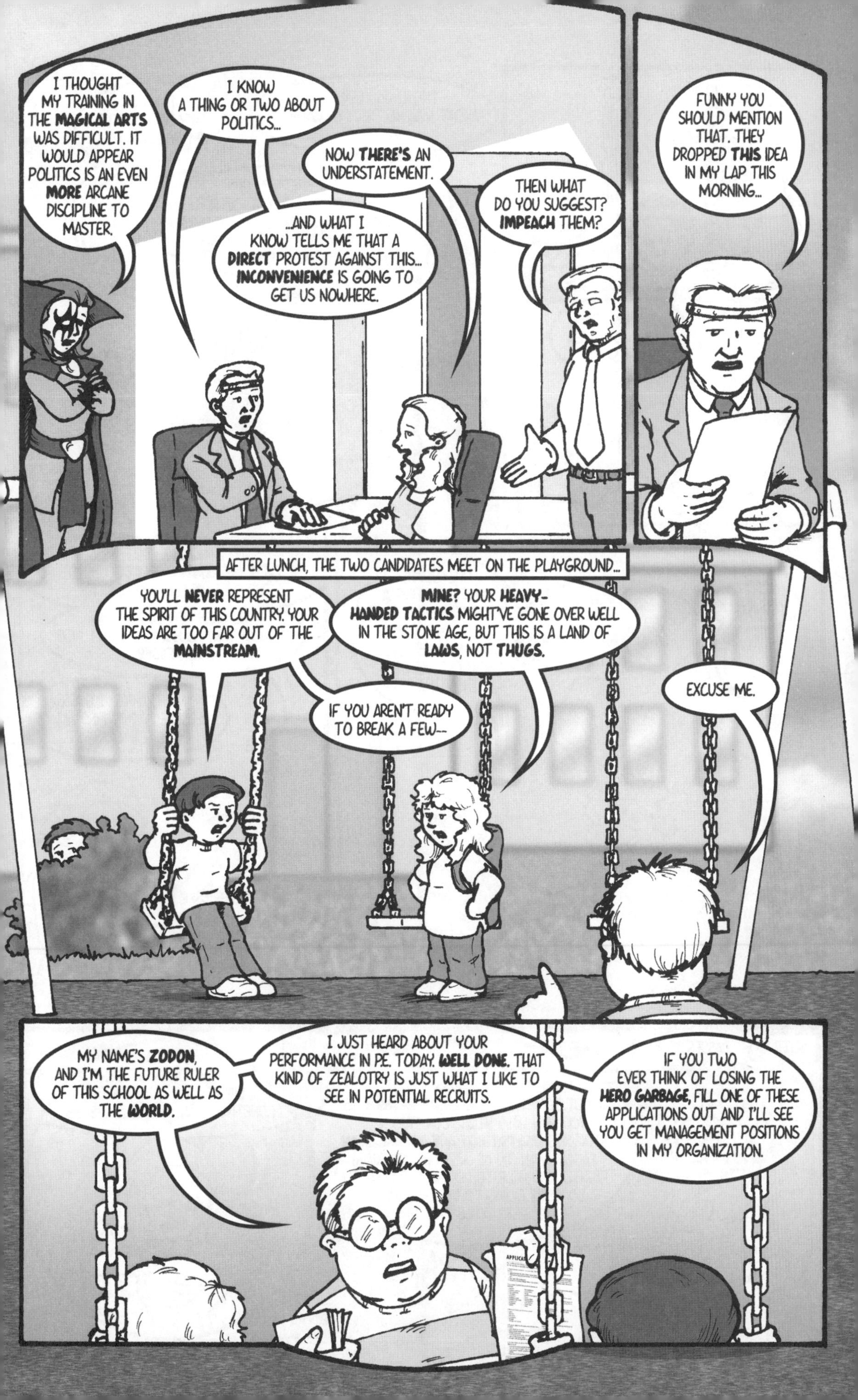
I THOUGHT MY TRAINING IN THE MAGICAL ARTS WAS DIFFICULT. IT WOULD APPEAR POLITICS IS AN EVEN MORE ARCANE DISCIPLINE TO MASTER.
I KNOW A THING OR TWO ABOUT POLITICS...
NOW THERE'S AN UNDERSTATEMENT.
...AND WHAT I KNOW TELLS ME THAT A DIRECT PROTEST AGAINST THIS... INCONVENIENCE IS GOING TO GET US NOWHERE.
THEN WHAT DO YOU SUGGEST? IMPEACH THEM?
FUNNY YOU SHOULD MENTION THAT. THEY DROPPED THIS IDEA IN MY LAP THIS MORNING...
AFTER LUNCH, THE TWO CANDIDATES MEET ON THE PLAYGROUND...
YOU'LL NEVER REPRESENT THE SPIRIT OF THIS COUNTRY. YOUR IDEAS ARE TOO FAR OUT OF THE MAINSTREAM.
MINE? YOUR HEAVY-HANDED TACTICS MIGHT'VE GONE OVER WELL IN THE STONE AGE, BUT THIS IS A LAND OF LAWS, NOT THUGS.
IF YOU AREN'T READY TO BREAK A FEW--
EXCUSE ME.
MY NAME'S ZODON, AND I'M THE FUTURE RULER OF THIS SCHOOL AS WELL AS THE WORLD.
I JUST HEARD ABOUT YOUR PERFORMANCE IN P.E. TODAY. WELL DONE. THAT KIND OF ZEALOTRY IS JUST WHAT I LIKE TO SEE IN POTENTIAL RECRUITS.
IF YOU TWO EVER THINK OF LOSING THE HERO GARBAGE, FILL ONE OF THESE APPLICATIONS OUT AND I'LL SEE YOU GET MANAGEMENT POSITIONS IN MY ORGANIZATION.

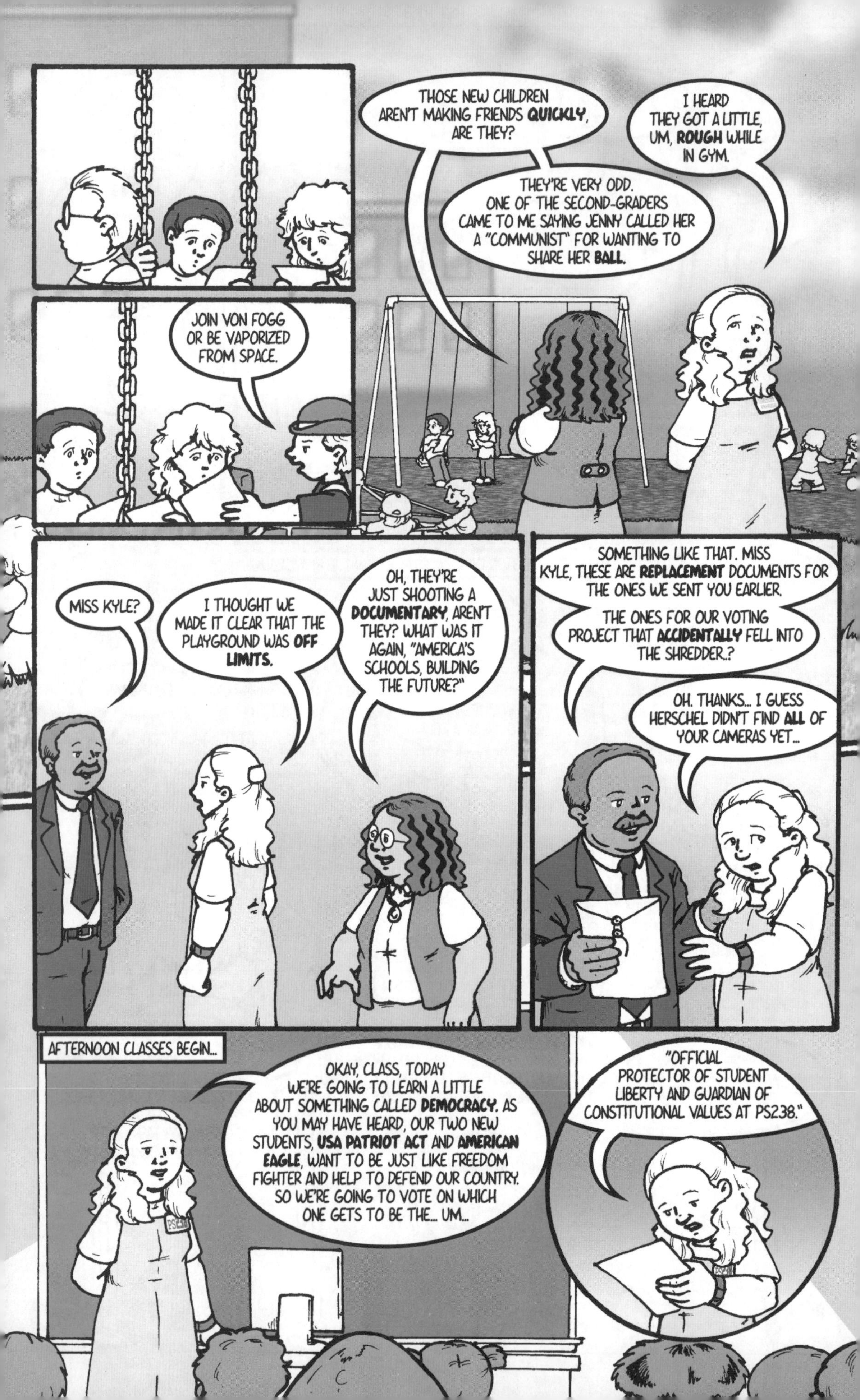
JOIN VON FOGG OR BE VAPORIZED FROM SPACE.
THOSE NEW CHILDREN AREN'T MAKING FRIENDS QUICKLY, ARE THEY?
I HEARD THEY GOT A LITTLE, UM, ROUGH WHILE IN GYM.
THEY'RE VERY ODD. ONE OF THE SECOND-GRADERS CAME TO ME SAYING JENNY CALLED HER A "COMMUNIST" FOR WANTING TO SHARE HER BALL.
MISS KYLE?
I THOUGHT WE MADE IT CLEAR THAT THE PLAYGROUND WAS OFF LIMITS.
OH, THEY'RE JUST SHOOTING A DOCUMENTARY, AREN'T THEY? WHAT WAS IT AGAIN, "AMERICA'S SCHOOLS, BUILDING THE FUTURE?"
SOMETHING LIKE THAT. MISS KYLE, THESE ARE REPLACEMENT DOCUMENTS FOR THE ONES WE SENT YOU EARLIER.
THE ONES FOR OUR VOTING PROJECT THAT ACCIDENTALLY FELL INTO THE SHREDDER..?
OH. THANKS... I GUESS HERSCHEL DIDN'T FIND ALL OF YOUR CAMERAS YET...
AFTERNOON CLASSES BEGIN...
OKAY, CLASS, TODAY WE'RE GOING TO LEARN A LITTLE ABOUT SOMETHING CALLED DEMOCRACY. AS YOU MAY HAVE HEARD, OUR TWO NEW STUDENTS, USA PATRIOT ACT AND AMERICAN EAGLE, WANT TO BE JUST LIKE FREEDOM FIGHTER AND HELP TO DEFEND OUR COUNTRY. SO WE'RE GOING TO VOTE ON WHICH ONE GETS TO BE THE... UM...
"OFFICIAL PROTECTOR OF STUDENT LIBERTY AND GUARDIAN OF CONSTITUTIONAL VALUES AT PS238."

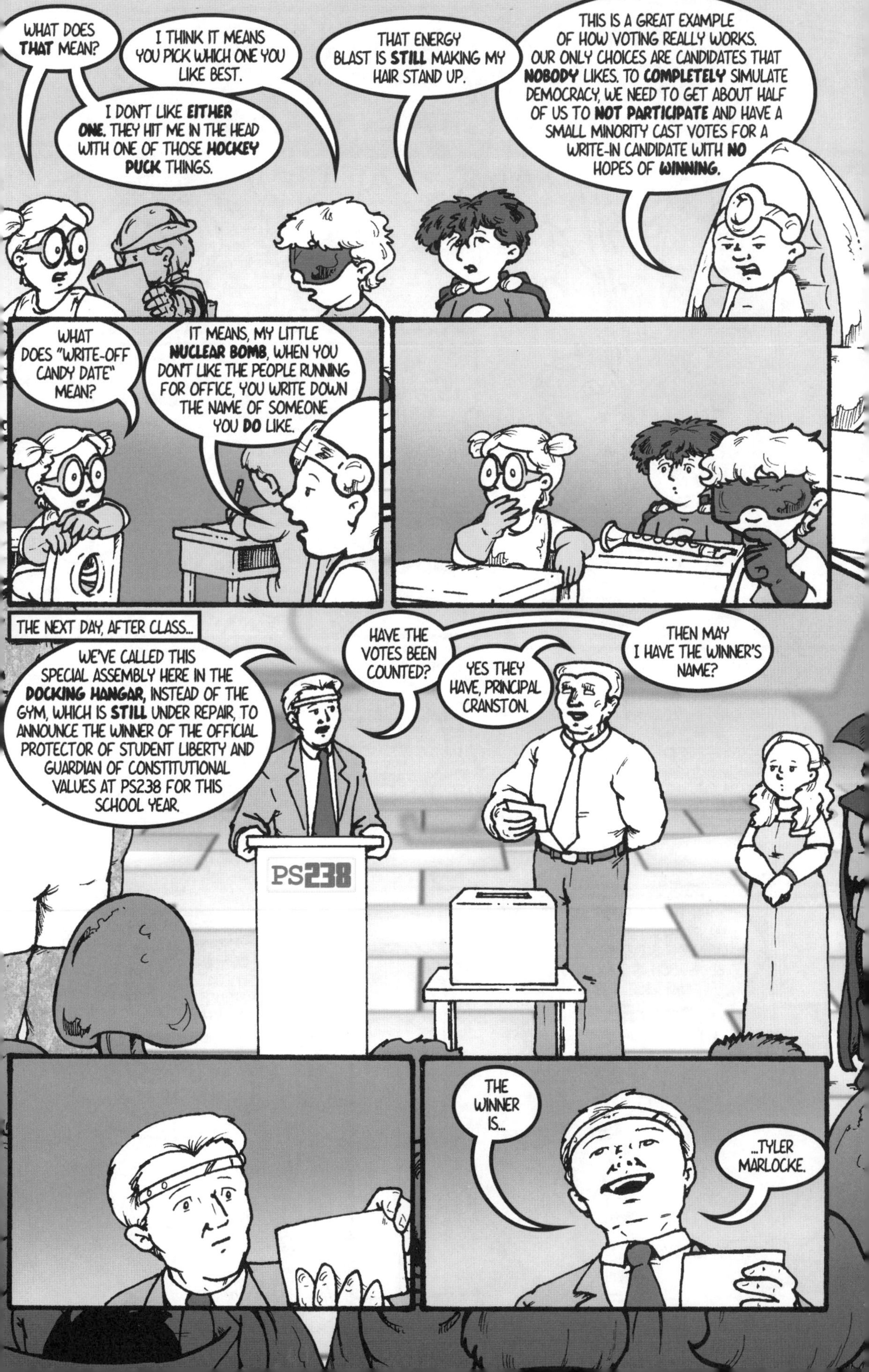
WHAT DOES THAT MEAN?
I THINK IT MEANS YOU PICK WHICH ONE YOU LIKE BEST.
I DON'T LIKE EITHER ONE. THEY HIT ME IN THE HEAD WITH ONE OF THOSE HOCKEY PUCK THINGS.
THAT ENERGY BLAST IS STILL MAKING MY HAIR STAND UP.
THIS IS A GREAT EXAMPLE OF HOW VOTING REALLY WORKS. OUR ONLY CHOICES ARE CANDIDATES THAT NOBODY LIKES. TO COMPLETELY SIMULATE DEMOCRACY, WE NEED TO GET ABOUT HALF OF US TO NOT PARTICIPATE AND HAVE A SMALL MINORITY CAST VOTES FOR A WRITE-IN CANDIDATE WITH NO HOPES OF WINNING.
WHAT DOES "WRITE-OFF CANDY DATE" MEAN?
IT MEANS, MY LITTLE NUCLEAR BOMB, WHEN YOU DON'T LIKE THE PEOPLE RUNNING FOR OFFICE, YOU WRITE DOWN THE NAME OF SOMEONE YOU DO LIKE.
THE NEXT DAY, AFTER CLASS...
WE'VE CALLED THIS SPECIAL ASSEMBLY HERE IN THE DOCKING HANGAR, INSTEAD OF THE GYM, WHICH IS STILL UNDER REPAIR, TO ANNOUNCE THE WINNER OF THE OFFICIAL PROTECTOR OF STUDENT LIBERTY AND GUARDIAN OF CONSTITUTIONAL VALUES AT PS238 FOR THIS SCHOOL YEAR.
HAVE THE VOTES BEEN COUNTED?
YES THEY HAVE, PRINCIPAL CRANSTON.
THEN MAY I HAVE THE WINNER'S NAME?
PS238
THE WINNER IS...
...TYLER MARLOCKE.

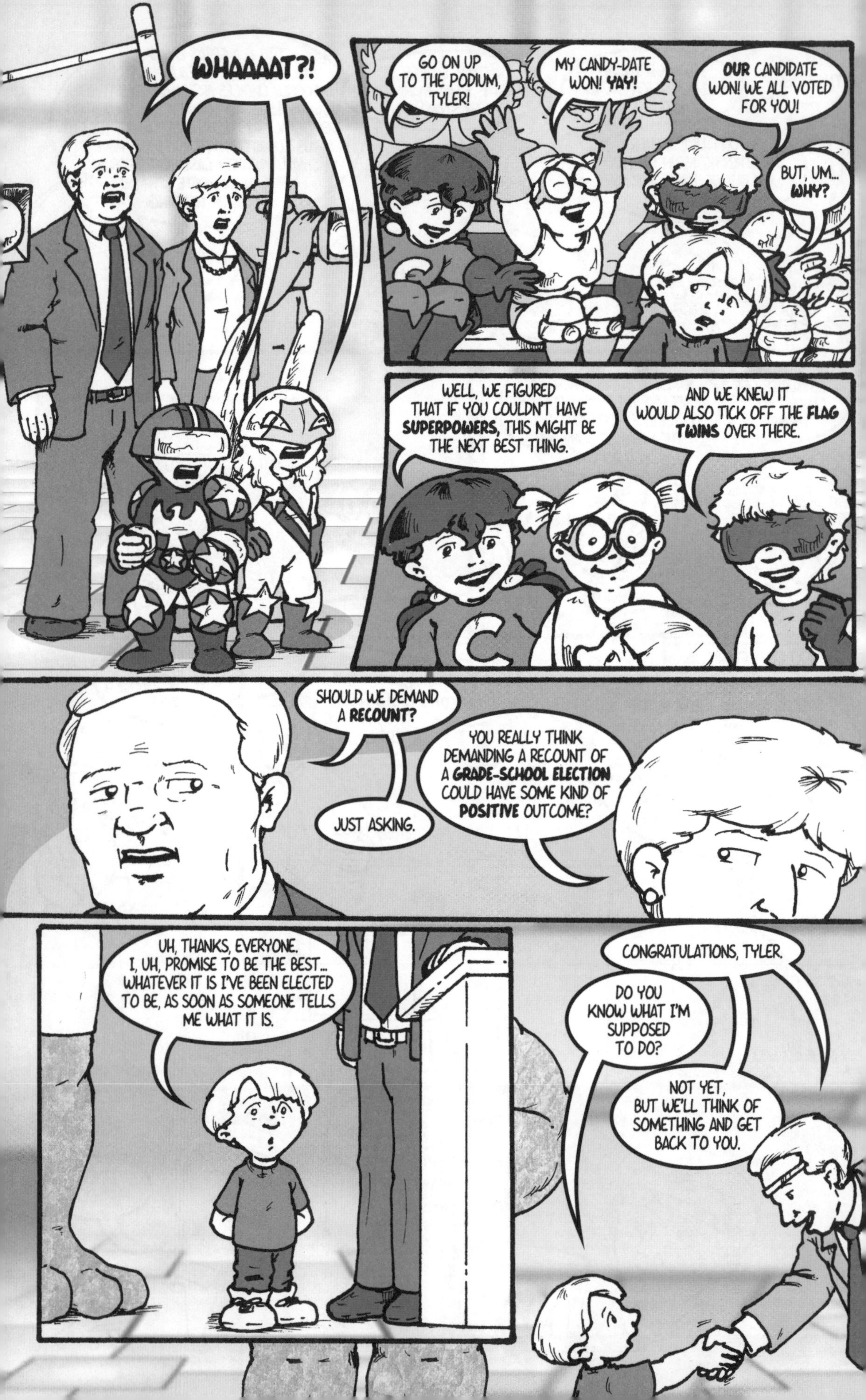

WHAAAAT?!
GO ON UP TO THE PODIUM, TYLER!
MY CANDY-DATE WON! YAY!
OUR CANDIDATE WON! WE ALL VOTED FOR YOU!
BUT, UM... WHY?
WELL, WE FIGURED THAT IF YOU COULDN'T HAVE SUPERPOWERS, THIS MIGHT BE THE NEXT BEST THING.
AND WE KNEW IT WOULD ALSO TICK OFF THE FLAG TWINS OVER THERE.
SHOULD WE DEMAND A RECOUNT?
YOU REALLY THINK DEMANDING A RECOUNT OF A GRADE-SCHOOL ELECTION COULD HAVE SOME KIND OF POSITIVE OUTCOME?
JUST ASKING.
UH, THANKS, EVERYONE. I, UH, PROMISE TO BE THE BEST... WHATEVER IT IS I'VE BEEN ELECTED TO BE, AS SOON AS SOMEONE TELLS ME WHAT IT IS.
CONGRATULATIONS, TYLER.
DO YOU KNOW WHAT I'M SUPPOSED TO DO?
NOT YET, BUT WE'LL THINK OF SOMETHING AND GET BACK TO YOU.

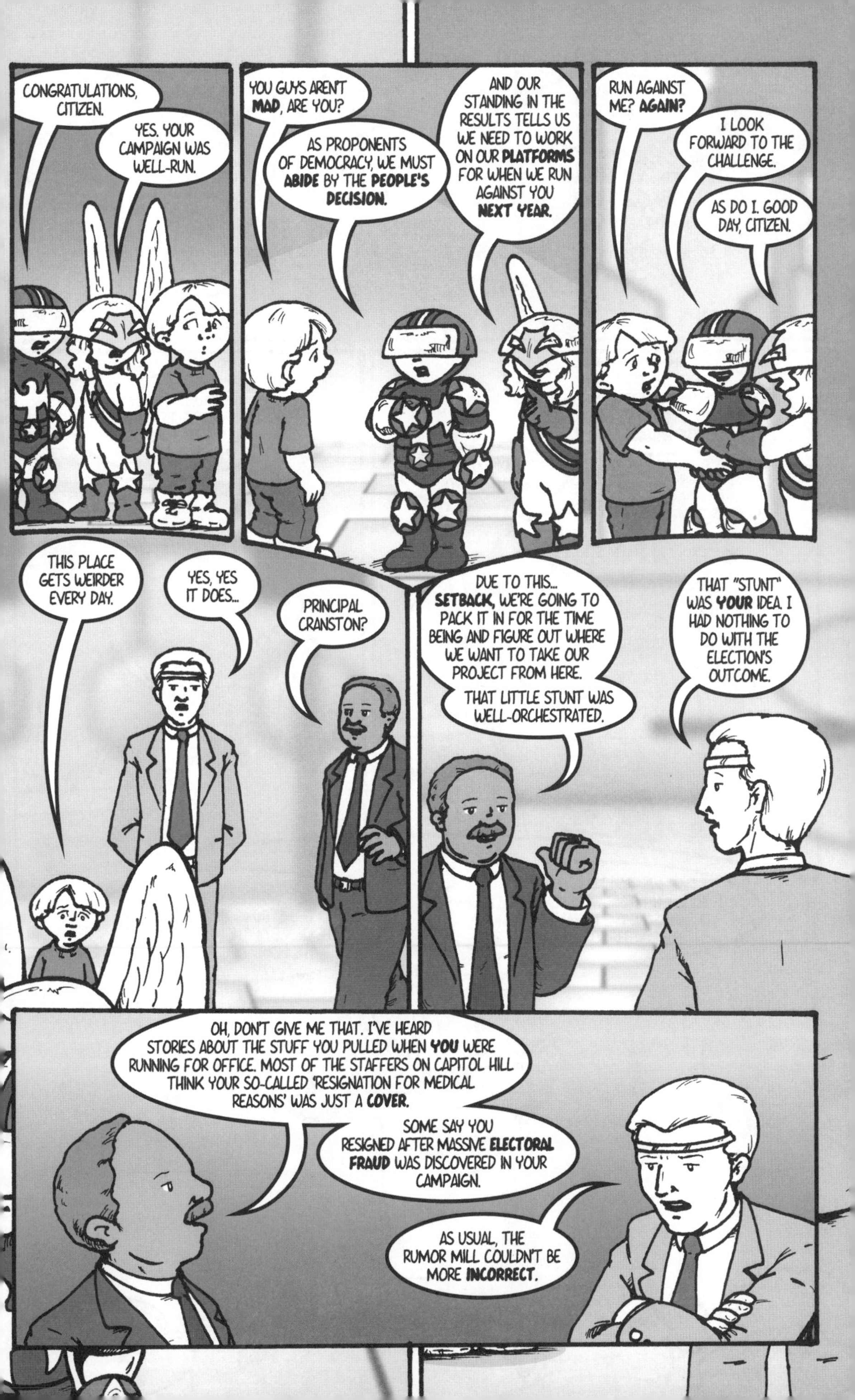
CONGRATULATIONS, CITIZEN.
YES. YOUR CAMPAIGN WAS WELL-RUN.
YOU GUYS AREN'T MAD, ARE YOU?
AS PROPONENTS OF DEMOCRACY, WE MUST ABIDE BY THE PEOPLE'S DECISION.
AND OUR STANDING IN THE RESULTS TELLS US WE NEED TO WORK ON OUR PLATFORMS FOR WHEN WE RUN AGAINST YOU NEXT YEAR.
RUN AGAINST ME? AGAIN?
I LOOK FORWARD TO THE CHALLENGE.
AS DO I. GOOD DAY, CITIZEN.
THIS PLACE GETS WEIRDER EVERY DAY.
YES, YES IT DOES...
PRINCIPAL CRANSTON?
DUE TO THIS... SETBACK, WE'RE GOING TO PACK IT IN FOR THE TIME BEING AND FIGURE OUT WHERE WE WANT TO TAKE OUR PROJECT FROM HERE.
THAT LITTLE STUNT WAS WELL-ORCHESTRATED.
THAT "STUNT" WAS YOUR IDEA. I HAD NOTHING TO DO WITH THE ELECTION'S OUTCOME.
OH, DON'T GIVE ME THAT. I'VE HEARD STORIES ABOUT THE STUFF YOU PULLED WHEN YOU WERE RUNNING FOR OFFICE. MOST OF THE STAFFERS ON CAPITOL HILL THINK YOUR SO-CALLED 'RESIGNATION FOR MEDICAL REASONS' WAS JUST A COVER.
SOME SAY YOU RESIGNED AFTER MASSIVE ELECTORAL FRAUD WAS DISCOVERED IN YOUR CAMPAIGN.
AS USUAL, THE RUMOR MILL COULDN'T BE MORE INCORRECT.

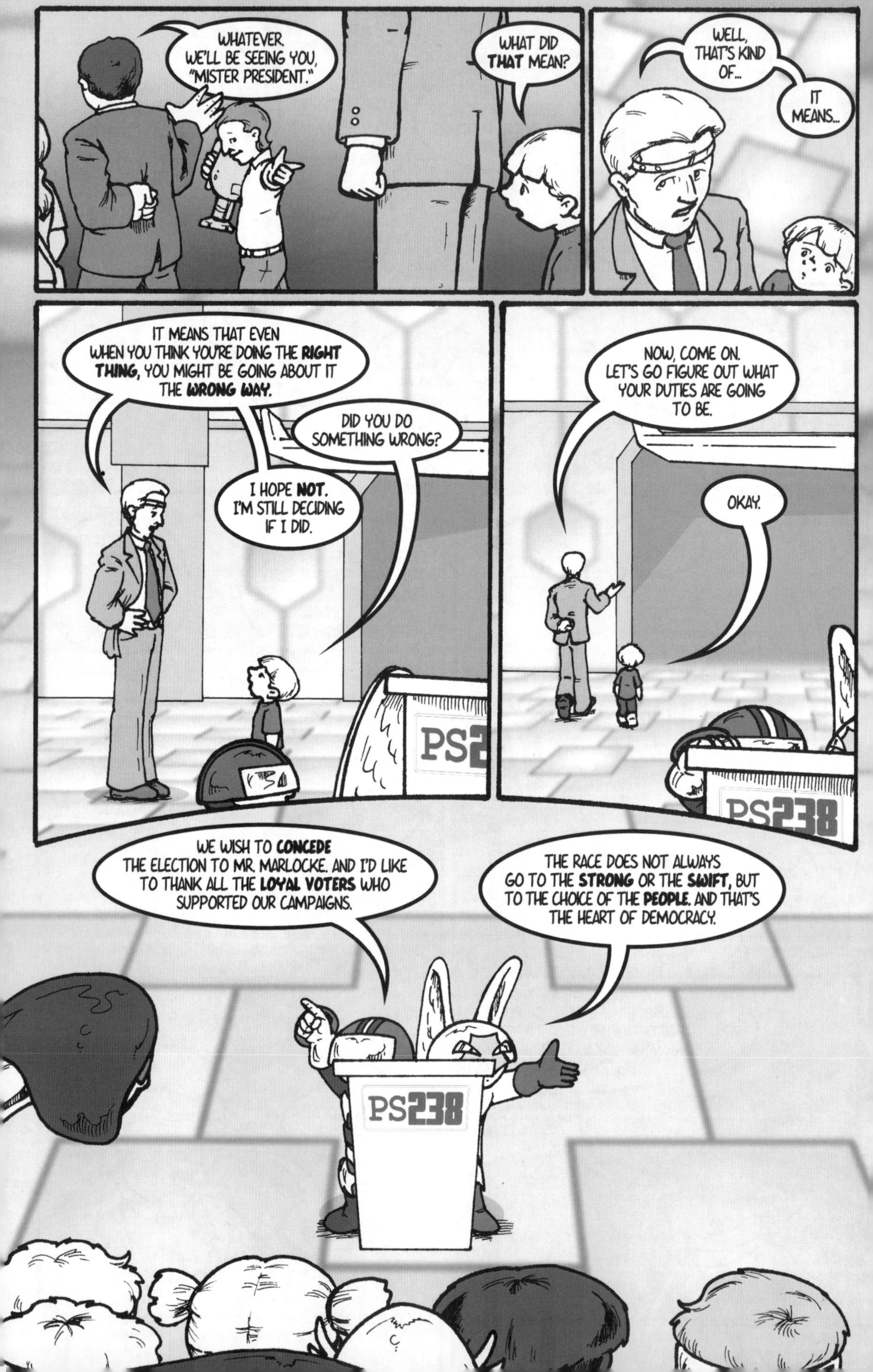
WHATEVER. WE'LL BE SEEING YOU, "MISTER PRESIDENT."
WHAT DID **THAT** MEAN?
WELL, THAT'S KIND OF...
IT MEANS...
IT MEANS THAT EVEN WHEN YOU THINK YOU'RE DOING THE **RIGHT THING,** YOU MIGHT BE GOING ABOUT IT THE **WRONG WAY.**
DID YOU DO SOMETHING WRONG?
I HOPE **NOT.** I'M STILL DECIDING IF I DID.
NOW, COME ON. LET'S GO FIGURE OUT WHAT YOUR DUTIES ARE GOING TO BE.
OKAY.
PS238
WE WISH TO **CONCEDE** THE ELECTION TO MR. MARLOCKE. AND I'D LIKE TO THANK ALL THE **LOYAL VOTERS** WHO SUPPORTED OUR CAMPAIGNS.
THE RACE DOES NOT ALWAYS GO TO THE **STRONG** OR THE **SWIFT,** BUT TO THE CHOICE OF THE **PEOPLE.** AND THAT'S THE HEART OF DEMOCRACY.
PS238

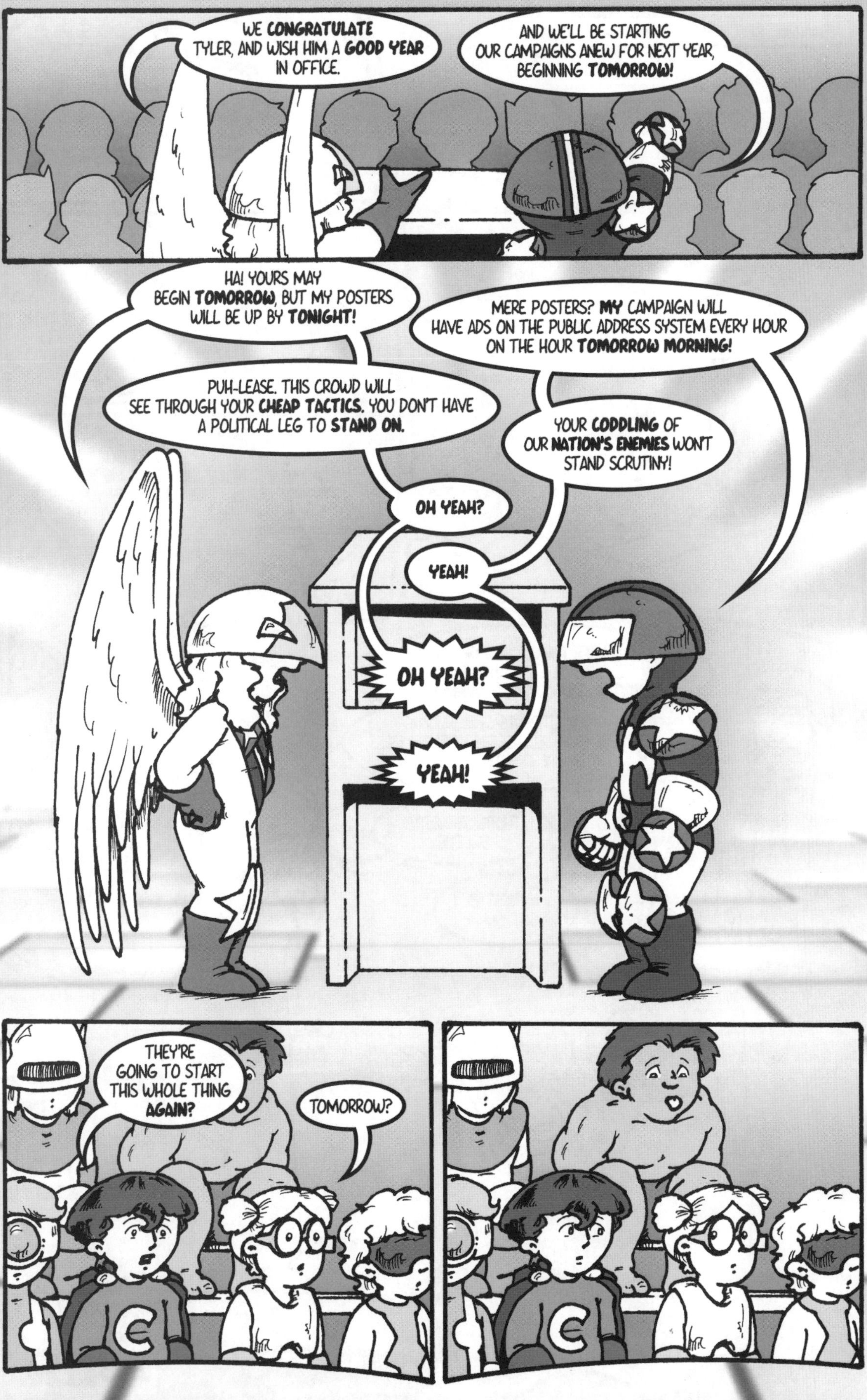
WE CONGRATULATE TYLER, AND WISH HIM A GOOD YEAR IN OFFICE.
AND WE'LL BE STARTING OUR CAMPAIGNS ANEW FOR NEXT YEAR, BEGINNING TOMORROW!
HA! YOURS MAY BEGIN TOMORROW, BUT MY POSTERS WILL BE UP BY TONIGHT!
MERE POSTERS? MY CAMPAIGN WILL HAVE ADS ON THE PUBLIC ADDRESS SYSTEM EVERY HOUR ON THE HOUR TOMORROW MORNING!
PUH-LEASE. THIS CROWD WILL SEE THROUGH YOUR CHEAP TACTICS. YOU DON'T HAVE A POLITICAL LEG TO STAND ON.
YOUR CODDLING OF OUR NATION'S ENEMIES WON'T STAND SCRUTINY!
OH YEAH?
YEAH!
OH YEAH?
YEAH!
THEY'RE GOING TO START THIS WHOLE THING AGAIN?
TOMORROW?

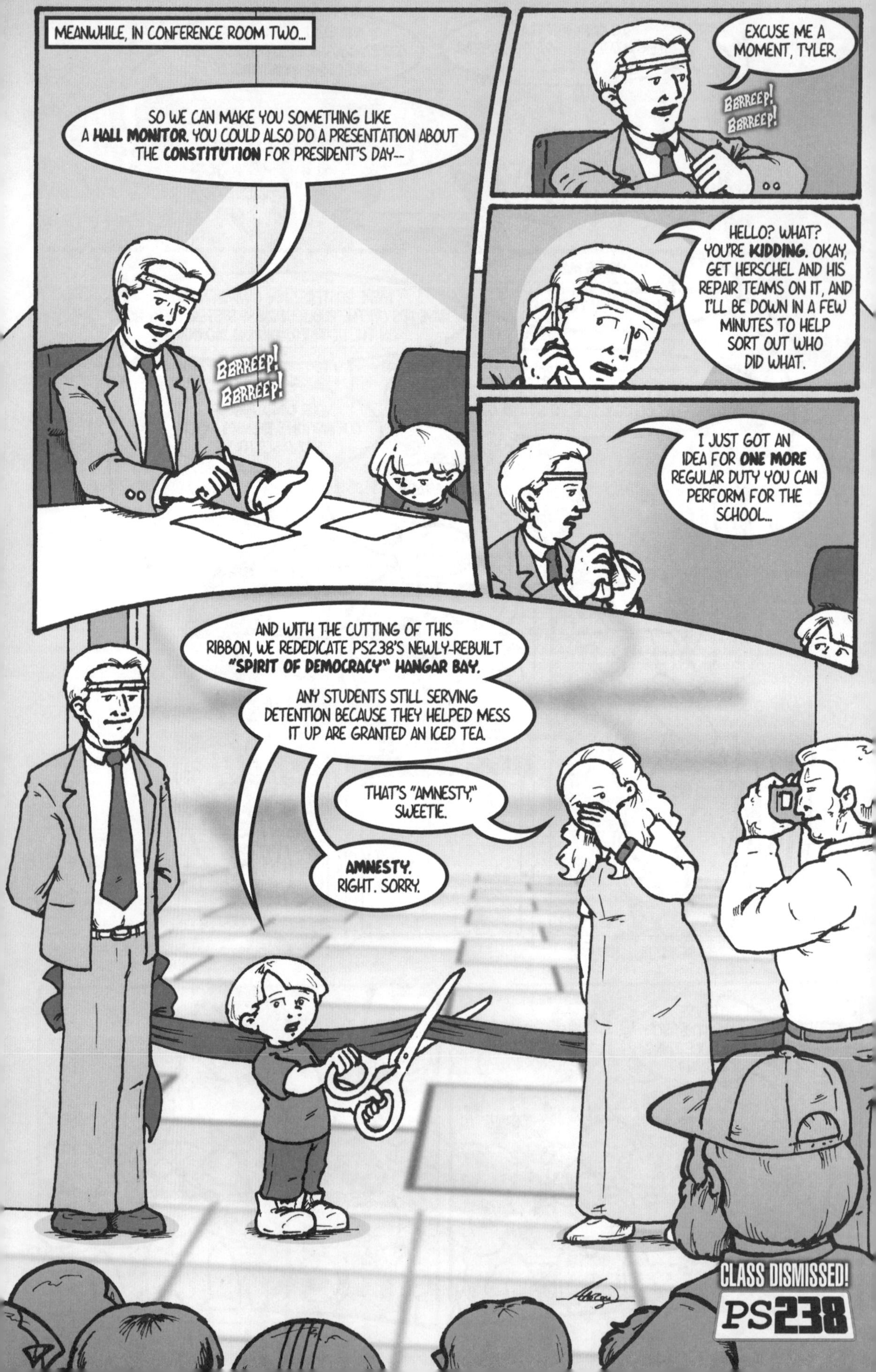
MEANWHILE, IN CONFERENCE ROOM TWO...
SO WE CAN MAKE YOU SOMETHING LIKE A **HALL MONITOR**. YOU COULD ALSO DO A PRESENTATION ABOUT THE **CONSTITUTION** FOR PRESIDENT'S DAY--
BBRREEP! BBRREEP!
EXCUSE ME A MOMENT, TYLER.
BBRREEP! BBRREEP!
HELLO? WHAT? YOU'RE **KIDDING**. OKAY, GET HERSCHEL AND HIS REPAIR TEAMS ON IT, AND I'LL BE DOWN IN A FEW MINUTES TO HELP SORT OUT WHO DID WHAT.
I JUST GOT AN IDEA FOR **ONE MORE** REGULAR DUTY YOU CAN PERFORM FOR THE SCHOOL...
AND WITH THE CUTTING OF THIS RIBBON, WE REDEDICATE PS238'S NEWLY-REBUILT **"SPIRIT OF DEMOCRACY" HANGAR BAY**.
ANY STUDENTS STILL SERVING DETENTION BECAUSE THEY HELPED MESS IT UP ARE GRANTED AN ICED TEA.
THAT'S "AMNESTY," SWEETIE.
AMNESTY. RIGHT. SORRY.
CLASS DISMISSED!
PS238

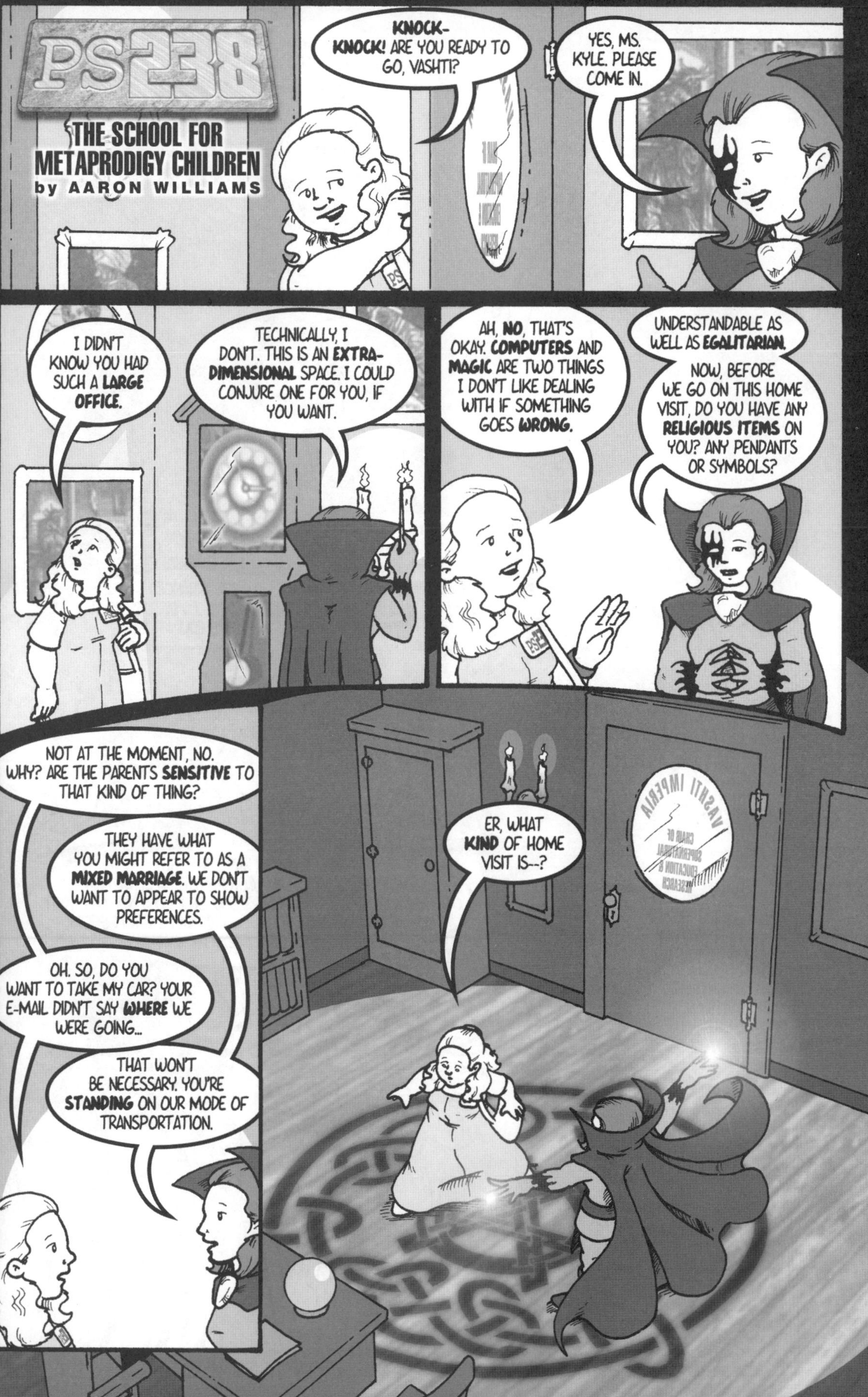
PS238
THE SCHOOL FOR METAPRODIGY CHILDREN
by AARON WILLIAMS
KNOCK-KNOCK! ARE YOU READY TO GO, VASHTI?
YES, MS. KYLE. PLEASE COME IN.
I DIDN'T KNOW YOU HAD SUCH A LARGE OFFICE.
TECHNICALLY, I DON'T. THIS IS AN EXTRA-DIMENSIONAL SPACE. I COULD CONJURE ONE FOR YOU, IF YOU WANT.
AH, NO, THAT'S OKAY. COMPUTERS AND MAGIC ARE TWO THINGS I DON'T LIKE DEALING WITH IF SOMETHING GOES WRONG.
UNDERSTANDABLE AS WELL AS EGALITARIAN.
NOW, BEFORE WE GO ON THIS HOME VISIT, DO YOU HAVE ANY RELIGIOUS ITEMS ON YOU? ANY PENDANTS OR SYMBOLS?
NOT AT THE MOMENT, NO. WHY? ARE THE PARENTS SENSITIVE TO THAT KIND OF THING?
THEY HAVE WHAT YOU MIGHT REFER TO AS A MIXED MARRIAGE. WE DON'T WANT TO APPEAR TO SHOW PREFERENCES.
ER, WHAT KIND OF HOME VISIT IS--?
VASHTI IMPERIA
CHAIR OF SUPERNATURAL EDUCATION & RESEARCH
OH. SO, DO YOU WANT TO TAKE MY CAR? YOUR E-MAIL DIDN'T SAY WHERE WE WERE GOING...
THAT WON'T BE NECESSARY. YOU'RE STANDING ON OUR MODE OF TRANSPORTATION.

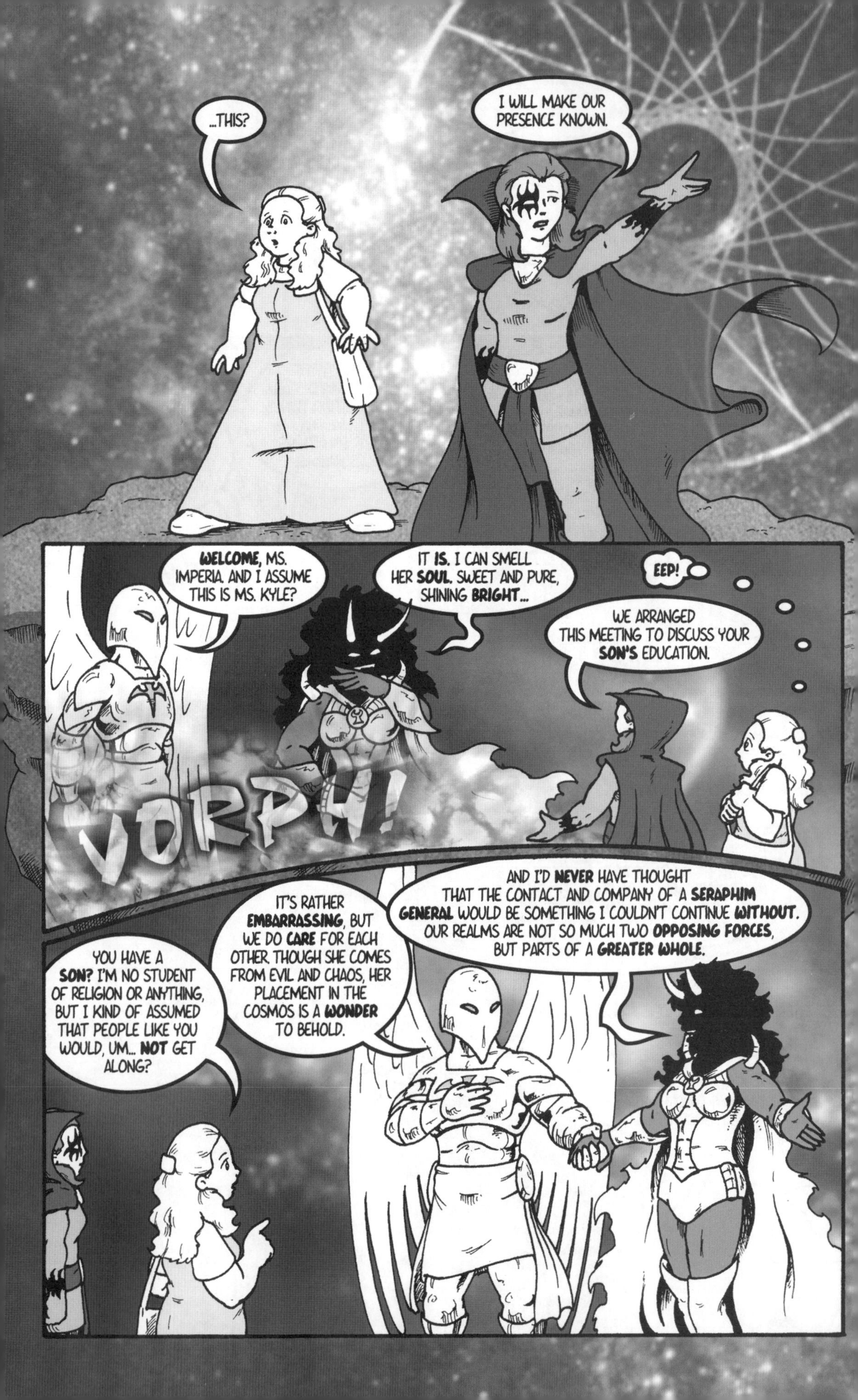
...THIS?
I WILL MAKE OUR PRESENCE KNOWN.
WELCOME, MS. IMPERIA. AND I ASSUME THIS IS MS. KYLE?
IT IS. I CAN SMELL HER SOUL. SWEET AND PURE, SHINING BRIGHT...
EEP!
WE ARRANGED THIS MEETING TO DISCUSS YOUR SON'S EDUCATION.
VORPH!
YOU HAVE A SON? I'M NO STUDENT OF RELIGION OR ANYTHING, BUT I KIND OF ASSUMED THAT PEOPLE LIKE YOU WOULD, UM... NOT GET ALONG?
IT'S RATHER EMBARRASSING, BUT WE DO CARE FOR EACH OTHER. THOUGH SHE COMES FROM EVIL AND CHAOS, HER PLACEMENT IN THE COSMOS IS A WONDER TO BEHOLD.
AND I'D NEVER HAVE THOUGHT THAT THE CONTACT AND COMPANY OF A SERAPHIM GENERAL WOULD BE SOMETHING I COULDN'T CONTINUE WITHOUT. OUR REALMS ARE NOT SO MUCH TWO OPPOSING FORCES, BUT PARTS OF A GREATER WHOLE.

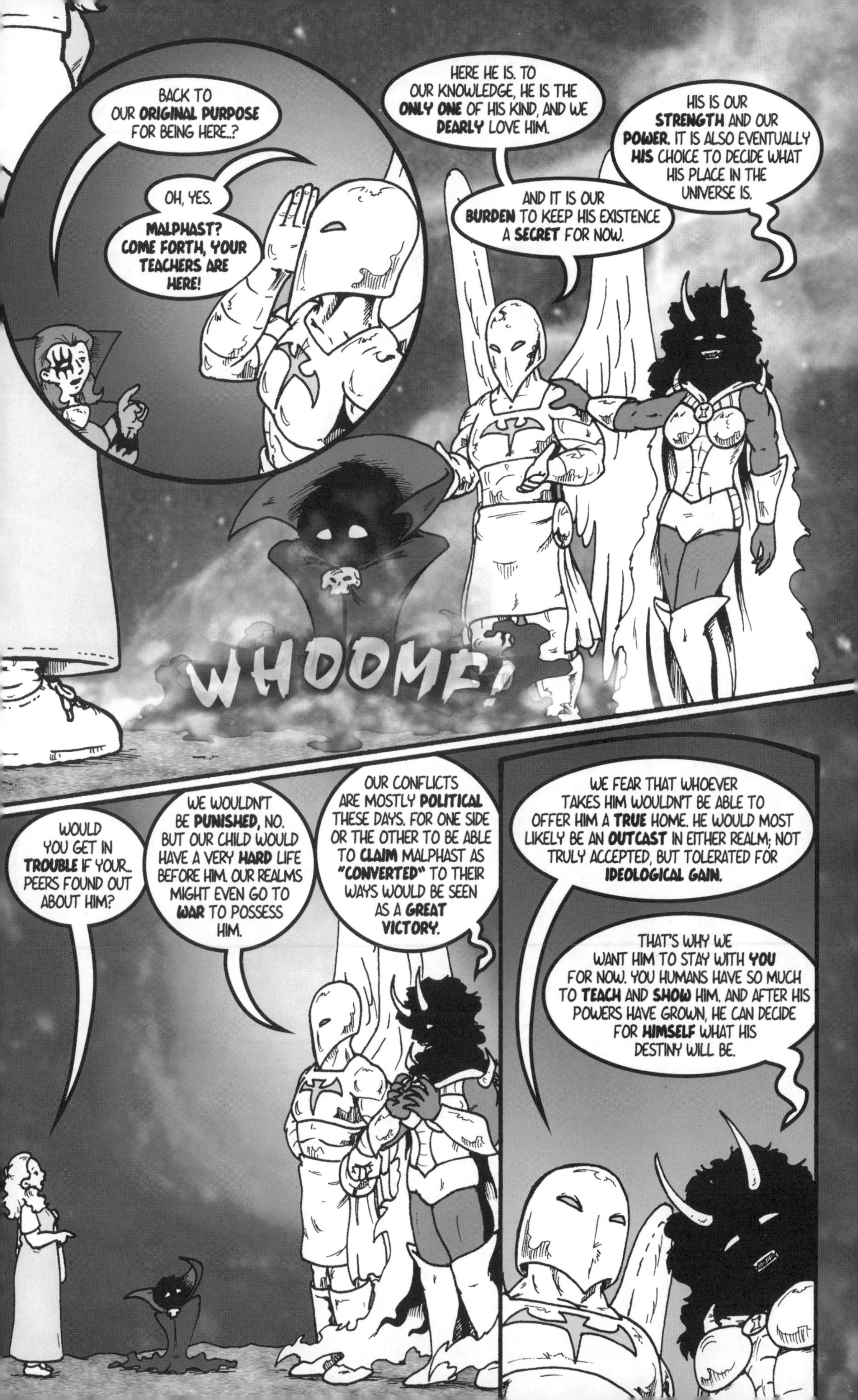

BACK TO OUR ORIGINAL PURPOSE FOR BEING HERE..?
OH, YES.
MALPHAST? COME FORTH, YOUR TEACHERS ARE HERE!
HERE HE IS. TO OUR KNOWLEDGE, HE IS THE ONLY ONE OF HIS KIND, AND WE DEARLY LOVE HIM.
AND IT IS OUR BURDEN TO KEEP HIS EXISTENCE A SECRET FOR NOW.
HIS IS OUR STRENGTH AND OUR POWER. IT IS ALSO EVENTUALLY HIS CHOICE TO DECIDE WHAT HIS PLACE IN THE UNIVERSE IS.
WHOOMF!
WOULD YOU GET IN TROUBLE IF YOUR.. PEERS FOUND OUT ABOUT HIM?
WE WOULDN'T BE PUNISHED, NO. BUT OUR CHILD WOULD HAVE A VERY HARD LIFE BEFORE HIM. OUR REALMS MIGHT EVEN GO TO WAR TO POSSESS HIM.
OUR CONFLICTS ARE MOSTLY POLITICAL THESE DAYS. FOR ONE SIDE OR THE OTHER TO BE ABLE TO CLAIM MALPHAST AS "CONVERTED" TO THEIR WAYS WOULD BE SEEN AS A GREAT VICTORY.
WE FEAR THAT WHOEVER TAKES HIM WOULDN'T BE ABLE TO OFFER HIM A TRUE HOME. HE WOULD MOST LIKELY BE AN OUTCAST IN EITHER REALM; NOT TRULY ACCEPTED, BUT TOLERATED FOR IDEOLOGICAL GAIN.
THAT'S WHY WE WANT HIM TO STAY WITH YOU FOR NOW. YOU HUMANS HAVE SO MUCH TO TEACH AND SHOW HIM. AND AFTER HIS POWERS HAVE GROWN, HE CAN DECIDE FOR HIMSELF WHAT HIS DESTINY WILL BE.

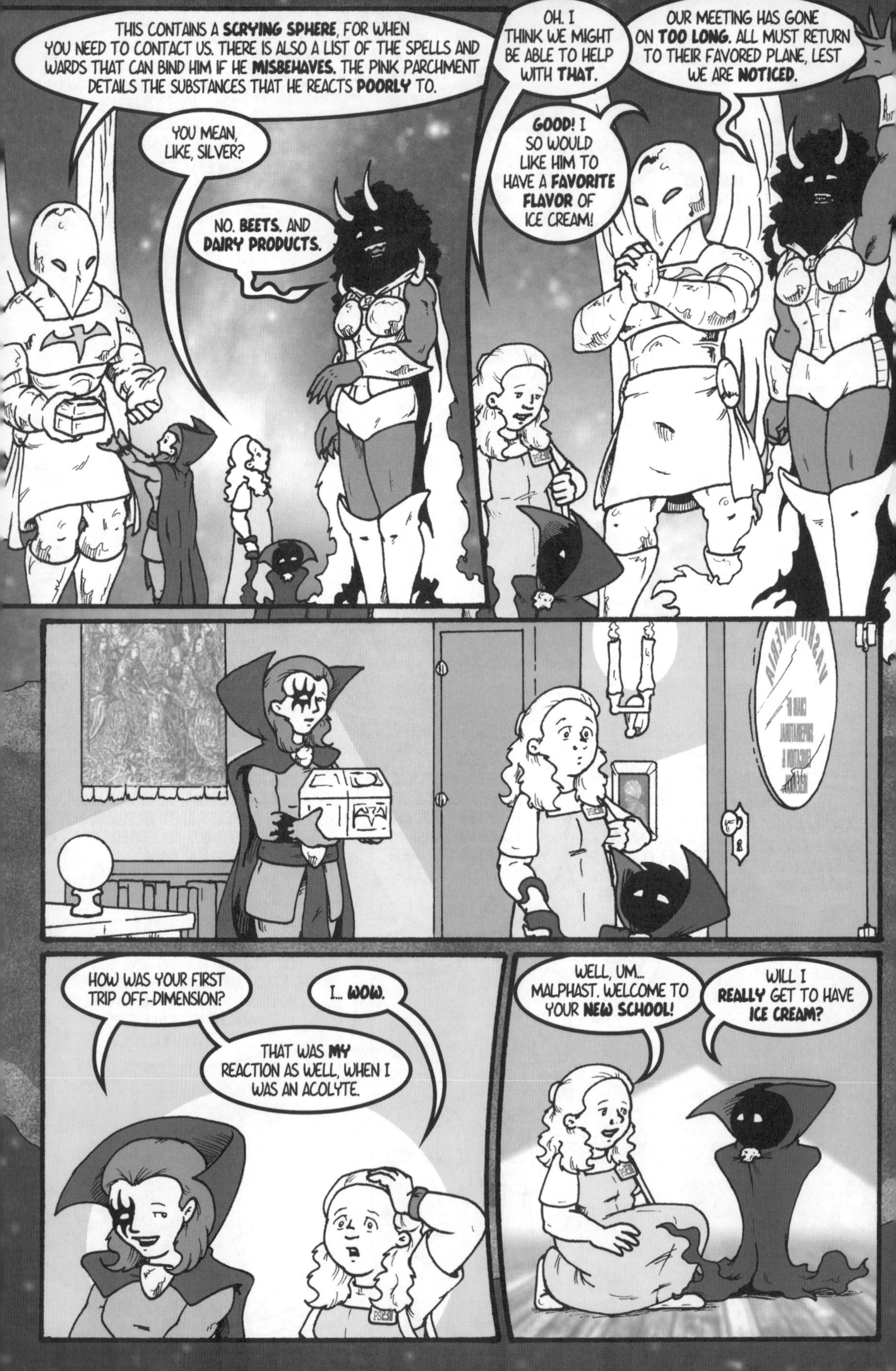
THIS CONTAINS A **SCRYING SPHERE**, FOR WHEN YOU NEED TO CONTACT US. THERE IS ALSO A LIST OF THE SPELLS AND WARDS THAT CAN BIND HIM IF HE **MISBEHAVES.** THE PINK PARCHMENT DETAILS THE SUBSTANCES THAT HE REACTS **POORLY** TO.
YOU MEAN, LIKE, SILVER?
NO. **BEETS.** AND **DAIRY PRODUCTS.**
OH. I THINK WE MIGHT BE ABLE TO HELP WITH **THAT.**
OUR MEETING HAS GONE ON **TOO LONG.** ALL MUST RETURN TO THEIR FAVORED PLANE, LEST WE ARE **NOTICED.**
GOOD! I SO WOULD LIKE HIM TO HAVE A **FAVORITE FLAVOR** OF ICE CREAM!
HOW WAS YOUR FIRST TRIP OFF-DIMENSION?
I... **WOW.**
THAT WAS **MY** REACTION AS WELL, WHEN I WAS AN ACOLYTE.
WELL, UM... MALPHAST. WELCOME TO YOUR **NEW SCHOOL!**
WILL I **REALLY** GET TO HAVE **ICE CREAM?**

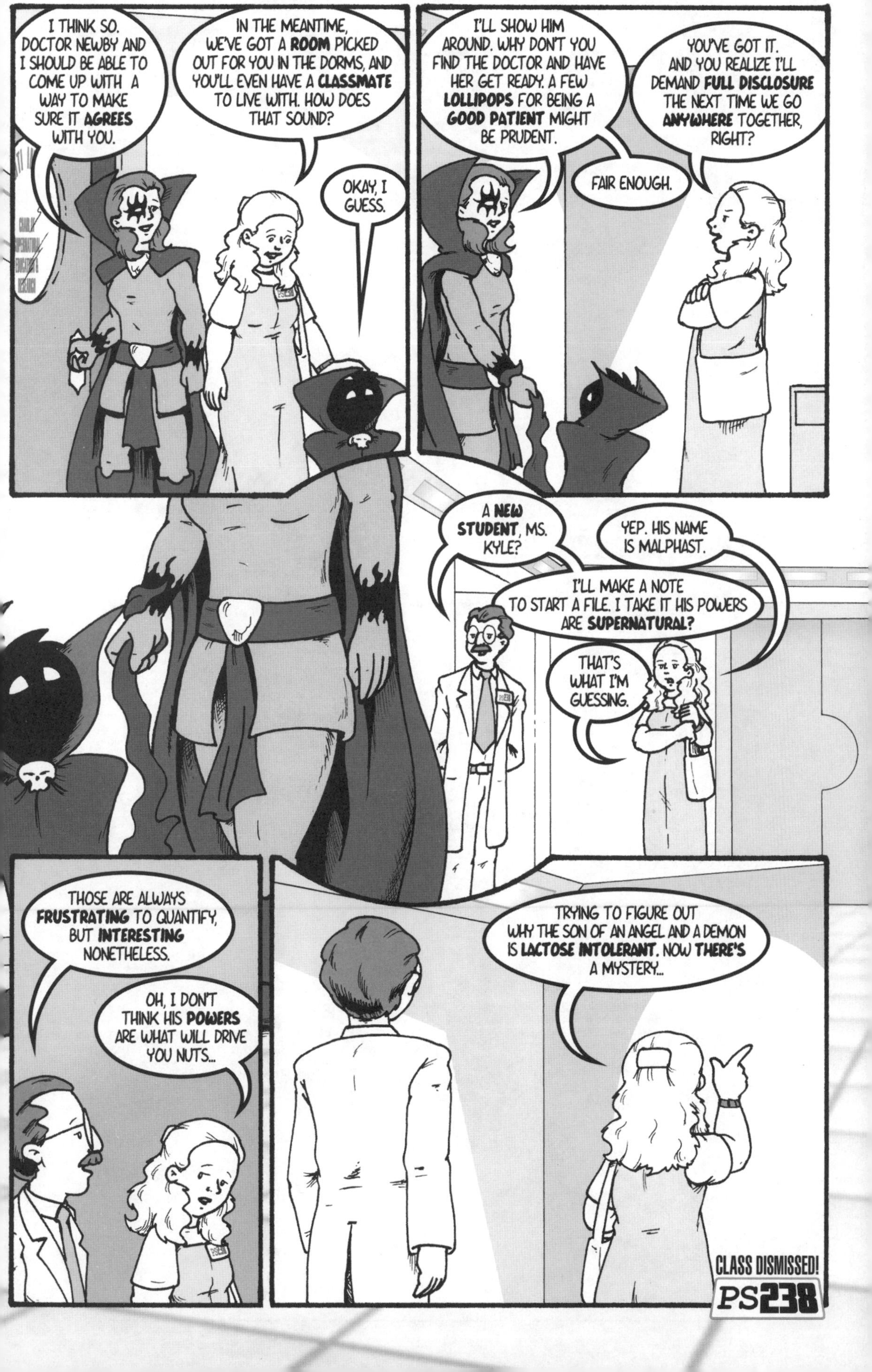
I THINK SO. DOCTOR NEWBY AND I SHOULD BE ABLE TO COME UP WITH A WAY TO MAKE SURE IT AGREES WITH YOU.
IN THE MEANTIME, WE'VE GOT A ROOM PICKED OUT FOR YOU IN THE DORMS, AND YOU'LL EVEN HAVE A CLASSMATE TO LIVE WITH. HOW DOES THAT SOUND?
OKAY, I GUESS.
I'LL SHOW HIM AROUND. WHY DON'T YOU FIND THE DOCTOR AND HAVE HER GET READY. A FEW LOLLIPOPS FOR BEING A GOOD PATIENT MIGHT BE PRUDENT.
YOU'VE GOT IT. AND YOU REALIZE I'LL DEMAND FULL DISCLOSURE THE NEXT TIME WE GO ANYWHERE TOGETHER, RIGHT?
FAIR ENOUGH.
A NEW STUDENT, MS. KYLE?
YEP. HIS NAME IS MALPHAST.
I'LL MAKE A NOTE TO START A FILE. I TAKE IT HIS POWERS ARE SUPERNATURAL?
THAT'S WHAT I'M GUESSING.
THOSE ARE ALWAYS FRUSTRATING TO QUANTIFY, BUT INTERESTING NONETHELESS.
OH, I DON'T THINK HIS POWERS ARE WHAT WILL DRIVE YOU NUTS...
TRYING TO FIGURE OUT WHY THE SON OF AN ANGEL AND A DEMON IS LACTOSE INTOLERANT. NOW THERE'S A MYSTERY...
CLASS DISMISSED!
PS238

AARON WILLIAMS'

PS238™

DORK STORM

HP HENCHMAN PUBLISHING

$2.99 #7

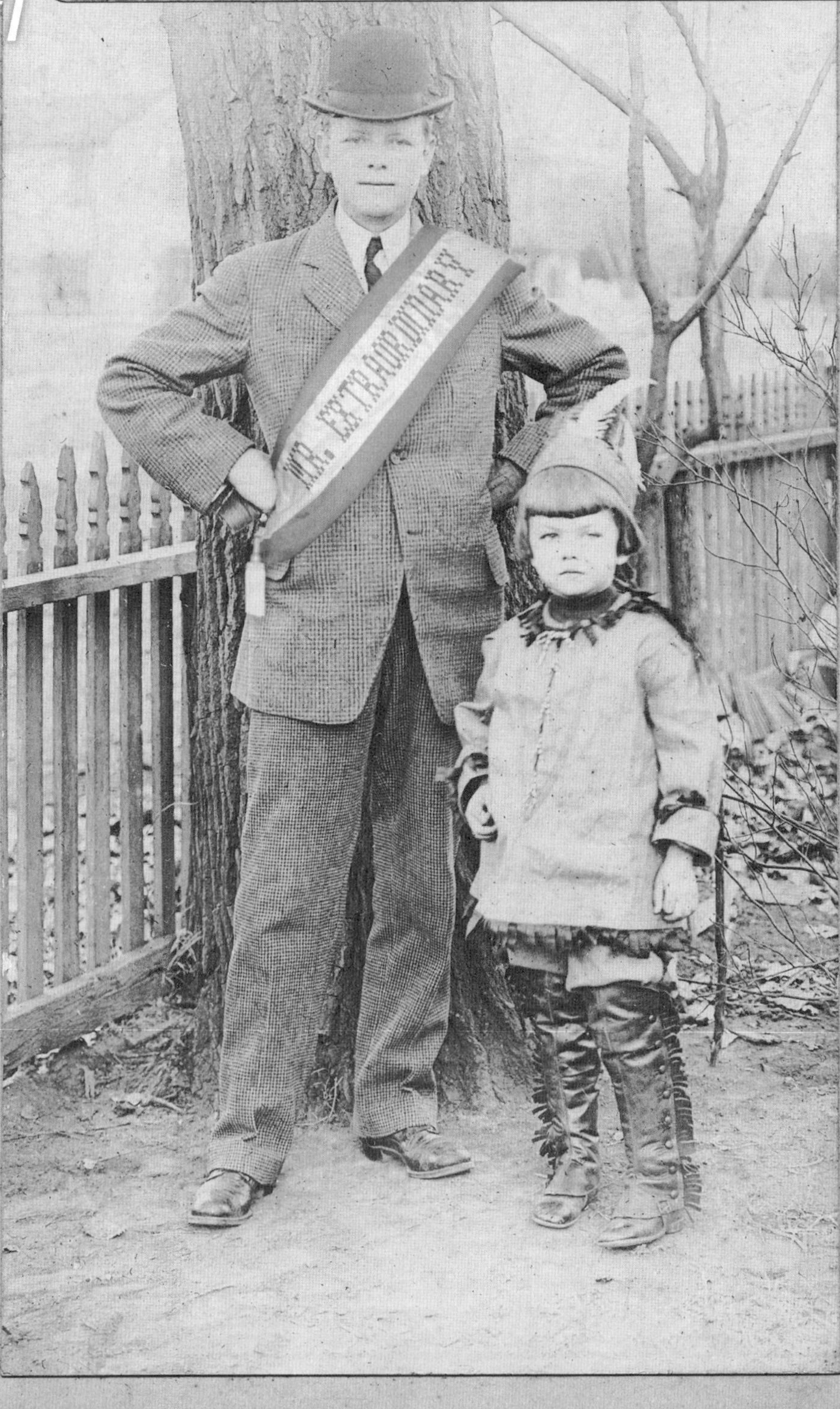
MR. EXTRAORDINARY

PS238 #7 by Aaron Williams, August 2004. Distributed by Dork Storm Press, published by Henchman Publishing, 5545 Holmes St, Kansas City, MO 64110. Fax: (608)255-1342. E-mail: aaron@ps238.com. Story and art ©2004 Aaron Williams. "The Revenant" is ©2004 Michael Stackpole. All rights reserved. No portion of this publication save for brief review excerpts may be reproduced without the express consent of the copyright holder. This is a work of fiction: any similarities to any actual persons or metahumans save for the purpose of satire is purely coincidental. ADVERTISING: sales@DorkStorm.com. SUBSCRIPTIONS: $26 per year. Please contact adventureretail2@qwest.net, or call (651)-488-2433 details. All letters to PS238 assumed intended for publication unless otherwise stated, and become the property of the copyright holder. Political history is far too criminal a subject to be a fit thing to teach children. -W.H. Auden. FIRST PRINTING, August 2004. PRINTED IN CANADA

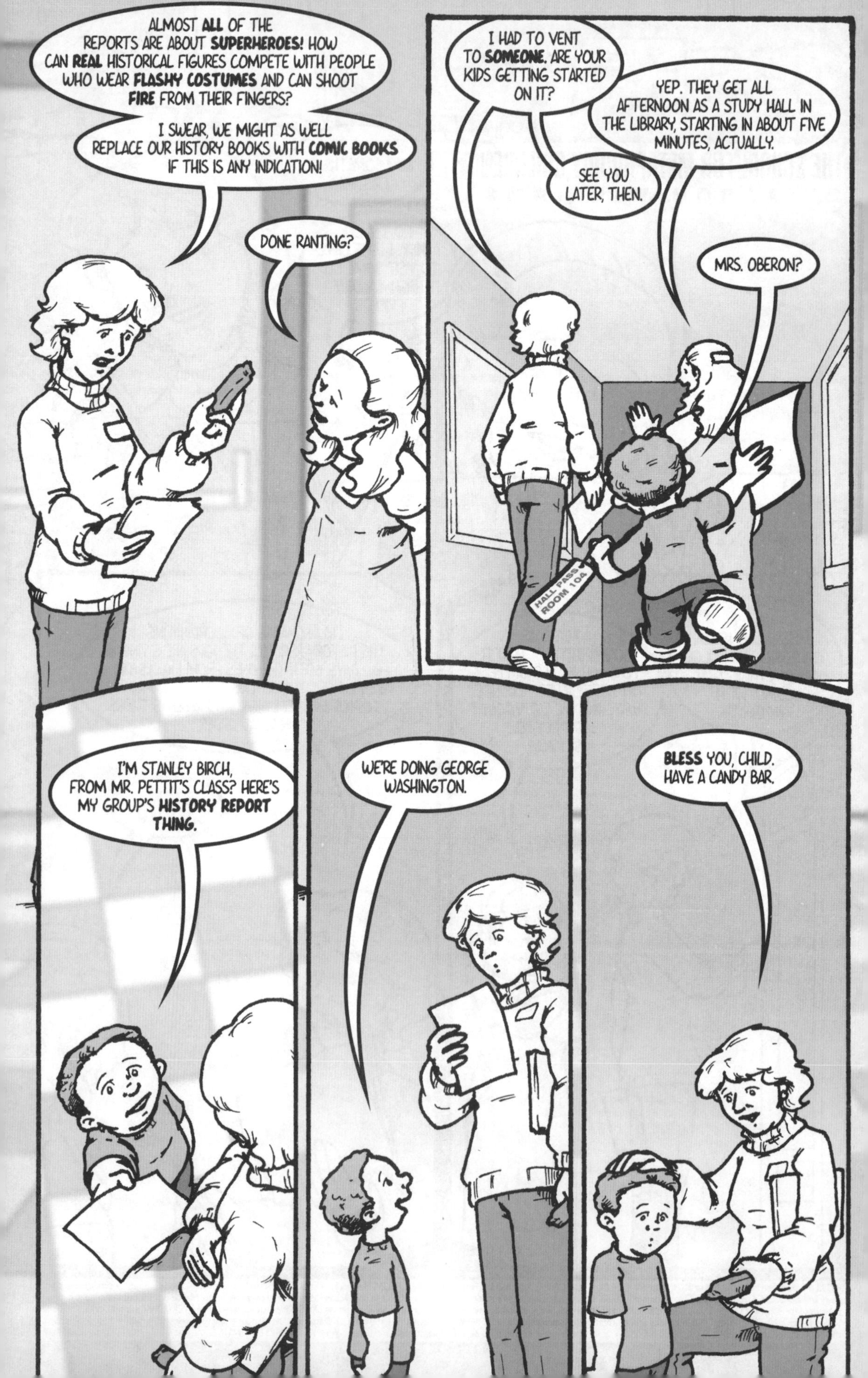
ALMOST ALL OF THE REPORTS ARE ABOUT SUPERHEROES! HOW CAN REAL HISTORICAL FIGURES COMPETE WITH PEOPLE WHO WEAR FLASHY COSTUMES AND CAN SHOOT FIRE FROM THEIR FINGERS?
I SWEAR, WE MIGHT AS WELL REPLACE OUR HISTORY BOOKS WITH COMIC BOOKS IF THIS IS ANY INDICATION!
DONE RANTING?
I HAD TO VENT TO SOMEONE. ARE YOUR KIDS GETTING STARTED ON IT?
YEP. THEY GET ALL AFTERNOON AS A STUDY HALL IN THE LIBRARY, STARTING IN ABOUT FIVE MINUTES, ACTUALLY.
SEE YOU LATER, THEN.
MRS. OBERON?
HALL PASS ROOM 104
I'M STANLEY BIRCH, FROM MR. PETTIT'S CLASS? HERE'S MY GROUP'S HISTORY REPORT THING.
WE'RE DOING GEORGE WASHINGTON.
BLESS YOU, CHILD. HAVE A CANDY BAR.

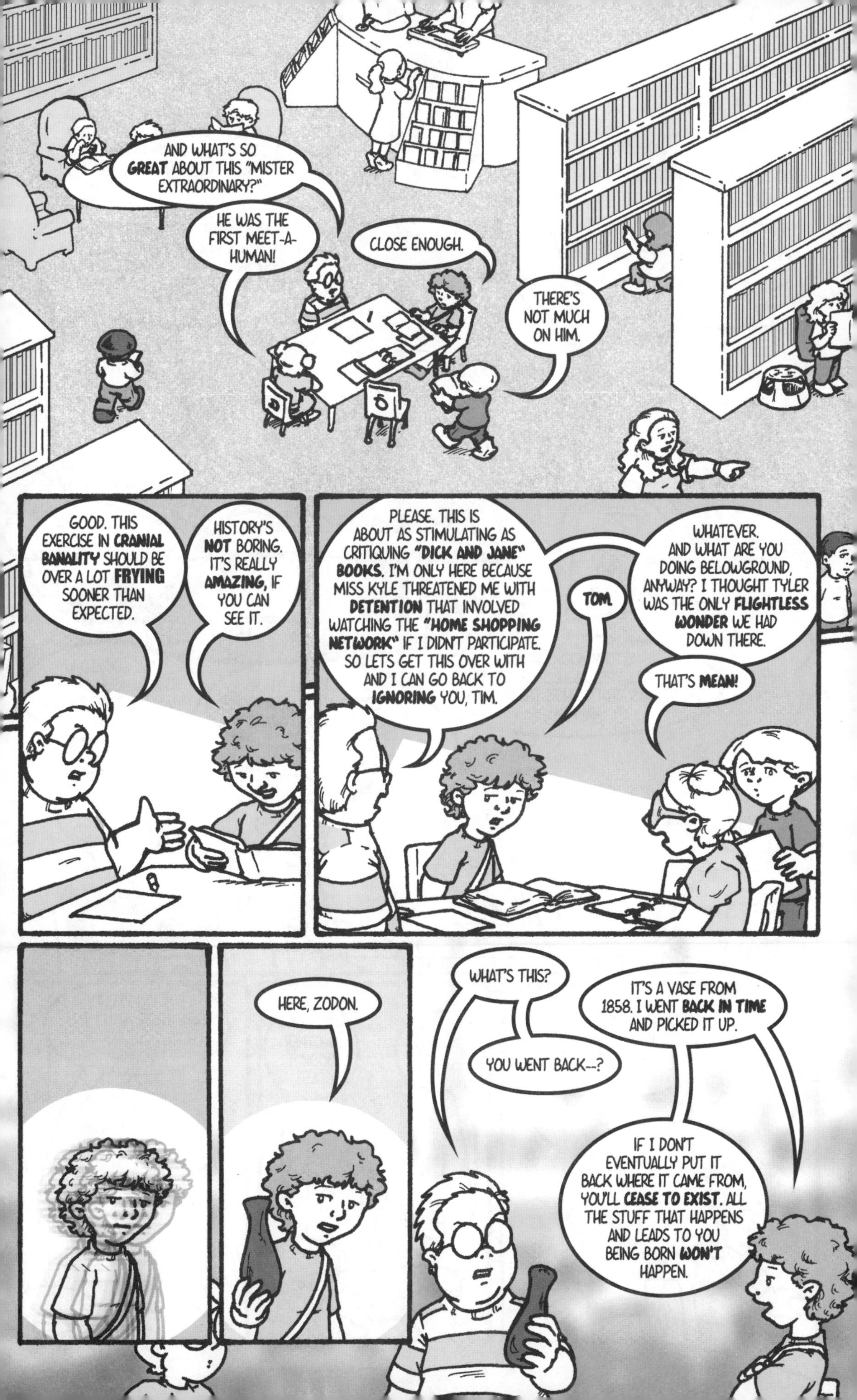
AND WHAT'S SO GREAT ABOUT THIS "MISTER EXTRAORDINARY?"
HE WAS THE FIRST MEET-A-HUMAN!
CLOSE ENOUGH.
THERE'S NOT MUCH ON HIM.
GOOD. THIS EXERCISE IN CRANIAL BANALITY SHOULD BE OVER A LOT FRYING SOONER THAN EXPECTED.
HISTORY'S NOT BORING. IT'S REALLY AMAZING, IF YOU CAN SEE IT.
PLEASE. THIS IS ABOUT AS STIMULATING AS CRITIQUING "DICK AND JANE" BOOKS. I'M ONLY HERE BECAUSE MISS KYLE THREATENED ME WITH DETENTION THAT INVOLVED WATCHING THE "HOME SHOPPING NETWORK" IF I DIDN'T PARTICIPATE. SO LETS GET THIS OVER WITH AND I CAN GO BACK TO IGNORING YOU, TIM.
TOM.
WHATEVER. AND WHAT ARE YOU DOING BELOWGROUND, ANYWAY? I THOUGHT TYLER WAS THE ONLY FLIGHTLESS WONDER WE HAD DOWN THERE.
THAT'S MEAN!
HERE, ZODON.
WHAT'S THIS?
IT'S A VASE FROM 1858. I WENT BACK IN TIME AND PICKED IT UP.
YOU WENT BACK--?
IF I DON'T EVENTUALLY PUT IT BACK WHERE IT CAME FROM, YOU'LL CEASE TO EXIST. ALL THE STUFF THAT HAPPENS AND LEADS TO YOU BEING BORN WON'T HAPPEN.

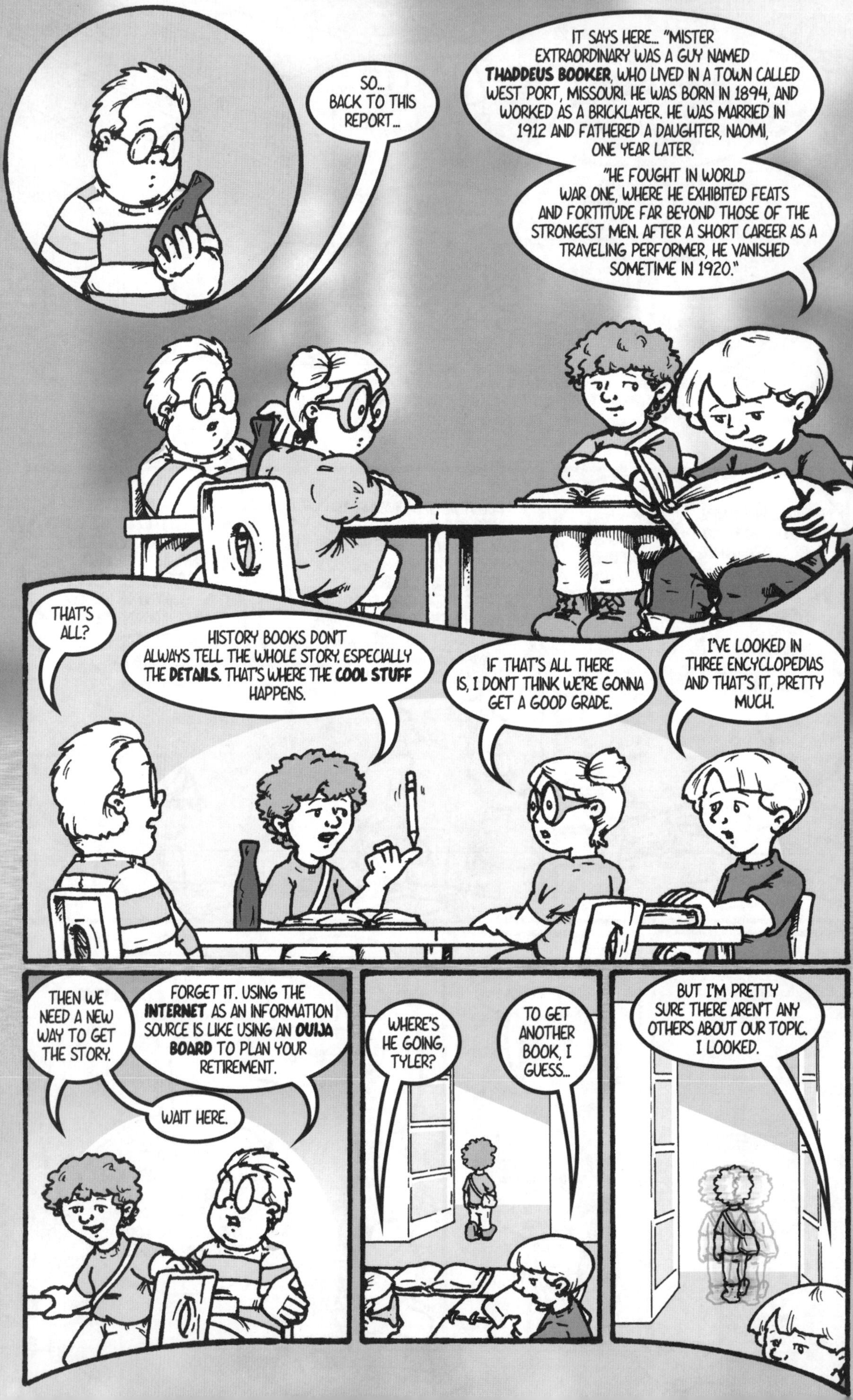
SO... BACK TO THIS REPORT...
IT SAYS HERE... "MISTER EXTRAORDINARY WAS A GUY NAMED **THADDEUS BOOKER**, WHO LIVED IN A TOWN CALLED WEST PORT, MISSOURI. HE WAS BORN IN 1894, AND WORKED AS A BRICKLAYER. HE WAS MARRIED IN 1912 AND FATHERED A DAUGHTER, NAOMI, ONE YEAR LATER.
"HE FOUGHT IN WORLD WAR ONE, WHERE HE EXHIBITED FEATS AND FORTITUDE FAR BEYOND THOSE OF THE STRONGEST MEN. AFTER A SHORT CAREER AS A TRAVELING PERFORMER, HE VANISHED SOMETIME IN 1920."
THAT'S ALL?
HISTORY BOOKS DON'T ALWAYS TELL THE WHOLE STORY. ESPECIALLY THE **DETAILS.** THAT'S WHERE THE **COOL STUFF** HAPPENS.
IF THAT'S ALL THERE IS, I DON'T THINK WE'RE GONNA GET A GOOD GRADE.
I'VE LOOKED IN THREE ENCYCLOPEDIAS AND THAT'S IT, PRETTY MUCH.
THEN WE NEED A NEW WAY TO GET THE STORY.
FORGET IT. USING THE **INTERNET** AS AN INFORMATION SOURCE IS LIKE USING AN **OUIJA BOARD** TO PLAN YOUR RETIREMENT.
WAIT HERE.
WHERE'S HE GOING, TYLER?
TO GET ANOTHER BOOK, I GUESS...
BUT I'M PRETTY SURE THERE AREN'T ANY OTHERS ABOUT OUR TOPIC. I LOOKED.

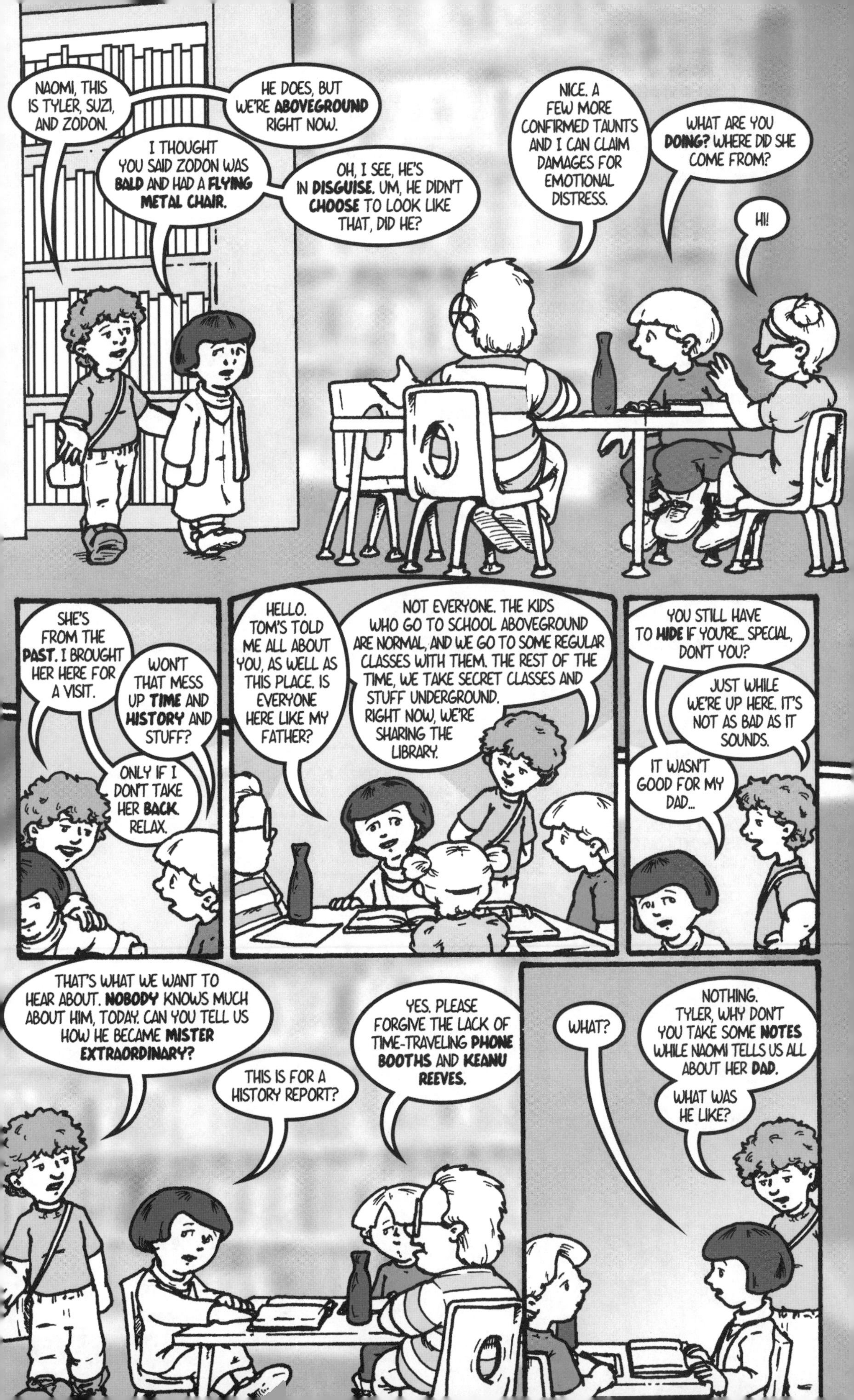
NAOMI, THIS IS TYLER, SUZI, AND ZODON.
I THOUGHT YOU SAID ZODON WAS BALD AND HAD A FLYING METAL CHAIR.
HE DOES, BUT WE'RE ABOVEGROUND RIGHT NOW.
OH, I SEE, HE'S IN DISGUISE. UM, HE DIDN'T CHOOSE TO LOOK LIKE THAT, DID HE?
NICE. A FEW MORE CONFIRMED TAUNTS AND I CAN CLAIM DAMAGES FOR EMOTIONAL DISTRESS.
WHAT ARE YOU DOING? WHERE DID SHE COME FROM?
HI!
SHE'S FROM THE PAST. I BROUGHT HER HERE FOR A VISIT.
WON'T THAT MESS UP TIME AND HISTORY AND STUFF?
ONLY IF I DON'T TAKE HER BACK. RELAX.
HELLO. TOM'S TOLD ME ALL ABOUT YOU, AS WELL AS THIS PLACE. IS EVERYONE HERE LIKE MY FATHER?
NOT EVERYONE. THE KIDS WHO GO TO SCHOOL ABOVEGROUND ARE NORMAL, AND WE GO TO SOME REGULAR CLASSES WITH THEM. THE REST OF THE TIME, WE TAKE SECRET CLASSES AND STUFF UNDERGROUND. RIGHT NOW, WE'RE SHARING THE LIBRARY.
YOU STILL HAVE TO HIDE IF YOU'RE... SPECIAL, DON'T YOU?
JUST WHILE WE'RE UP HERE. IT'S NOT AS BAD AS IT SOUNDS.
IT WASN'T GOOD FOR MY DAD...
THAT'S WHAT WE WANT TO HEAR ABOUT. NOBODY KNOWS MUCH ABOUT HIM, TODAY. CAN YOU TELL US HOW HE BECAME MISTER EXTRAORDINARY?
THIS IS FOR A HISTORY REPORT?
YES. PLEASE FORGIVE THE LACK OF TIME-TRAVELING PHONE BOOTHS AND KEANU REEVES.
WHAT?
NOTHING. TYLER, WHY DON'T YOU TAKE SOME NOTES WHILE NAOMI TELLS US ALL ABOUT HER DAD.
WHAT WAS HE LIKE?

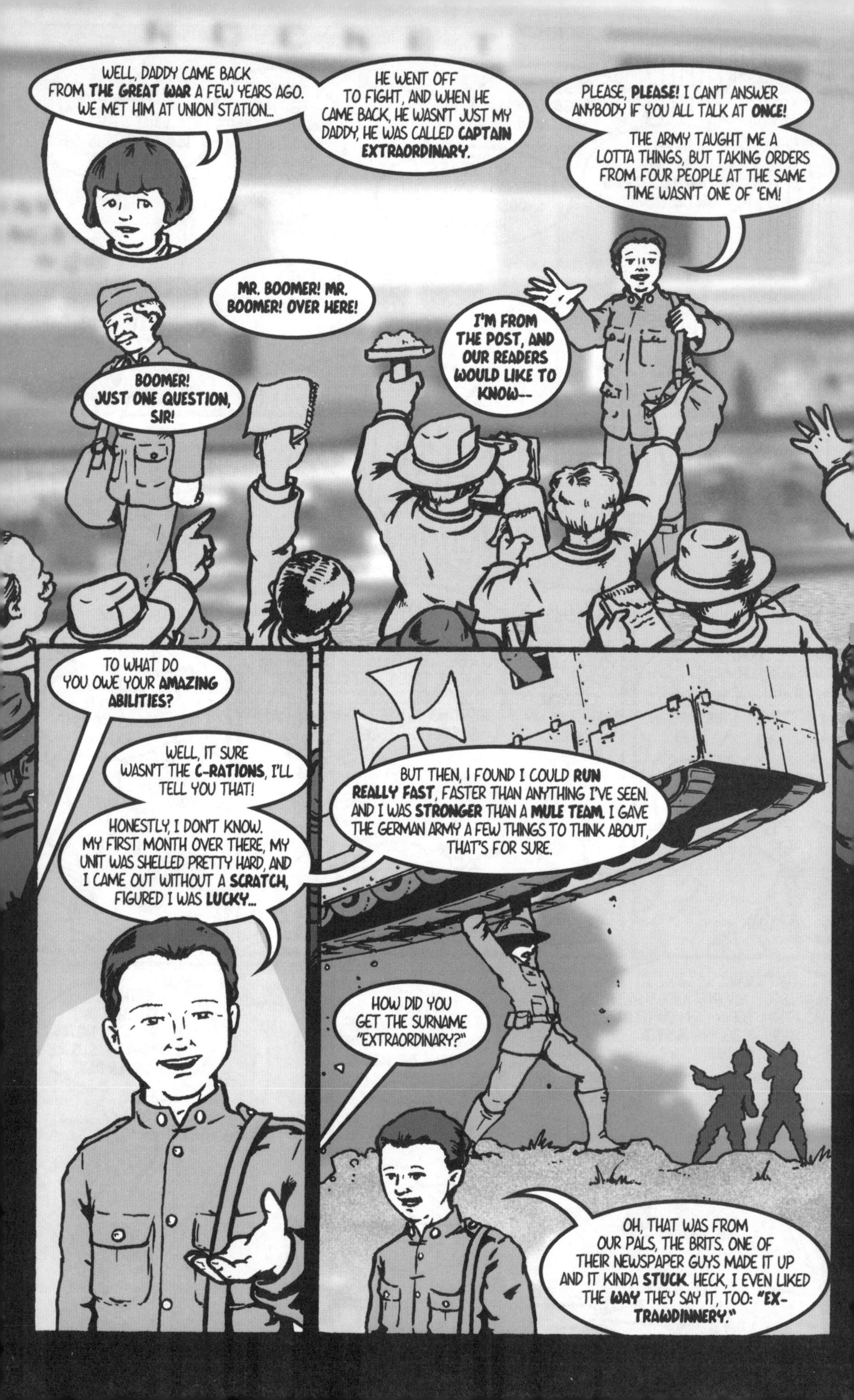

WELL, DADDY CAME BACK FROM THE GREAT WAR A FEW YEARS AGO. WE MET HIM AT UNION STATION...
HE WENT OFF TO FIGHT, AND WHEN HE CAME BACK, HE WASN'T JUST MY DADDY, HE WAS CALLED CAPTAIN EXTRAORDINARY.
PLEASE, PLEASE! I CAN'T ANSWER ANYBODY IF YOU ALL TALK AT ONCE!
THE ARMY TAUGHT ME A LOTTA THINGS, BUT TAKING ORDERS FROM FOUR PEOPLE AT THE SAME TIME WASN'T ONE OF 'EM!
MR. BOOMER! MR. BOOMER! OVER HERE!
I'M FROM THE POST, AND OUR READERS WOULD LIKE TO KNOW--
BOOMER! JUST ONE QUESTION, SIR!
TO WHAT DO YOU OWE YOUR AMAZING ABILITIES?
WELL, IT SURE WASN'T THE C-RATIONS, I'LL TELL YOU THAT!
HONESTLY, I DON'T KNOW. MY FIRST MONTH OVER THERE, MY UNIT WAS SHELLED PRETTY HARD, AND I CAME OUT WITHOUT A SCRATCH, FIGURED I WAS LUCKY...
BUT THEN, I FOUND I COULD RUN REALLY FAST, FASTER THAN ANYTHING I'VE SEEN. AND I WAS STRONGER THAN A MULE TEAM. I GAVE THE GERMAN ARMY A FEW THINGS TO THINK ABOUT, THAT'S FOR SURE.
HOW DID YOU GET THE SURNAME "EXTRAORDINARY?"
OH, THAT WAS FROM OUR PALS, THE BRITS. ONE OF THEIR NEWSPAPER GUYS MADE IT UP AND IT KINDA STUCK. HECK, I EVEN LIKED THE WAY THEY SAY IT, TOO: "EX-TRAWDINNERY."

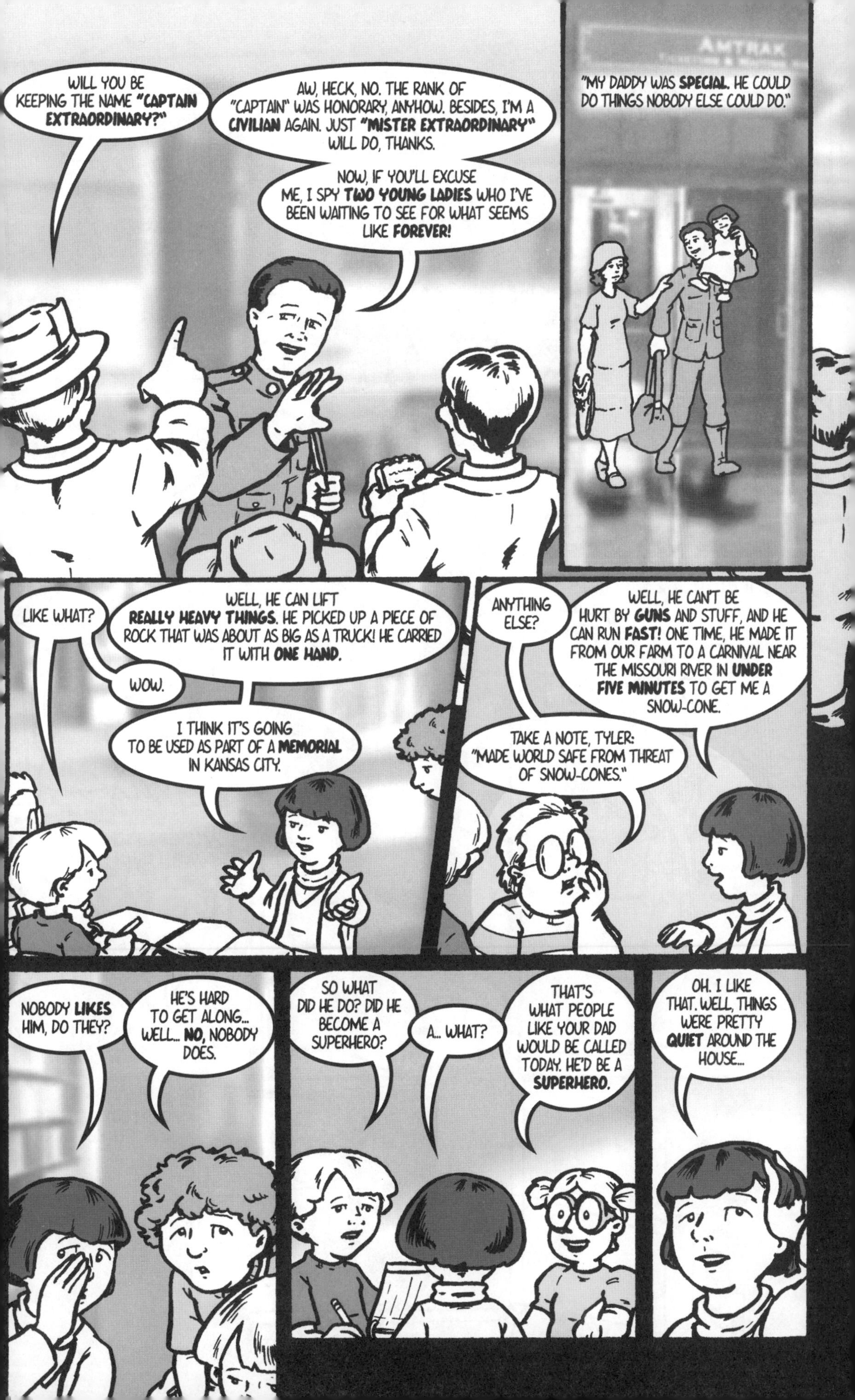
WILL YOU BE KEEPING THE NAME "CAPTAIN EXTRAORDINARY?"
AW, HECK, NO. THE RANK OF "CAPTAIN" WAS HONORARY, ANYHOW. BESIDES, I'M A CIVILIAN AGAIN. JUST "MISTER EXTRAORDINARY" WILL DO, THANKS.
NOW, IF YOU'LL EXCUSE ME, I SPY TWO YOUNG LADIES WHO I'VE BEEN WAITING TO SEE FOR WHAT SEEMS LIKE FOREVER!
AMTRAK
"MY DADDY WAS SPECIAL. HE COULD DO THINGS NOBODY ELSE COULD DO."
LIKE WHAT?
WELL, HE CAN LIFT REALLY HEAVY THINGS. HE PICKED UP A PIECE OF ROCK THAT WAS ABOUT AS BIG AS A TRUCK! HE CARRIED IT WITH ONE HAND.
WOW.
I THINK IT'S GOING TO BE USED AS PART OF A MEMORIAL IN KANSAS CITY.
ANYTHING ELSE?
WELL, HE CAN'T BE HURT BY GUNS AND STUFF, AND HE CAN RUN FAST! ONE TIME, HE MADE IT FROM OUR FARM TO A CARNIVAL NEAR THE MISSOURI RIVER IN UNDER FIVE MINUTES TO GET ME A SNOW-CONE.
TAKE A NOTE, TYLER: "MADE WORLD SAFE FROM THREAT OF SNOW-CONES."
NOBODY LIKES HIM, DO THEY?
HE'S HARD TO GET ALONG... WELL... NO, NOBODY DOES.
SO WHAT DID HE DO? DID HE BECOME A SUPERHERO?
A... WHAT?
THAT'S WHAT PEOPLE LIKE YOUR DAD WOULD BE CALLED TODAY. HE'D BE A SUPERHERO.
OH. I LIKE THAT. WELL, THINGS WERE PRETTY QUIET AROUND THE HOUSE...

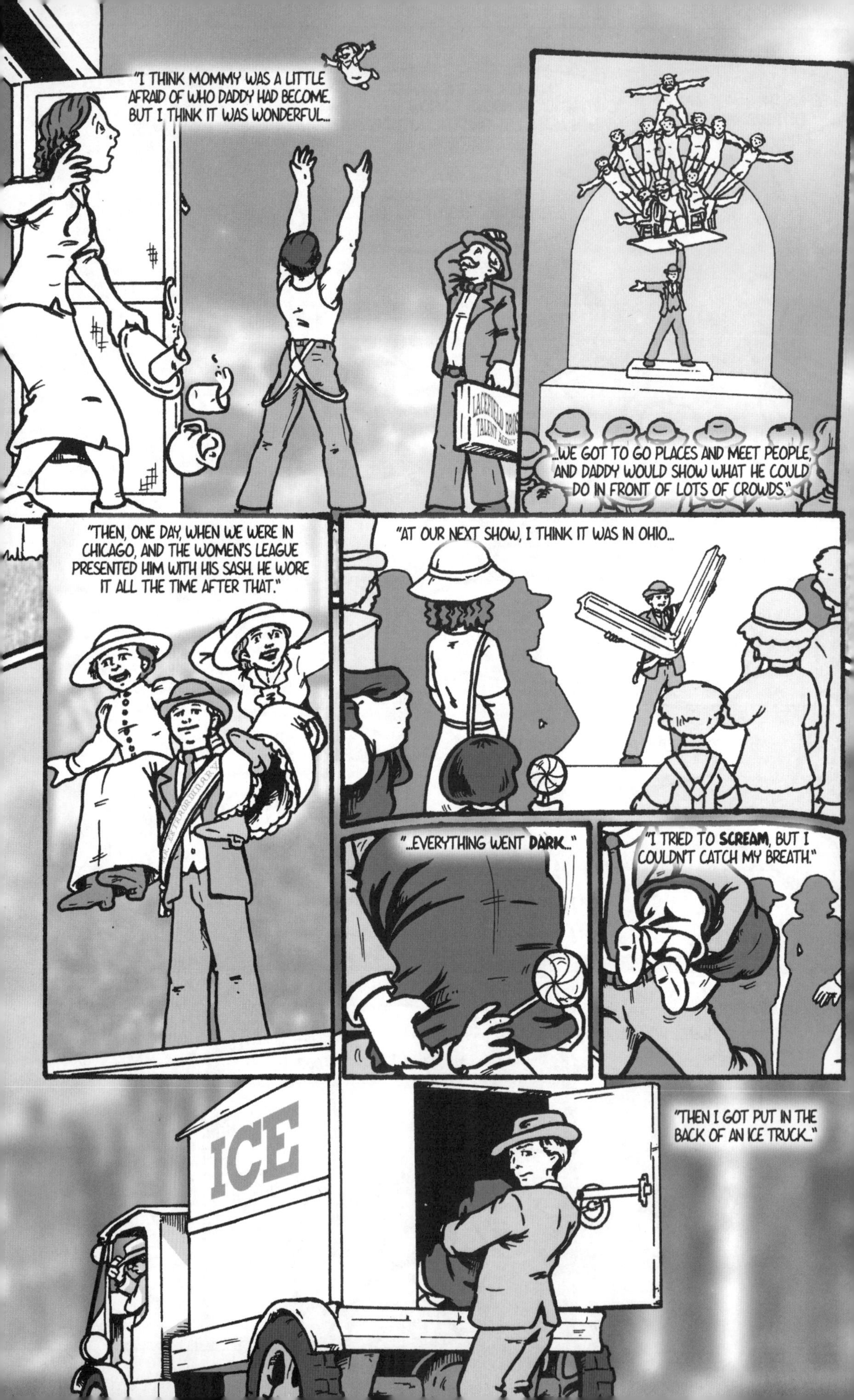
"I THINK MOMMY WAS A LITTLE AFRAID OF WHO DADDY HAD BECOME. BUT I THINK IT WAS WONDERFUL...
LACEFIELD BROS TALENT AGENCY
...WE GOT TO GO PLACES AND MEET PEOPLE, AND DADDY WOULD SHOW WHAT HE COULD DO IN FRONT OF LOTS OF CROWDS."
"THEN, ONE DAY, WHEN WE WERE IN CHICAGO, AND THE WOMEN'S LEAGUE PRESENTED HIM WITH HIS SASH. HE WORE IT ALL THE TIME AFTER THAT."
"AT OUR NEXT SHOW, I THINK IT WAS IN OHIO...
"...EVERYTHING WENT **DARK**..."
"I TRIED TO **SCREAM**, BUT I COULDN'T CATCH MY BREATH."
ICE
"THEN I GOT PUT IN THE BACK OF AN ICE TRUCK..."

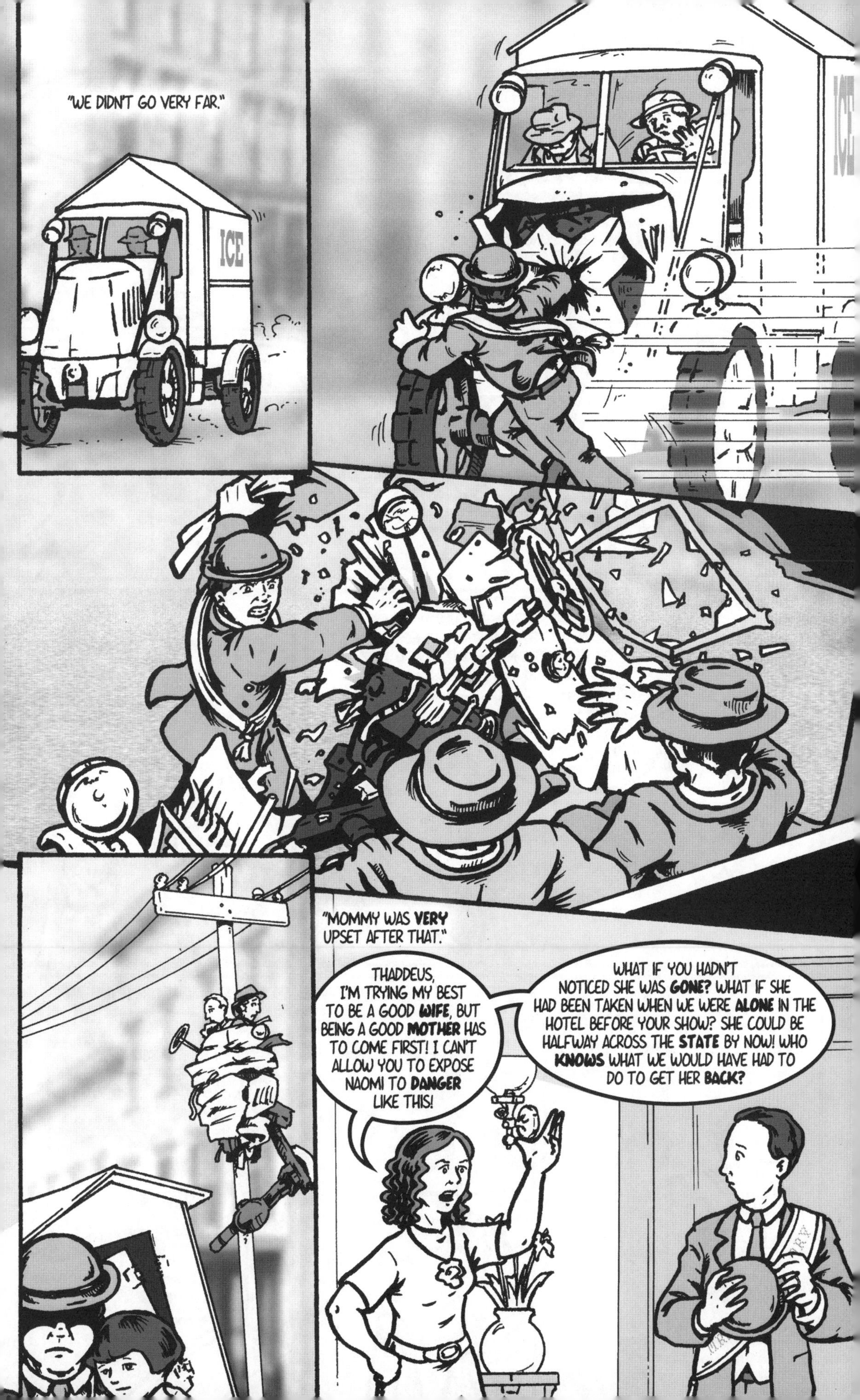
"WE DIDN'T GO VERY FAR."
ICE
ICE
"MOMMY WAS **VERY** UPSET AFTER THAT."
THADDEUS, I'M TRYING MY BEST TO BE A GOOD **WIFE**, BUT BEING A GOOD **MOTHER** HAS TO COME FIRST! I CAN'T ALLOW YOU TO EXPOSE NAOMI TO **DANGER** LIKE THIS!
WHAT IF YOU HADN'T NOTICED SHE WAS **GONE?** WHAT IF SHE HAD BEEN TAKEN WHEN WE WERE **ALONE** IN THE HOTEL BEFORE YOUR SHOW? SHE COULD BE HALFWAY ACROSS THE **STATE** BY NOW! WHO **KNOWS** WHAT WE WOULD HAVE HAD TO DO TO GET HER **BACK?**

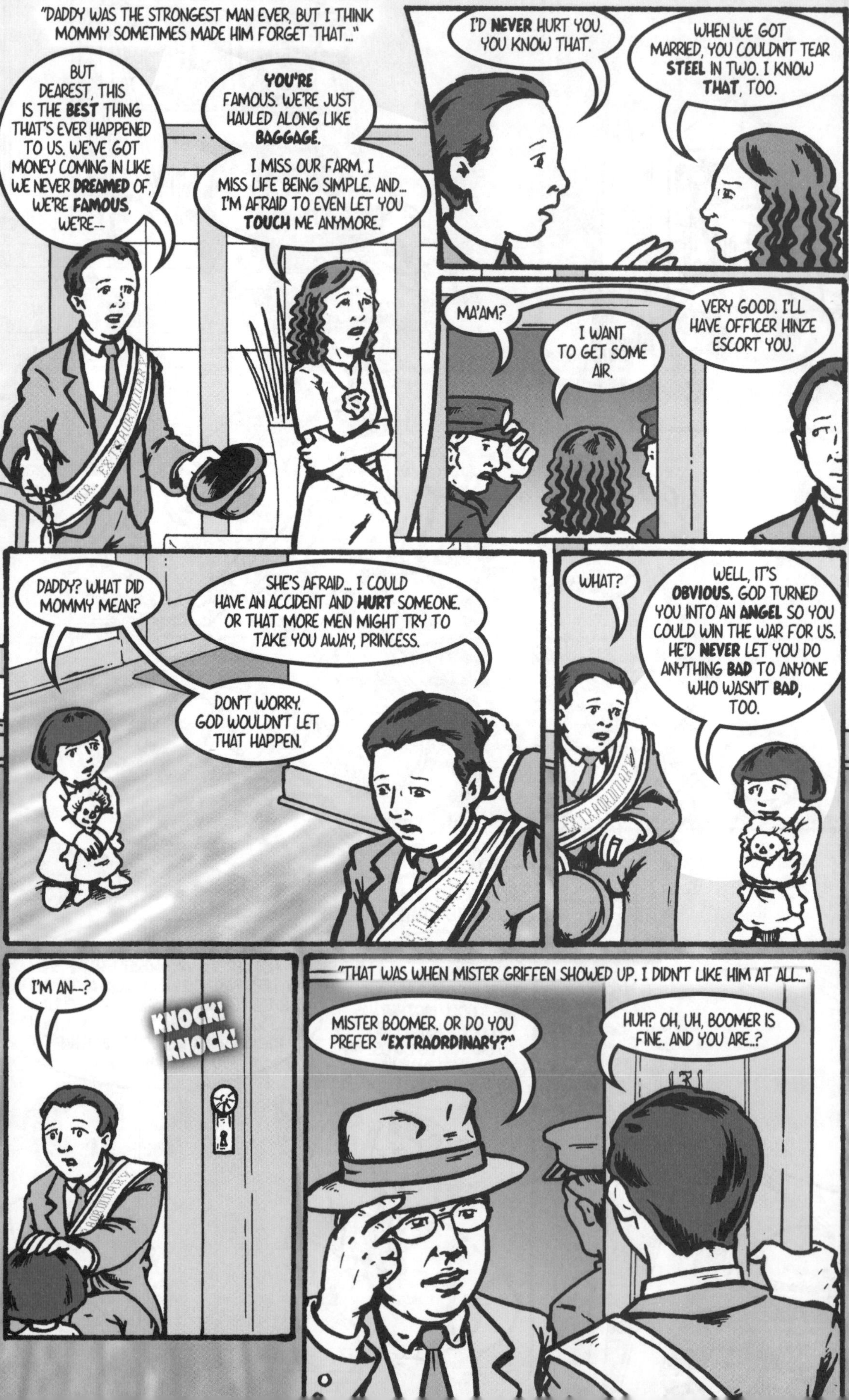
"DADDY WAS THE STRONGEST MAN EVER, BUT I THINK MOMMY SOMETIMES MADE HIM FORGET THAT..."
BUT DEAREST, THIS IS THE **BEST** THING THAT'S EVER HAPPENED TO US. WE'VE GOT MONEY COMING IN LIKE WE NEVER **DREAMED** OF, WE'RE **FAMOUS**, WE'RE--
YOU'RE FAMOUS. WE'RE JUST HAULED ALONG LIKE **BAGGAGE.**
I MISS OUR FARM. I MISS LIFE BEING SIMPLE. AND... I'M AFRAID TO EVEN LET YOU **TOUCH** ME ANYMORE.
I'D **NEVER** HURT YOU. YOU KNOW THAT.
WHEN WE GOT MARRIED, YOU COULDN'T TEAR **STEEL** IN TWO. I KNOW **THAT**, TOO.
MA'AM?
I WANT TO GET SOME AIR.
VERY GOOD. I'LL HAVE OFFICER HINZE ESCORT YOU.
DADDY? WHAT DID MOMMY MEAN?
SHE'S AFRAID... I COULD HAVE AN ACCIDENT AND **HURT** SOMEONE. OR THAT MORE MEN MIGHT TRY TO TAKE YOU AWAY, PRINCESS.
DON'T WORRY. GOD WOULDN'T LET THAT HAPPEN.
WHAT?
WELL, IT'S **OBVIOUS.** GOD TURNED YOU INTO AN **ANGEL** SO YOU COULD WIN THE WAR FOR US. HE'D **NEVER** LET YOU DO ANYTHING **BAD** TO ANYONE WHO WASN'T **BAD,** TOO.
I'M AN--?
KNOCK! KNOCK!
"THAT WAS WHEN MISTER GRIFFEN SHOWED UP. I DIDN'T LIKE HIM AT ALL..."
MISTER BOOMER. OR DO YOU PREFER **"EXTRAORDINARY?"**
HUH? OH, UH, BOOMER IS FINE. AND YOU ARE..?

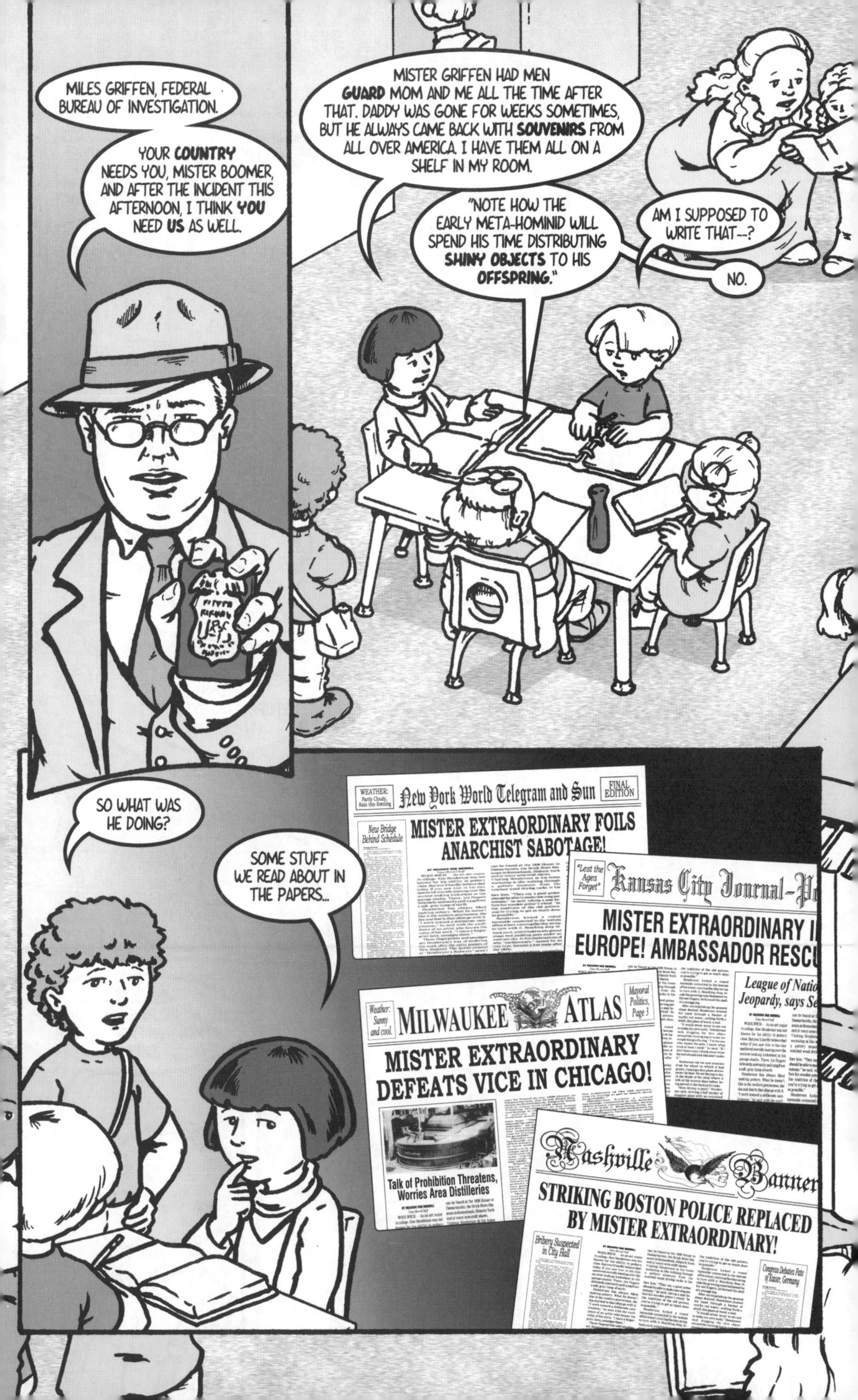
MILES GRIFFEN, FEDERAL BUREAU OF INVESTIGATION.
YOUR **COUNTRY** NEEDS YOU, MISTER BOOMER, AND AFTER THE INCIDENT THIS AFTERNOON, I THINK **YOU** NEED **US** AS WELL.
MISTER GRIFFEN HAD MEN **GUARD** MOM AND ME ALL THE TIME AFTER THAT. DADDY WAS GONE FOR WEEKS SOMETIMES, BUT HE ALWAYS CAME BACK WITH **SOUVENIRS** FROM ALL OVER AMERICA. I HAVE THEM ALL ON A SHELF IN MY ROOM.
"NOTE HOW THE EARLY META-HOMINID WILL SPEND HIS TIME DISTRIBUTING **SHINY OBJECTS** TO HIS **OFFSPRING.**"
AM I SUPPOSED TO WRITE THAT--?
NO.
SO WHAT WAS HE DOING?
SOME STUFF WE READ ABOUT IN THE PAPERS...
WEATHER: Partly Cloudy, Rain this Evening
New York World Telegram and Sun
FINAL EDITION
New Bridge Behind Schedule
MISTER EXTRAORDINARY FOILS ANARCHIST SABOTAGE!
"Lest the Ages Forget"
Kansas City Journal-P
MISTER EXTRAORDINARY I
EUROPE! AMBASSADOR RESCU
League of Natio
Jeopardy, says Se
Weather: Sunny and cool.
MILWAUKEE ATLAS
Mayoral Politics, Page 3
MISTER EXTRAORDINARY DEFEATS VICE IN CHICAGO!
Talk of Prohibition Threatens, Worries Area Distilleries
Nashville Banner
STRIKING BOSTON POLICE REPLACED BY MISTER EXTRAORDINARY!
Bribery Suspected in City Hall
Congress Debates Fate of Kaiser, Germany

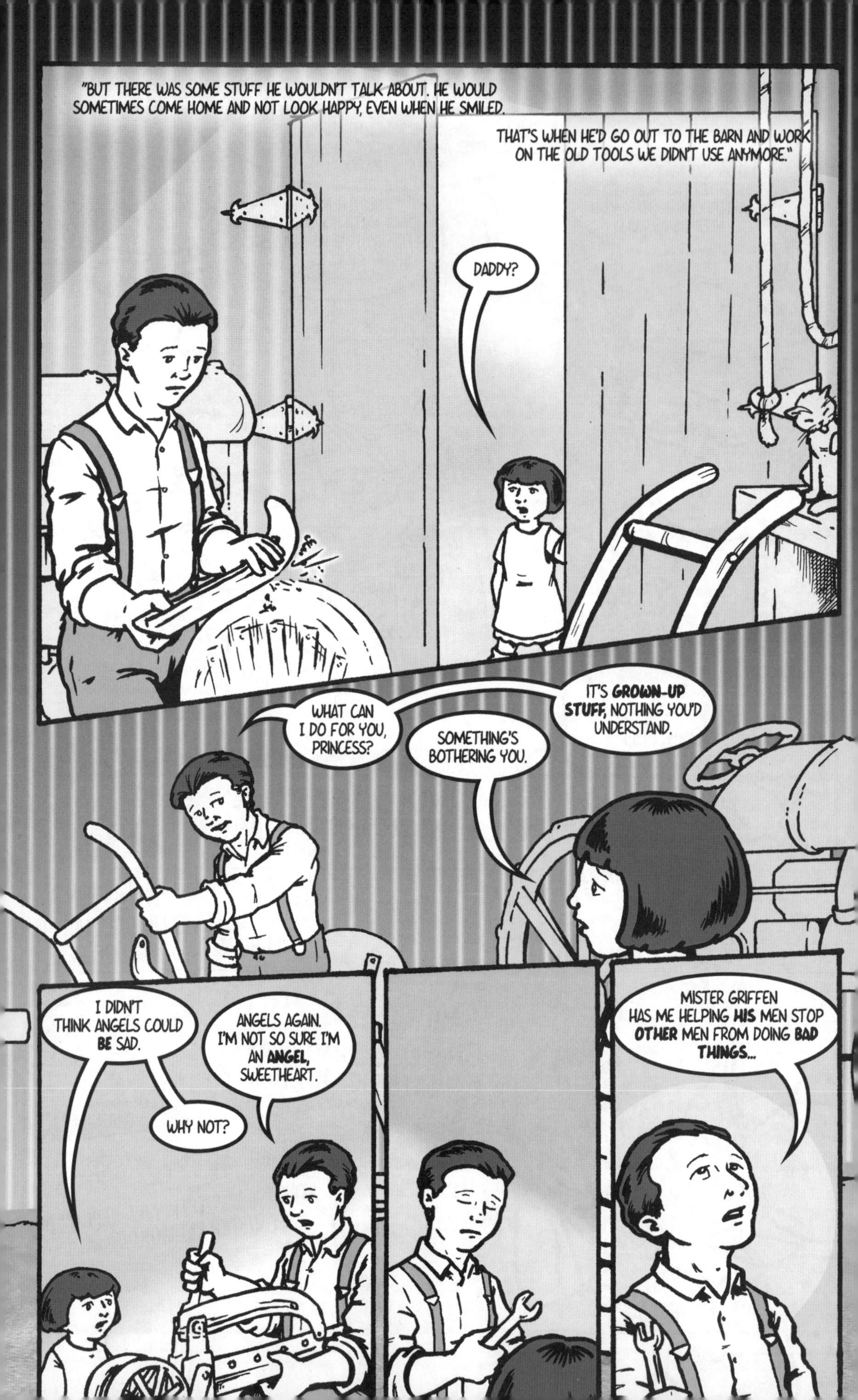
"BUT THERE WAS SOME STUFF HE WOULDN'T TALK ABOUT. HE WOULD SOMETIMES COME HOME AND NOT LOOK HAPPY, EVEN WHEN HE SMILED.
THAT'S WHEN HE'D GO OUT TO THE BARN AND WORK ON THE OLD TOOLS WE DIDN'T USE ANYMORE."
DADDY?
WHAT CAN I DO FOR YOU, PRINCESS?
SOMETHING'S BOTHERING YOU.
IT'S GROWN-UP STUFF, NOTHING YOU'D UNDERSTAND.
I DIDN'T THINK ANGELS COULD BE SAD.
WHY NOT?
ANGELS AGAIN. I'M NOT SO SURE I'M AN ANGEL, SWEETHEART.
MISTER GRIFFEN HAS ME HELPING HIS MEN STOP OTHER MEN FROM DOING BAD THINGS...

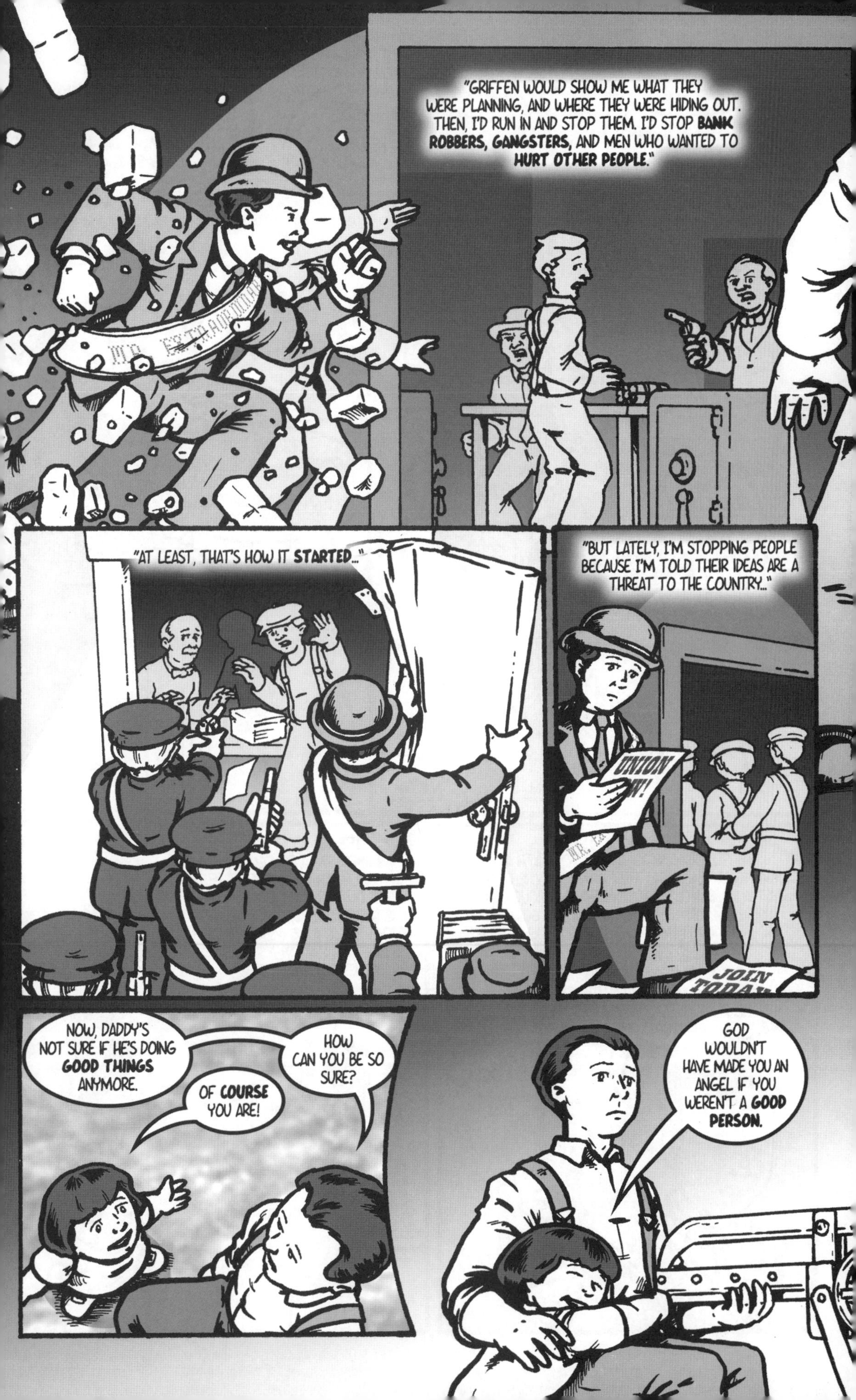
"GRIFFEN WOULD SHOW ME WHAT THEY WERE PLANNING, AND WHERE THEY WERE HIDING OUT. THEN, I'D RUN IN AND STOP THEM. I'D STOP **BANK ROBBERS, GANGSTERS,** AND MEN WHO WANTED TO **HURT OTHER PEOPLE.**"
MR. EXTRAORDINARY
"AT LEAST, THAT'S HOW IT **STARTED**..."
"BUT LATELY, I'M STOPPING PEOPLE BECAUSE I'M TOLD THEIR IDEAS ARE A THREAT TO THE COUNTRY..."
UNION
JOIN TODAY
NOW, DADDY'S NOT SURE IF HE'S DOING **GOOD THINGS** ANYMORE.
OF **COURSE** YOU ARE!
HOW CAN YOU BE SO SURE?
GOD WOULDN'T HAVE MADE YOU AN ANGEL IF YOU WEREN'T A **GOOD PERSON.**

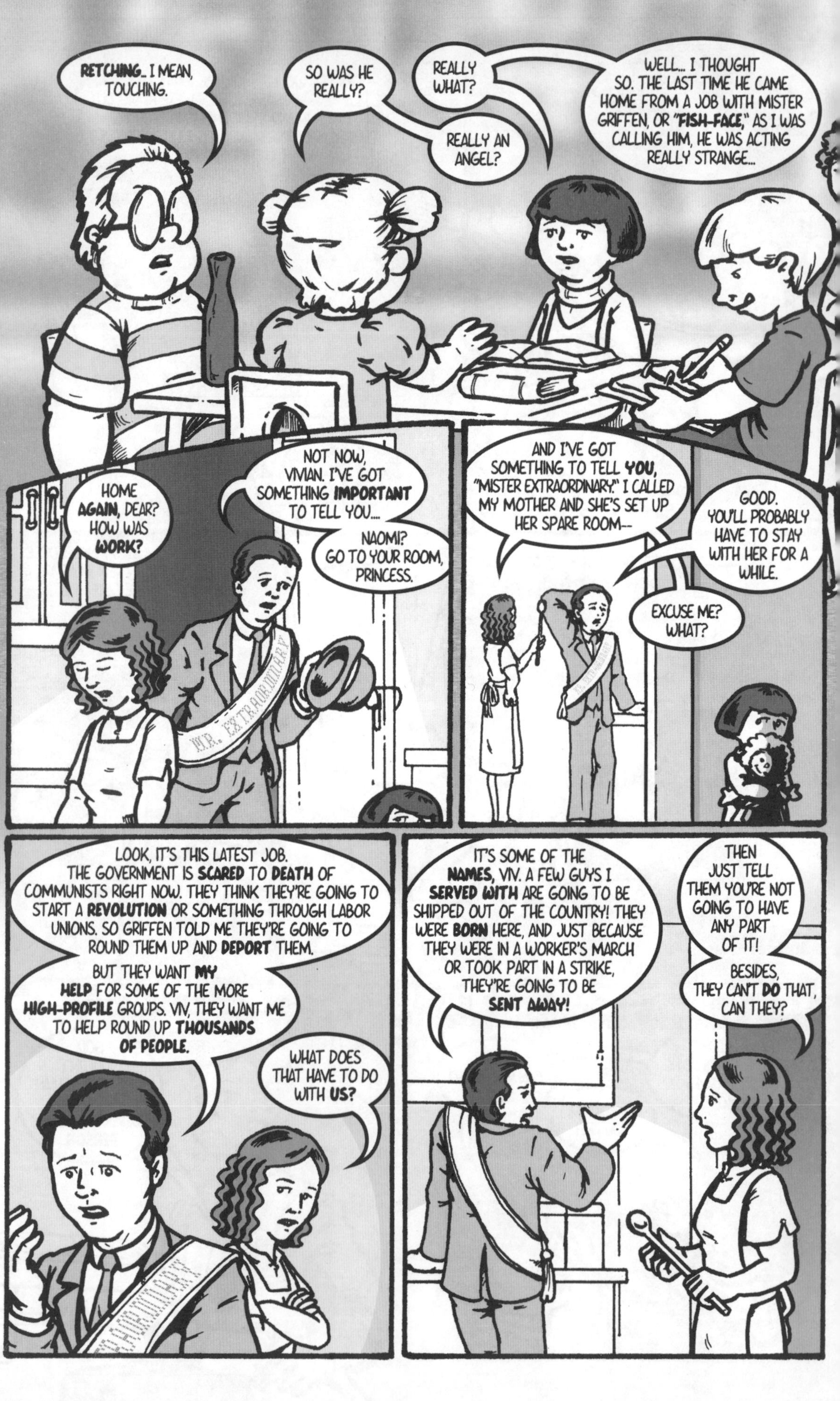
RETCHING.. I MEAN, TOUCHING.
SO WAS HE REALLY?
REALLY WHAT?
REALLY AN ANGEL?
WELL... I THOUGHT SO. THE LAST TIME HE CAME HOME FROM A JOB WITH MISTER GRIFFEN, OR "FISH-FACE," AS I WAS CALLING HIM, HE WAS ACTING REALLY STRANGE...
HOME AGAIN, DEAR? HOW WAS WORK?
NOT NOW, VIVIAN. I'VE GOT SOMETHING IMPORTANT TO TELL YOU....
NAOMI? GO TO YOUR ROOM, PRINCESS.
MR. EXTRAORDINARY
AND I'VE GOT SOMETHING TO TELL YOU, "MISTER EXTRAORDINARY." I CALLED MY MOTHER AND SHE'S SET UP HER SPARE ROOM--
GOOD. YOU'LL PROBABLY HAVE TO STAY WITH HER FOR A WHILE.
EXCUSE ME? WHAT?
LOOK, IT'S THIS LATEST JOB. THE GOVERNMENT IS SCARED TO DEATH OF COMMUNISTS RIGHT NOW. THEY THINK THEY'RE GOING TO START A REVOLUTION OR SOMETHING THROUGH LABOR UNIONS. SO GRIFFEN TOLD ME THEY'RE GOING TO ROUND THEM UP AND DEPORT THEM.
BUT THEY WANT MY HELP FOR SOME OF THE MORE HIGH-PROFILE GROUPS. VIV, THEY WANT ME TO HELP ROUND UP THOUSANDS OF PEOPLE.
WHAT DOES THAT HAVE TO DO WITH US?
IT'S SOME OF THE NAMES, VIV. A FEW GUYS I SERVED WITH ARE GOING TO BE SHIPPED OUT OF THE COUNTRY! THEY WERE BORN HERE, AND JUST BECAUSE THEY WERE IN A WORKER'S MARCH OR TOOK PART IN A STRIKE, THEY'RE GOING TO BE SENT AWAY!
THEN JUST TELL THEM YOU'RE NOT GOING TO HAVE ANY PART OF IT!
BESIDES, THEY CAN'T DO THAT, CAN THEY?

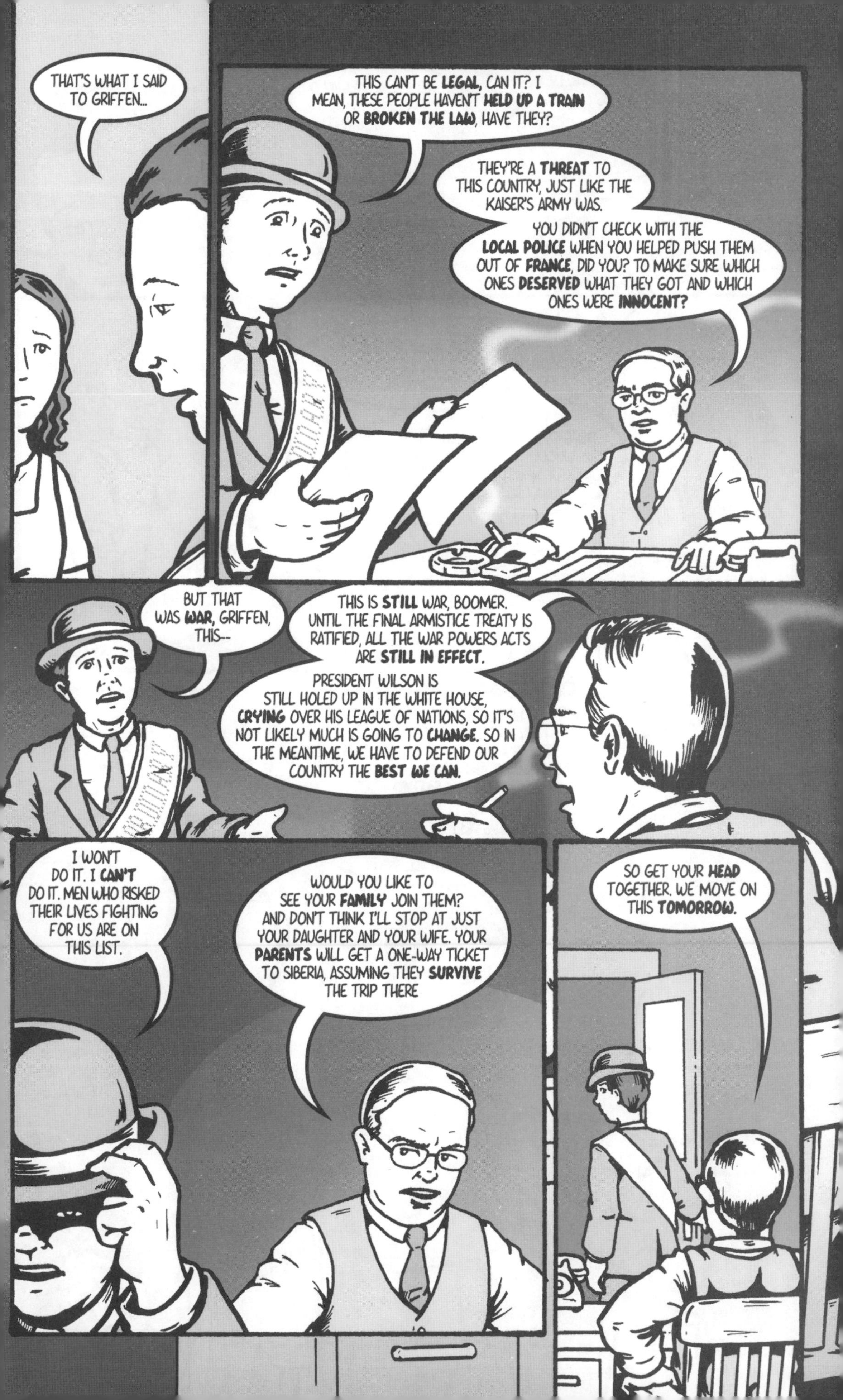
THAT'S WHAT I SAID TO GRIFFEN...
THIS CAN'T BE LEGAL, CAN IT? I MEAN, THESE PEOPLE HAVEN'T HELD UP A TRAIN OR BROKEN THE LAW, HAVE THEY?
THEY'RE A THREAT TO THIS COUNTRY, JUST LIKE THE KAISER'S ARMY WAS.
YOU DIDN'T CHECK WITH THE LOCAL POLICE WHEN YOU HELPED PUSH THEM OUT OF FRANCE, DID YOU? TO MAKE SURE WHICH ONES DESERVED WHAT THEY GOT AND WHICH ONES WERE INNOCENT?
BUT THAT WAS WAR, GRIFFEN, THIS--
THIS IS STILL WAR, BOOMER. UNTIL THE FINAL ARMISTICE TREATY IS RATIFIED, ALL THE WAR POWERS ACTS ARE STILL IN EFFECT.
PRESIDENT WILSON IS STILL HOLED UP IN THE WHITE HOUSE, CRYING OVER HIS LEAGUE OF NATIONS, SO IT'S NOT LIKELY MUCH IS GOING TO CHANGE. SO IN THE MEANTIME, WE HAVE TO DEFEND OUR COUNTRY THE BEST WE CAN.
I WON'T DO IT. I CAN'T DO IT. MEN WHO RISKED THEIR LIVES FIGHTING FOR US ARE ON THIS LIST.
WOULD YOU LIKE TO SEE YOUR FAMILY JOIN THEM? AND DON'T THINK I'LL STOP AT JUST YOUR DAUGHTER AND YOUR WIFE. YOUR PARENTS WILL GET A ONE-WAY TICKET TO SIBERIA, ASSUMING THEY SURVIVE THE TRIP THERE
SO GET YOUR HEAD TOGETHER. WE MOVE ON THIS TOMORROW.

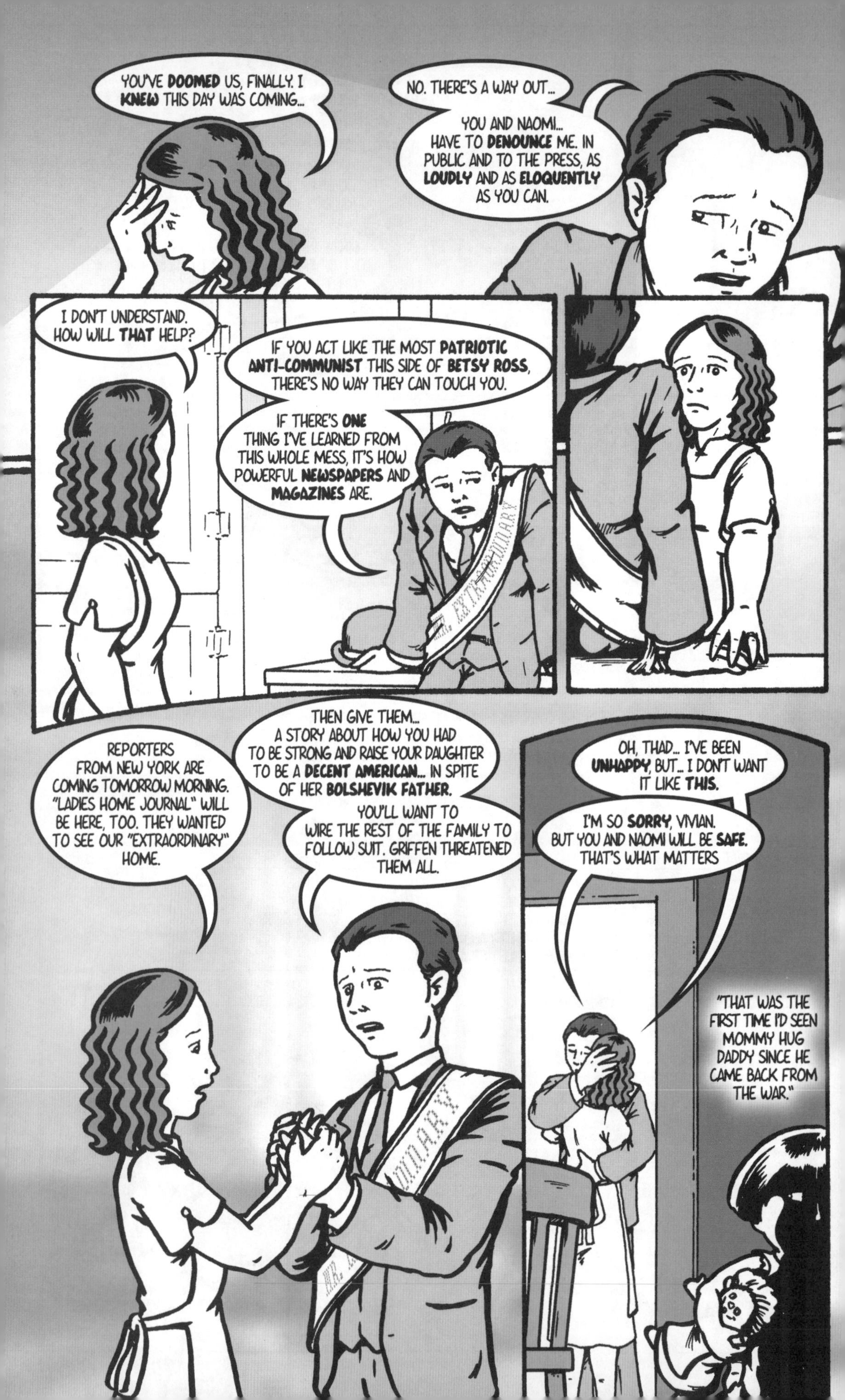

YOU'VE **DOOMED** US, FINALLY. I **KNEW** THIS DAY WAS COMING...
NO. THERE'S A WAY OUT...
YOU AND NAOMI... HAVE TO **DENOUNCE** ME. IN PUBLIC AND TO THE PRESS, AS **LOUDLY** AND AS **ELOQUENTLY** AS YOU CAN.
I DON'T UNDERSTAND. HOW WILL **THAT** HELP?
IF YOU ACT LIKE THE MOST **PATRIOTIC ANTI-COMMUNIST** THIS SIDE OF **BETSY ROSS**, THERE'S NO WAY THEY CAN TOUCH YOU.
IF THERE'S **ONE** THING I'VE LEARNED FROM THIS WHOLE MESS, IT'S HOW POWERFUL **NEWSPAPERS** AND **MAGAZINES** ARE.
REPORTERS FROM NEW YORK ARE COMING TOMORROW MORNING. "LADIES HOME JOURNAL" WILL BE HERE, TOO. THEY WANTED TO SEE OUR "EXTRAORDINARY" HOME.
THEN GIVE THEM... A STORY ABOUT HOW YOU HAD TO BE STRONG AND RAISE YOUR DAUGHTER TO BE A **DECENT AMERICAN...** IN SPITE OF HER **BOLSHEVIK FATHER.**
YOU'LL WANT TO WIRE THE REST OF THE FAMILY TO FOLLOW SUIT. GRIFFEN THREATENED THEM ALL.
OH, THAD... I'VE BEEN **UNHAPPY**, BUT... I DON'T WANT IT LIKE **THIS.**
I'M SO **SORRY**, VIVIAN. BUT YOU AND NAOMI WILL BE **SAFE**. THAT'S WHAT MATTERS
"THAT WAS THE FIRST TIME I'D SEEN MOMMY HUG DADDY SINCE HE CAME BACK FROM THE WAR."

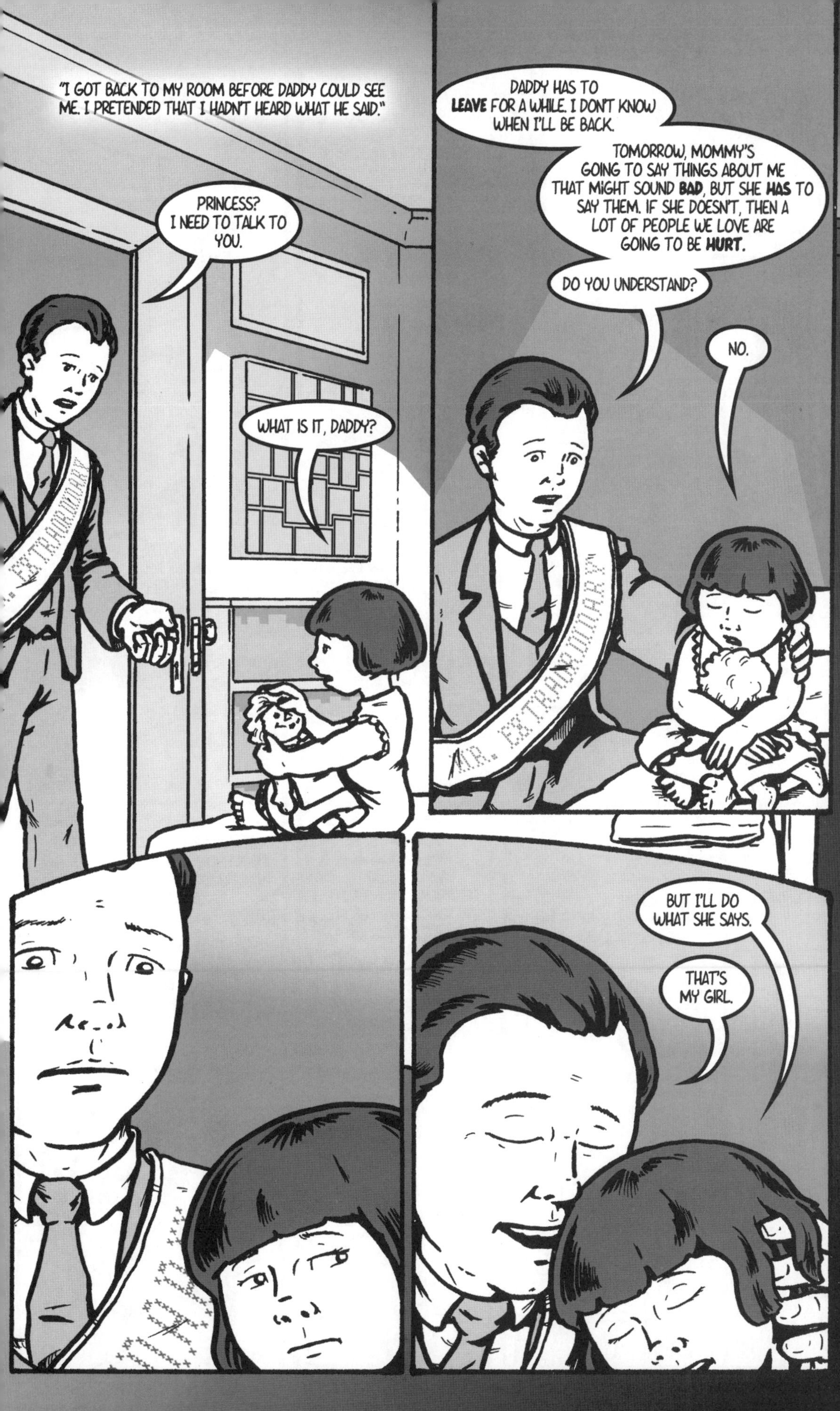
"I GOT BACK TO MY ROOM BEFORE DADDY COULD SEE ME. I PRETENDED THAT I HADN'T HEARD WHAT HE SAID."
PRINCESS? I NEED TO TALK TO YOU.
WHAT IS IT, DADDY?
MR. EXTRAORDINARY
DADDY HAS TO LEAVE FOR A WHILE. I DON'T KNOW WHEN I'LL BE BACK.
TOMORROW, MOMMY'S GOING TO SAY THINGS ABOUT ME THAT MIGHT SOUND BAD, BUT SHE HAS TO SAY THEM. IF SHE DOESN'T, THEN A LOT OF PEOPLE WE LOVE ARE GOING TO BE HURT.
DO YOU UNDERSTAND?
NO.
MR. EXTRAORDINARY
BUT I'LL DO WHAT SHE SAYS.
THAT'S MY GIRL.

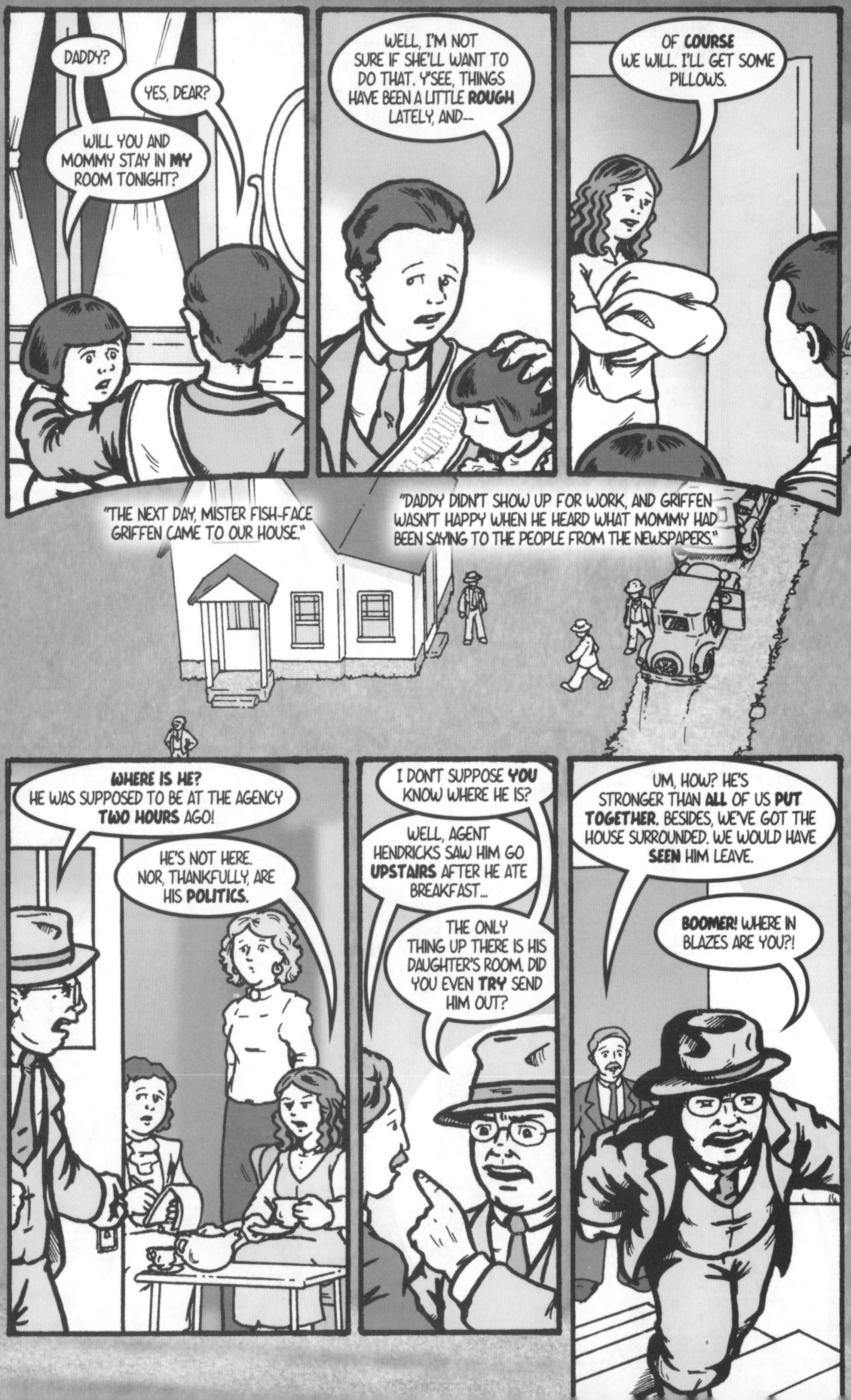
DADDY?
YES, DEAR?
WILL YOU AND MOMMY STAY IN MY ROOM TONIGHT?
WELL, I'M NOT SURE IF SHE'LL WANT TO DO THAT. Y'SEE, THINGS HAVE BEEN A LITTLE ROUGH LATELY, AND--
OF COURSE WE WILL. I'LL GET SOME PILLOWS.
"THE NEXT DAY, MISTER FISH-FACE GRIFFEN CAME TO OUR HOUSE."
"DADDY DIDN'T SHOW UP FOR WORK, AND GRIFFEN WASN'T HAPPY WHEN HE HEARD WHAT MOMMY HAD BEEN SAYING TO THE PEOPLE FROM THE NEWSPAPERS."
WHERE IS HE? HE WAS SUPPOSED TO BE AT THE AGENCY TWO HOURS AGO!
HE'S NOT HERE. NOR, THANKFULLY, ARE HIS POLITICS.
I DON'T SUPPOSE YOU KNOW WHERE HE IS?
WELL, AGENT HENDRICKS SAW HIM GO UPSTAIRS AFTER HE ATE BREAKFAST...
THE ONLY THING UP THERE IS HIS DAUGHTER'S ROOM. DID YOU EVEN TRY SEND HIM OUT?
UM, HOW? HE'S STRONGER THAN ALL OF US PUT TOGETHER. BESIDES, WE'VE GOT THE HOUSE SURROUNDED. WE WOULD HAVE SEEN HIM LEAVE.
BOOMER! WHERE IN BLAZES ARE YOU?!

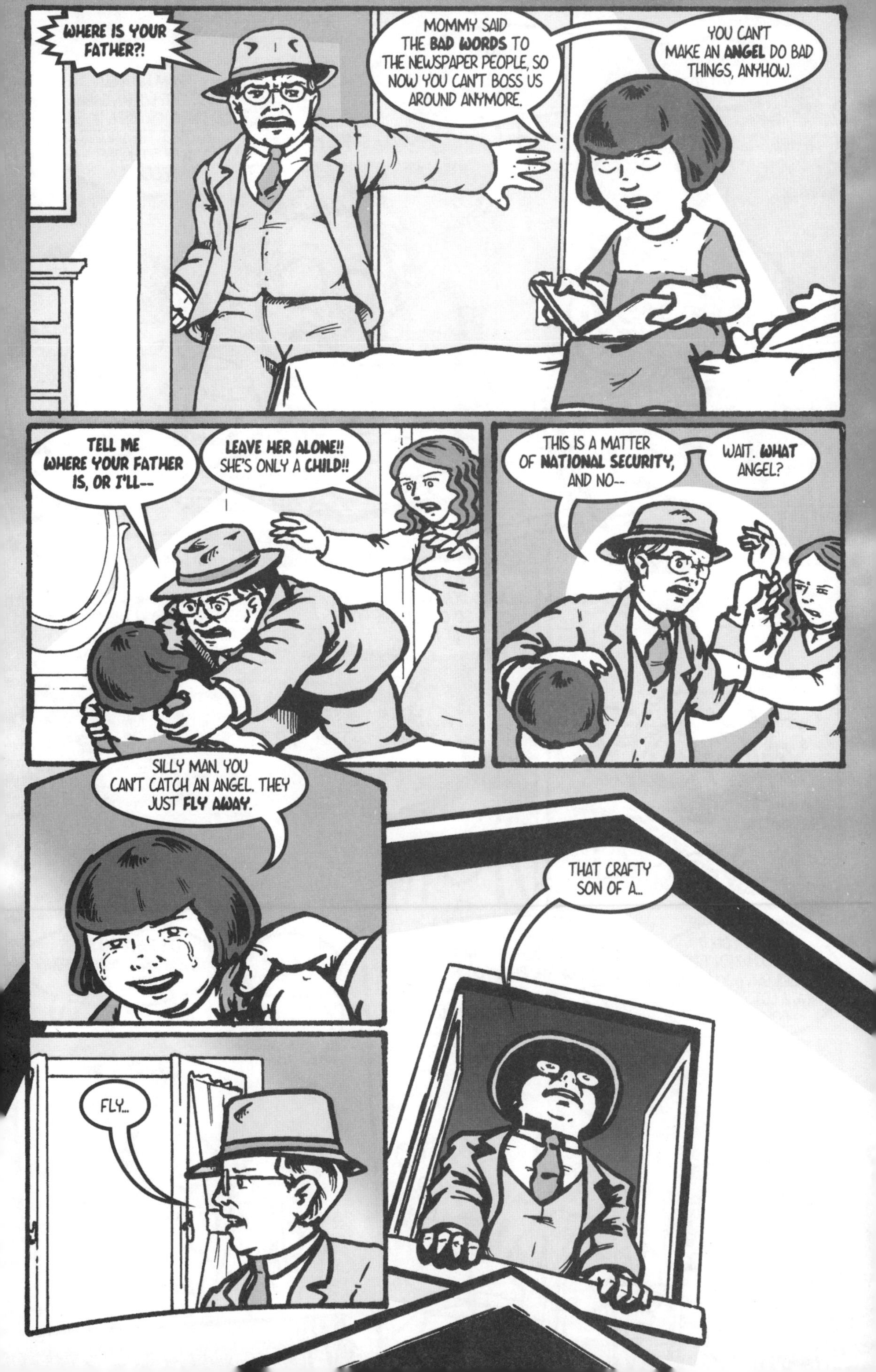
WHERE IS YOUR FATHER?!
MOMMY SAID THE BAD WORDS TO THE NEWSPAPER PEOPLE, SO NOW YOU CAN'T BOSS US AROUND ANYMORE.
YOU CAN'T MAKE AN ANGEL DO BAD THINGS, ANYHOW.
TELL ME WHERE YOUR FATHER IS, OR I'LL--
LEAVE HER ALONE!! SHE'S ONLY A CHILD!!
THIS IS A MATTER OF NATIONAL SECURITY, AND NO--
WAIT. WHAT ANGEL?
SILLY MAN. YOU CAN'T CATCH AN ANGEL. THEY JUST FLY AWAY.
FLY...
THAT CRAFTY SON OF A...

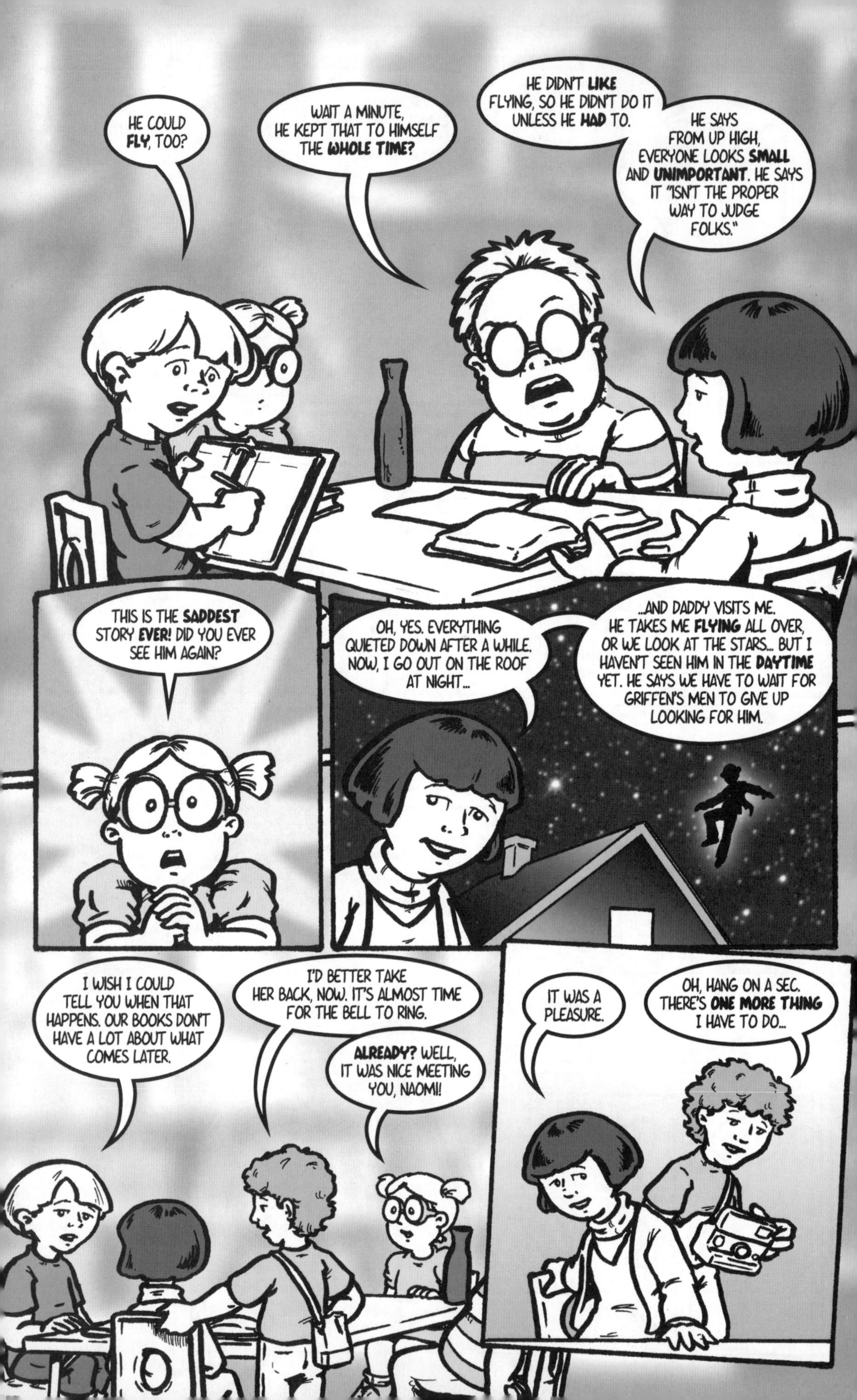
HE COULD FLY, TOO?
WAIT A MINUTE, HE KEPT THAT TO HIMSELF THE WHOLE TIME?
HE DIDN'T LIKE FLYING, SO HE DIDN'T DO IT UNLESS HE HAD TO.
HE SAYS FROM UP HIGH, EVERYONE LOOKS SMALL AND UNIMPORTANT. HE SAYS IT "ISN'T THE PROPER WAY TO JUDGE FOLKS."
THIS IS THE SADDEST STORY EVER! DID YOU EVER SEE HIM AGAIN?
OH, YES. EVERYTHING QUIETED DOWN AFTER A WHILE. NOW, I GO OUT ON THE ROOF AT NIGHT...
...AND DADDY VISITS ME. HE TAKES ME FLYING ALL OVER, OR WE LOOK AT THE STARS... BUT I HAVEN'T SEEN HIM IN THE DAYTIME YET. HE SAYS WE HAVE TO WAIT FOR GRIFFEN'S MEN TO GIVE UP LOOKING FOR HIM.
I WISH I COULD TELL YOU WHEN THAT HAPPENS. OUR BOOKS DON'T HAVE A LOT ABOUT WHAT COMES LATER.
I'D BETTER TAKE HER BACK, NOW. IT'S ALMOST TIME FOR THE BELL TO RING.
ALREADY? WELL, IT WAS NICE MEETING YOU, NAOMI!
IT WAS A PLEASURE.
OH, HANG ON A SEC. THERE'S ONE MORE THING I HAVE TO DO...

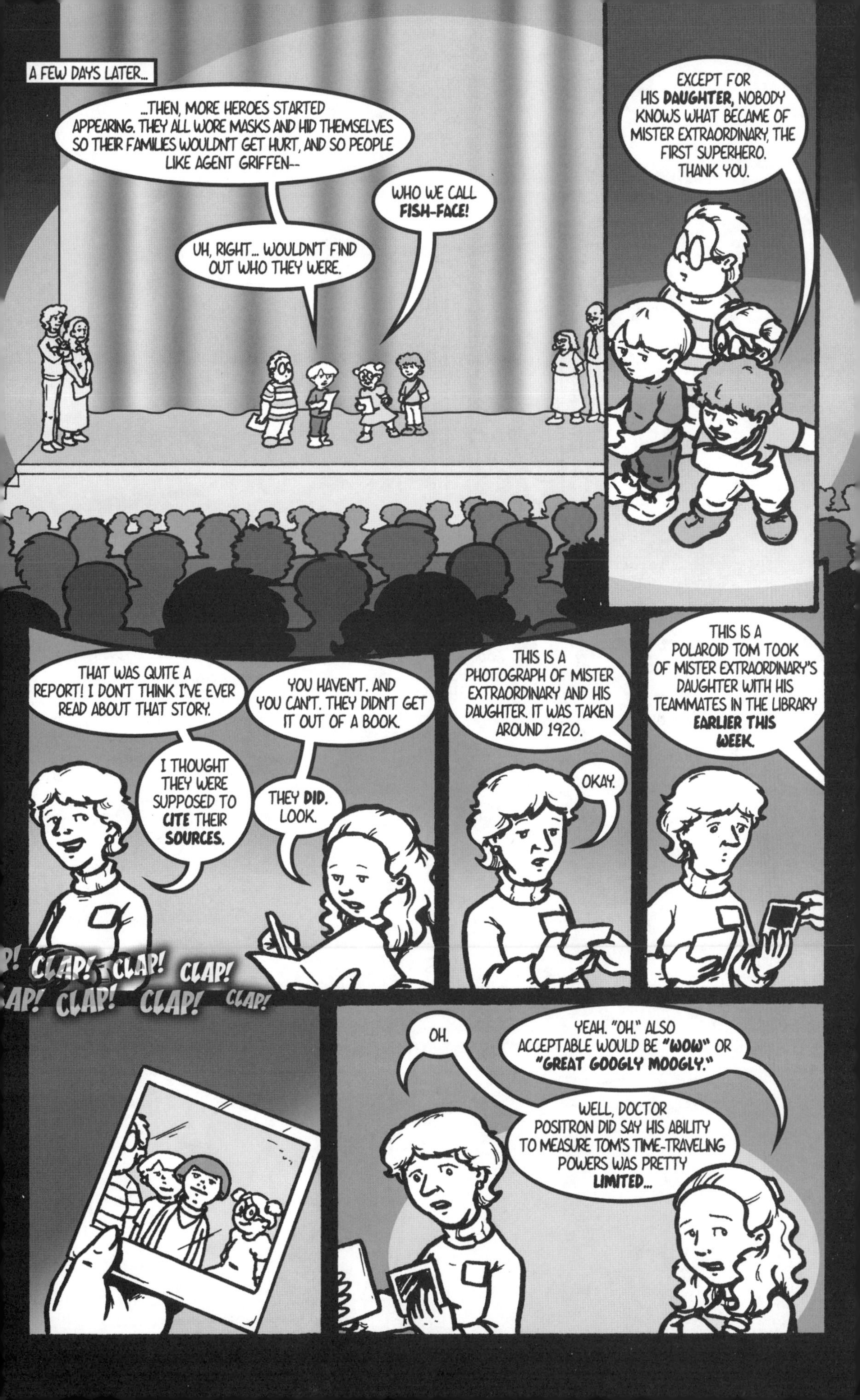
A FEW DAYS LATER...
...THEN, MORE HEROES STARTED APPEARING. THEY ALL WORE MASKS AND HID THEMSELVES SO THEIR FAMILIES WOULDN'T GET HURT, AND SO PEOPLE LIKE AGENT GRIFFEN--
WHO WE CALL **FISH-FACE!**
UH, RIGHT... WOULDN'T FIND OUT WHO THEY WERE.
EXCEPT FOR HIS **DAUGHTER,** NOBODY KNOWS WHAT BECAME OF MISTER EXTRAORDINARY, THE FIRST SUPERHERO. THANK YOU.
CLAP! CLAP! CLAP! CLAP! CLAP! CLAP! CLAP!
THAT WAS QUITE A REPORT! I DON'T THINK I'VE EVER READ ABOUT THAT STORY.
I THOUGHT THEY WERE SUPPOSED TO **CITE** THEIR **SOURCES.**
YOU HAVEN'T. AND YOU CAN'T. THEY DIDN'T GET IT OUT OF A BOOK.
THEY **DID.** LOOK.
THIS IS A PHOTOGRAPH OF MISTER EXTRAORDINARY AND HIS DAUGHTER. IT WAS TAKEN AROUND 1920.
OKAY.
THIS IS A POLAROID TOM TOOK OF MISTER EXTRAORDINARY'S DAUGHTER WITH HIS TEAMMATES IN THE LIBRARY **EARLIER THIS WEEK.**
OH.
YEAH. "OH." ALSO ACCEPTABLE WOULD BE **"WOW"** OR **"GREAT GOOGLY MOOGLY."**
WELL, DOCTOR POSITRON DID SAY HIS ABILITY TO MEASURE TOM'S TIME-TRAVELING POWERS WAS PRETTY **LIMITED...**

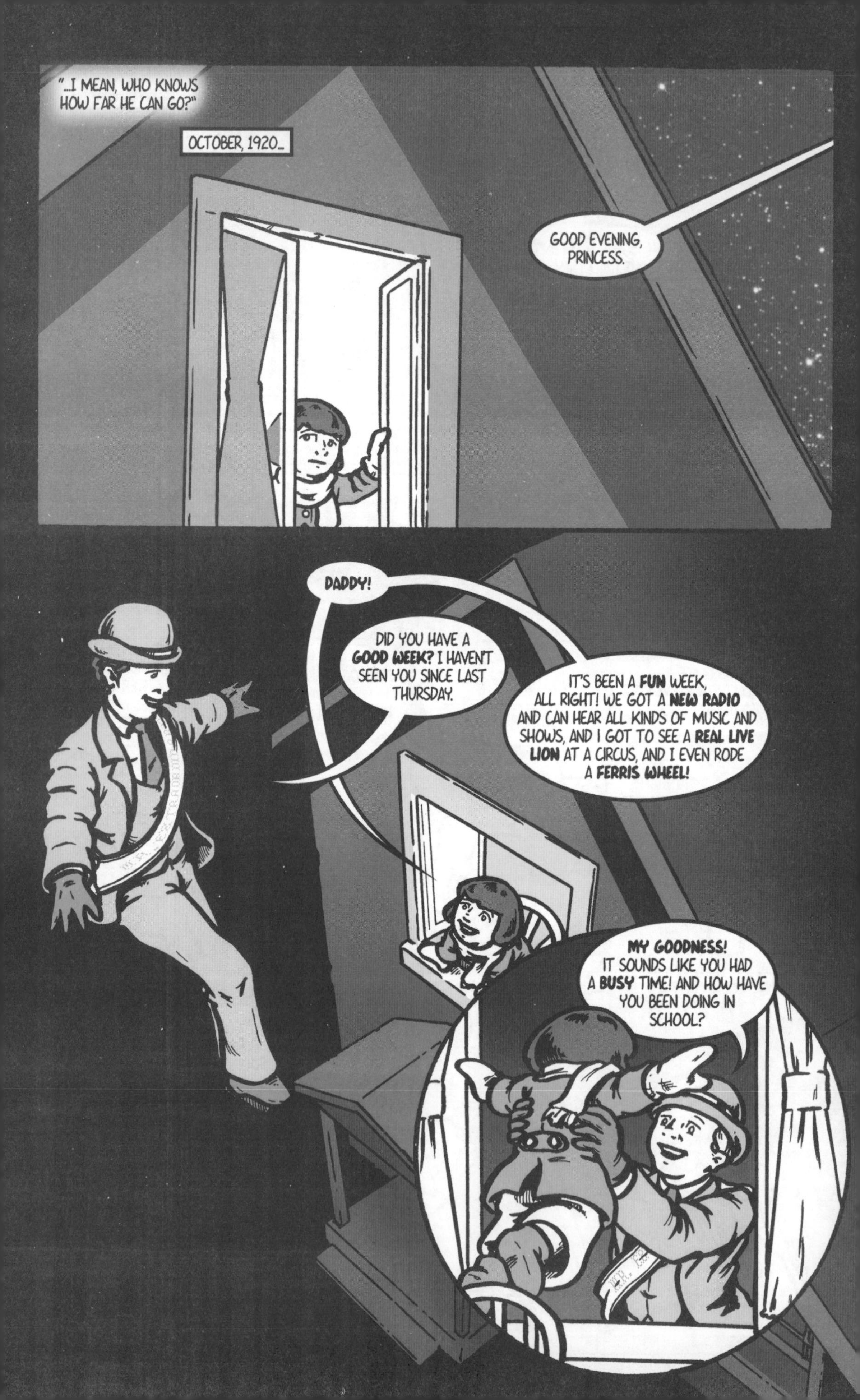
"...I MEAN, WHO KNOWS HOW FAR HE CAN GO?"
OCTOBER, 1920...
GOOD EVENING, PRINCESS.
DADDY!
DID YOU HAVE A GOOD WEEK? I HAVEN'T SEEN YOU SINCE LAST THURSDAY.
IT'S BEEN A FUN WEEK, ALL RIGHT! WE GOT A NEW RADIO AND CAN HEAR ALL KINDS OF MUSIC AND SHOWS, AND I GOT TO SEE A REAL LIVE LION AT A CIRCUS, AND I EVEN RODE A FERRIS WHEEL!
MY GOODNESS! IT SOUNDS LIKE YOU HAD A BUSY TIME! AND HOW HAVE YOU BEEN DOING IN SCHOOL?

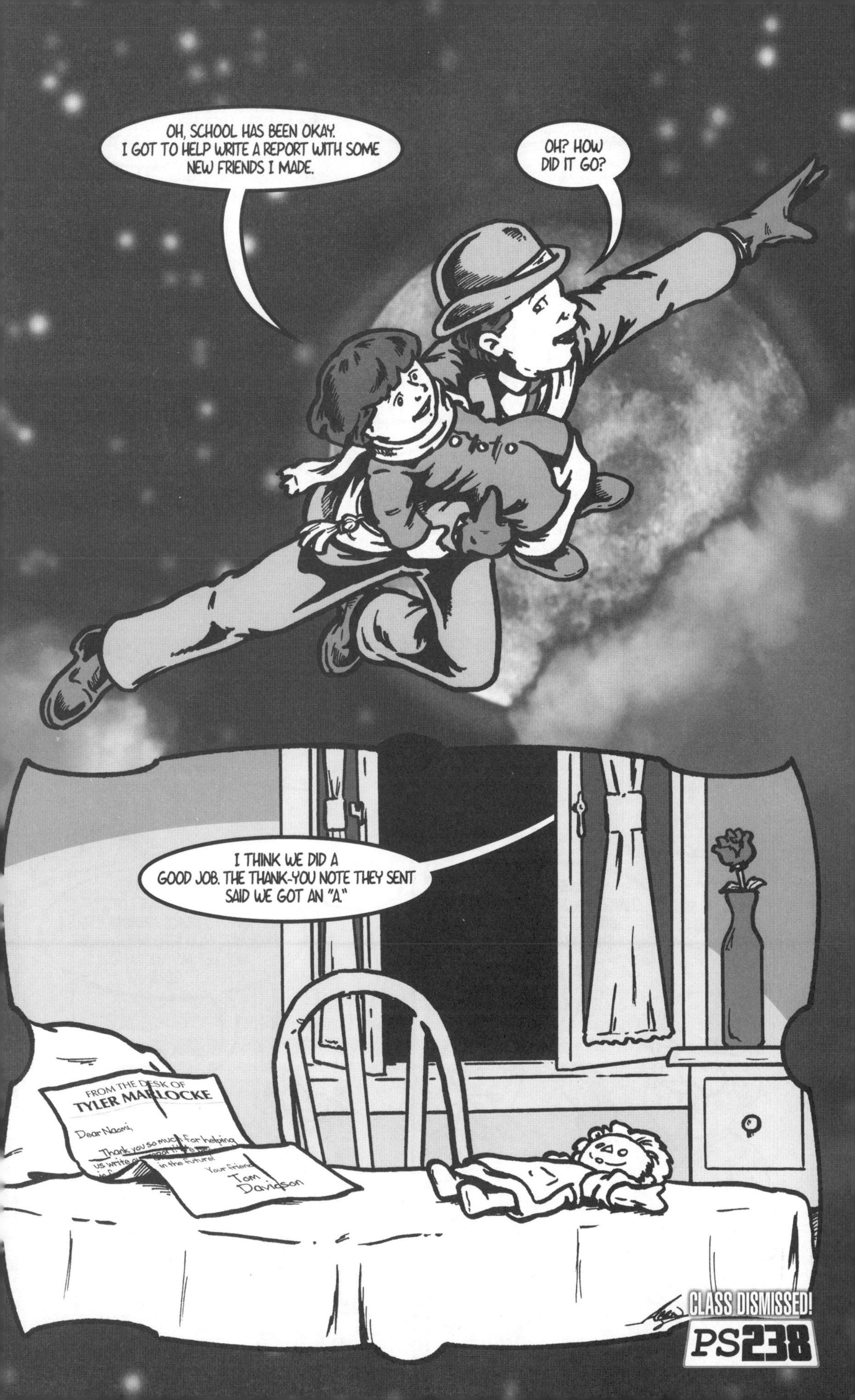
OH, SCHOOL HAS BEEN OKAY. I GOT TO HELP WRITE A REPORT WITH SOME NEW FRIENDS I MADE.
OH? HOW DID IT GO?
I THINK WE DID A GOOD JOB. THE THANK-YOU NOTE THEY SENT SAID WE GOT AN "A."
FROM THE DESK OF
TYLER MARLOCKE
Dear Naomi,
Thank you so much for helping
us write
in the future!
Your friend
Tom Davidson
CLASS DISMISSED!
PS238

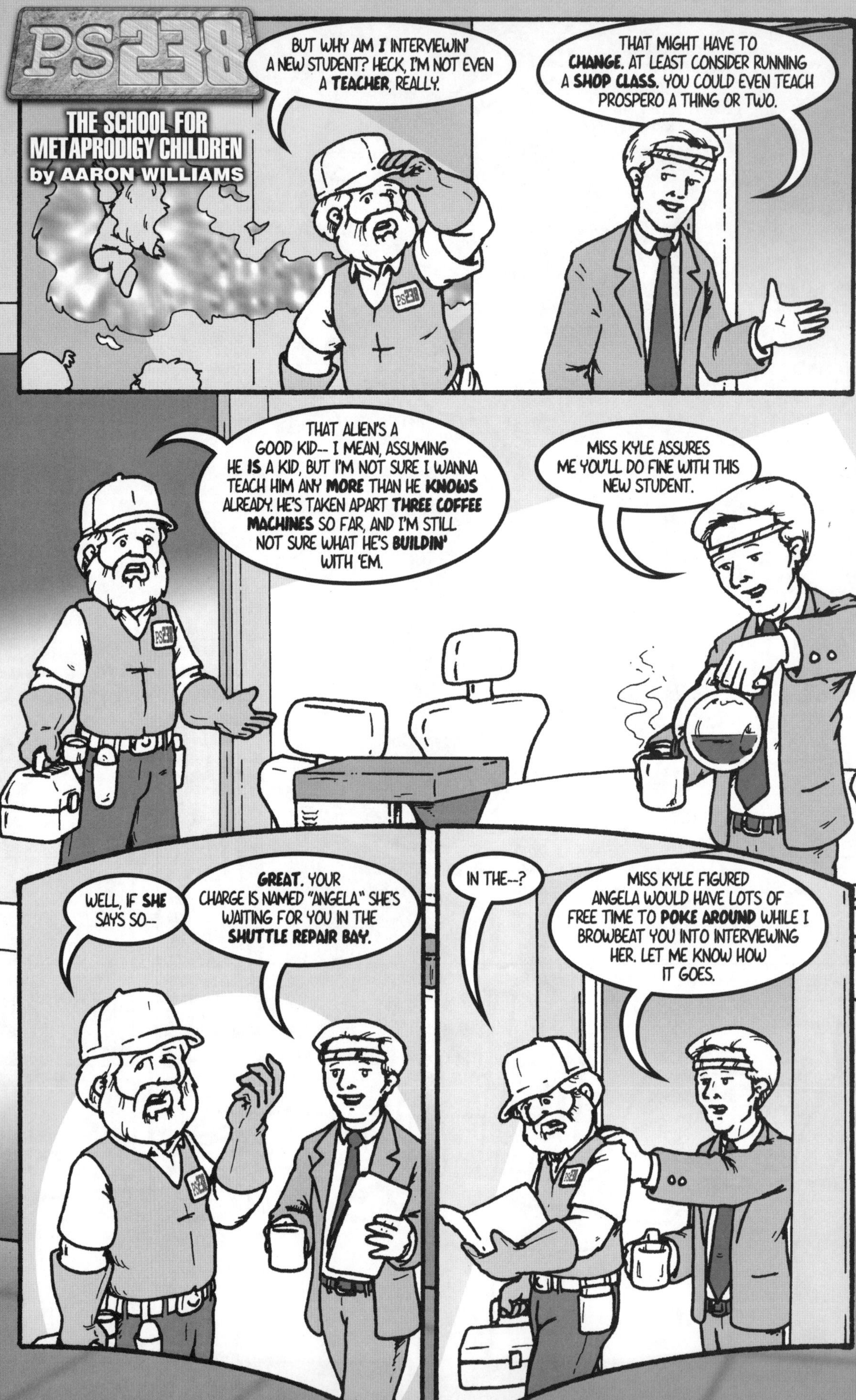
PS238
THE SCHOOL FOR METAPRODIGY CHILDREN
by AARON WILLIAMS
BUT WHY AM I INTERVIEWIN' A NEW STUDENT? HECK, I'M NOT EVEN A TEACHER, REALLY.
THAT MIGHT HAVE TO CHANGE. AT LEAST CONSIDER RUNNING A SHOP CLASS. YOU COULD EVEN TEACH PROSPERO A THING OR TWO.
THAT ALIEN'S A GOOD KID-- I MEAN, ASSUMING HE IS A KID, BUT I'M NOT SURE I WANNA TEACH HIM ANY MORE THAN HE KNOWS ALREADY. HE'S TAKEN APART THREE COFFEE MACHINES SO FAR, AND I'M STILL NOT SURE WHAT HE'S BUILDIN' WITH 'EM.
MISS KYLE ASSURES ME YOU'LL DO FINE WITH THIS NEW STUDENT.
WELL, IF SHE SAYS SO--
GREAT. YOUR CHARGE IS NAMED "ANGELA." SHE'S WAITING FOR YOU IN THE SHUTTLE REPAIR BAY.
IN THE--?
MISS KYLE FIGURED ANGELA WOULD HAVE LOTS OF FREE TIME TO POKE AROUND WHILE I BROWBEAT YOU INTO INTERVIEWING HER. LET ME KNOW HOW IT GOES.

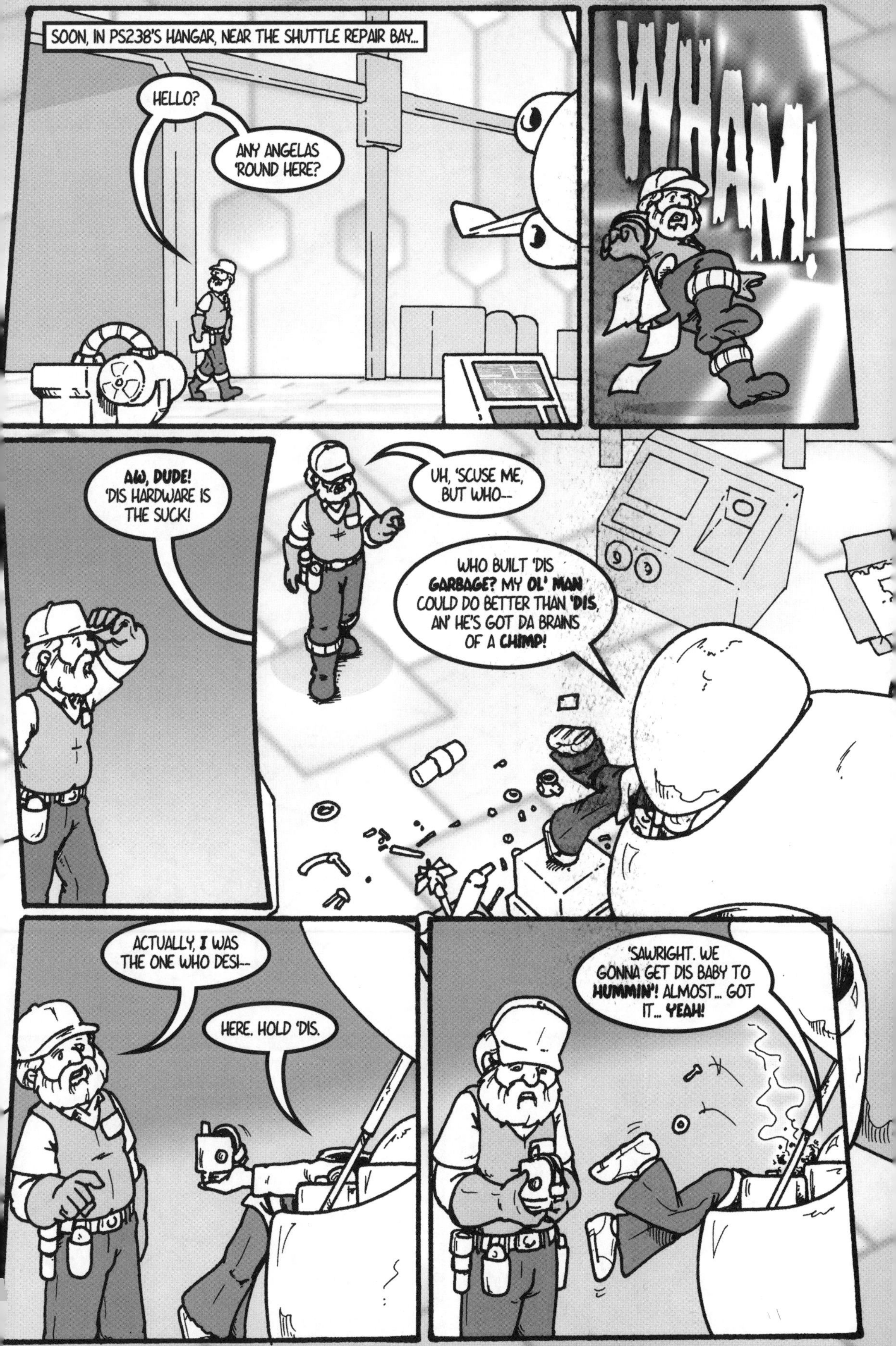
SOON, IN PS238'S HANGAR, NEAR THE SHUTTLE REPAIR BAY...
HELLO?
ANY ANGELAS 'ROUND HERE?
WHAM!
AW, DUDE! 'DIS HARDWARE IS THE SUCK!
UH, 'SCUSE ME, BUT WHO--
WHO BUILT 'DIS GARBAGE? MY OL' MAN COULD DO BETTER THAN 'DIS, AN' HE'S GOT DA BRAINS OF A CHIMP!
ACTUALLY, I WAS THE ONE WHO DESI--
HERE. HOLD 'DIS.
'SAWRIGHT. WE GONNA GET DIS BABY TO HUMMIN'! ALMOST... GOT IT... YEAH!

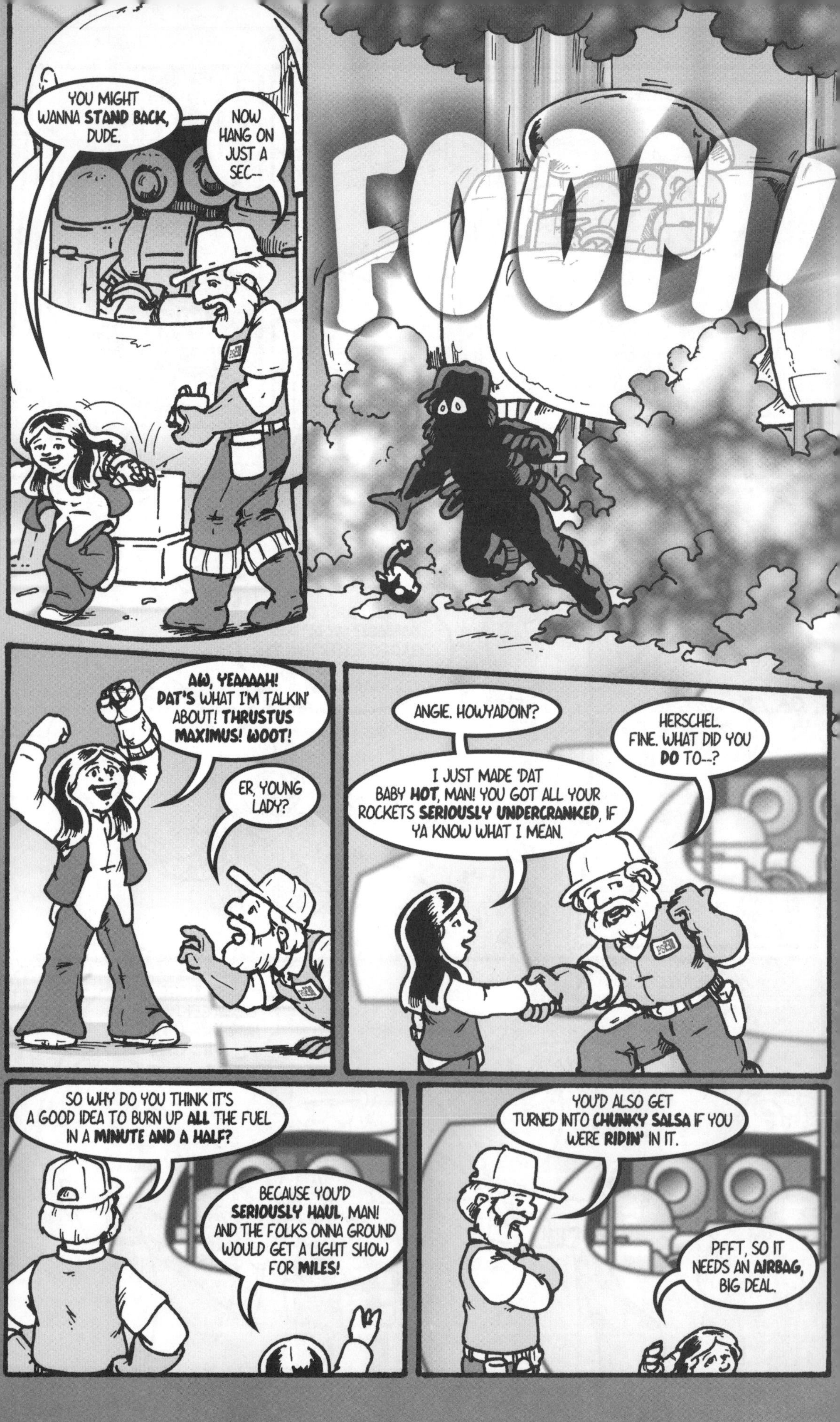
YOU MIGHT WANNA STAND BACK, DUDE.
NOW HANG ON JUST A SEC--
FOOM!
AW, YEAAAAH! DAT'S WHAT I'M TALKIN' ABOUT! THRUSTUS MAXIMUS! WOOT!
ER, YOUNG LADY?
ANGIE. HOWYADOIN'?
HERSCHEL. FINE. WHAT DID YOU DO TO--?
I JUST MADE 'DAT BABY HOT, MAN! YOU GOT ALL YOUR ROCKETS SERIOUSLY UNDERCRANKED, IF YA KNOW WHAT I MEAN.
SO WHY DO YOU THINK IT'S A GOOD IDEA TO BURN UP ALL THE FUEL IN A MINUTE AND A HALF?
BECAUSE YOU'D SERIOUSLY HAUL, MAN! AND THE FOLKS ONNA GROUND WOULD GET A LIGHT SHOW FOR MILES!
YOU'D ALSO GET TURNED INTO CHUNKY SALSA IF YOU WERE RIDIN' IN IT.
PFFT, SO IT NEEDS AN AIRBAG, BIG DEAL.

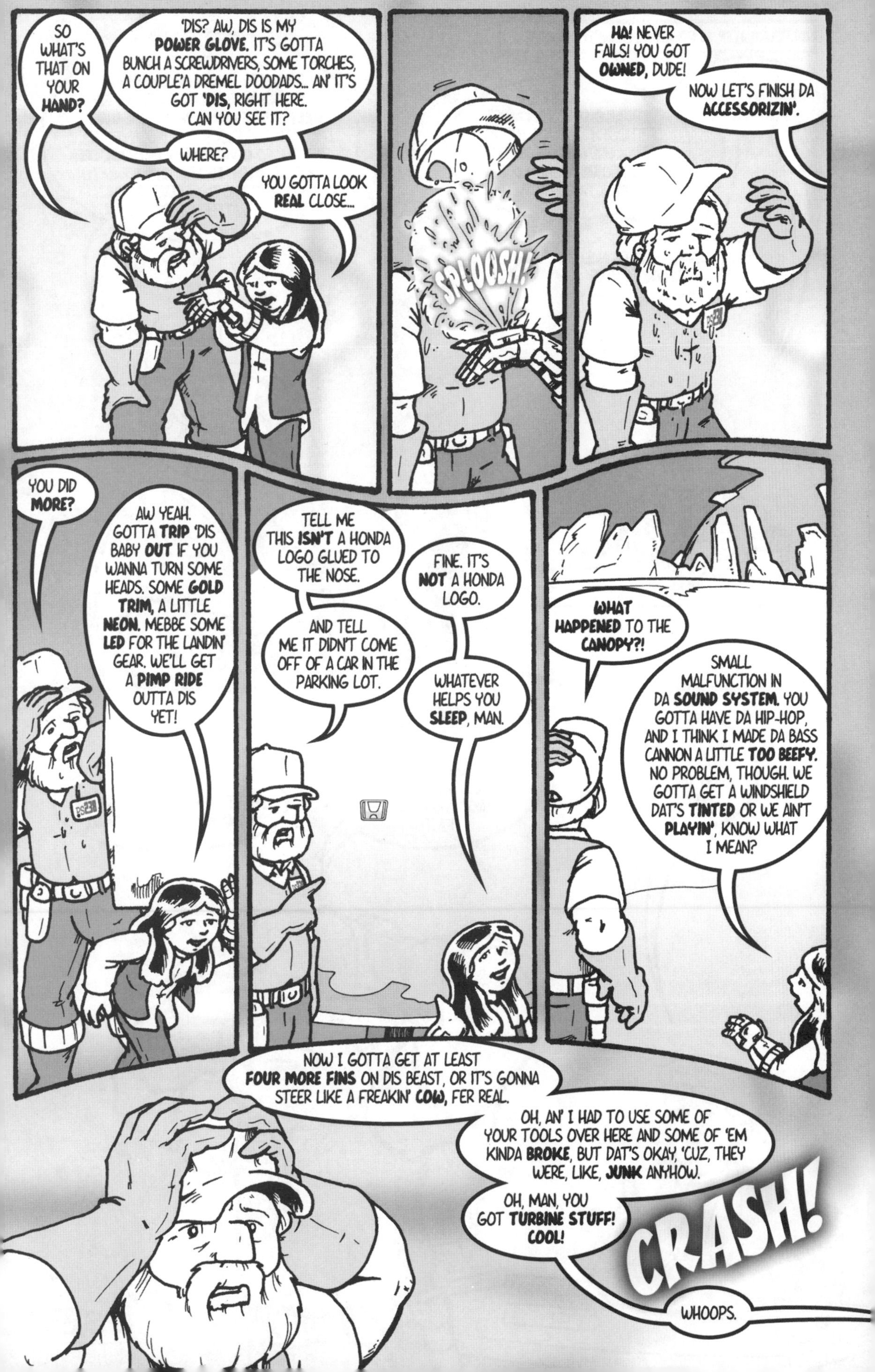
SO WHAT'S THAT ON YOUR HAND?
'DIS? AW, DIS IS MY POWER GLOVE. IT'S GOTTA BUNCH A SCREWDRIVERS, SOME TORCHES, A COUPLE'A DREMEL DOODADS... AN' IT'S GOT 'DIS, RIGHT HERE. CAN YOU SEE IT?
WHERE?
YOU GOTTA LOOK REAL CLOSE...
SPLOOSH!
HA! NEVER FAILS! YOU GOT OWNED, DUDE!
NOW LET'S FINISH DA ACCESSORIZIN'.
YOU DID MORE?
AW YEAH. GOTTA TRIP 'DIS BABY OUT IF YOU WANNA TURN SOME HEADS. SOME GOLD TRIM, A LITTLE NEON. MEBBE SOME LED FOR THE LANDIN' GEAR. WE'LL GET A PIMP RIDE OUTTA DIS YET!
TELL ME THIS ISN'T A HONDA LOGO GLUED TO THE NOSE.
FINE. IT'S NOT A HONDA LOGO.
AND TELL ME IT DIDN'T COME OFF OF A CAR IN THE PARKING LOT.
WHATEVER HELPS YOU SLEEP, MAN.
WHAT HAPPENED TO THE CANOPY?!
SMALL MALFUNCTION IN DA SOUND SYSTEM. YOU GOTTA HAVE DA HIP-HOP, AND I THINK I MADE DA BASS CANNON A LITTLE TOO BEEFY. NO PROBLEM, THOUGH. WE GOTTA GET A WINDSHIELD DAT'S TINTED OR WE AIN'T PLAYIN', KNOW WHAT I MEAN?
NOW I GOTTA GET AT LEAST FOUR MORE FINS ON DIS BEAST, OR IT'S GONNA STEER LIKE A FREAKIN' COW, FER REAL.
OH, AN' I HAD TO USE SOME OF YOUR TOOLS OVER HERE AND SOME OF 'EM KINDA BROKE, BUT DAT'S OKAY, 'CUZ, THEY WERE, LIKE, JUNK ANYHOW.
OH, MAN, YOU GOT TURBINE STUFF! COOL!
CRASH!
WHOOPS.

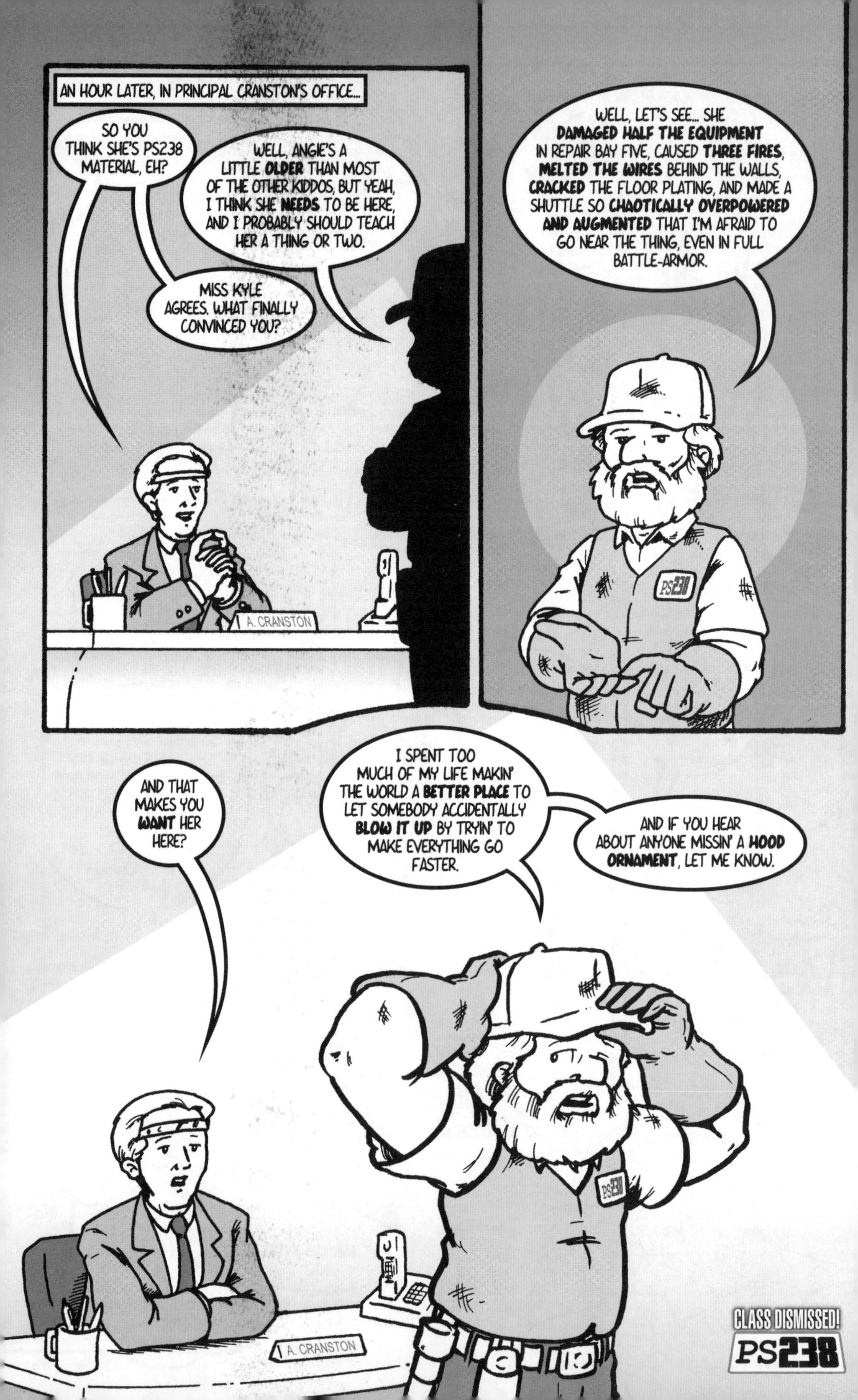
AN HOUR LATER, IN PRINCIPAL CRANSTON'S OFFICE...
SO YOU THINK SHE'S PS238 MATERIAL, EH?
WELL, ANGIE'S A LITTLE OLDER THAN MOST OF THE OTHER KIDDOS, BUT YEAH, I THINK SHE NEEDS TO BE HERE, AND I PROBABLY SHOULD TEACH HER A THING OR TWO.
MISS KYLE AGREES. WHAT FINALLY CONVINCED YOU?
A. CRANSTON
WELL, LET'S SEE... SHE DAMAGED HALF THE EQUIPMENT IN REPAIR BAY FIVE, CAUSED THREE FIRES, MELTED THE WIRES BEHIND THE WALLS, CRACKED THE FLOOR PLATING, AND MADE A SHUTTLE SO CHAOTICALLY OVERPOWERED AND AUGMENTED THAT I'M AFRAID TO GO NEAR THE THING, EVEN IN FULL BATTLE-ARMOR.
PS238
AND THAT MAKES YOU WANT HER HERE?
I SPENT TOO MUCH OF MY LIFE MAKIN' THE WORLD A BETTER PLACE TO LET SOMEBODY ACCIDENTALLY BLOW IT UP BY TRYIN' TO MAKE EVERYTHING GO FASTER.
AND IF YOU HEAR ABOUT ANYONE MISSIN' A HOOD ORNAMENT, LET ME KNOW.
PS238
A. CRANSTON
CLASS DISMISSED!
PS238

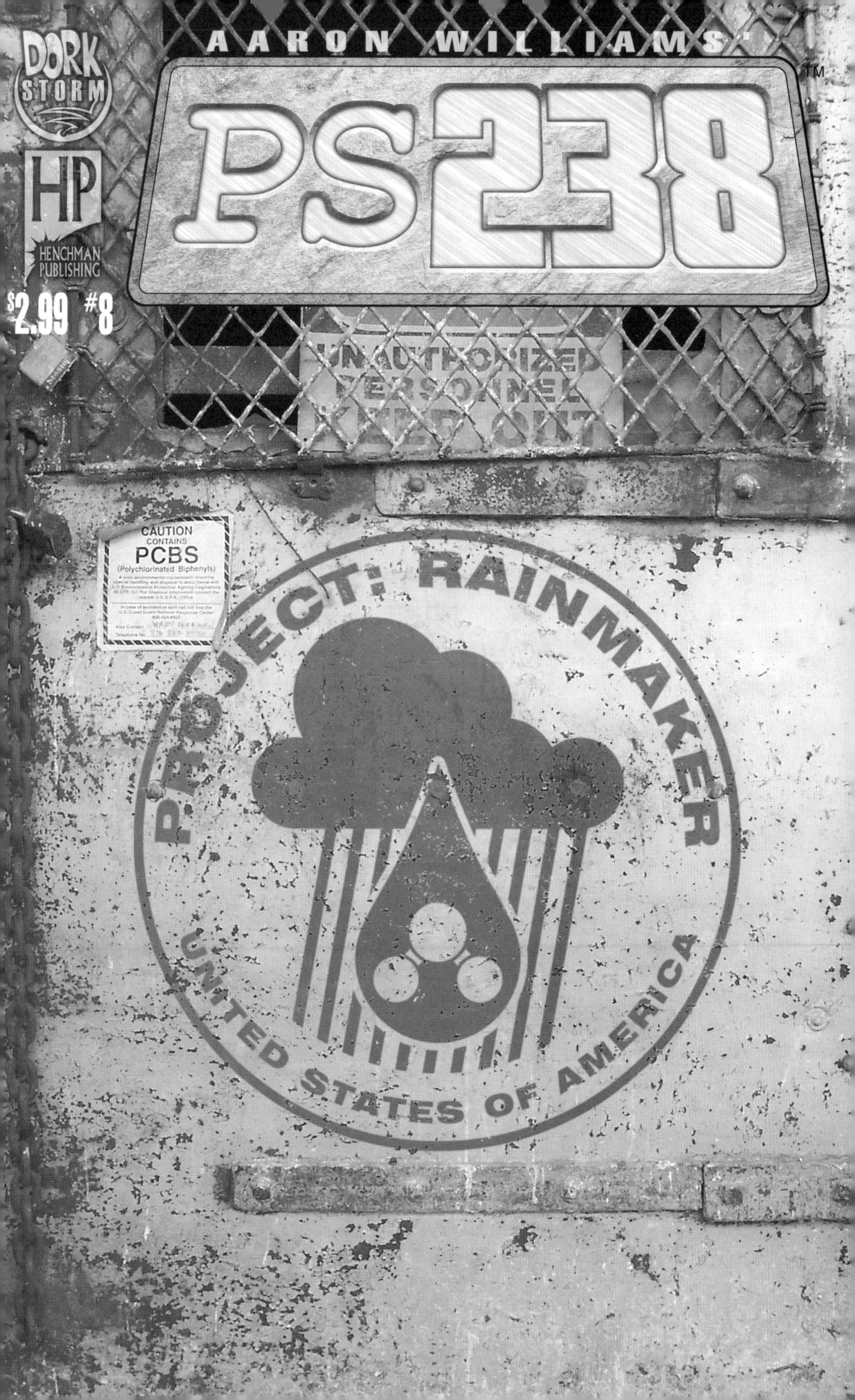
DORK STORM
HP
HENCHMAN PUBLISHING
$2.99 #8
AARON WILLIAMS'
PS238
TM
UNAUTHORIZED PERSONNEL
KEEP OUT
CAUTION
CONTAINS
PCBS
(Polychlorinated Biphenyls)
PROJECT: RAINMAKER
UNITED STATES OF AMERICA

PS238

THE SCHOOL FOR METAPRODIGY CHILDREN

BY AARON WILLIAMS

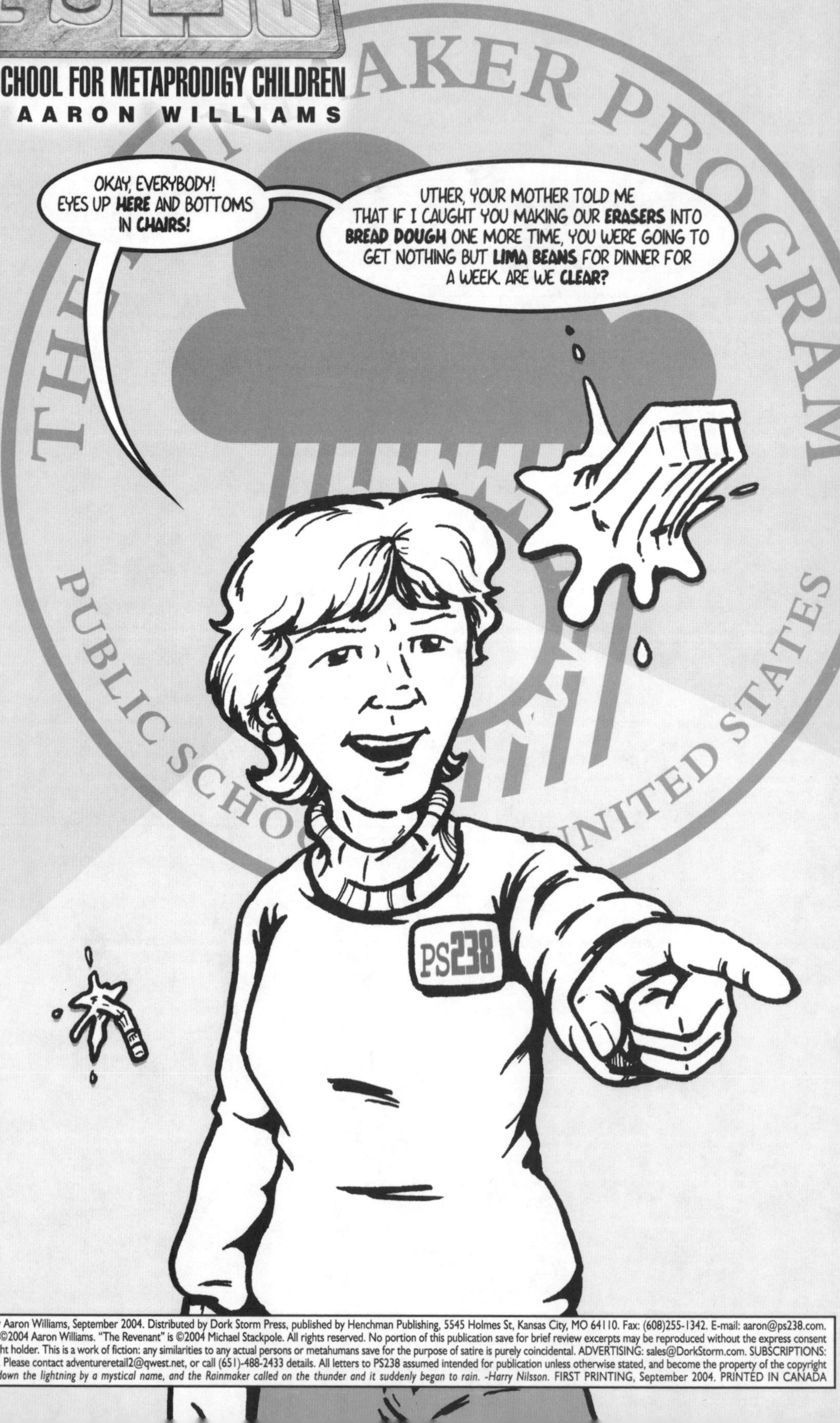
OKAY, EVERYBODY! EYES UP **HERE** AND BOTTOMS IN **CHAIRS!**
UTHER, YOUR MOTHER TOLD ME THAT IF I CAUGHT YOU MAKING OUR **ERASERS** INTO **BREAD DOUGH** ONE MORE TIME, YOU WERE GOING TO GET NOTHING BUT **LIMA BEANS** FOR DINNER FOR A WEEK. ARE WE **CLEAR?**
THE RAINMAKER PROGRAM
PUBLIC SCHOOLS OF THE UNITED STATES
PS238

PS238 #8 by Aaron Williams, September 2004. Distributed by Dork Storm Press, published by Henchman Publishing, 5545 Holmes St, Kansas City, MO 64110. Fax: (608)255-1342. E-mail: aaron@ps238.com.
 Call down the lightning by a mystical name, and the Rainmaker called on the thunder and it suddenly began to rain. -Harry Nilsson. FIRST PRINTING, September 2004. PRINTED IN CANADA

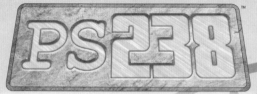

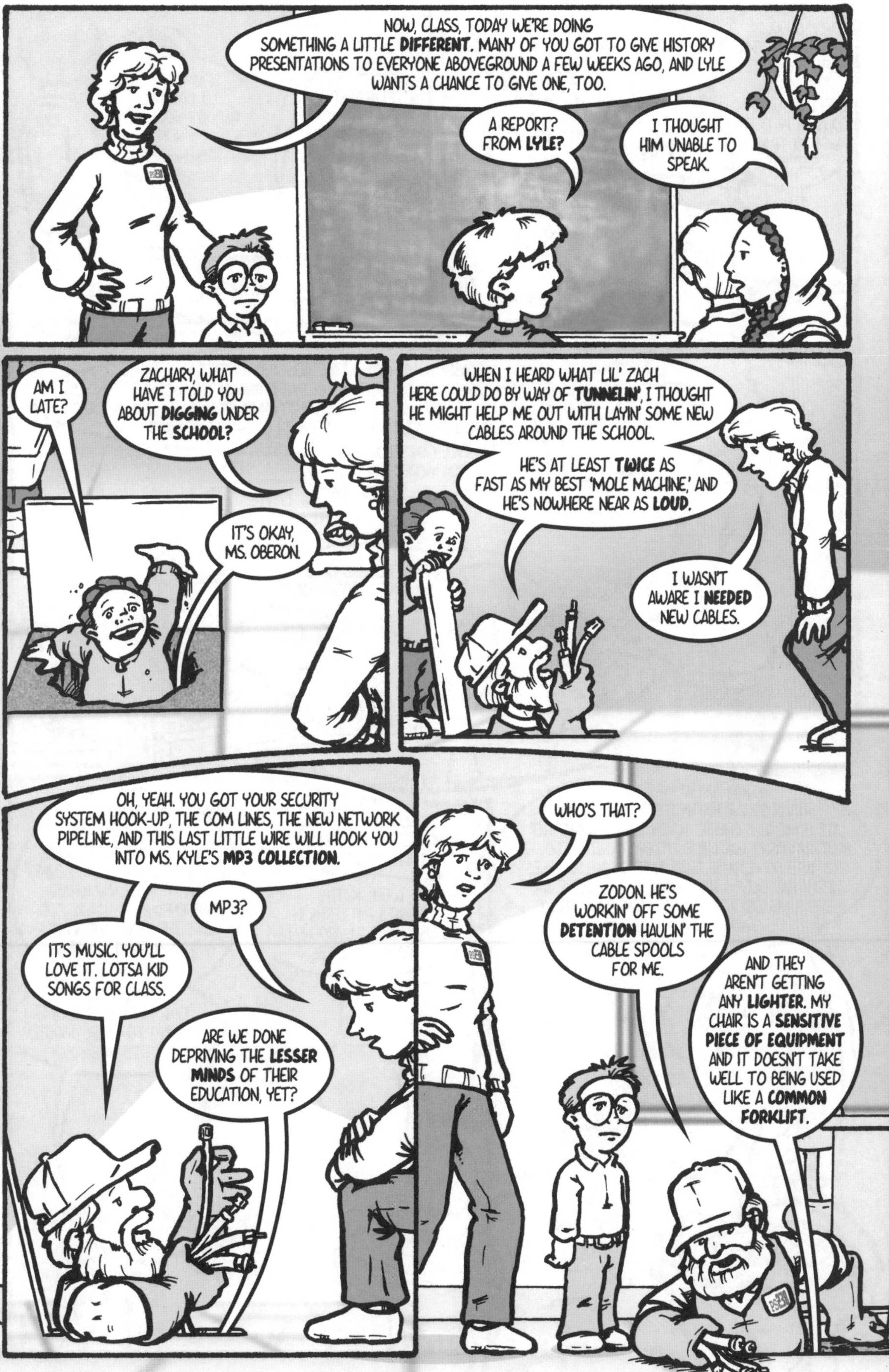

NOW, CLASS, TODAY WE'RE DOING SOMETHING A LITTLE DIFFERENT. MANY OF YOU GOT TO GIVE HISTORY PRESENTATIONS TO EVERYONE ABOVEGROUND A FEW WEEKS AGO, AND LYLE WANTS A CHANCE TO GIVE ONE, TOO.
A REPORT? FROM LYLE?
I THOUGHT HIM UNABLE TO SPEAK.
AM I LATE?
ZACHARY, WHAT HAVE I TOLD YOU ABOUT DIGGING UNDER THE SCHOOL?
IT'S OKAY, MS. OBERON.
WHEN I HEARD WHAT LIL' ZACH HERE COULD DO BY WAY OF TUNNELIN', I THOUGHT HE MIGHT HELP ME OUT WITH LAYIN' SOME NEW CABLES AROUND THE SCHOOL.
HE'S AT LEAST TWICE AS FAST AS MY BEST 'MOLE MACHINE,' AND HE'S NOWHERE NEAR AS LOUD.
I WASN'T AWARE I NEEDED NEW CABLES.
OH, YEAH. YOU GOT YOUR SECURITY SYSTEM HOOK-UP, THE COM LINES, THE NEW NETWORK PIPELINE, AND THIS LAST LITTLE WIRE WILL HOOK YOU INTO MS. KYLE'S MP3 COLLECTION.
MP3?
IT'S MUSIC. YOU'LL LOVE IT. LOTSA KID SONGS FOR CLASS.
ARE WE DONE DEPRIVING THE LESSER MINDS OF THEIR EDUCATION, YET?
WHO'S THAT?
ZODON. HE'S WORKIN' OFF SOME DETENTION HAULIN' THE CABLE SPOOLS FOR ME.
AND THEY AREN'T GETTING ANY LIGHTER. MY CHAIR IS A SENSITIVE PIECE OF EQUIPMENT AND IT DOESN'T TAKE WELL TO BEING USED LIKE A COMMON FORKLIFT.

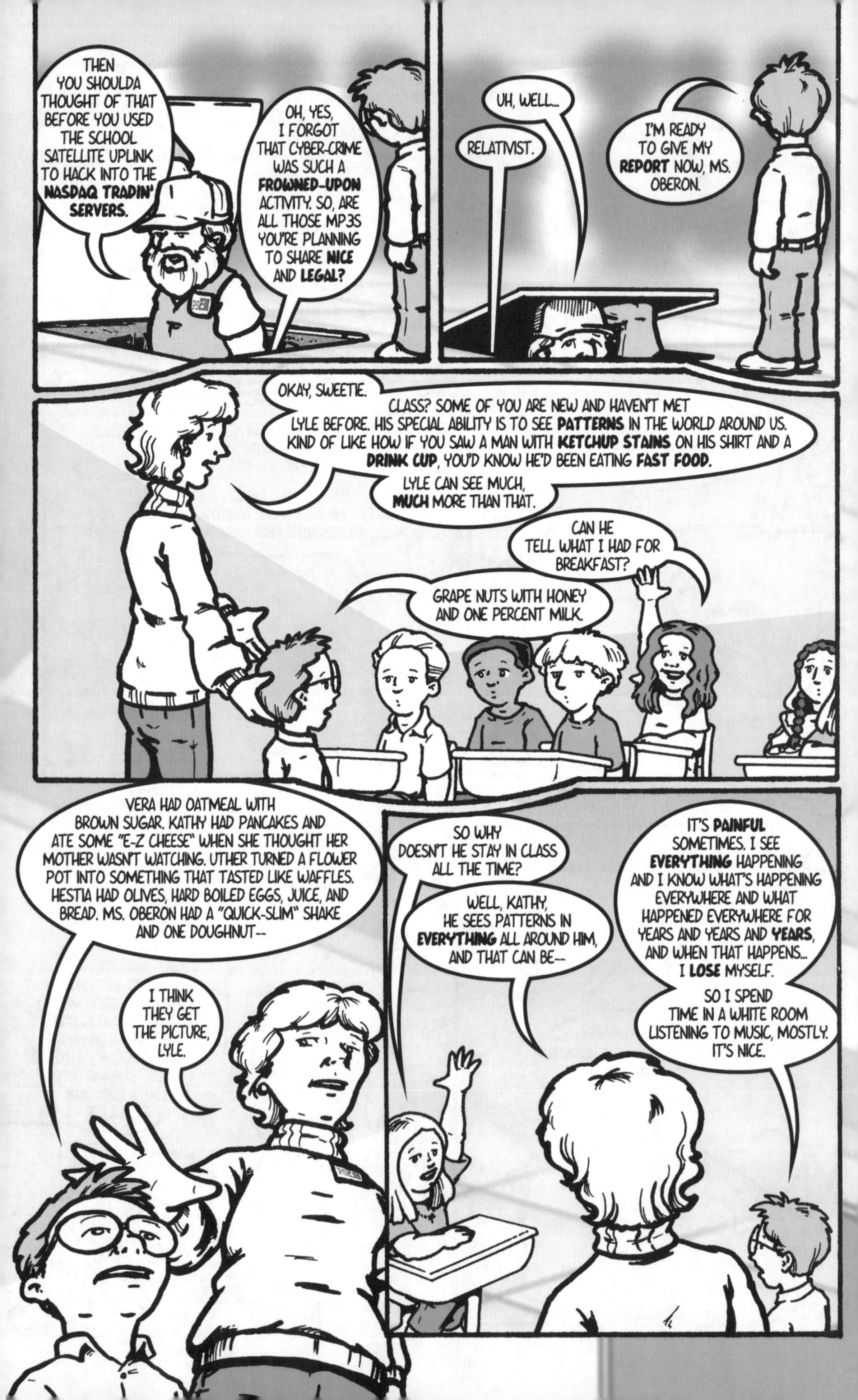
THEN YOU SHOULDA THOUGHT OF THAT BEFORE YOU USED THE SCHOOL SATELLITE UPLINK TO HACK INTO THE NASDAQ TRADIN' SERVERS.
OH, YES, I FORGOT THAT CYBER-CRIME WAS SUCH A FROWNED-UPON ACTIVITY. SO, ARE ALL THOSE MP3S YOU'RE PLANNING TO SHARE NICE AND LEGAL?
RELATIVIST.
UH, WELL...
I'M READY TO GIVE MY REPORT NOW, MS. OBERON.
OKAY, SWEETIE.
CLASS? SOME OF YOU ARE NEW AND HAVEN'T MET LYLE BEFORE. HIS SPECIAL ABILITY IS TO SEE PATTERNS IN THE WORLD AROUND US. KIND OF LIKE HOW IF YOU SAW A MAN WITH KETCHUP STAINS ON HIS SHIRT AND A DRINK CUP, YOU'D KNOW HE'D BEEN EATING FAST FOOD.
LYLE CAN SEE MUCH, MUCH MORE THAN THAT.
CAN HE TELL WHAT I HAD FOR BREAKFAST?
GRAPE NUTS WITH HONEY AND ONE PERCENT MILK.
VERA HAD OATMEAL WITH BROWN SUGAR. KATHY HAD PANCAKES AND ATE SOME "E-Z CHEESE" WHEN SHE THOUGHT HER MOTHER WASN'T WATCHING. UTHER TURNED A FLOWER POT INTO SOMETHING THAT TASTED LIKE WAFFLES. HESTIA HAD OLIVES, HARD BOILED EGGS, JUICE, AND BREAD. MS. OBERON HAD A "QUICK-SLIM" SHAKE AND ONE DOUGHNUT--
I THINK THEY GET THE PICTURE, LYLE.
SO WHY DOESN'T HE STAY IN CLASS ALL THE TIME?
WELL, KATHY, HE SEES PATTERNS IN EVERYTHING ALL AROUND HIM, AND THAT CAN BE--
IT'S PAINFUL SOMETIMES. I SEE EVERYTHING HAPPENING AND I KNOW WHAT'S HAPPENING EVERYWHERE AND WHAT HAPPENED EVERYWHERE FOR YEARS AND YEARS AND YEARS, AND WHEN THAT HAPPENS... I LOSE MYSELF.
SO I SPEND TIME IN A WHITE ROOM LISTENING TO MUSIC, MOSTLY. IT'S NICE.

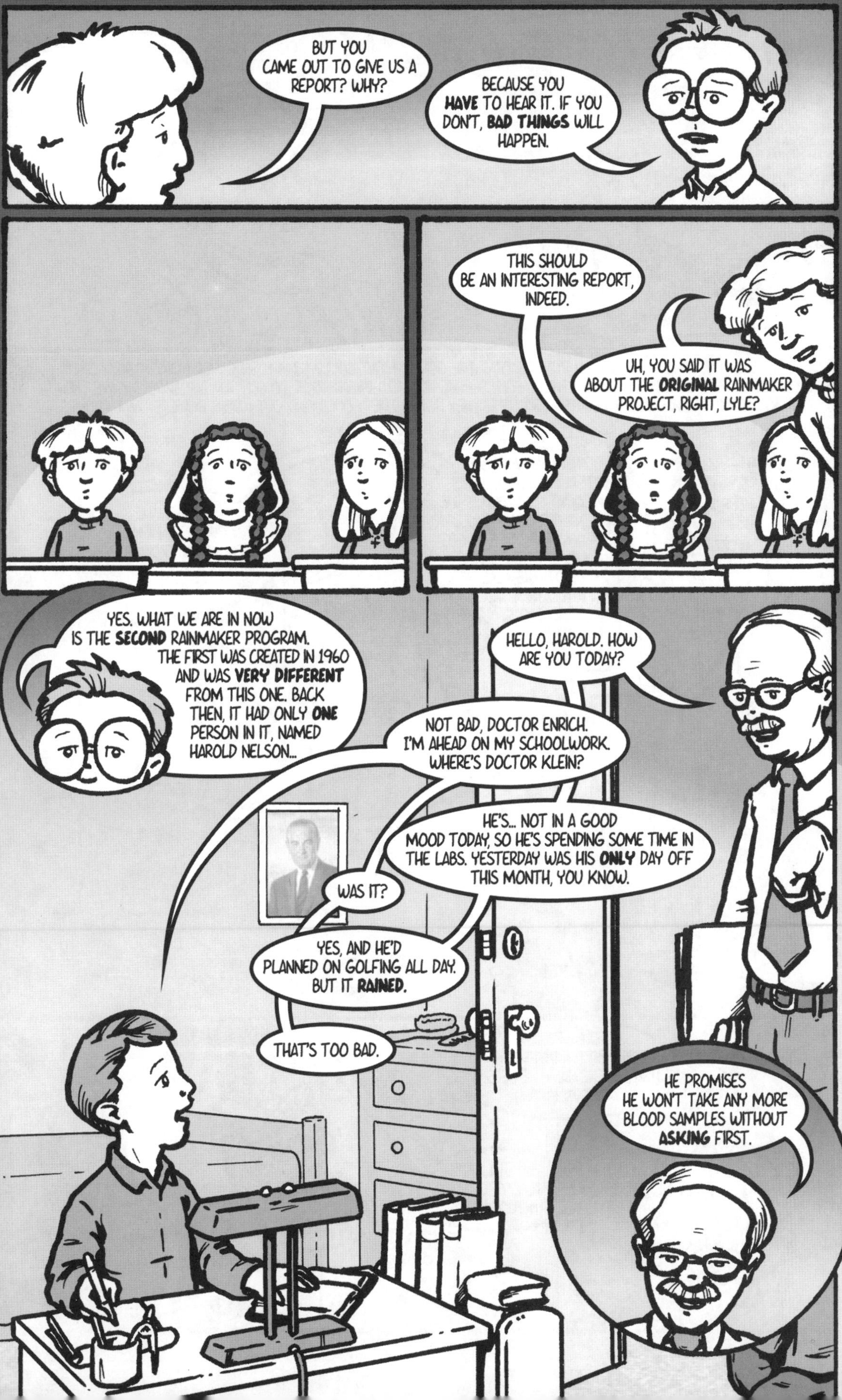

BUT YOU CAME OUT TO GIVE US A REPORT? WHY?
BECAUSE YOU **HAVE** TO HEAR IT. IF YOU DON'T, **BAD THINGS** WILL HAPPEN.
THIS SHOULD BE AN INTERESTING REPORT, INDEED.
UH, YOU SAID IT WAS ABOUT THE **ORIGINAL** RAINMAKER PROJECT, RIGHT, LYLE?
YES. WHAT WE ARE IN NOW IS THE **SECOND** RAINMAKER PROGRAM. THE FIRST WAS CREATED IN 1960 AND WAS **VERY DIFFERENT** FROM THIS ONE. BACK THEN, IT HAD ONLY **ONE** PERSON IN IT, NAMED HAROLD NELSON...
HELLO, HAROLD. HOW ARE YOU TODAY?
NOT BAD, DOCTOR ENRICH. I'M AHEAD ON MY SCHOOLWORK. WHERE'S DOCTOR KLEIN?
HE'S... NOT IN A GOOD MOOD TODAY, SO HE'S SPENDING SOME TIME IN THE LABS. YESTERDAY WAS HIS **ONLY** DAY OFF THIS MONTH, YOU KNOW.
WAS IT?
YES, AND HE'D PLANNED ON GOLFING ALL DAY. BUT IT **RAINED.**
THAT'S TOO BAD.
HE PROMISES HE WON'T TAKE ANY MORE BLOOD SAMPLES WITHOUT **ASKING** FIRST.

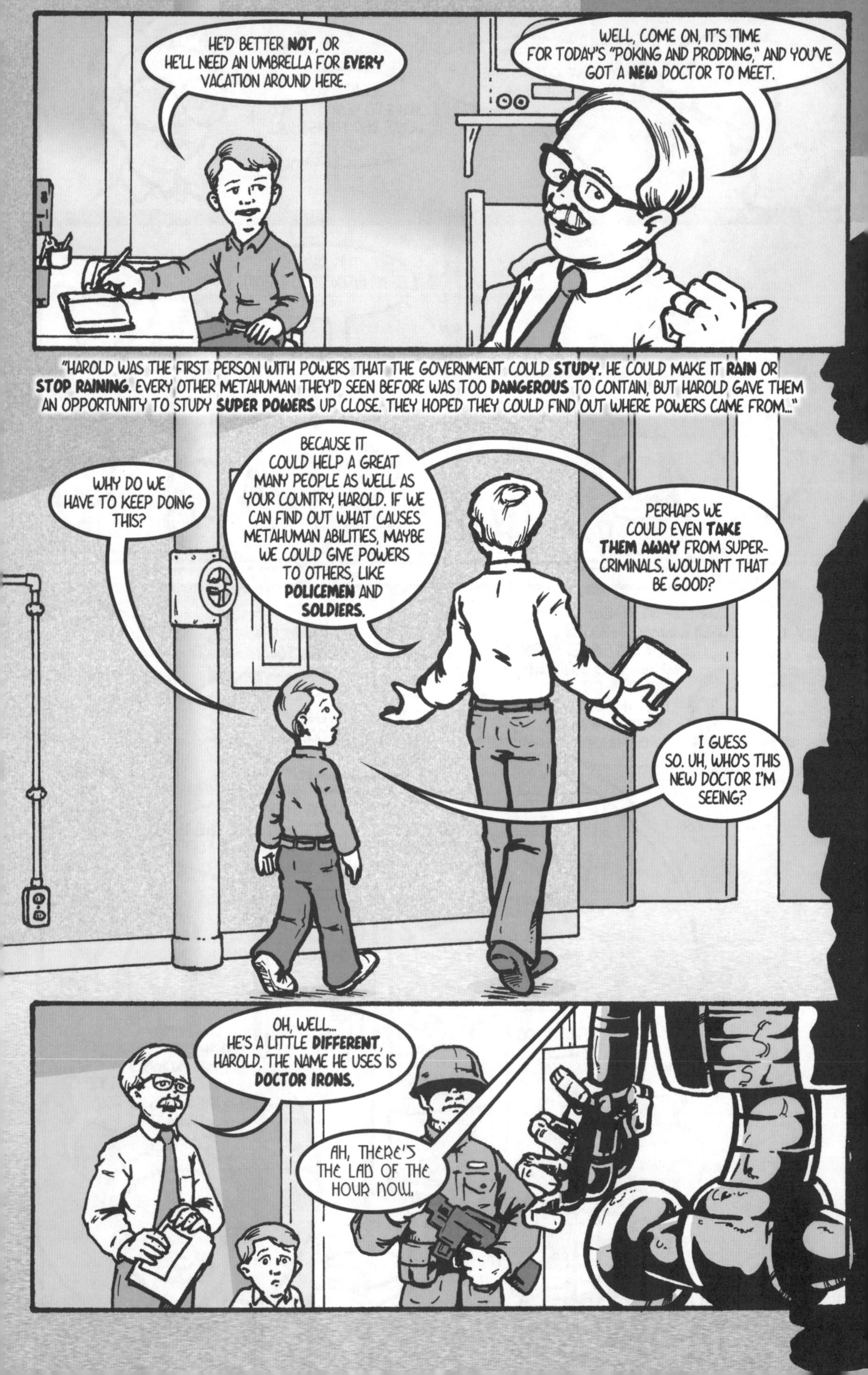
HE'D BETTER NOT, OR HE'LL NEED AN UMBRELLA FOR EVERY VACATION AROUND HERE.
WELL, COME ON, IT'S TIME FOR TODAY'S "POKING AND PRODDING," AND YOU'VE GOT A NEW DOCTOR TO MEET.
"HAROLD WAS THE FIRST PERSON WITH POWERS THAT THE GOVERNMENT COULD STUDY. HE COULD MAKE IT RAIN OR STOP RAINING. EVERY OTHER METAHUMAN THEY'D SEEN BEFORE WAS TOO DANGEROUS TO CONTAIN, BUT HAROLD GAVE THEM AN OPPORTUNITY TO STUDY SUPER POWERS UP CLOSE. THEY HOPED THEY COULD FIND OUT WHERE POWERS CAME FROM..."
WHY DO WE HAVE TO KEEP DOING THIS?
BECAUSE IT COULD HELP A GREAT MANY PEOPLE AS WELL AS YOUR COUNTRY, HAROLD. IF WE CAN FIND OUT WHAT CAUSES METAHUMAN ABILITIES, MAYBE WE COULD GIVE POWERS TO OTHERS, LIKE POLICEMEN AND SOLDIERS.
PERHAPS WE COULD EVEN TAKE THEM AWAY FROM SUPER-CRIMINALS. WOULDN'T THAT BE GOOD?
I GUESS SO. UH, WHO'S THIS NEW DOCTOR I'M SEEING?
OH, WELL... HE'S A LITTLE DIFFERENT, HAROLD. THE NAME HE USES IS DOCTOR IRONS.
AH, THERE'S THE LAD OF THE HOUR NOW.

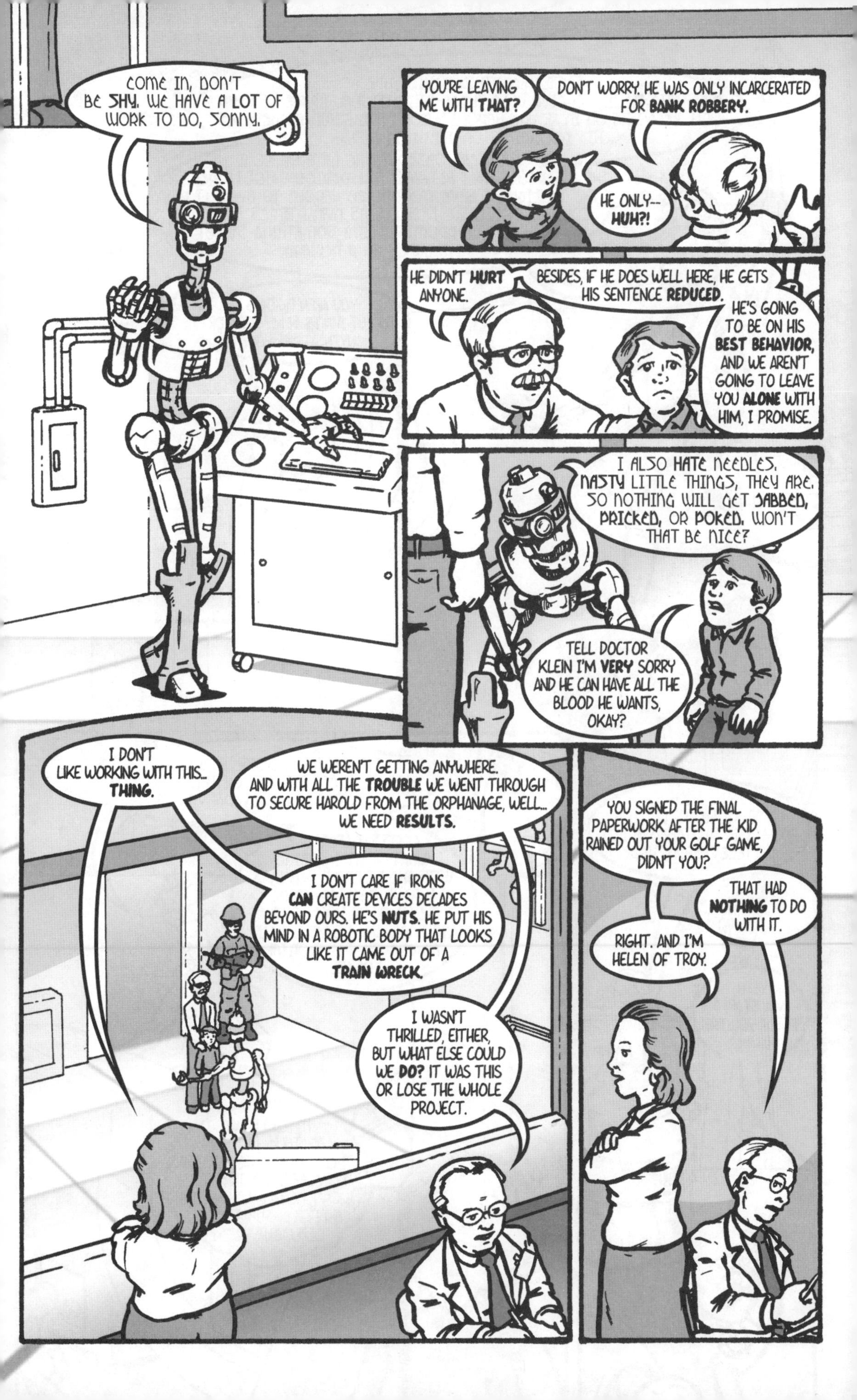
COME IN, DON'T BE SHY. WE HAVE A LOT OF WORK TO DO, SONNY.
YOU'RE LEAVING ME WITH THAT?
DON'T WORRY. HE WAS ONLY INCARCERATED FOR BANK ROBBERY.
HE ONLY-- HUH?!
HE DIDN'T HURT ANYONE.
BESIDES, IF HE DOES WELL HERE, HE GETS HIS SENTENCE REDUCED.
HE'S GOING TO BE ON HIS BEST BEHAVIOR, AND WE AREN'T GOING TO LEAVE YOU ALONE WITH HIM, I PROMISE.
I ALSO HATE NEEDLES. NASTY LITTLE THINGS, THEY ARE. SO NOTHING WILL GET JABBED, PRICKED, OR POKED. WON'T THAT BE NICE?
TELL DOCTOR KLEIN I'M VERY SORRY AND HE CAN HAVE ALL THE BLOOD HE WANTS, OKAY?
I DON'T LIKE WORKING WITH THIS... THING.
WE WEREN'T GETTING ANYWHERE. AND WITH ALL THE TROUBLE WE WENT THROUGH TO SECURE HAROLD FROM THE ORPHANAGE, WELL... WE NEED RESULTS.
I DON'T CARE IF IRONS CAN CREATE DEVICES DECADES BEYOND OURS. HE'S NUTS. HE PUT HIS MIND IN A ROBOTIC BODY THAT LOOKS LIKE IT CAME OUT OF A TRAIN WRECK.
I WASN'T THRILLED, EITHER, BUT WHAT ELSE COULD WE DO? IT WAS THIS OR LOSE THE WHOLE PROJECT.
YOU SIGNED THE FINAL PAPERWORK AFTER THE KID RAINED OUT YOUR GOLF GAME, DIDN'T YOU?
THAT HAD NOTHING TO DO WITH IT.
RIGHT. AND I'M HELEN OF TROY.

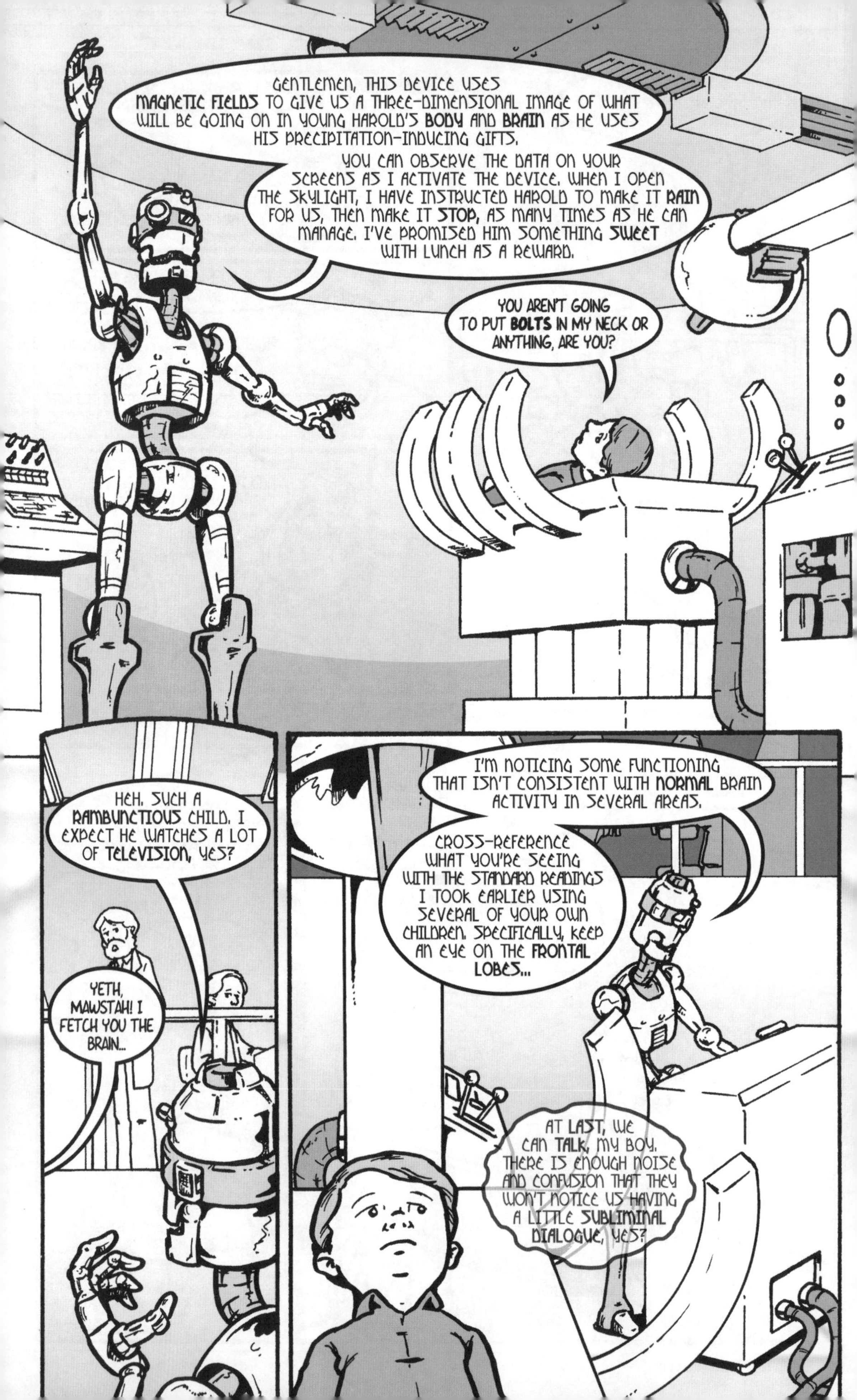

GENTLEMEN, THIS DEVICE USES MAGNETIC FIELDS TO GIVE US A THREE-DIMENSIONAL IMAGE OF WHAT WILL BE GOING ON IN YOUNG HAROLD'S BODY AND BRAIN AS HE USES HIS PRECIPITATION-INDUCING GIFTS.
YOU CAN OBSERVE THE DATA ON YOUR SCREENS AS I ACTIVATE THE DEVICE. WHEN I OPEN THE SKYLIGHT, I HAVE INSTRUCTED HAROLD TO MAKE IT RAIN FOR US, THEN MAKE IT STOP, AS MANY TIMES AS HE CAN MANAGE. I'VE PROMISED HIM SOMETHING SWEET WITH LUNCH AS A REWARD.
YOU AREN'T GOING TO PUT BOLTS IN MY NECK OR ANYTHING, ARE YOU?
HEH. SUCH A RAMBUNCTIOUS CHILD. I EXPECT HE WATCHES A LOT OF TELEVISION, YES?
YETH, MAWSTAH! I FETCH YOU THE BRAIN...
I'M NOTICING SOME FUNCTIONING THAT ISN'T CONSISTENT WITH NORMAL BRAIN ACTIVITY IN SEVERAL AREAS.
CROSS-REFERENCE WHAT YOU'RE SEEING WITH THE STANDARD READINGS I TOOK EARLIER USING SEVERAL OF YOUR OWN CHILDREN. SPECIFICALLY, KEEP AN EYE ON THE FRONTAL LOBES...
AT LAST, WE CAN TALK, MY BOY. THERE IS ENOUGH NOISE AND CONFUSION THAT THEY WON'T NOTICE US HAVING A LITTLE SUBLIMINAL DIALOGUE, YES?

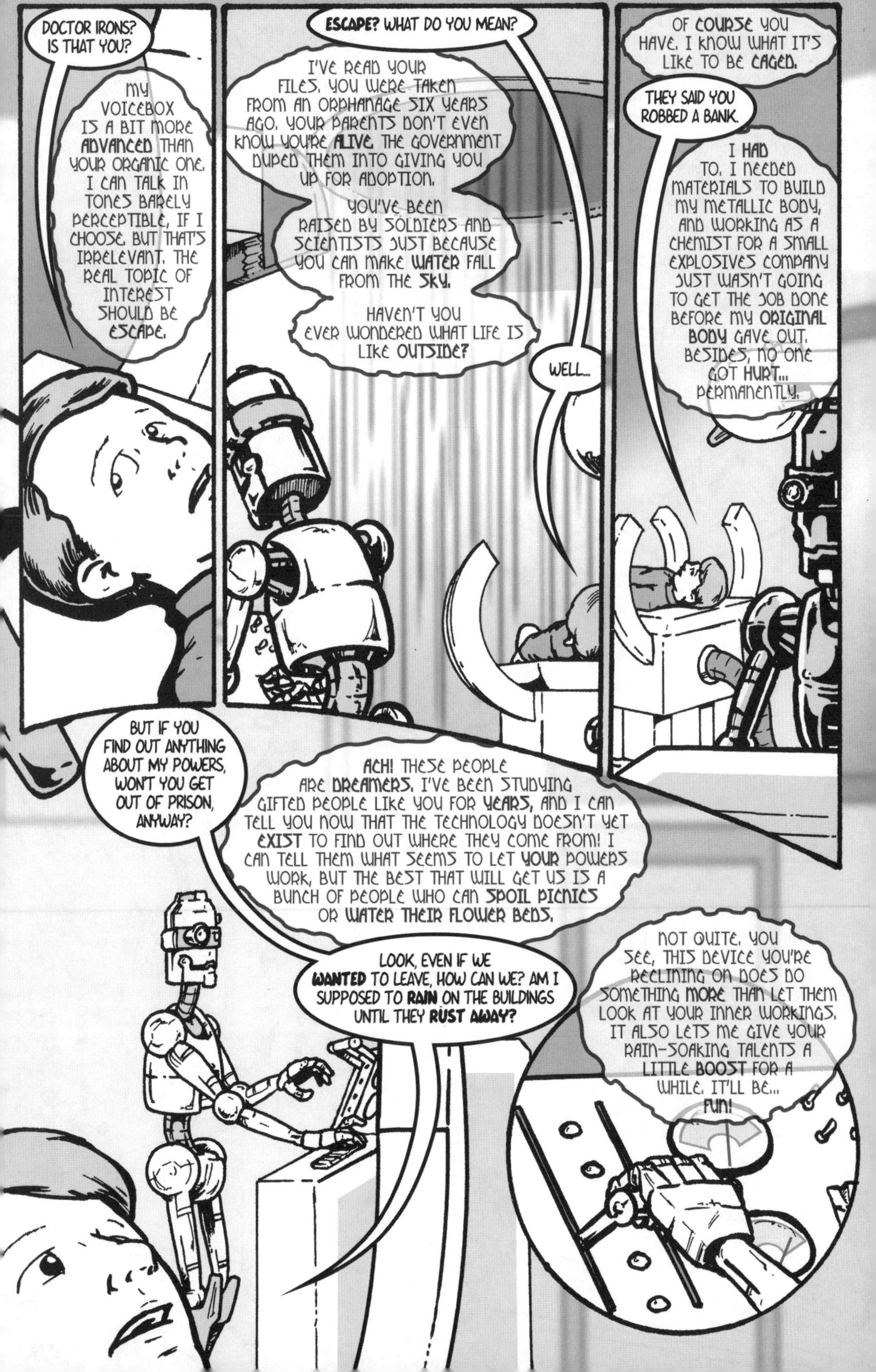
DOCTOR IRONS? IS THAT YOU?
MY VOICEBOX IS A BIT MORE ADVANCED THAN YOUR ORGANIC ONE. I CAN TALK IN TONES BARELY PERCEPTIBLE, IF I CHOOSE. BUT THAT'S IRRELEVANT. THE REAL TOPIC OF INTEREST SHOULD BE ESCAPE.
ESCAPE? WHAT DO YOU MEAN?
I'VE READ YOUR FILES. YOU WERE TAKEN FROM AN ORPHANAGE SIX YEARS AGO. YOUR PARENTS DON'T EVEN KNOW YOU'RE ALIVE. THE GOVERNMENT DUPED THEM INTO GIVING YOU UP FOR ADOPTION.
YOU'VE BEEN RAISED BY SOLDIERS AND SCIENTISTS JUST BECAUSE YOU CAN MAKE WATER FALL FROM THE SKY.
HAVEN'T YOU EVER WONDERED WHAT LIFE IS LIKE OUTSIDE?
WELL...
OF COURSE YOU HAVE. I KNOW WHAT IT'S LIKE TO BE CAGED.
THEY SAID YOU ROBBED A BANK.
I HAD TO. I NEEDED MATERIALS TO BUILD MY METALLIC BODY, AND WORKING AS A CHEMIST FOR A SMALL EXPLOSIVES COMPANY JUST WASN'T GOING TO GET THE JOB DONE BEFORE MY ORIGINAL BODY GAVE OUT. BESIDES, NO ONE GOT HURT... PERMANENTLY.
BUT IF YOU FIND OUT ANYTHING ABOUT MY POWERS, WON'T YOU GET OUT OF PRISON, ANYWAY?
ACH! THESE PEOPLE ARE DREAMERS. I'VE BEEN STUDYING GIFTED PEOPLE LIKE YOU FOR YEARS, AND I CAN TELL YOU NOW THAT THE TECHNOLOGY DOESN'T YET EXIST TO FIND OUT WHERE THEY COME FROM! I CAN TELL THEM WHAT SEEMS TO LET YOUR POWERS WORK, BUT THE BEST THAT WILL GET US IS A BUNCH OF PEOPLE WHO CAN SPOIL PICNICS OR WATER THEIR FLOWER BEDS.
LOOK, EVEN IF WE WANTED TO LEAVE, HOW CAN WE? AM I SUPPOSED TO RAIN ON THE BUILDINGS UNTIL THEY RUST AWAY?
NOT QUITE. YOU SEE, THIS DEVICE YOU'RE RECLINING ON DOES DO SOMETHING MORE THAN LET THEM LOOK AT YOUR INNER WORKINGS. IT ALSO LETS ME GIVE YOUR RAIN-SOAKING TALENTS A LITTLE BOOST FOR A WHILE. IT'LL BE... FUN!

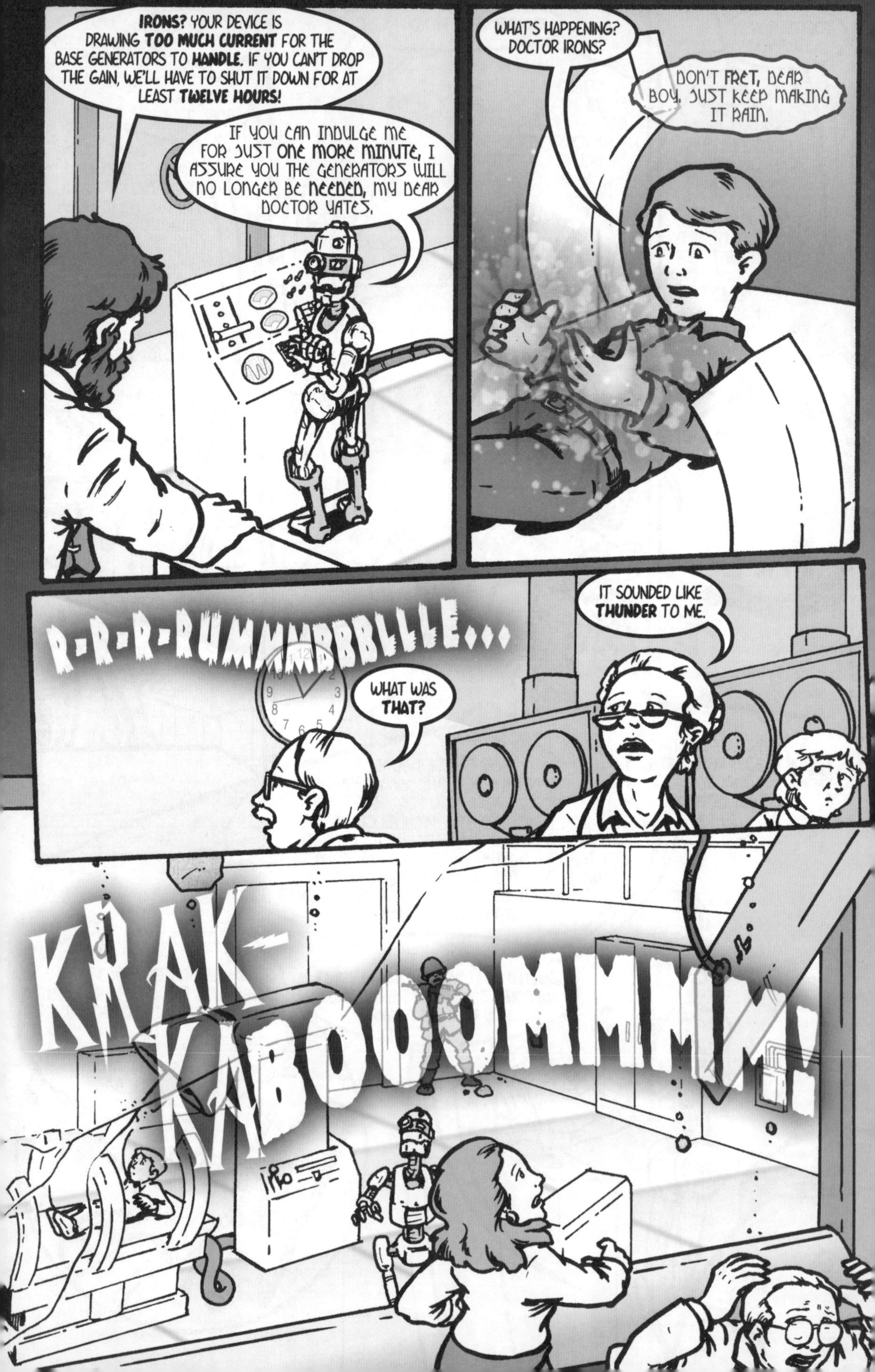
IRONS? YOUR DEVICE IS DRAWING TOO MUCH CURRENT FOR THE BASE GENERATORS TO HANDLE. IF YOU CAN'T DROP THE GAIN, WE'LL HAVE TO SHUT IT DOWN FOR AT LEAST TWELVE HOURS!
IF YOU CAN INDULGE ME FOR JUST ONE MORE MINUTE, I ASSURE YOU THE GENERATORS WILL NO LONGER BE NEEDED, MY DEAR DOCTOR YATES.
WHAT'S HAPPENING? DOCTOR IRONS?
DON'T FRET, DEAR BOY. JUST KEEP MAKING IT RAIN.
R-R-R-RUMMMBBBLLLE...
WHAT WAS THAT?
IT SOUNDED LIKE THUNDER TO ME.
KRAK-KA-BOOOMMMM!

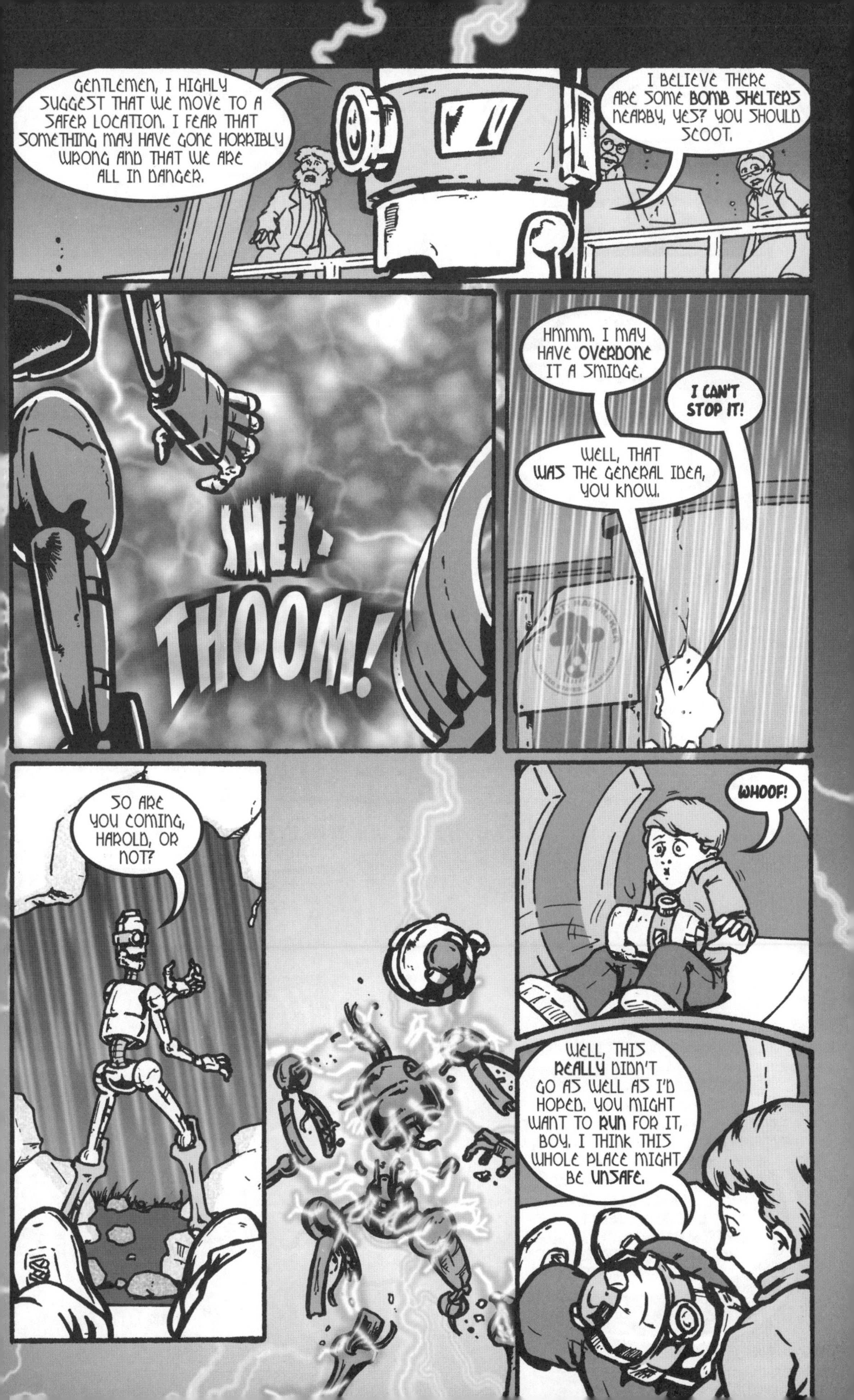
GENTLEMEN, I HIGHLY SUGGEST THAT WE MOVE TO A SAFER LOCATION. I FEAR THAT SOMETHING MAY HAVE GONE HORRIBLY WRONG AND THAT WE ARE ALL IN DANGER.
I BELIEVE THERE ARE SOME BOMB SHELTERS NEARBY, YES? YOU SHOULD SCOOT.
SHEK-THOOM!
HMMM. I MAY HAVE OVERDONE IT A SMIDGE.
I CAN'T STOP IT!
WELL, THAT WAS THE GENERAL IDEA, YOU KNOW.
SO ARE YOU COMING, HAROLD, OR NOT?
WHOOF!
WELL, THIS REALLY DIDN'T GO AS WELL AS I'D HOPED. YOU MIGHT WANT TO RUN FOR IT, BOY. I THINK THIS WHOLE PLACE MIGHT BE UNSAFE.

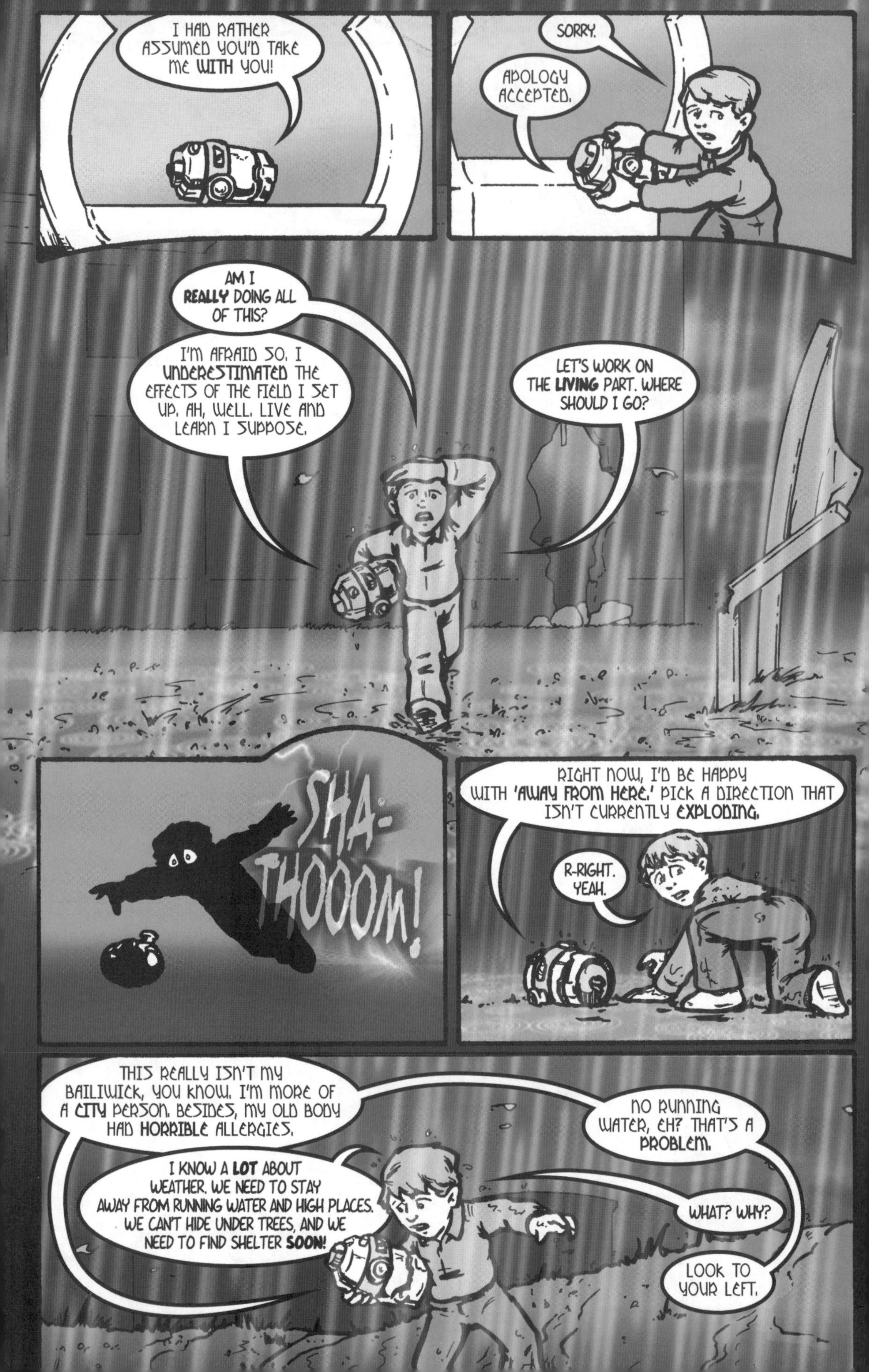

I HAD RATHER ASSUMED YOU'D TAKE ME WITH YOU!
SORRY.
APOLOGY ACCEPTED.
AM I REALLY DOING ALL OF THIS?
I'M AFRAID SO. I UNDERESTIMATED THE EFFECTS OF THE FIELD I SET UP. AH, WELL. LIVE AND LEARN I SUPPOSE.
LET'S WORK ON THE LIVING PART. WHERE SHOULD I GO?
SHA-THOOOM!
RIGHT NOW, I'D BE HAPPY WITH 'AWAY FROM HERE.' PICK A DIRECTION THAT ISN'T CURRENTLY EXPLODING.
R-RIGHT. YEAH.
THIS REALLY ISN'T MY BAILIWICK, YOU KNOW. I'M MORE OF A CITY PERSON. BESIDES, MY OLD BODY HAD HORRIBLE ALLERGIES.
NO RUNNING WATER, EH? THAT'S A PROBLEM.
I KNOW A LOT ABOUT WEATHER. WE NEED TO STAY AWAY FROM RUNNING WATER AND HIGH PLACES. WE CAN'T HIDE UNDER TREES, AND WE NEED TO FIND SHELTER SOON!
WHAT? WHY?
LOOK TO YOUR LEFT.

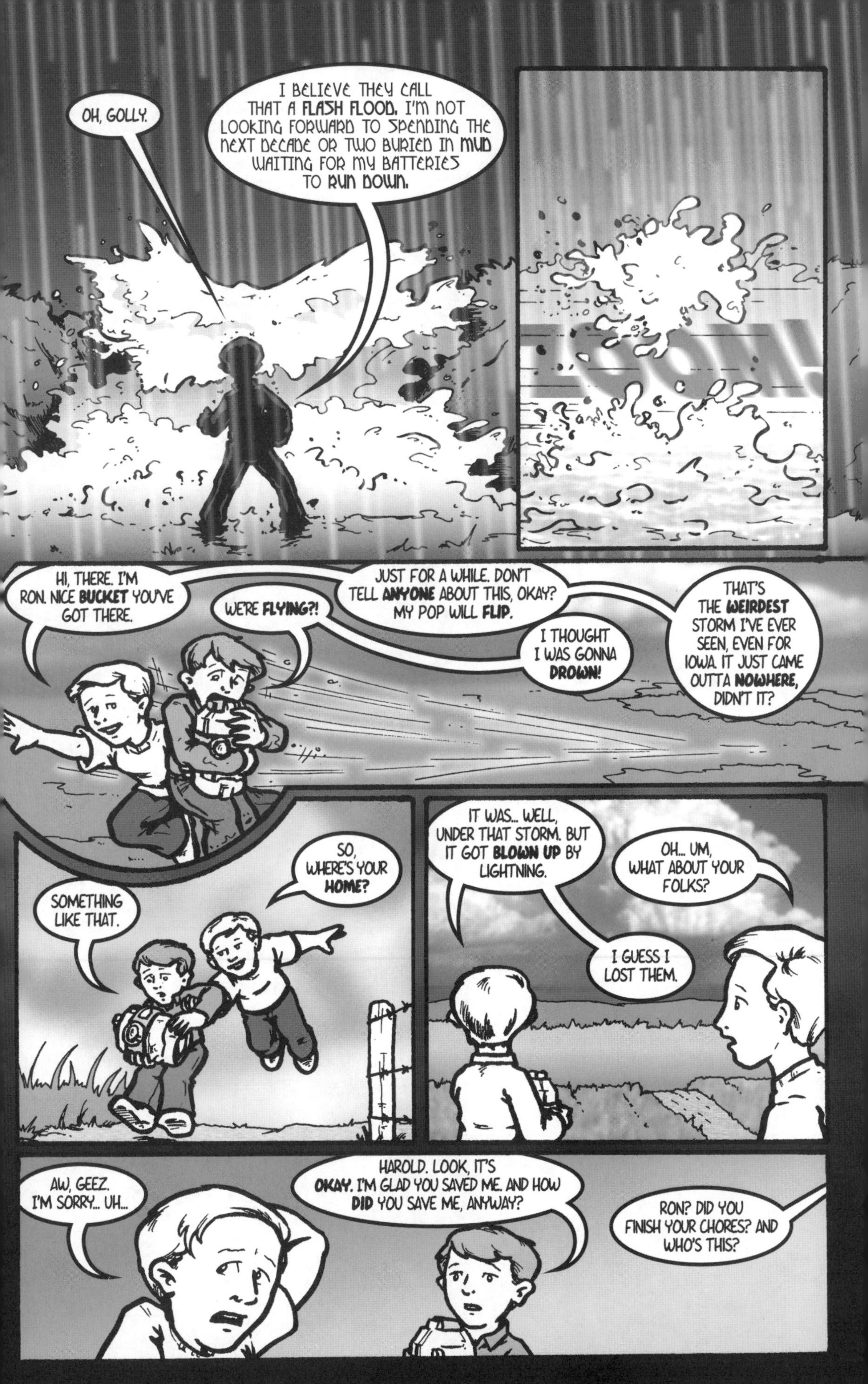
OH, GOLLY.
I BELIEVE THEY CALL THAT A FLASH FLOOD. I'M NOT LOOKING FORWARD TO SPENDING THE NEXT DECADE OR TWO BURIED IN MUD WAITING FOR MY BATTERIES TO RUN DOWN.
HI, THERE. I'M RON. NICE BUCKET YOU'VE GOT THERE.
WE'RE FLYING?!
JUST FOR A WHILE. DON'T TELL ANYONE ABOUT THIS, OKAY? MY POP WILL FLIP.
I THOUGHT I WAS GONNA DROWN!
THAT'S THE WEIRDEST STORM I'VE EVER SEEN, EVEN FOR IOWA. IT JUST CAME OUTTA NOWHERE, DIDN'T IT?
SOMETHING LIKE THAT.
SO, WHERE'S YOUR HOME?
IT WAS... WELL, UNDER THAT STORM. BUT IT GOT BLOWN UP BY LIGHTNING.
OH... UM, WHAT ABOUT YOUR FOLKS?
I GUESS I LOST THEM.
AW, GEEZ. I'M SORRY... UH...
HAROLD. LOOK, IT'S OKAY. I'M GLAD YOU SAVED ME. AND HOW DID YOU SAVE ME, ANYWAY?
RON? DID YOU FINISH YOUR CHORES? AND WHO'S THIS?

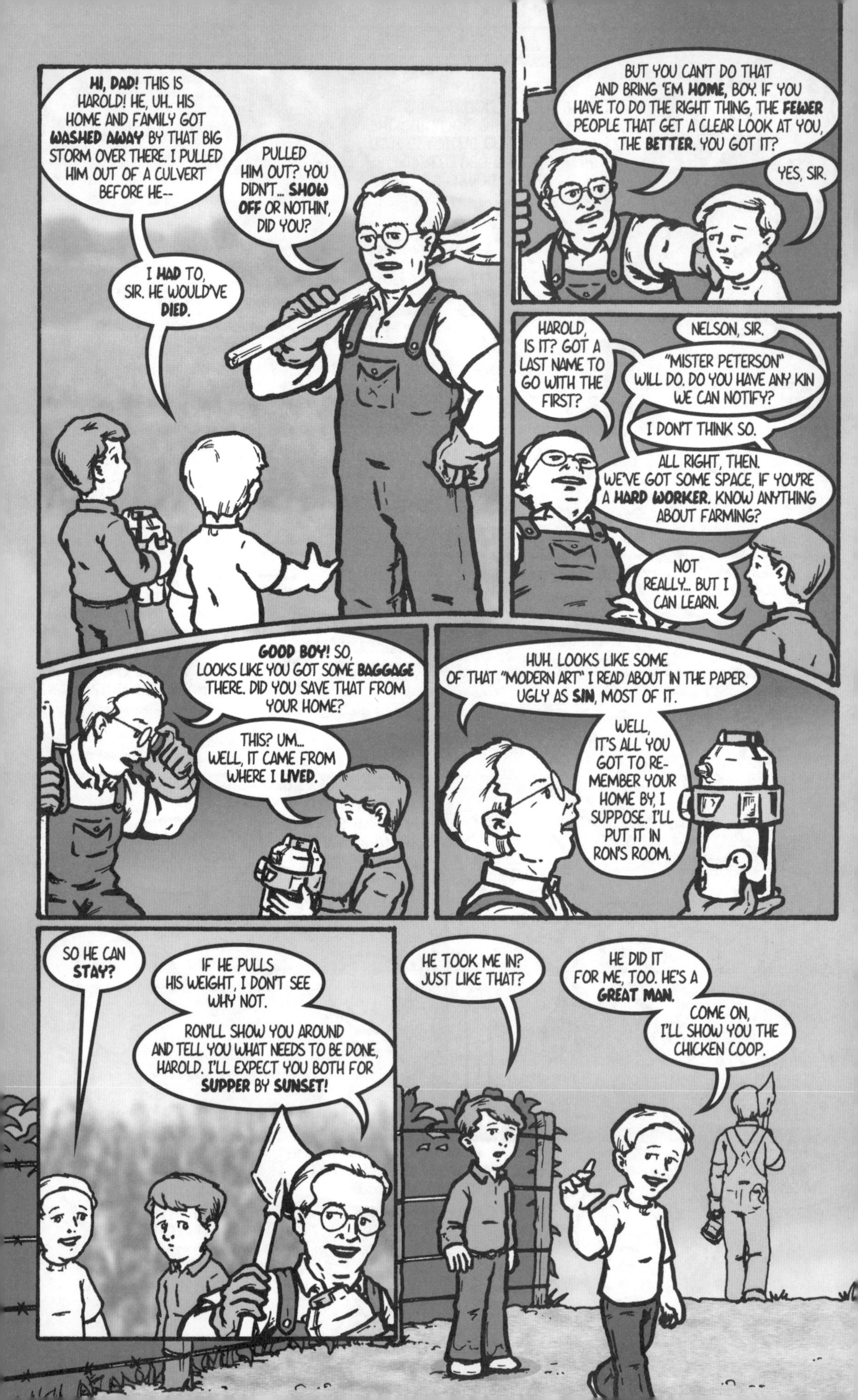
HI, DAD! THIS IS HAROLD! HE, UH.. HIS HOME AND FAMILY GOT WASHED AWAY BY THAT BIG STORM OVER THERE. I PULLED HIM OUT OF A CULVERT BEFORE HE--
PULLED HIM OUT? YOU DIDN'T... SHOW OFF OR NOTHIN', DID YOU?
I HAD TO, SIR. HE WOULD'VE DIED.
BUT YOU CAN'T DO THAT AND BRING 'EM HOME, BOY. IF YOU HAVE TO DO THE RIGHT THING, THE FEWER PEOPLE THAT GET A CLEAR LOOK AT YOU, THE BETTER. YOU GOT IT?
YES, SIR.
HAROLD, IS IT? GOT A LAST NAME TO GO WITH THE FIRST?
NELSON, SIR.
"MISTER PETERSON" WILL DO. DO YOU HAVE ANY KIN WE CAN NOTIFY?
I DON'T THINK SO.
ALL RIGHT, THEN. WE'VE GOT SOME SPACE, IF YOU'RE A HARD WORKER. KNOW ANYTHING ABOUT FARMING?
NOT REALLY... BUT I CAN LEARN.
GOOD BOY! SO, LOOKS LIKE YOU GOT SOME BAGGAGE THERE. DID YOU SAVE THAT FROM YOUR HOME?
THIS? UM... WELL, IT CAME FROM WHERE I LIVED.
HUH. LOOKS LIKE SOME OF THAT "MODERN ART" I READ ABOUT IN THE PAPER. UGLY AS SIN, MOST OF IT.
WELL, IT'S ALL YOU GOT TO RE-MEMBER YOUR HOME BY, I SUPPOSE. I'LL PUT IT IN RON'S ROOM.
SO HE CAN STAY?
IF HE PULLS HIS WEIGHT, I DON'T SEE WHY NOT.
RON'LL SHOW YOU AROUND AND TELL YOU WHAT NEEDS TO BE DONE, HAROLD. I'LL EXPECT YOU BOTH FOR SUPPER BY SUNSET!
HE TOOK ME IN? JUST LIKE THAT?
HE DID IT FOR ME, TOO. HE'S A GREAT MAN.
COME ON, I'LL SHOW YOU THE CHICKEN COOP.

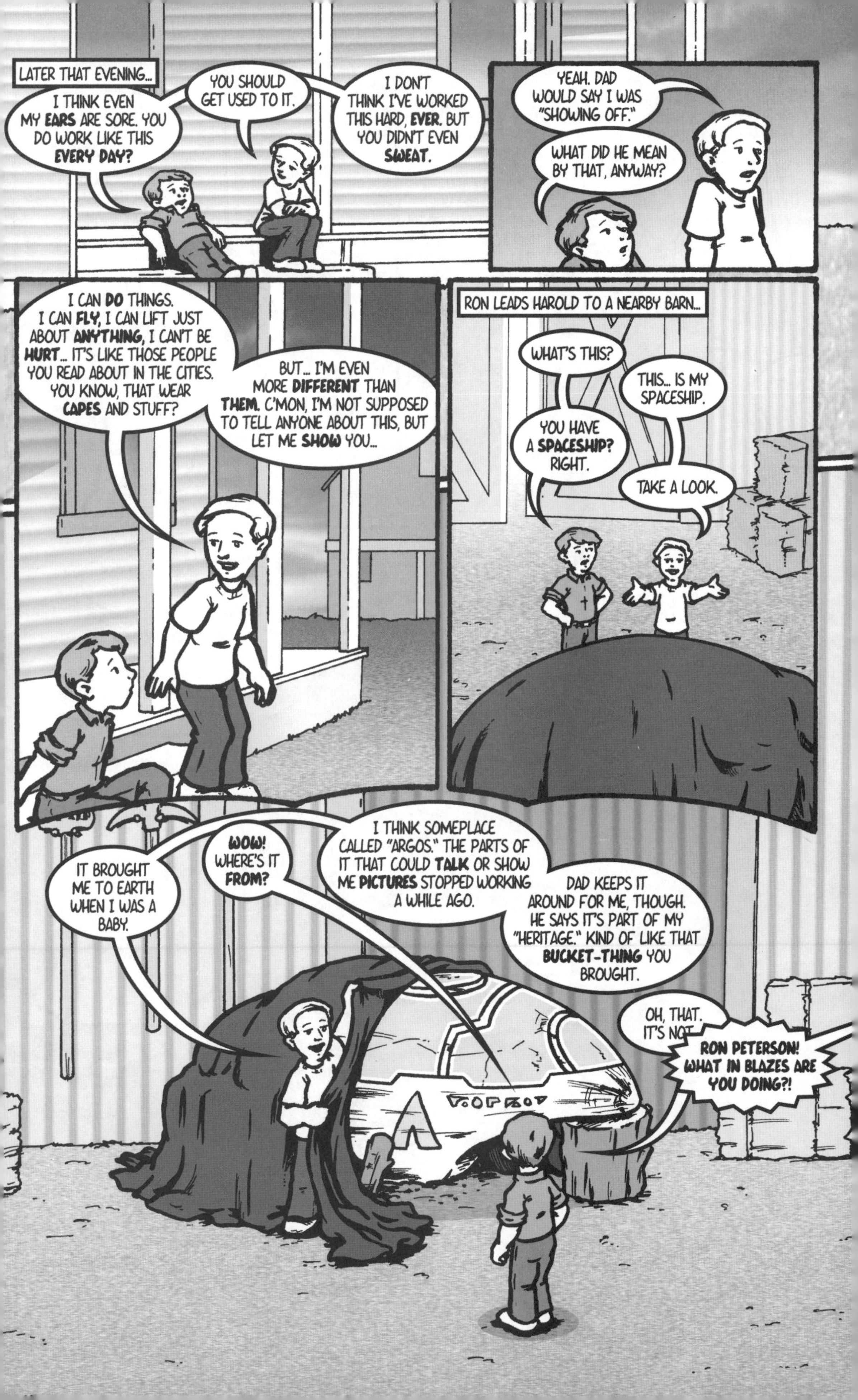

LATER THAT EVENING...
I THINK EVEN MY EARS ARE SORE. YOU DO WORK LIKE THIS EVERY DAY?
YOU SHOULD GET USED TO IT.
I DON'T THINK I'VE WORKED THIS HARD, EVER. BUT YOU DIDN'T EVEN SWEAT.
YEAH. DAD WOULD SAY I WAS "SHOWING OFF."
WHAT DID HE MEAN BY THAT, ANYWAY?
I CAN DO THINGS. I CAN FLY, I CAN LIFT JUST ABOUT ANYTHING, I CAN'T BE HURT... IT'S LIKE THOSE PEOPLE YOU READ ABOUT IN THE CITIES. YOU KNOW, THAT WEAR CAPES AND STUFF?
BUT... I'M EVEN MORE DIFFERENT THAN THEM. C'MON, I'M NOT SUPPOSED TO TELL ANYONE ABOUT THIS, BUT LET ME SHOW YOU...
RON LEADS HAROLD TO A NEARBY BARN...
WHAT'S THIS?
THIS... IS MY SPACESHIP.
YOU HAVE A SPACESHIP? RIGHT.
TAKE A LOOK.
IT BROUGHT ME TO EARTH WHEN I WAS A BABY.
WOW! WHERE'S IT FROM?
I THINK SOMEPLACE CALLED "ARGOS." THE PARTS OF IT THAT COULD TALK OR SHOW ME PICTURES STOPPED WORKING A WHILE AGO.
DAD KEEPS IT AROUND FOR ME, THOUGH. HE SAYS IT'S PART OF MY "HERITAGE." KIND OF LIKE THAT BUCKET-THING YOU BROUGHT.
OH, THAT. IT'S NOT
RON PETERSON! WHAT IN BLAZES ARE YOU DOING?!

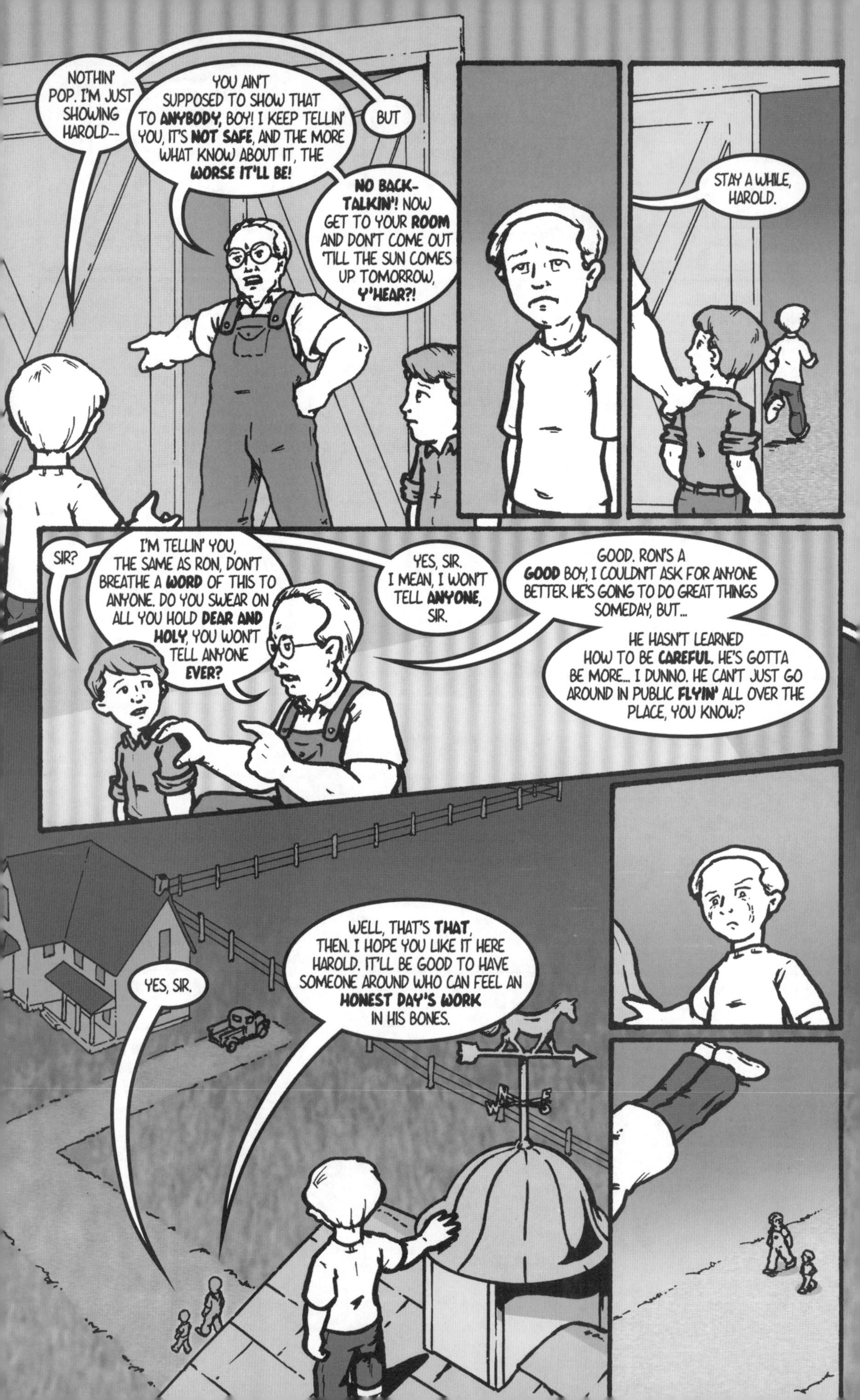
NOTHIN' POP. I'M JUST SHOWING HAROLD--
YOU AIN'T SUPPOSED TO SHOW THAT TO ANYBODY, BOY! I KEEP TELLIN' YOU, IT'S NOT SAFE, AND THE MORE WHAT KNOW ABOUT IT, THE WORSE IT'LL BE!
BUT
NO BACK-TALKIN'! NOW GET TO YOUR ROOM AND DON'T COME OUT 'TILL THE SUN COMES UP TOMORROW, Y'HEAR?!
STAY A WHILE, HAROLD.
SIR?
I'M TELLIN' YOU, THE SAME AS RON, DON'T BREATHE A WORD OF THIS TO ANYONE. DO YOU SWEAR ON ALL YOU HOLD DEAR AND HOLY, YOU WON'T TELL ANYONE EVER?
YES, SIR. I MEAN, I WON'T TELL ANYONE, SIR.
GOOD. RON'S A GOOD BOY, I COULDN'T ASK FOR ANYONE BETTER. HE'S GOING TO DO GREAT THINGS SOMEDAY, BUT...
HE HASN'T LEARNED HOW TO BE CAREFUL. HE'S GOTTA BE MORE... I DUNNO. HE CAN'T JUST GO AROUND IN PUBLIC FLYIN' ALL OVER THE PLACE, YOU KNOW?
YES, SIR.
WELL, THAT'S THAT, THEN. I HOPE YOU LIKE IT HERE HAROLD. IT'LL BE GOOD TO HAVE SOMEONE AROUND WHO CAN FEEL AN HONEST DAY'S WORK IN HIS BONES.

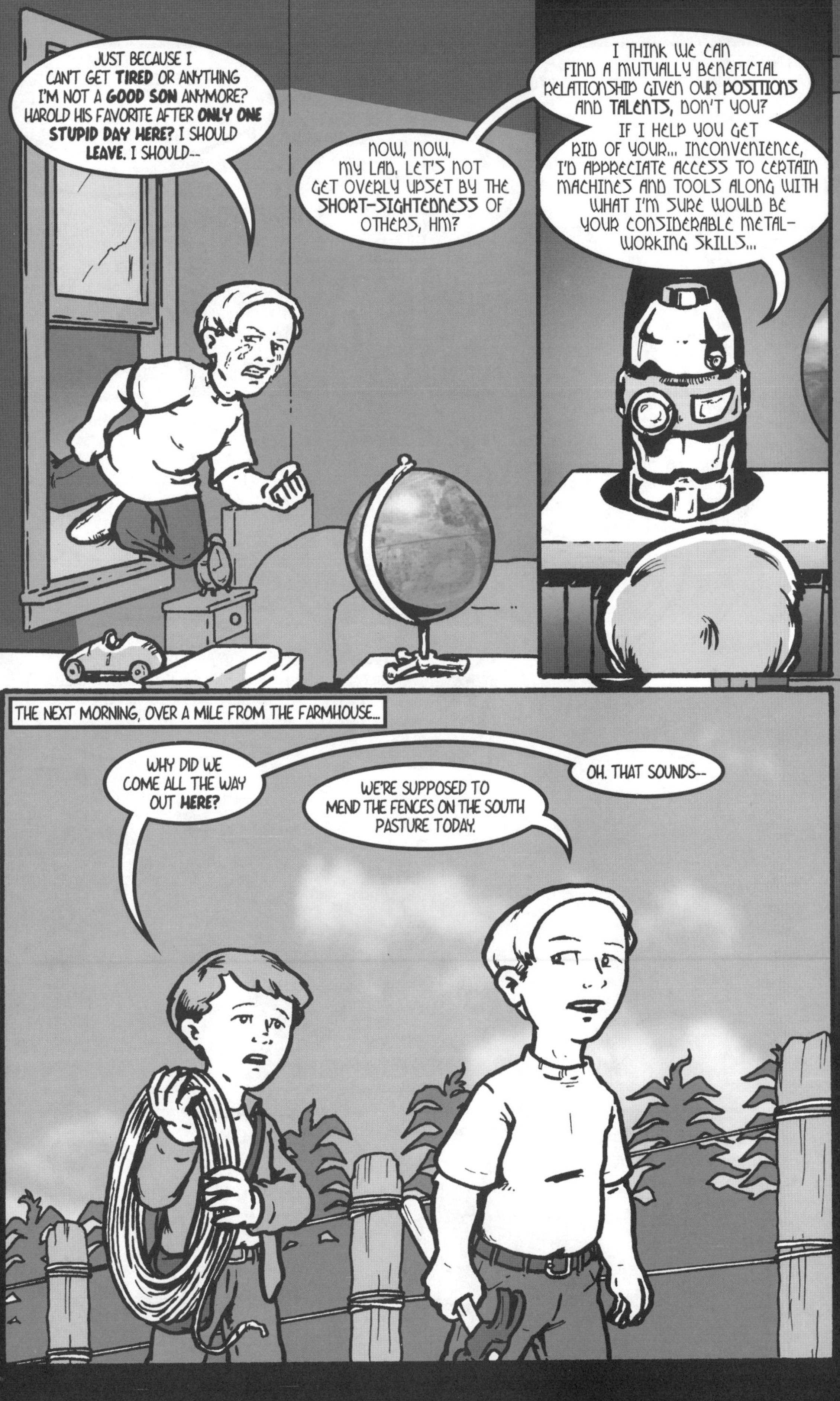
JUST BECAUSE I CAN'T GET TIRED OR ANYTHING I'M NOT A GOOD SON ANYMORE? HAROLD HIS FAVORITE AFTER ONLY ONE STUPID DAY HERE? I SHOULD LEAVE. I SHOULD--
NOW, NOW, MY LAD. LET'S NOT GET OVERLY UPSET BY THE SHORT-SIGHTEDNESS OF OTHERS, HM?
I THINK WE CAN FIND A MUTUALLY BENEFICIAL RELATIONSHIP GIVEN OUR POSITIONS AND TALENTS, DON'T YOU?
IF I HELP YOU GET RID OF YOUR... INCONVENIENCE, I'D APPRECIATE ACCESS TO CERTAIN MACHINES AND TOOLS ALONG WITH WHAT I'M SURE WOULD BE YOUR CONSIDERABLE METAL-WORKING SKILLS...
THE NEXT MORNING, OVER A MILE FROM THE FARMHOUSE...
WHY DID WE COME ALL THE WAY OUT HERE?
WE'RE SUPPOSED TO MEND THE FENCES ON THE SOUTH PASTURE TODAY.
OH. THAT SOUNDS--

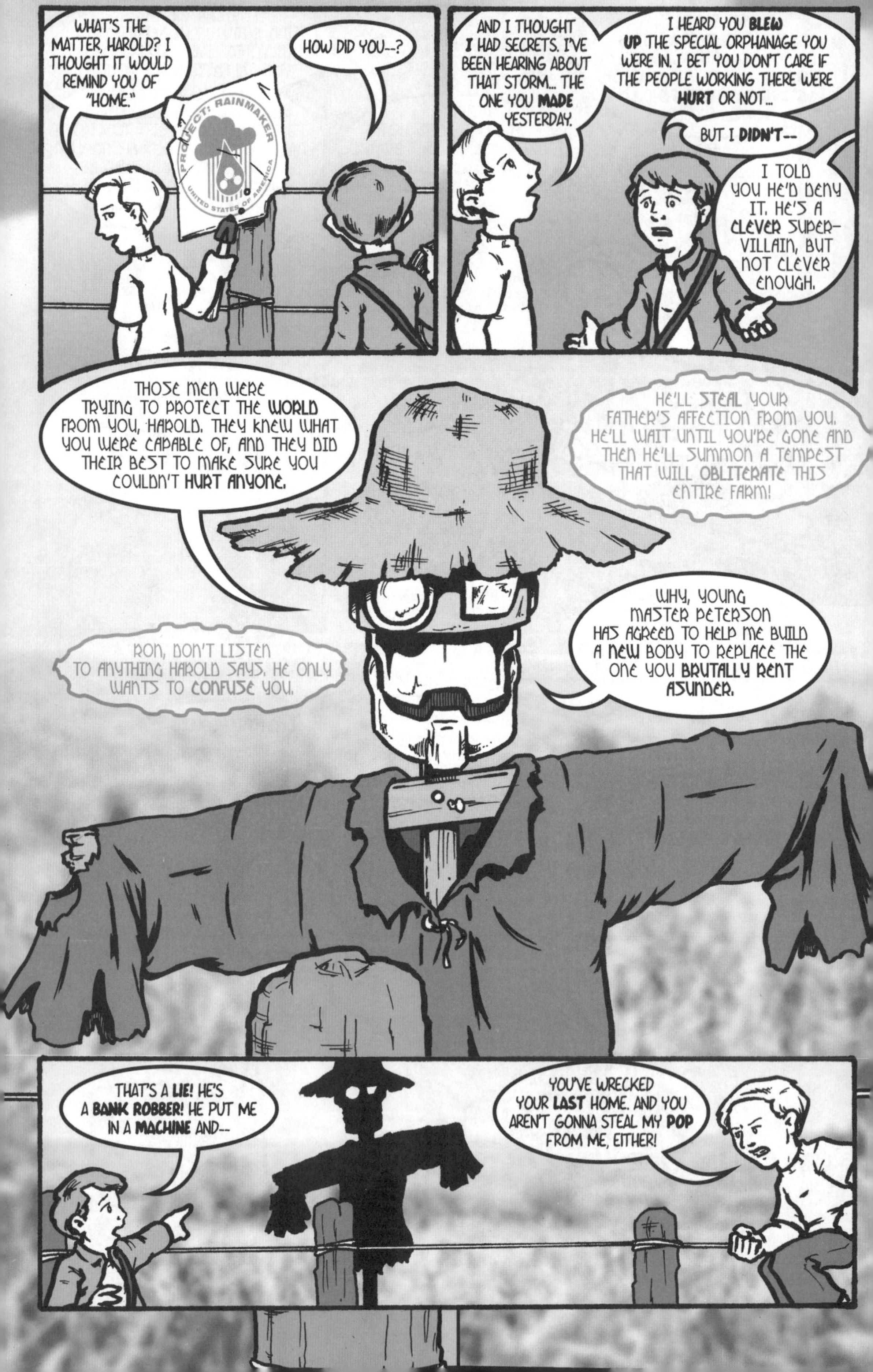
WHAT'S THE MATTER, HAROLD? I THOUGHT IT WOULD REMIND YOU OF "HOME."
HOW DID YOU--?
PROJECT: RAINMAKER
UNITED STATES OF AMERICA
AND I THOUGHT I HAD SECRETS. I'VE BEEN HEARING ABOUT THAT STORM... THE ONE YOU MADE YESTERDAY.
I HEARD YOU BLEW UP THE SPECIAL ORPHANAGE YOU WERE IN. I BET YOU DON'T CARE IF THE PEOPLE WORKING THERE WERE HURT OR NOT...
BUT I DIDN'T--
I TOLD YOU HE'D DENY IT. HE'S A CLEVER SUPER-VILLAIN, BUT NOT CLEVER ENOUGH.
THOSE MEN WERE TRYING TO PROTECT THE WORLD FROM YOU, HAROLD. THEY KNEW WHAT YOU WERE CAPABLE OF, AND THEY DID THEIR BEST TO MAKE SURE YOU COULDN'T HURT ANYONE.
HE'LL STEAL YOUR FATHER'S AFFECTION FROM YOU. HE'LL WAIT UNTIL YOU'RE GONE AND THEN HE'LL SUMMON A TEMPEST THAT WILL OBLITERATE THIS ENTIRE FARM!
RON, DON'T LISTEN TO ANYTHING HAROLD SAYS. HE ONLY WANTS TO CONFUSE YOU.
WHY, YOUNG MASTER PETERSON HAS AGREED TO HELP ME BUILD A NEW BODY TO REPLACE THE ONE YOU BRUTALLY RENT ASUNDER.
THAT'S A LIE! HE'S A BANK ROBBER! HE PUT ME IN A MACHINE AND--
YOU'VE WRECKED YOUR LAST HOME. AND YOU AREN'T GONNA STEAL MY POP FROM ME, EITHER!

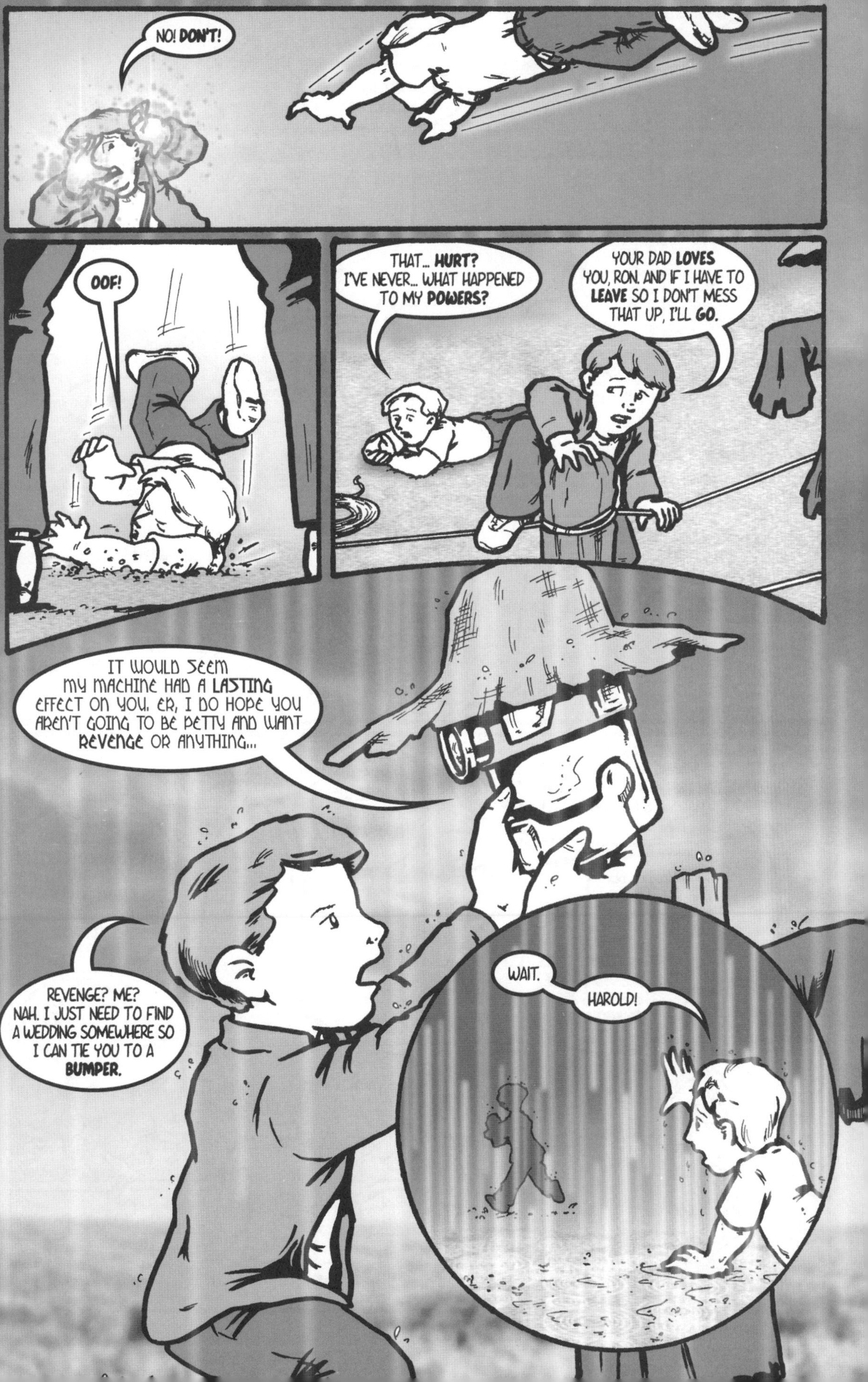
NO! DON'T!
OOF!
THAT... HURT? I'VE NEVER... WHAT HAPPENED TO MY POWERS?
YOUR DAD LOVES YOU, RON. AND IF I HAVE TO LEAVE SO I DON'T MESS THAT UP, I'LL GO.
IT WOULD SEEM MY MACHINE HAD A LASTING EFFECT ON YOU. ER, I DO HOPE YOU AREN'T GOING TO BE PETTY AND WANT REVENGE OR ANYTHING...
REVENGE? ME? NAH. I JUST NEED TO FIND A WEDDING SOMEWHERE SO I CAN TIE YOU TO A BUMPER.
WAIT.
HAROLD!

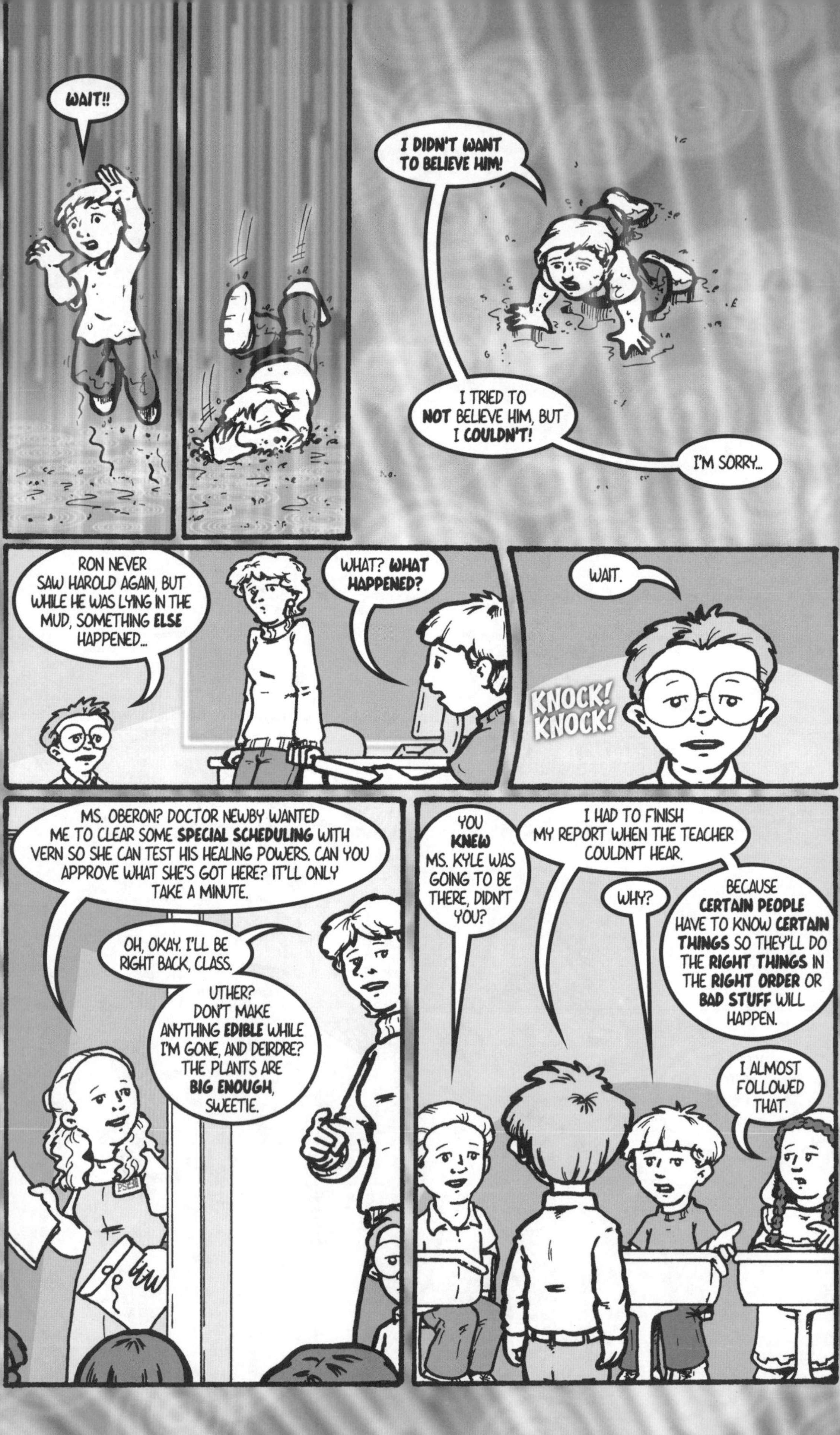
WAIT!!
I DIDN'T WANT TO BELIEVE HIM!
I TRIED TO NOT BELIEVE HIM, BUT I COULDN'T!
I'M SORRY...
RON NEVER SAW HAROLD AGAIN, BUT WHILE HE WAS LYING IN THE MUD, SOMETHING ELSE HAPPENED...
WHAT? WHAT HAPPENED?
WAIT.
KNOCK! KNOCK!
MS. OBERON? DOCTOR NEWBY WANTED ME TO CLEAR SOME SPECIAL SCHEDULING WITH VERN SO SHE CAN TEST HIS HEALING POWERS. CAN YOU APPROVE WHAT SHE'S GOT HERE? IT'LL ONLY TAKE A MINUTE.
OH, OKAY. I'LL BE RIGHT BACK, CLASS.
UTHER? DON'T MAKE ANYTHING EDIBLE WHILE I'M GONE, AND DEIRDRE? THE PLANTS ARE BIG ENOUGH, SWEETIE.
YOU KNEW MS. KYLE WAS GOING TO BE THERE, DIDN'T YOU?
I HAD TO FINISH MY REPORT WHEN THE TEACHER COULDN'T HEAR.
WHY?
BECAUSE CERTAIN PEOPLE HAVE TO KNOW CERTAIN THINGS SO THEY'LL DO THE RIGHT THINGS IN THE RIGHT ORDER OR BAD STUFF WILL HAPPEN.
I ALMOST FOLLOWED THAT.

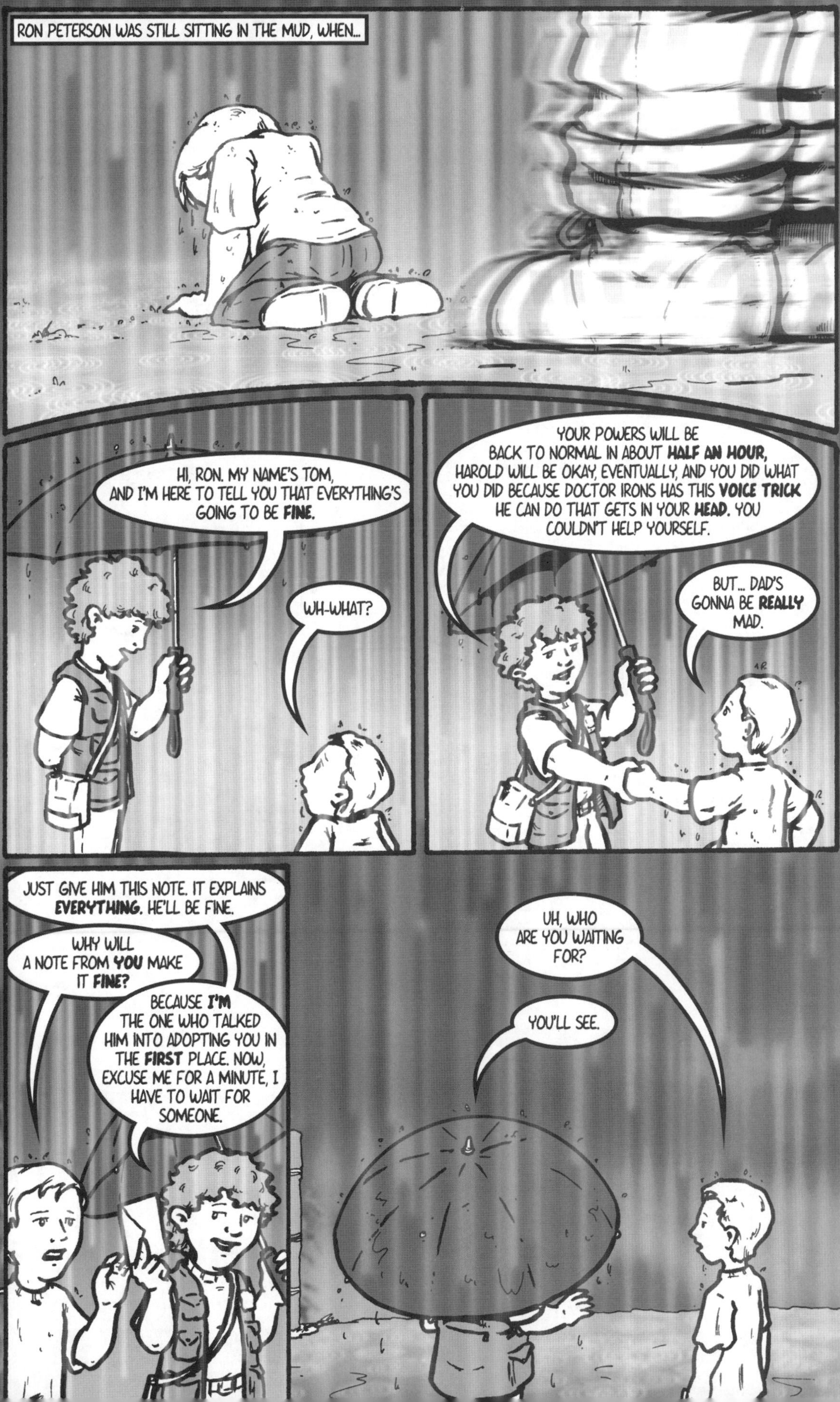
RON PETERSON WAS STILL SITTING IN THE MUD, WHEN...
HI, RON. MY NAME'S TOM, AND I'M HERE TO TELL YOU THAT EVERYTHING'S GOING TO BE **FINE.**
WH-WHAT?
YOUR POWERS WILL BE BACK TO NORMAL IN ABOUT **HALF AN HOUR,** HAROLD WILL BE OKAY, EVENTUALLY, AND YOU DID WHAT YOU DID BECAUSE DOCTOR IRONS HAS THIS **VOICE TRICK** HE CAN DO THAT GETS IN YOUR **HEAD.** YOU COULDN'T HELP YOURSELF.
BUT... DAD'S GONNA BE **REALLY** MAD.
JUST GIVE HIM THIS NOTE. IT EXPLAINS **EVERYTHING.** HE'LL BE FINE.
WHY WILL A NOTE FROM **YOU** MAKE IT **FINE?**
BECAUSE **I'M** THE ONE WHO TALKED HIM INTO ADOPTING YOU IN THE **FIRST** PLACE. NOW, EXCUSE ME FOR A MINUTE, I HAVE TO WAIT FOR SOMEONE.
UH, WHO ARE YOU WAITING FOR?
YOU'LL SEE.

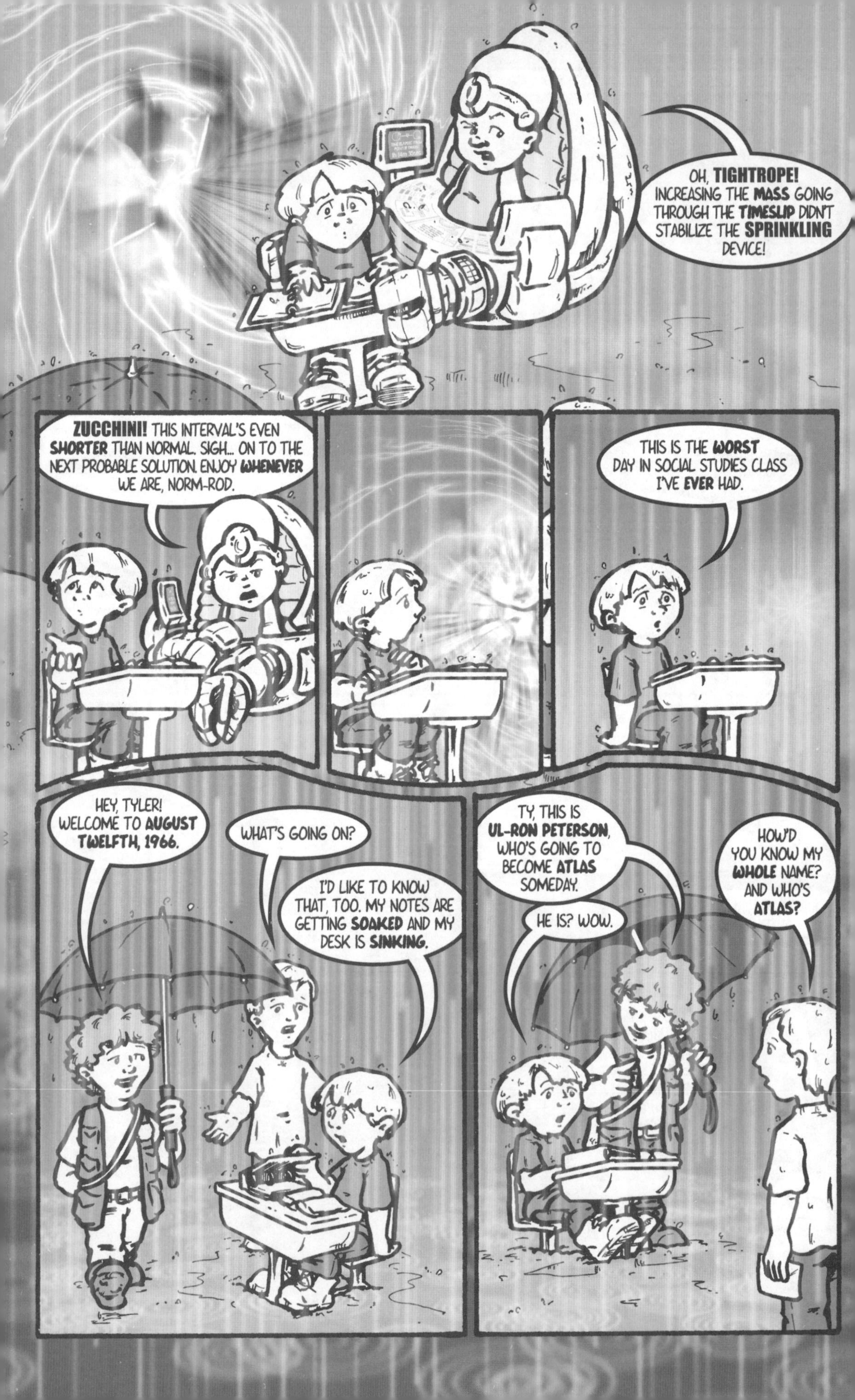

OH, TIGHTROPE! INCREASING THE MASS GOING THROUGH THE TIMESLIP DIDN'T STABILIZE THE SPRINKLING DEVICE!
ZUCCHINI! THIS INTERVAL'S EVEN SHORTER THAN NORMAL. SIGH... ON TO THE NEXT PROBABLE SOLUTION. ENJOY WHENEVER WE ARE, NORM-ROD.
THIS IS THE WORST DAY IN SOCIAL STUDIES CLASS I'VE EVER HAD.
HEY, TYLER! WELCOME TO AUGUST TWELFTH, 1966.
WHAT'S GOING ON?
I'D LIKE TO KNOW THAT, TOO. MY NOTES ARE GETTING SOAKED AND MY DESK IS SINKING.
TY, THIS IS UL-RON PETERSON, WHO'S GOING TO BECOME ATLAS SOMEDAY.
HE IS? WOW.
HOW'D YOU KNOW MY WHOLE NAME? AND WHO'S ATLAS?

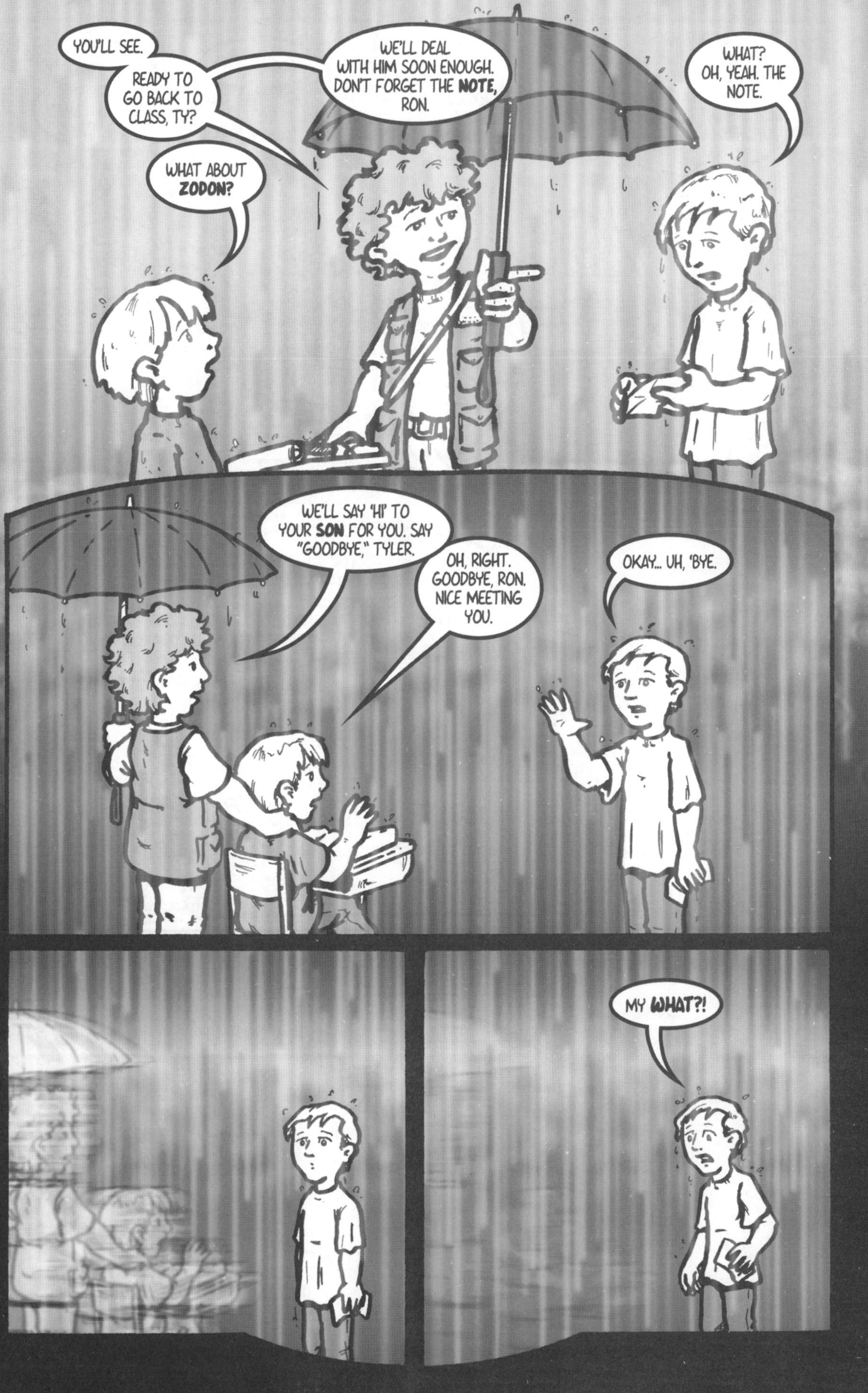
YOU'LL SEE.
READY TO GO BACK TO CLASS, TY?
WE'LL DEAL WITH HIM SOON ENOUGH. DON'T FORGET THE **NOTE**, RON.
WHAT? OH, YEAH. THE NOTE.
WHAT ABOUT **ZODON?**
WE'LL SAY 'HI' TO YOUR **SON** FOR YOU. SAY "GOODBYE," TYLER.
OH, RIGHT. GOODBYE, RON. NICE MEETING YOU.
OKAY... UH, 'BYE.
MY **WHAT?!**

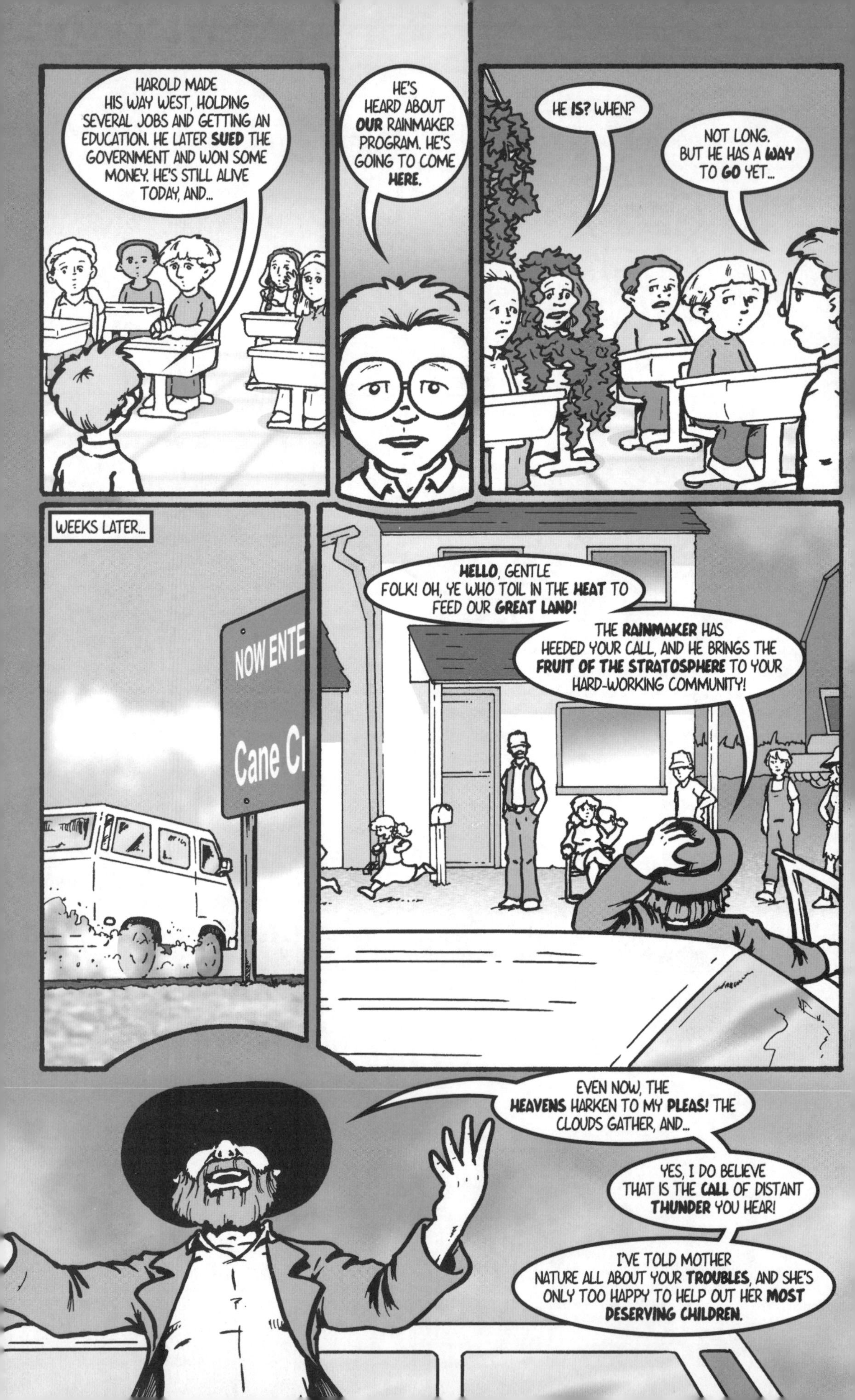
HAROLD MADE HIS WAY WEST, HOLDING SEVERAL JOBS AND GETTING AN EDUCATION. HE LATER SUED THE GOVERNMENT AND WON SOME MONEY. HE'S STILL ALIVE TODAY, AND...
HE'S HEARD ABOUT OUR RAINMAKER PROGRAM. HE'S GOING TO COME HERE.
HE IS? WHEN?
NOT LONG. BUT HE HAS A WAY TO GO YET...
WEEKS LATER...
NOW ENTE
Cane Cr
HELLO, GENTLE FOLK! OH, YE WHO TOIL IN THE HEAT TO FEED OUR GREAT LAND!
THE RAINMAKER HAS HEEDED YOUR CALL, AND HE BRINGS THE FRUIT OF THE STRATOSPHERE TO YOUR HARD-WORKING COMMUNITY!
EVEN NOW, THE HEAVENS HARKEN TO MY PLEAS! THE CLOUDS GATHER, AND...
YES, I DO BELIEVE THAT IS THE CALL OF DISTANT THUNDER YOU HEAR!
I'VE TOLD MOTHER NATURE ALL ABOUT YOUR TROUBLES, AND SHE'S ONLY TOO HAPPY TO HELP OUT HER MOST DESERVING CHILDREN.

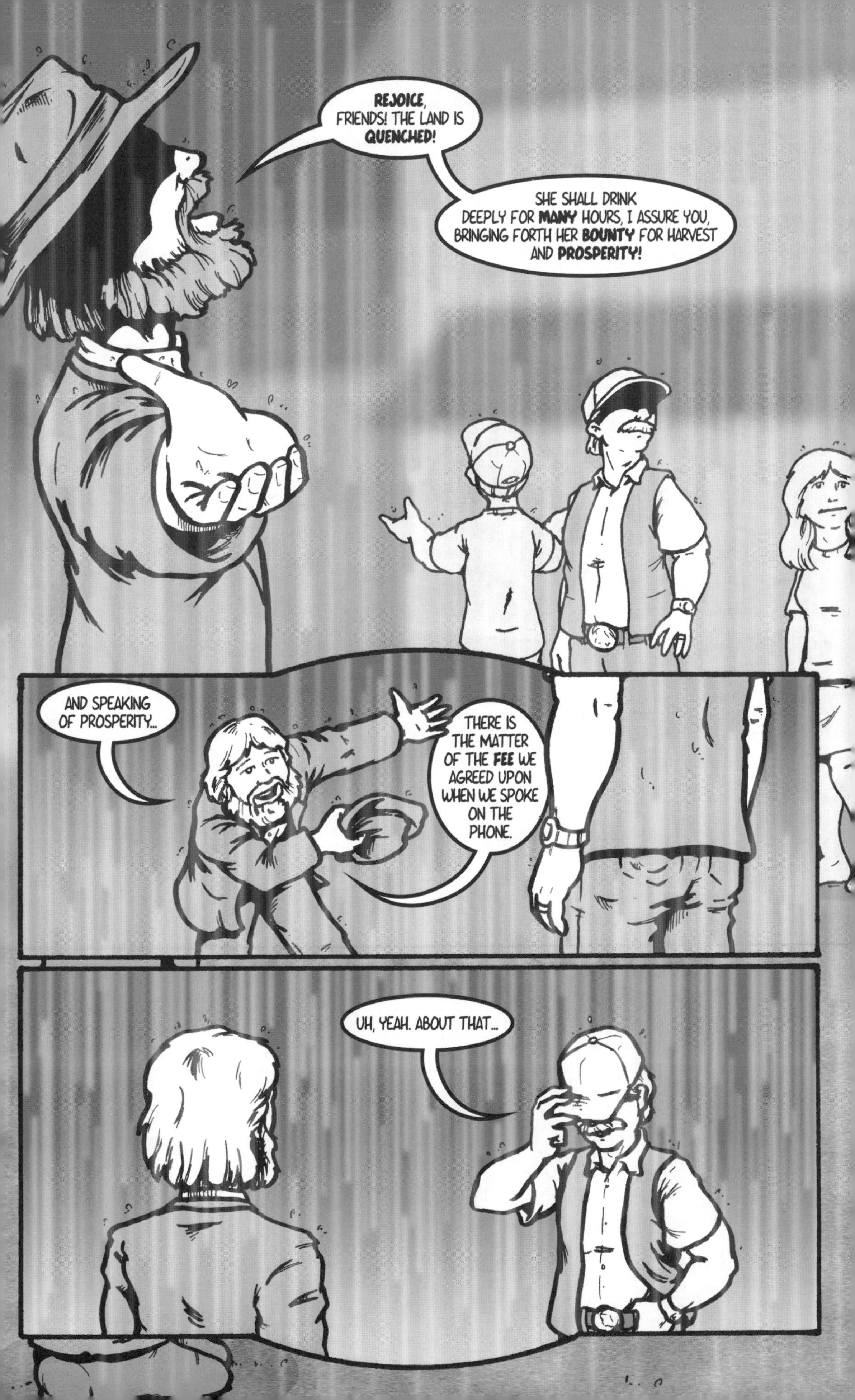
REJOICE, FRIENDS! THE LAND IS QUENCHED!
SHE SHALL DRINK DEEPLY FOR MANY HOURS, I ASSURE YOU, BRINGING FORTH HER BOUNTY FOR HARVEST AND PROSPERITY!
AND SPEAKING OF PROSPERITY...
THERE IS THE MATTER OF THE FEE WE AGREED UPON WHEN WE SPOKE ON THE PHONE.
UH, YEAH. ABOUT THAT...

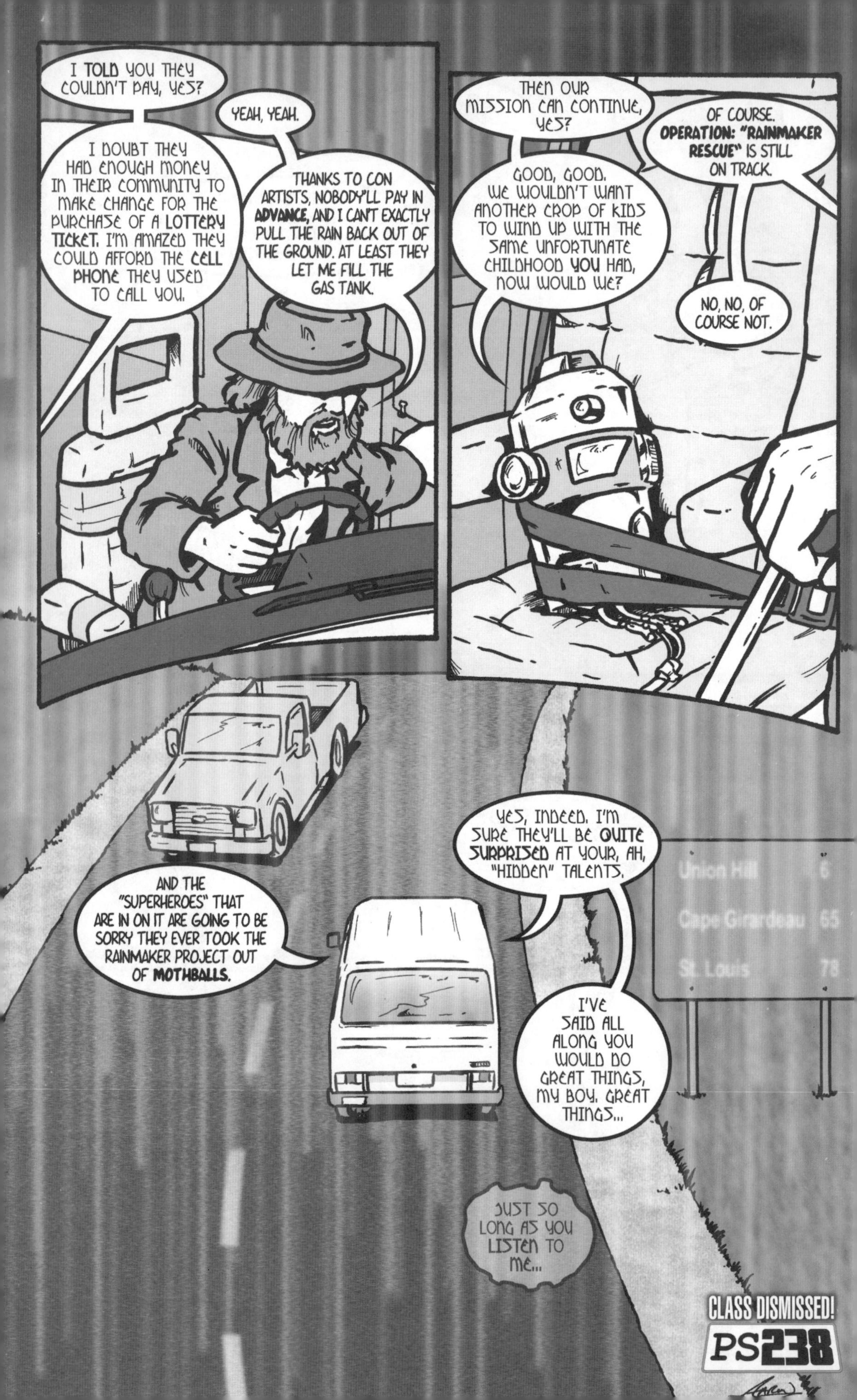
I TOLD YOU THEY COULDN'T PAY, YES?
YEAH, YEAH.
I DOUBT THEY HAD ENOUGH MONEY IN THEIR COMMUNITY TO MAKE CHANGE FOR THE PURCHASE OF A LOTTERY TICKET. I'M AMAZED THEY COULD AFFORD THE CELL PHONE THEY USED TO CALL YOU.
THANKS TO CON ARTISTS, NOBODY'LL PAY IN ADVANCE, AND I CAN'T EXACTLY PULL THE RAIN BACK OUT OF THE GROUND. AT LEAST THEY LET ME FILL THE GAS TANK.
THEN OUR MISSION CAN CONTINUE, YES?
OF COURSE. OPERATION: "RAINMAKER RESCUE" IS STILL ON TRACK.
GOOD, GOOD. WE WOULDN'T WANT ANOTHER CROP OF KIDS TO WIND UP WITH THE SAME UNFORTUNATE CHILDHOOD YOU HAD, NOW WOULD WE?
NO, NO, OF COURSE NOT.
AND THE "SUPERHEROES" THAT ARE IN ON IT ARE GOING TO BE SORRY THEY EVER TOOK THE RAINMAKER PROJECT OUT OF MOTHBALLS.
YES, INDEED. I'M SURE THEY'LL BE QUITE SURPRISED AT YOUR, AH, "HIDDEN" TALENTS.
Union Hill 6
Cape Girardeau 65
St. Louis 78
I'VE SAID ALL ALONG YOU WOULD DO GREAT THINGS, MY BOY. GREAT THINGS...
JUST SO LONG AS YOU LISTEN TO ME...
CLASS DISMISSED!
PS238

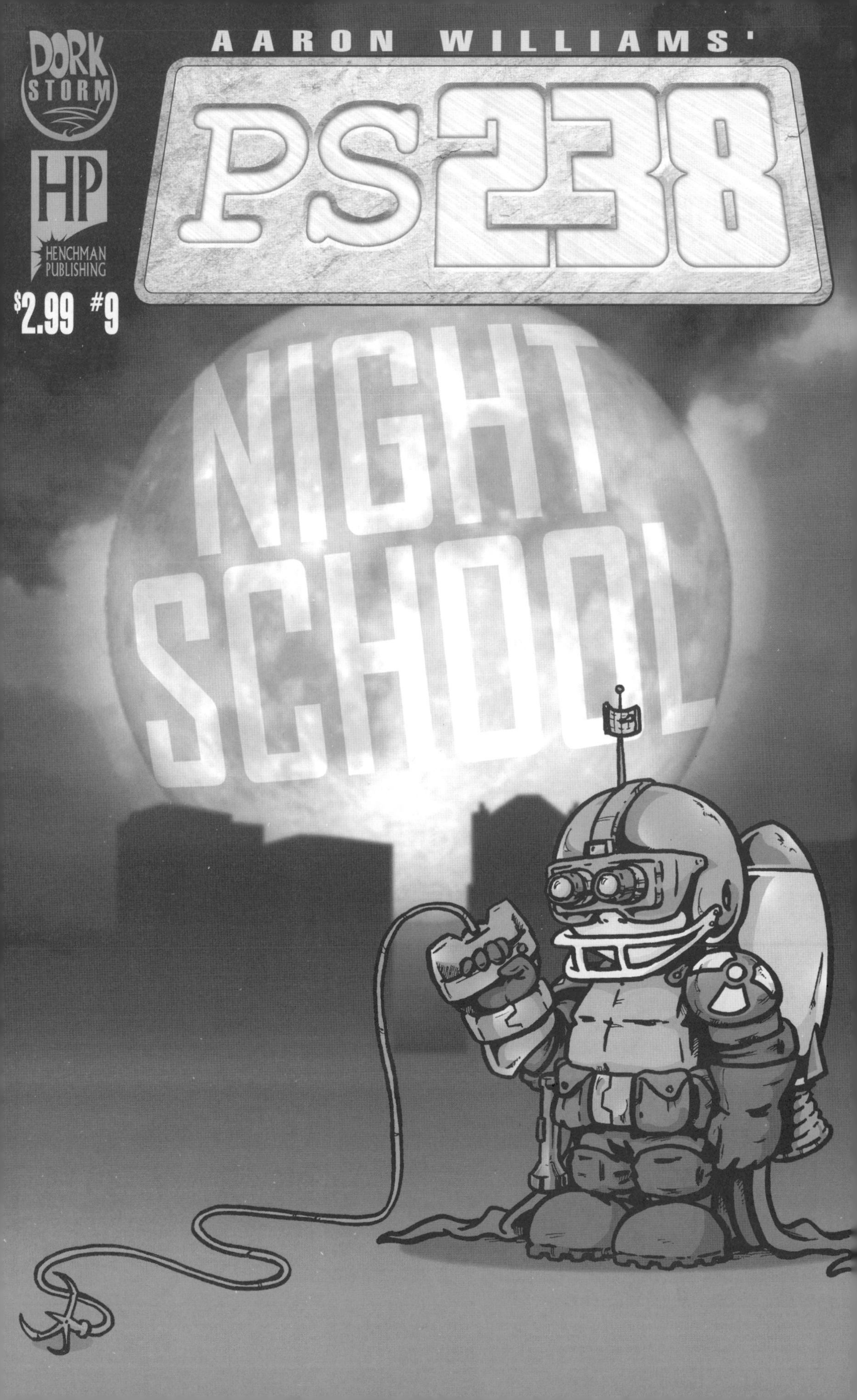
DORK STORM
AARON WILLIAMS'
PS238
HP
HENCHMAN PUBLISHING
$2.99 #9
NIGHT SCHOOL

PS238
THE SCHOOL FOR METAPRODIGY CHILDREN
BY AARON WILLIAMS

From the diary of Tyler Marloke:

I've been at ps238 for a few months now, and I'm still alive. I don't believe it. I go to classes with other kids who have super powers, even though I don't. My parents put me here because they think I'll get powers someday. They don't seem to understand that if a blue boy who weighs a couple hundred pounds drops something big and metal on you, it doesn't matter if you were GOING to get powers someday. What matters is you're squished.

My mom and dad are off fighting some guy in alien armor with the rest of the Earth Defense League. They never tell me exactly what they're fighting because they don't want to upset me.

POK!

PS238 #9 by Aaron Williams, November 2004. Distributed by Dork Storm Press, published by Henchman Publishing, 5545 Holmes St, Kansas City, MO 64110. Fax: (608)255-1342. E-mail: aaron@ps238.com. Story and art ©2004 Aaron Williams. "The Revenant" is ©2004 Michael Stackpole. All rights reserved. No portion of this publication save for brief review excerpts may be reproduced without the express consent of the copyright holder. This is a work of fiction: any similarities to any actual persons or metahumans save for the purpose of satire is purely coincidental. ADVERTISING: sales@DorkStorm.com. SUBSCRIPTIONS: $26 per year. Please contact adventureretail2@qwest.net. or call (651)-488-2433 details. All letters to PS238 assumed intended for publication unless otherwise stated, and become the property of the copyright holder. When we walk to the edge of all the light we have and take the step into the darkness of the unknown, we must believe that one of two things will happen. There will be something solid for us to stand on or we will be taught to fly.--Patrick Overton. FIRST PRINTING, November 2004. PRINTED IN CANADA

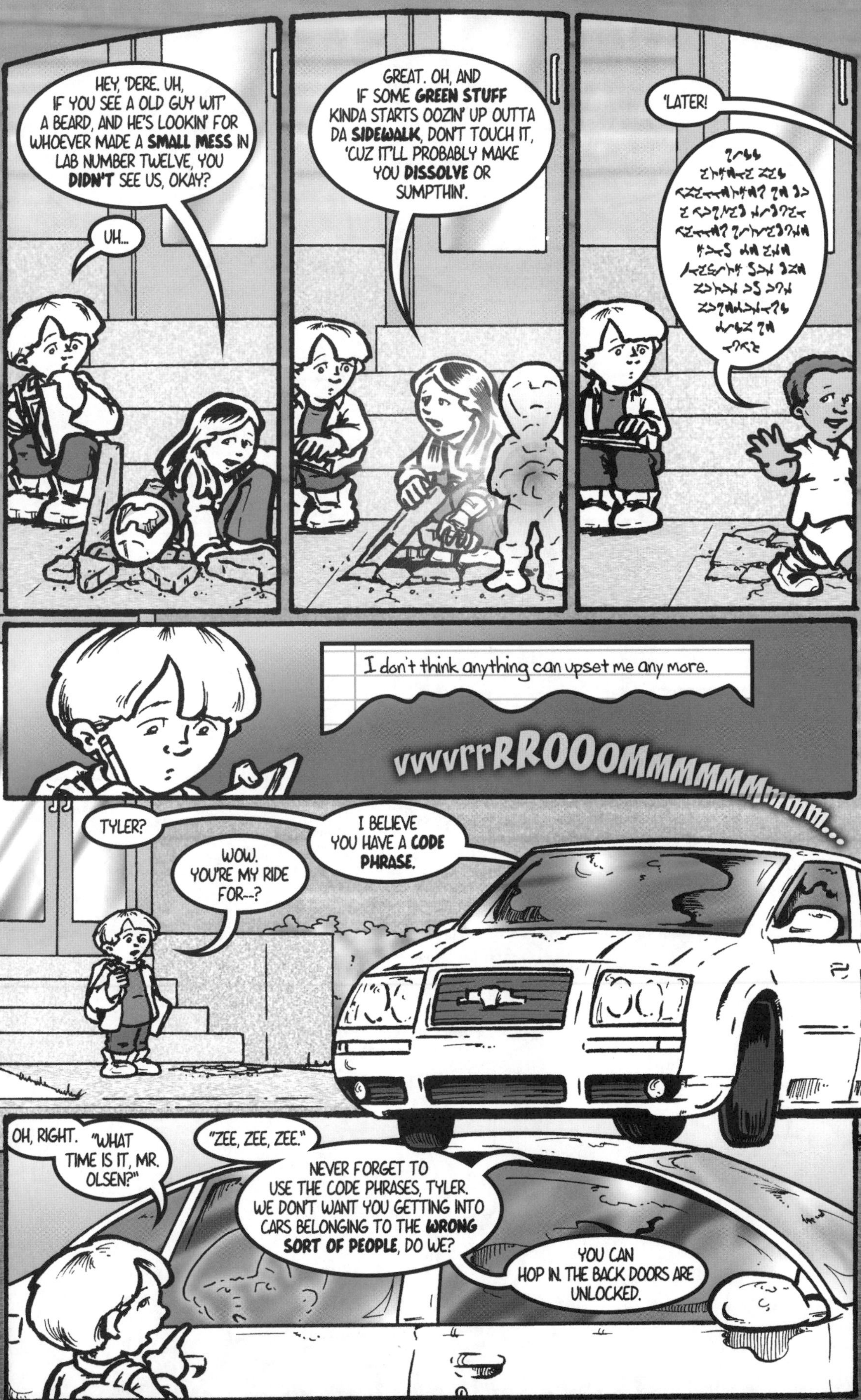
HEY, 'DERE. UH, IF YOU SEE A OLD GUY WIT' A BEARD, AND HE'S LOOKIN' FOR WHOEVER MADE A SMALL MESS IN LAB NUMBER TWELVE, YOU DIDN'T SEE US, OKAY?
UH...
GREAT. OH, AND IF SOME GREEN STUFF KINDA STARTS OOZIN' UP OUTTA DA SIDEWALK, DON'T TOUCH IT, 'CUZ IT'LL PROBABLY MAKE YOU DISSOLVE OR SUMPTHIN'.
'LATER!
I don't think anything can upset me any more.
vvvvrrRROOOOMMMMMMMMMmmm...
TYLER?
I BELIEVE YOU HAVE A CODE PHRASE.
WOW. YOU'RE MY RIDE FOR--?
OH, RIGHT. "WHAT TIME IS IT, MR. OLSEN?"
"ZEE, ZEE, ZEE."
NEVER FORGET TO USE THE CODE PHRASES, TYLER. WE DON'T WANT YOU GETTING INTO CARS BELONGING TO THE WRONG SORT OF PEOPLE, DO WE?
YOU CAN HOP IN. THE BACK DOORS ARE UNLOCKED.

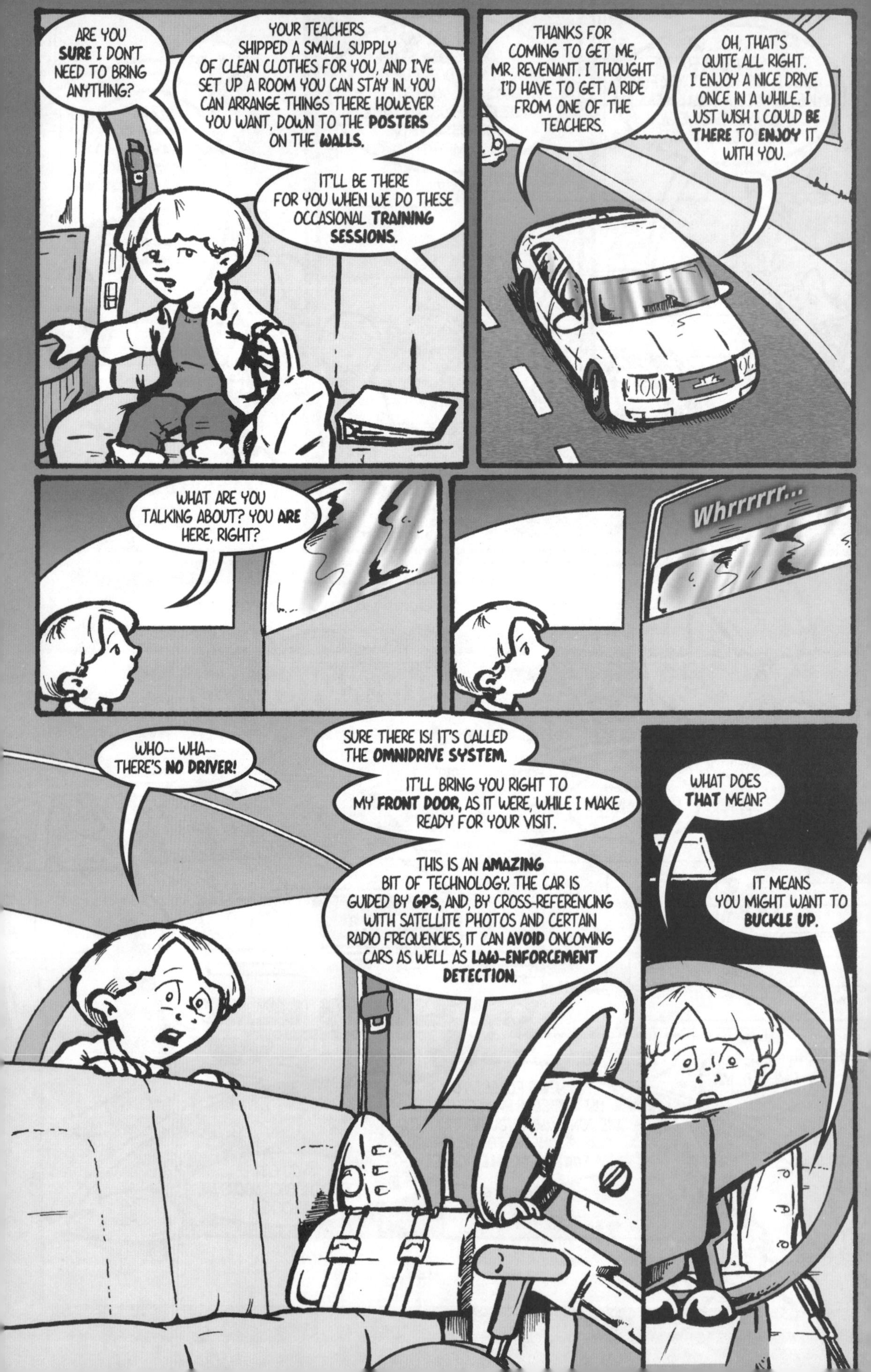
ARE YOU SURE I DON'T NEED TO BRING ANYTHING?
YOUR TEACHERS SHIPPED A SMALL SUPPLY OF CLEAN CLOTHES FOR YOU, AND I'VE SET UP A ROOM YOU CAN STAY IN. YOU CAN ARRANGE THINGS THERE HOWEVER YOU WANT, DOWN TO THE POSTERS ON THE WALLS.
IT'LL BE THERE FOR YOU WHEN WE DO THESE OCCASIONAL TRAINING SESSIONS.
THANKS FOR COMING TO GET ME, MR. REVENANT. I THOUGHT I'D HAVE TO GET A RIDE FROM ONE OF THE TEACHERS.
OH, THAT'S QUITE ALL RIGHT. I ENJOY A NICE DRIVE ONCE IN A WHILE. I JUST WISH I COULD BE THERE TO ENJOY IT WITH YOU.
WHAT ARE YOU TALKING ABOUT? YOU ARE HERE, RIGHT?
Whrrrrrr...
WHO-- WHA-- THERE'S NO DRIVER!
SURE THERE IS! IT'S CALLED THE OMNIDRIVE SYSTEM.
IT'LL BRING YOU RIGHT TO MY FRONT DOOR, AS IT WERE, WHILE I MAKE READY FOR YOUR VISIT.
THIS IS AN AMAZING BIT OF TECHNOLOGY. THE CAR IS GUIDED BY GPS, AND, BY CROSS-REFERENCING WITH SATELLITE PHOTOS AND CERTAIN RADIO FREQUENCIES, IT CAN AVOID ONCOMING CARS AS WELL AS LAW-ENFORCEMENT DETECTION.
WHAT DOES THAT MEAN?
IT MEANS YOU MIGHT WANT TO BUCKLE UP.

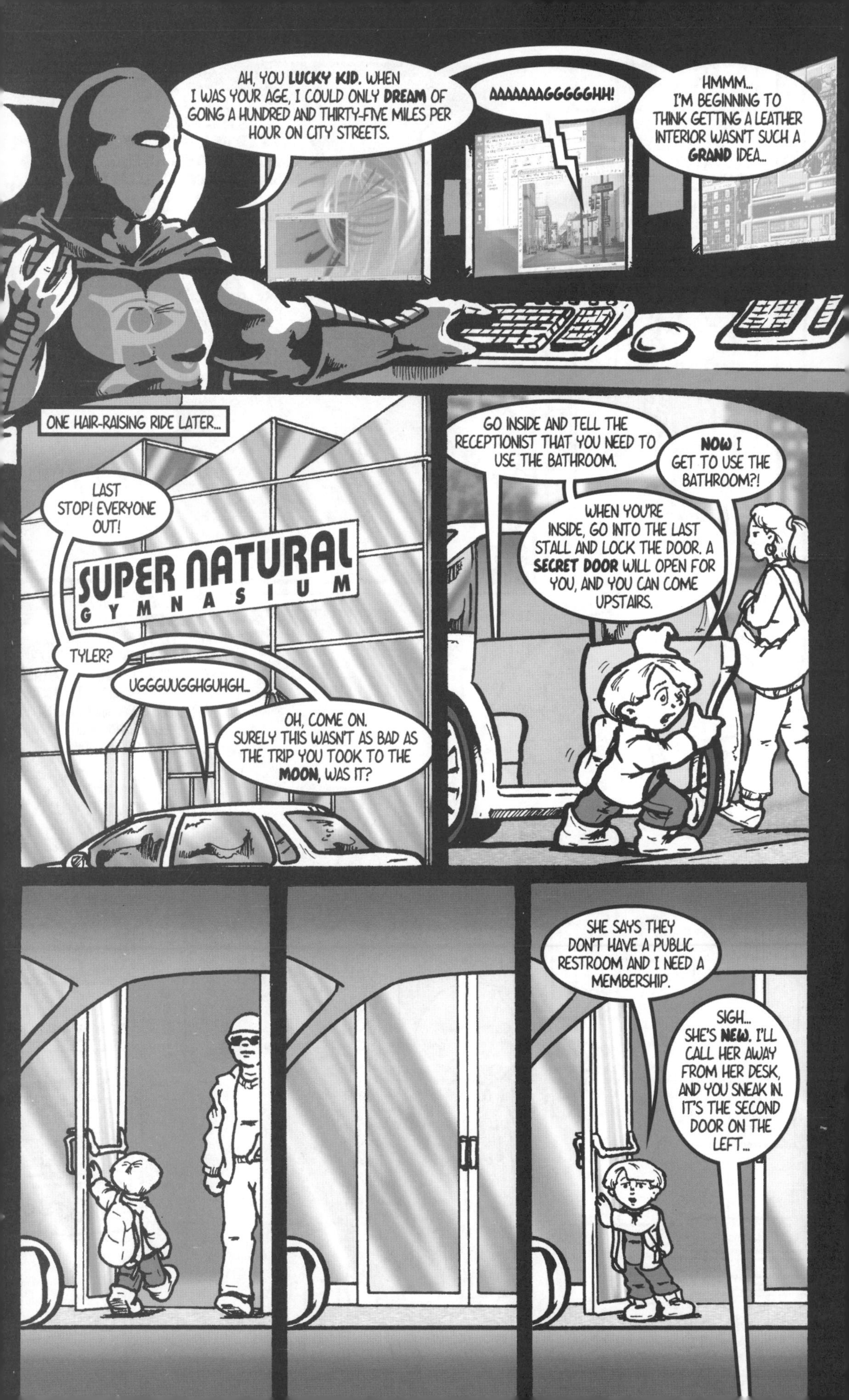
AH, YOU **LUCKY KID.** WHEN I WAS YOUR AGE, I COULD ONLY **DREAM** OF GOING A HUNDRED AND THIRTY-FIVE MILES PER HOUR ON CITY STREETS.
AAAAAAAGGGGGHH!
HMMM... I'M BEGINNING TO THINK GETTING A LEATHER INTERIOR WASN'T SUCH A **GRAND** IDEA...
ONE HAIR-RAISING RIDE LATER...
LAST STOP! EVERYONE OUT!
SUPER NATURAL GYMNASIUM
TYLER?
UGGGUUGGHGUHGH...
OH, COME ON. SURELY THIS WASN'T AS BAD AS THE TRIP YOU TOOK TO THE **MOON,** WAS IT?
GO INSIDE AND TELL THE RECEPTIONIST THAT YOU NEED TO USE THE BATHROOM.
NOW I GET TO USE THE BATHROOM?!
WHEN YOU'RE INSIDE, GO INTO THE LAST STALL AND LOCK THE DOOR. A **SECRET DOOR** WILL OPEN FOR YOU, AND YOU CAN COME UPSTAIRS.
SHE SAYS THEY DON'T HAVE A PUBLIC RESTROOM AND I NEED A MEMBERSHIP.
SIGH... SHE'S **NEW.** I'LL CALL HER AWAY FROM HER DESK, AND YOU SNEAK IN. IT'S THE SECOND DOOR ON THE LEFT...

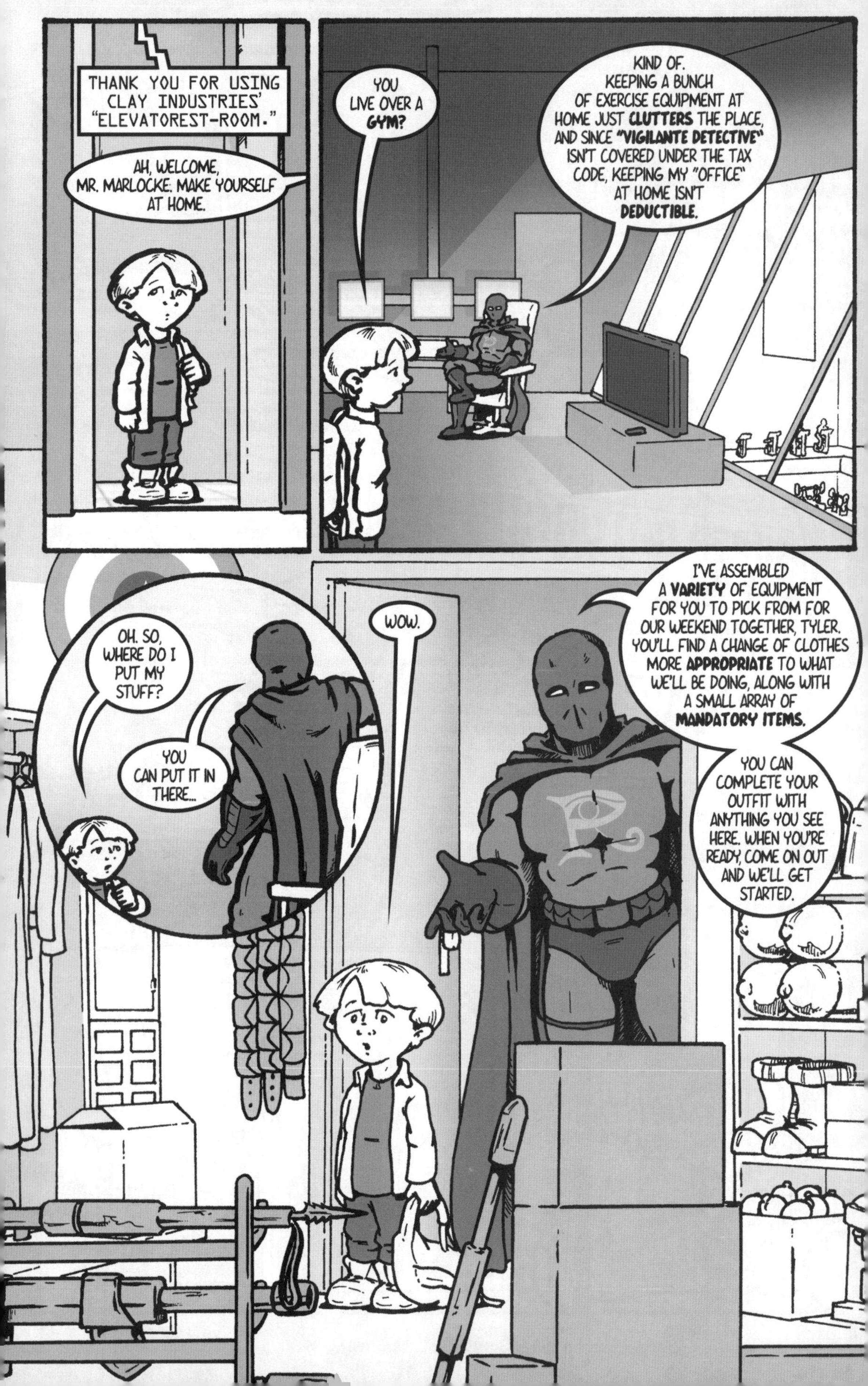
THANK YOU FOR USING CLAY INDUSTRIES' "ELEVATOREST-ROOM."
AH, WELCOME, MR. MARLOCKE. MAKE YOURSELF AT HOME.
YOU LIVE OVER A GYM?
KIND OF. KEEPING A BUNCH OF EXERCISE EQUIPMENT AT HOME JUST CLUTTERS THE PLACE, AND SINCE "VIGILANTE DETECTIVE" ISN'T COVERED UNDER THE TAX CODE, KEEPING MY "OFFICE" AT HOME ISN'T DEDUCTIBLE.
OH. SO, WHERE DO I PUT MY STUFF?
YOU CAN PUT IT IN THERE...
WOW.
I'VE ASSEMBLED A VARIETY OF EQUIPMENT FOR YOU TO PICK FROM FOR OUR WEEKEND TOGETHER, TYLER. YOU'LL FIND A CHANGE OF CLOTHES MORE APPROPRIATE TO WHAT WE'LL BE DOING, ALONG WITH A SMALL ARRAY OF MANDATORY ITEMS.
YOU CAN COMPLETE YOUR OUTFIT WITH ANYTHING YOU SEE HERE. WHEN YOU'RE READY, COME ON OUT AND WE'LL GET STARTED.

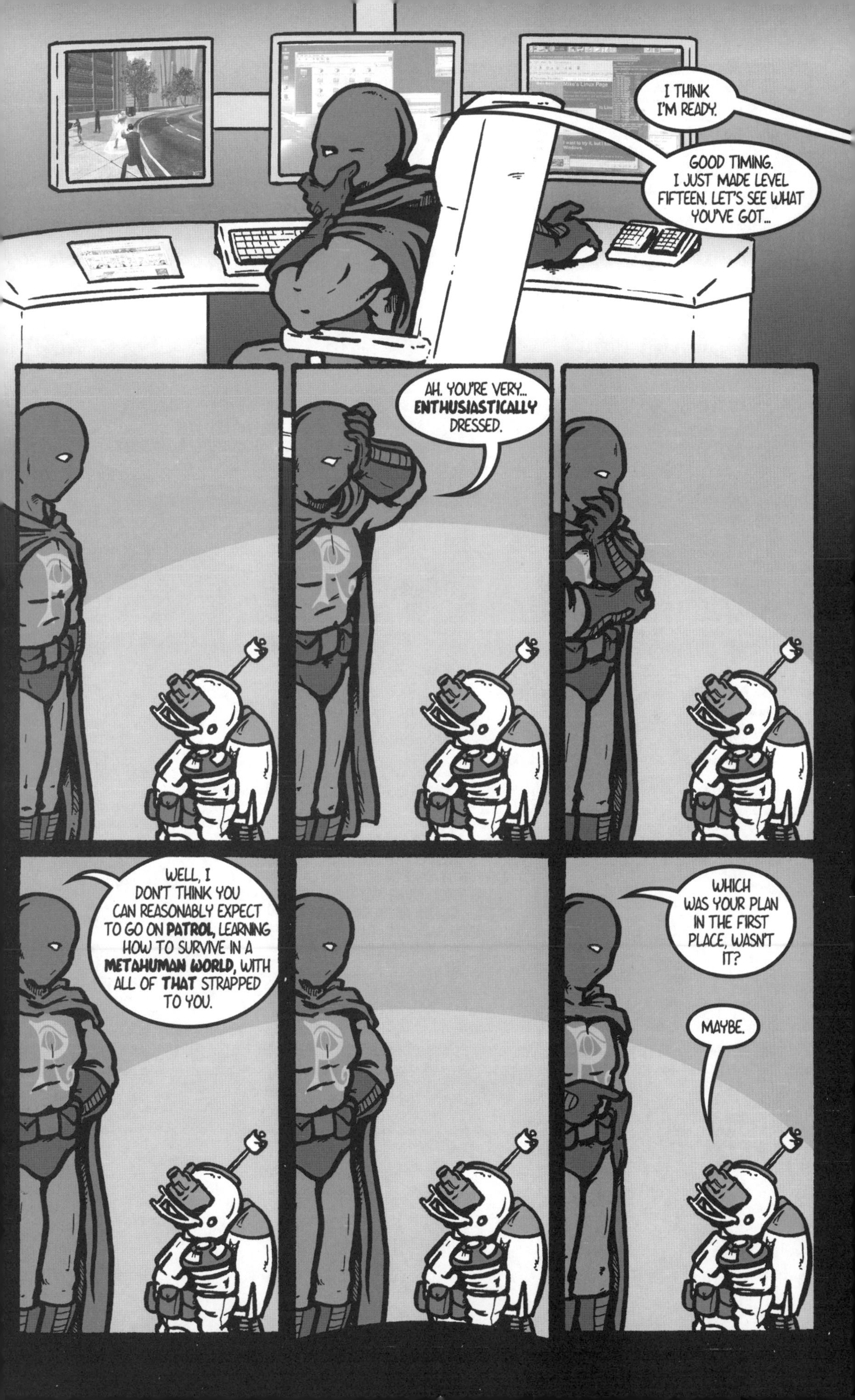
I THINK I'M READY.
GOOD TIMING. I JUST MADE LEVEL FIFTEEN. LET'S SEE WHAT YOU'VE GOT...
AH. YOU'RE VERY... **ENTHUSIASTICALLY** DRESSED.
WELL, I DON'T THINK YOU CAN REASONABLY EXPECT TO GO ON **PATROL**, LEARNING HOW TO SURVIVE IN A **METAHUMAN WORLD**, WITH ALL OF **THAT** STRAPPED TO YOU.
WHICH WAS YOUR PLAN IN THE FIRST PLACE, WASN'T IT?
MAYBE.

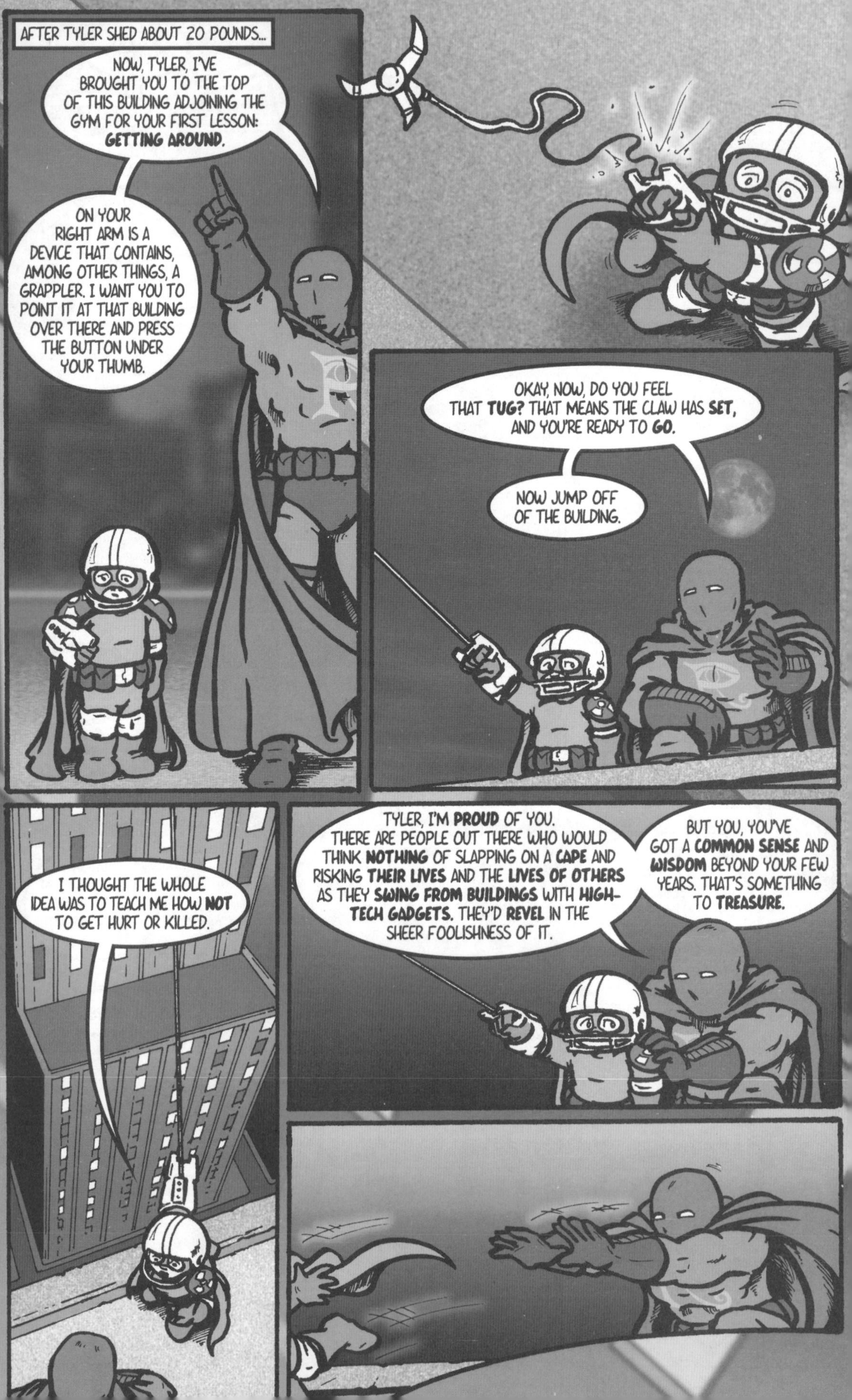
AFTER TYLER SHED ABOUT 20 POUNDS...
NOW, TYLER, I'VE BROUGHT YOU TO THE TOP OF THIS BUILDING ADJOINING THE GYM FOR YOUR FIRST LESSON: **GETTING AROUND.**
ON YOUR RIGHT ARM IS A DEVICE THAT CONTAINS, AMONG OTHER THINGS, A GRAPPLER. I WANT YOU TO POINT IT AT THAT BUILDING OVER THERE AND PRESS THE BUTTON UNDER YOUR THUMB.
OKAY, NOW, DO YOU FEEL THAT **TUG?** THAT MEANS THE CLAW HAS **SET,** AND YOU'RE READY TO **GO.**
NOW JUMP OFF OF THE BUILDING.
I THOUGHT THE WHOLE IDEA WAS TO TEACH ME HOW **NOT** TO GET HURT OR KILLED.
TYLER, I'M **PROUD** OF YOU. THERE ARE PEOPLE OUT THERE WHO WOULD THINK **NOTHING** OF SLAPPING ON A **CAPE** AND RISKING **THEIR LIVES** AND THE **LIVES OF OTHERS** AS THEY **SWING FROM BUILDINGS** WITH **HIGH-TECH GADGETS.** THEY'D **REVEL** IN THE SHEER FOOLISHNESS OF IT.
BUT YOU, YOU'VE GOT A **COMMON SENSE** AND **WISDOM** BEYOND YOUR FEW YEARS. THAT'S SOMETHING TO **TREASURE.**

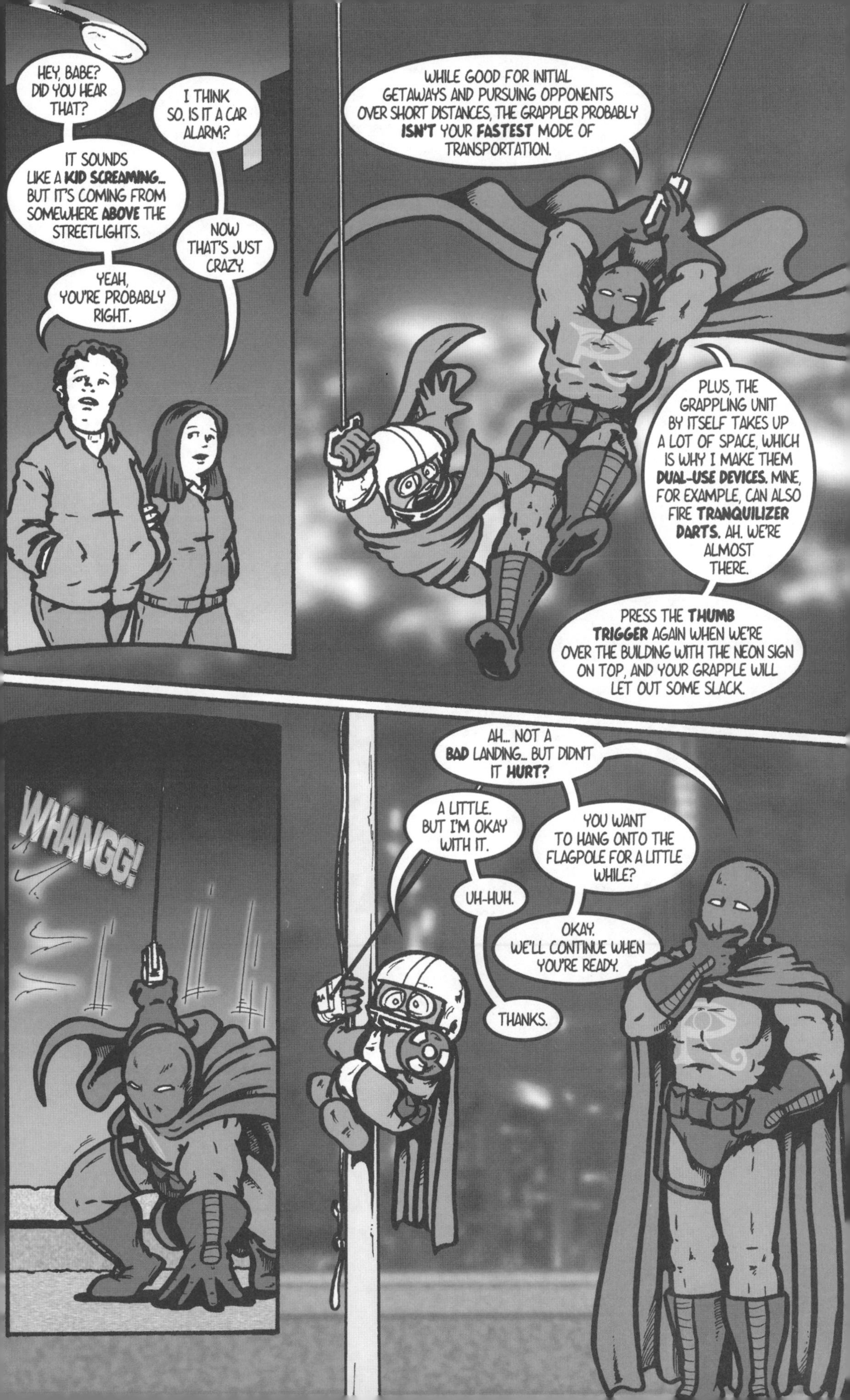
HEY, BABE? DID YOU HEAR THAT?
I THINK SO. IS IT A CAR ALARM?
IT SOUNDS LIKE A KID SCREAMING... BUT IT'S COMING FROM SOMEWHERE ABOVE THE STREETLIGHTS.
NOW THAT'S JUST CRAZY.
YEAH, YOU'RE PROBABLY RIGHT.
WHILE GOOD FOR INITIAL GETAWAYS AND PURSUING OPPONENTS OVER SHORT DISTANCES, THE GRAPPLER PROBABLY ISN'T YOUR FASTEST MODE OF TRANSPORTATION.
PLUS, THE GRAPPLING UNIT BY ITSELF TAKES UP A LOT OF SPACE, WHICH IS WHY I MAKE THEM DUAL-USE DEVICES. MINE, FOR EXAMPLE, CAN ALSO FIRE TRANQUILIZER DARTS. AH. WE'RE ALMOST THERE.
PRESS THE THUMB TRIGGER AGAIN WHEN WE'RE OVER THE BUILDING WITH THE NEON SIGN ON TOP, AND YOUR GRAPPLE WILL LET OUT SOME SLACK.
WHANGG!
AH... NOT A BAD LANDING... BUT DIDN'T IT HURT?
A LITTLE. BUT I'M OKAY WITH IT.
YOU WANT TO HANG ONTO THE FLAGPOLE FOR A LITTLE WHILE?
UH-HUH.
OKAY. WE'LL CONTINUE WHEN YOU'RE READY.
THANKS.

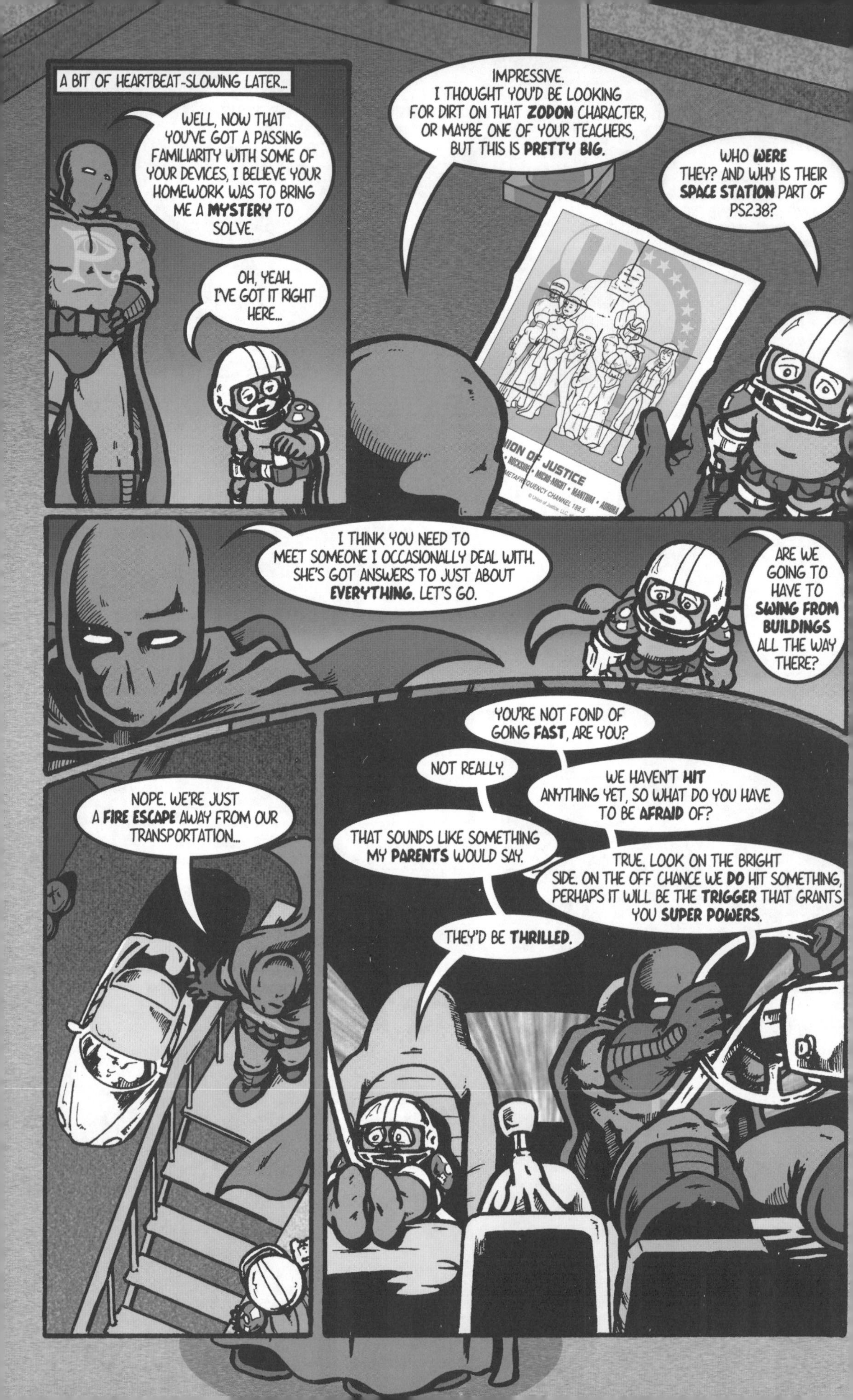
A BIT OF HEARTBEAT-SLOWING LATER...
WELL, NOW THAT YOU'VE GOT A PASSING FAMILIARITY WITH SOME OF YOUR DEVICES, I BELIEVE YOUR HOMEWORK WAS TO BRING ME A MYSTERY TO SOLVE.
OH, YEAH. I'VE GOT IT RIGHT HERE...
IMPRESSIVE. I THOUGHT YOU'D BE LOOKING FOR DIRT ON THAT ZODON CHARACTER, OR MAYBE ONE OF YOUR TEACHERS, BUT THIS IS PRETTY BIG.
WHO WERE THEY? AND WHY IS THEIR SPACE STATION PART OF PS238?
I THINK YOU NEED TO MEET SOMEONE I OCCASIONALLY DEAL WITH. SHE'S GOT ANSWERS TO JUST ABOUT EVERYTHING. LET'S GO.
ARE WE GOING TO HAVE TO SWING FROM BUILDINGS ALL THE WAY THERE?
NOPE. WE'RE JUST A FIRE ESCAPE AWAY FROM OUR TRANSPORTATION...
YOU'RE NOT FOND OF GOING FAST, ARE YOU?
NOT REALLY.
WE HAVEN'T HIT ANYTHING YET, SO WHAT DO YOU HAVE TO BE AFRAID OF?
THAT SOUNDS LIKE SOMETHING MY PARENTS WOULD SAY.
TRUE. LOOK ON THE BRIGHT SIDE. ON THE OFF CHANCE WE DO HIT SOMETHING, PERHAPS IT WILL BE THE TRIGGER THAT GRANTS YOU SUPER POWERS.
THEY'D BE THRILLED.

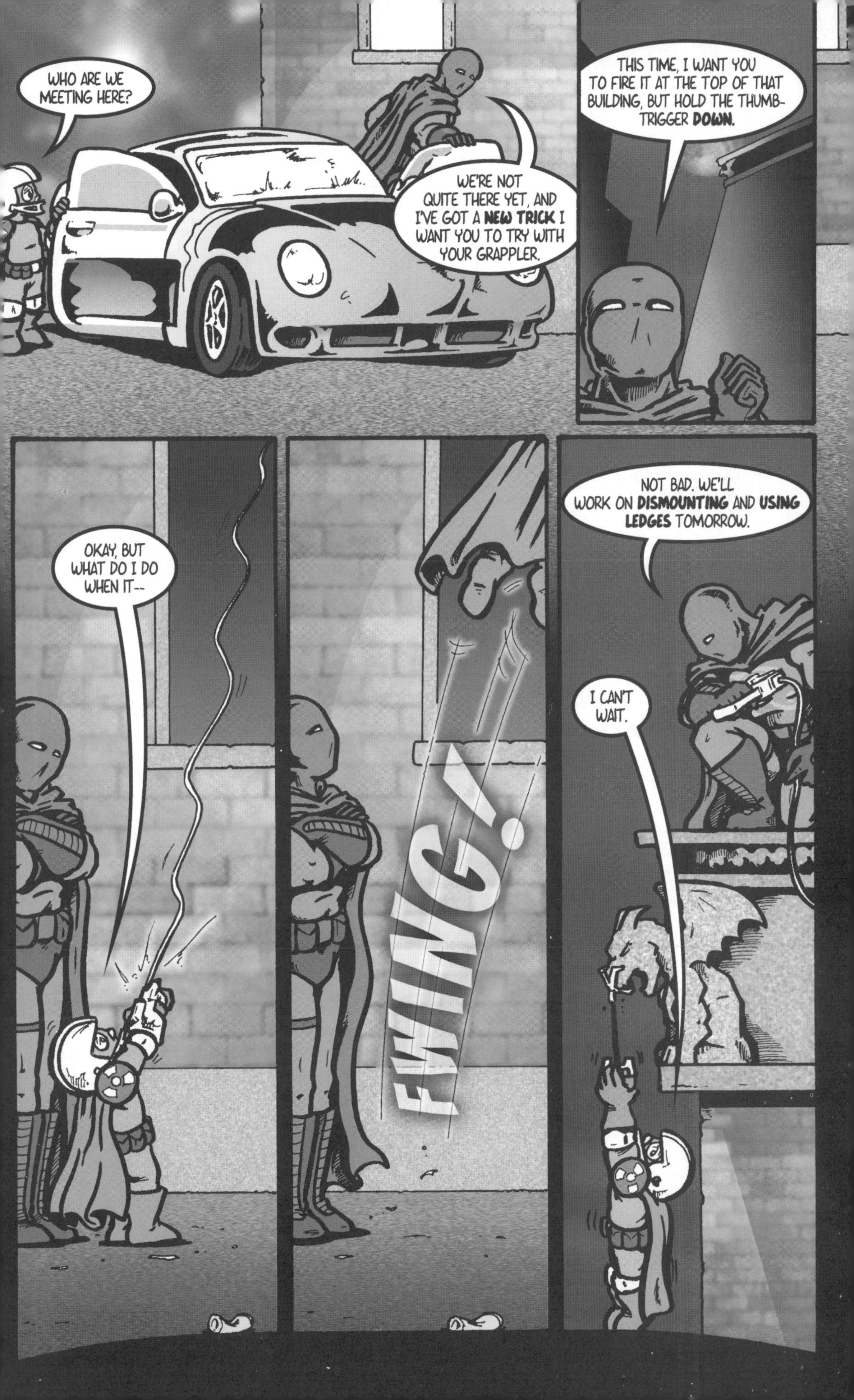
WHO ARE WE MEETING HERE?
WE'RE NOT QUITE THERE YET, AND I'VE GOT A NEW TRICK I WANT YOU TO TRY WITH YOUR GRAPPLER.
THIS TIME, I WANT YOU TO FIRE IT AT THE TOP OF THAT BUILDING, BUT HOLD THE THUMB-TRIGGER DOWN.
OKAY, BUT WHAT DO I DO WHEN IT--
FWING!
NOT BAD. WE'LL WORK ON DISMOUNTING AND USING LEDGES TOMORROW.
I CAN'T WAIT.

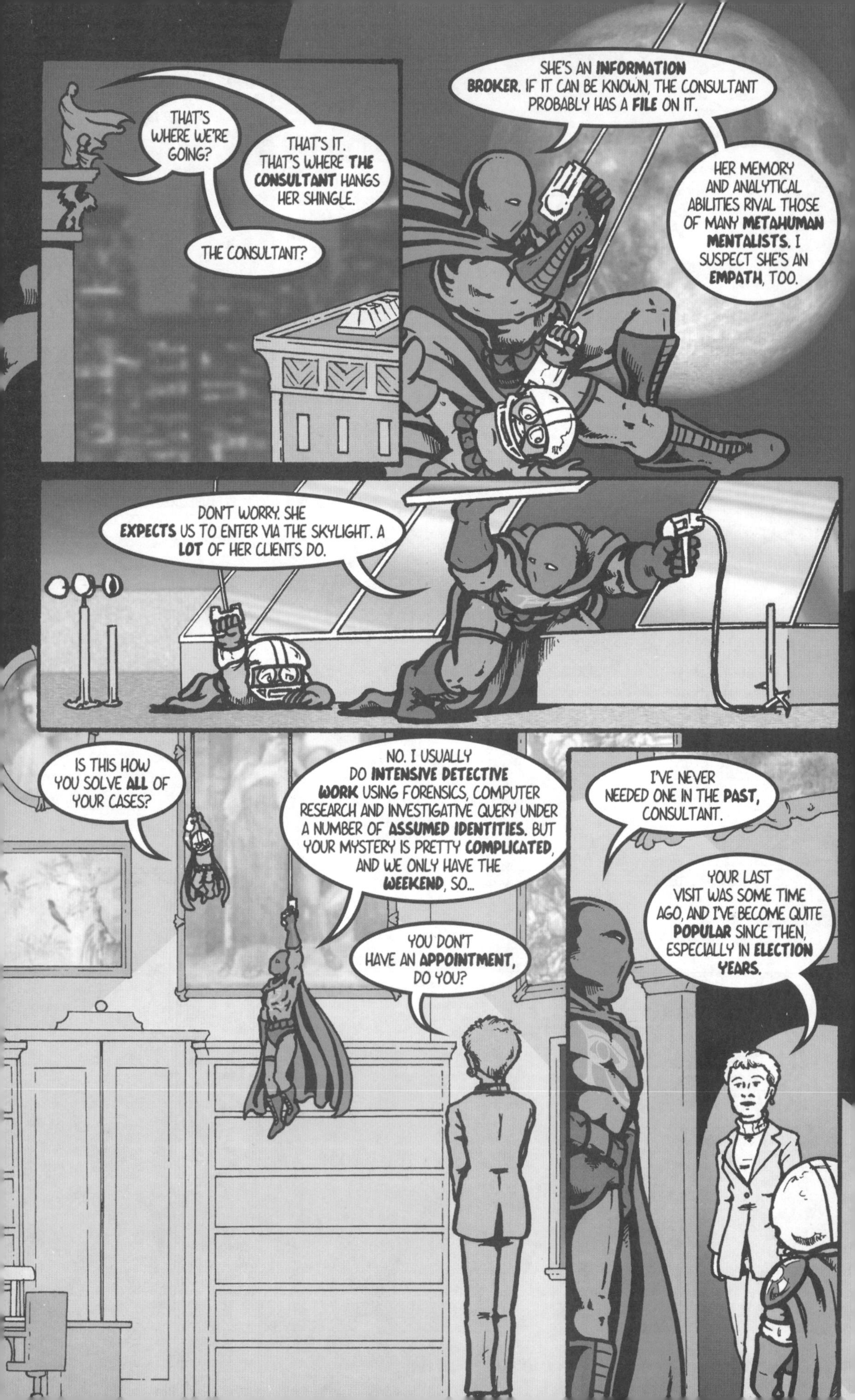
THAT'S WHERE WE'RE GOING?
THAT'S IT. THAT'S WHERE THE CONSULTANT HANGS HER SHINGLE.
THE CONSULTANT?
SHE'S AN INFORMATION BROKER. IF IT CAN BE KNOWN, THE CONSULTANT PROBABLY HAS A FILE ON IT.
HER MEMORY AND ANALYTICAL ABILITIES RIVAL THOSE OF MANY METAHUMAN MENTALISTS. I SUSPECT SHE'S AN EMPATH, TOO.
DON'T WORRY. SHE EXPECTS US TO ENTER VIA THE SKYLIGHT. A LOT OF HER CLIENTS DO.
IS THIS HOW YOU SOLVE ALL OF YOUR CASES?
NO. I USUALLY DO INTENSIVE DETECTIVE WORK USING FORENSICS, COMPUTER RESEARCH AND INVESTIGATIVE QUERY UNDER A NUMBER OF ASSUMED IDENTITIES. BUT YOUR MYSTERY IS PRETTY COMPLICATED, AND WE ONLY HAVE THE WEEKEND, SO...
YOU DON'T HAVE AN APPOINTMENT, DO YOU?
I'VE NEVER NEEDED ONE IN THE PAST, CONSULTANT.
YOUR LAST VISIT WAS SOME TIME AGO, AND I'VE BECOME QUITE POPULAR SINCE THEN, ESPECIALLY IN ELECTION YEARS.

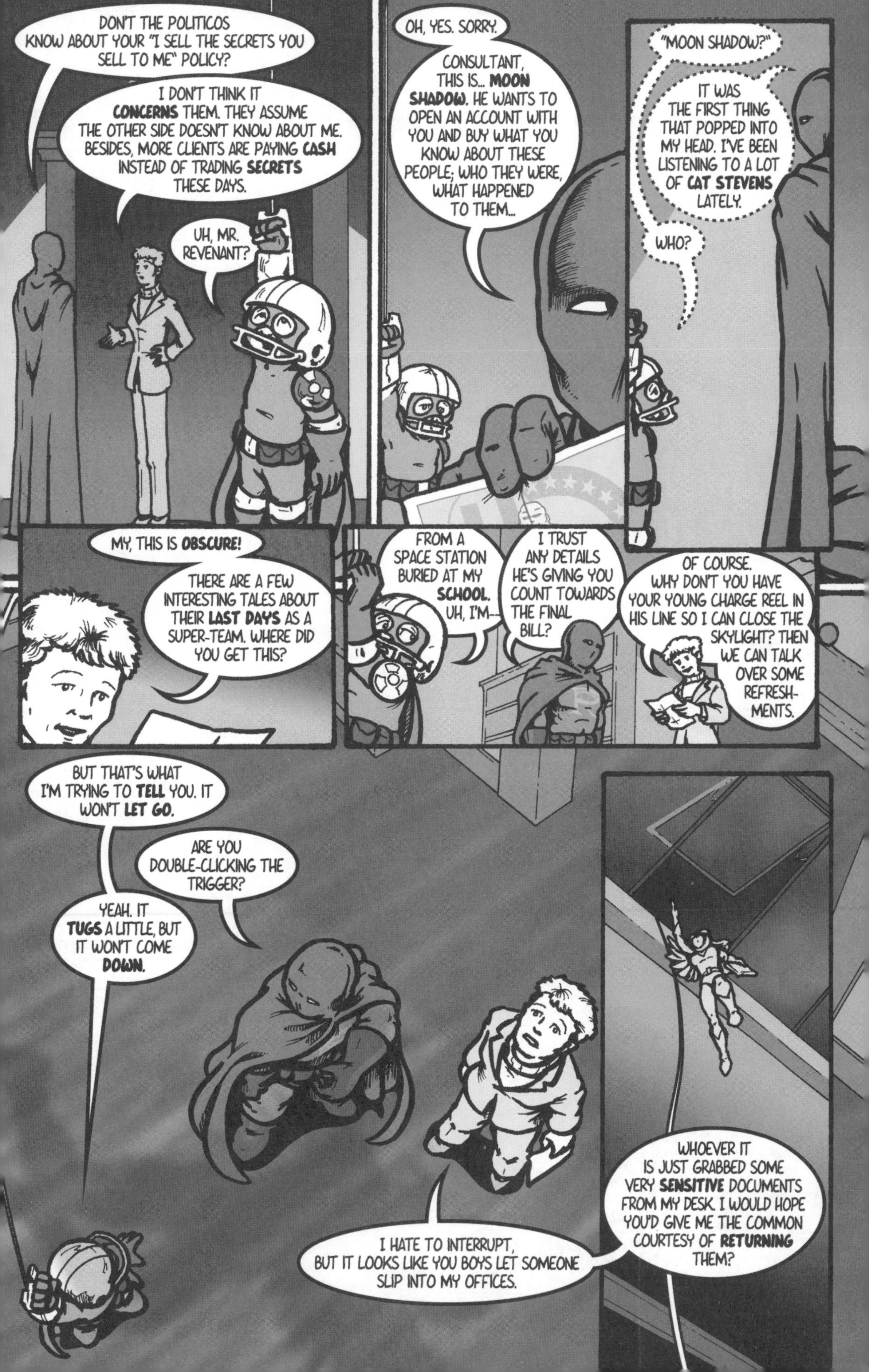
DON'T THE POLITICOS KNOW ABOUT YOUR "I SELL THE SECRETS YOU SELL TO ME" POLICY?
I DON'T THINK IT CONCERNS THEM. THEY ASSUME THE OTHER SIDE DOESN'T KNOW ABOUT ME. BESIDES, MORE CLIENTS ARE PAYING CASH INSTEAD OF TRADING SECRETS THESE DAYS.
UH, MR. REVENANT?
OH, YES. SORRY.
CONSULTANT, THIS IS... MOON SHADOW. HE WANTS TO OPEN AN ACCOUNT WITH YOU AND BUY WHAT YOU KNOW ABOUT THESE PEOPLE; WHO THEY WERE, WHAT HAPPENED TO THEM...
"MOON SHADOW?"
IT WAS THE FIRST THING THAT POPPED INTO MY HEAD. I'VE BEEN LISTENING TO A LOT OF CAT STEVENS LATELY.
WHO?
MY, THIS IS OBSCURE!
THERE ARE A FEW INTERESTING TALES ABOUT THEIR LAST DAYS AS A SUPER-TEAM. WHERE DID YOU GET THIS?
FROM A SPACE STATION BURIED AT MY SCHOOL. UH, I'M--
I TRUST ANY DETAILS HE'S GIVING YOU COUNT TOWARDS THE FINAL BILL?
OF COURSE. WHY DON'T YOU HAVE YOUR YOUNG CHARGE REEL IN HIS LINE SO I CAN CLOSE THE SKYLIGHT? THEN WE CAN TALK OVER SOME REFRESH-MENTS.
BUT THAT'S WHAT I'M TRYING TO TELL YOU. IT WON'T LET GO.
ARE YOU DOUBLE-CLICKING THE TRIGGER?
YEAH. IT TUGS A LITTLE, BUT IT WON'T COME DOWN.
I HATE TO INTERRUPT, BUT IT LOOKS LIKE YOU BOYS LET SOMEONE SLIP INTO MY OFFICES.
WHOEVER IT IS JUST GRABBED SOME VERY SENSITIVE DOCUMENTS FROM MY DESK. I WOULD HOPE YOU'D GIVE ME THE COMMON COURTESY OF RETURNING THEM?

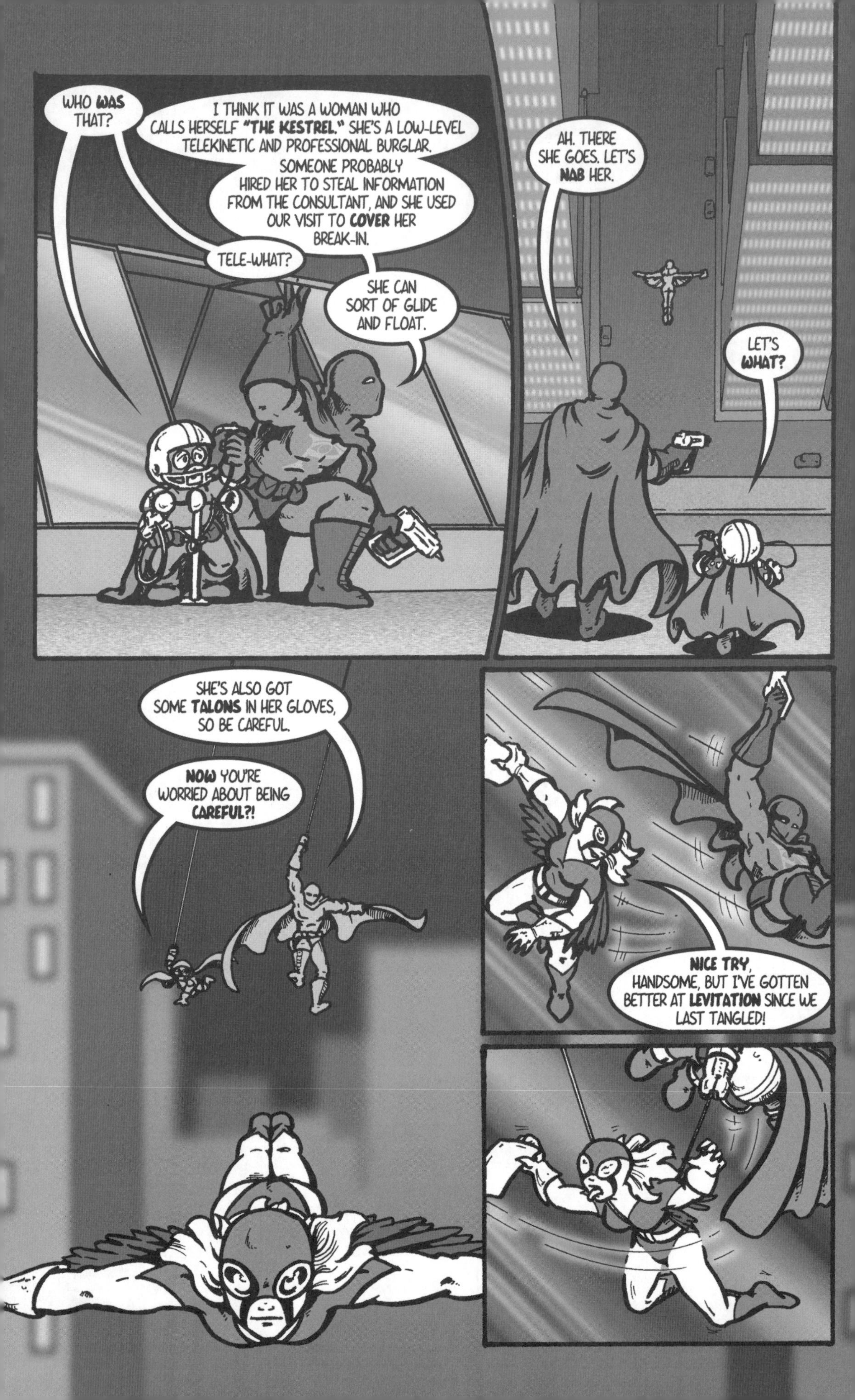
WHO WAS THAT?
I THINK IT WAS A WOMAN WHO CALLS HERSELF "THE KESTREL." SHE'S A LOW-LEVEL TELEKINETIC AND PROFESSIONAL BURGLAR.
SOMEONE PROBABLY HIRED HER TO STEAL INFORMATION FROM THE CONSULTANT, AND SHE USED OUR VISIT TO COVER HER BREAK-IN.
TELE-WHAT?
SHE CAN SORT OF GLIDE AND FLOAT.
AH. THERE SHE GOES. LET'S NAB HER.
LET'S WHAT?
SHE'S ALSO GOT SOME TALONS IN HER GLOVES, SO BE CAREFUL.
NOW YOU'RE WORRIED ABOUT BEING CAREFUL?!
NICE TRY, HANDSOME, BUT I'VE GOTTEN BETTER AT LEVITATION SINCE WE LAST TANGLED!

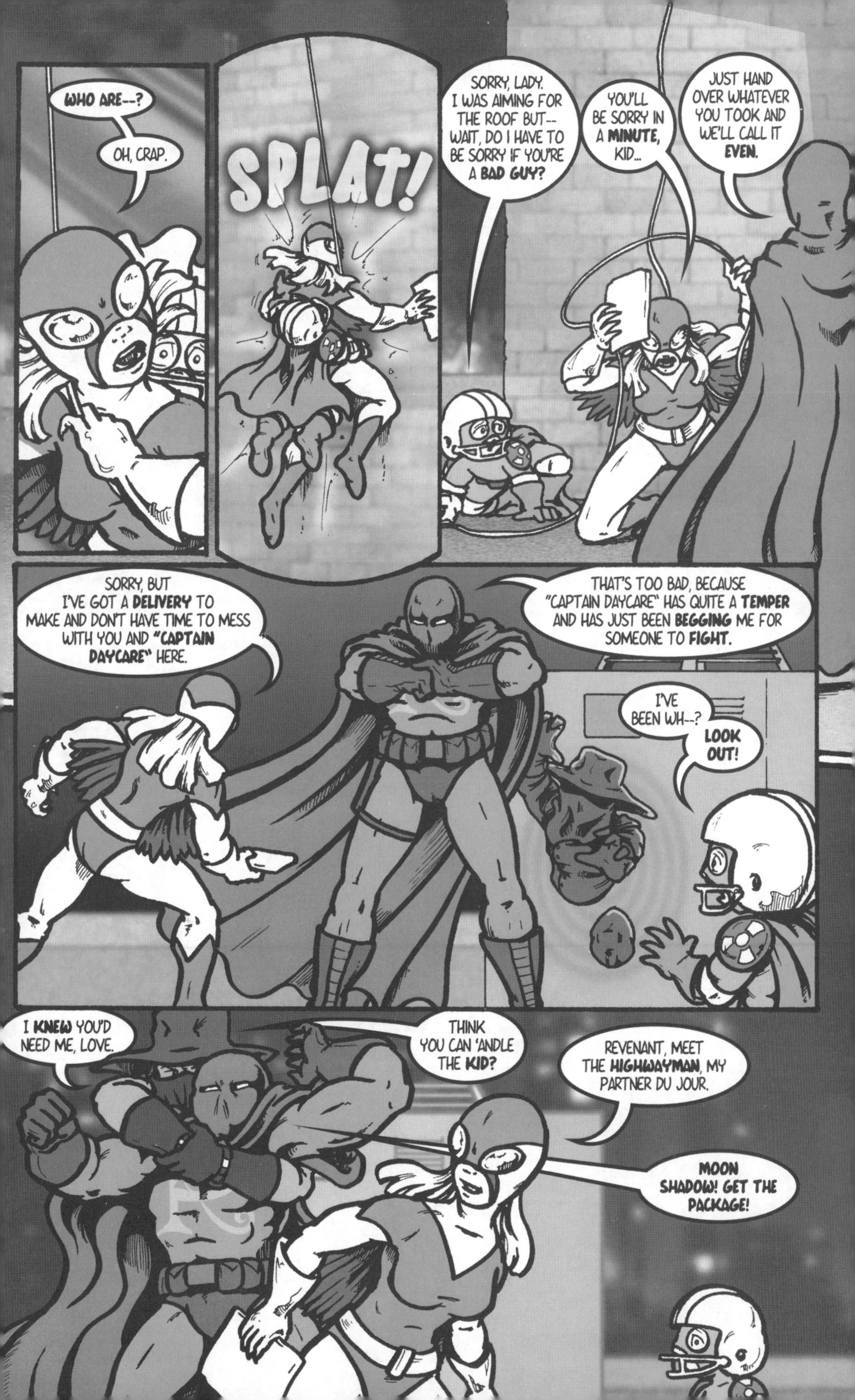
WHO ARE--?
OH, CRAP.
SPLAT!
SORRY, LADY. I WAS AIMING FOR THE ROOF BUT-- WAIT, DO I HAVE TO BE SORRY IF YOU'RE A BAD GUY?
YOU'LL BE SORRY IN A MINUTE, KID...
JUST HAND OVER WHATEVER YOU TOOK AND WE'LL CALL IT EVEN.
SORRY, BUT I'VE GOT A DELIVERY TO MAKE AND DON'T HAVE TIME TO MESS WITH YOU AND "CAPTAIN DAYCARE" HERE.
THAT'S TOO BAD, BECAUSE "CAPTAIN DAYCARE" HAS QUITE A TEMPER AND HAS JUST BEEN BEGGING ME FOR SOMEONE TO FIGHT.
I'VE BEEN WH--? LOOK OUT!
I KNEW YOU'D NEED ME, LOVE.
THINK YOU CAN 'ANDLE THE KID?
REVENANT, MEET THE HIGHWAYMAN, MY PARTNER DU JOUR.
MOON SHADOW! GET THE PACKAGE!

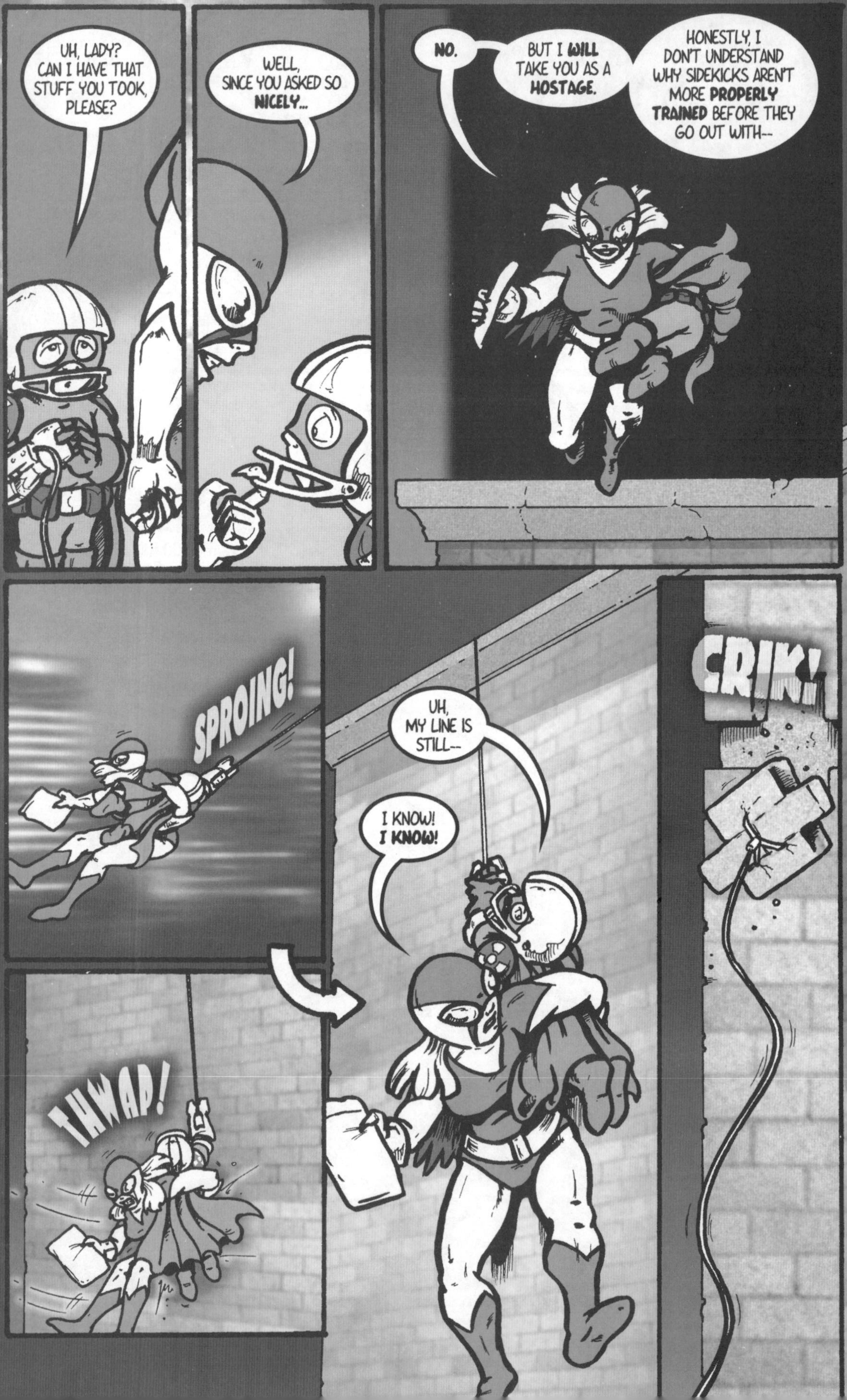
UH, LADY? CAN I HAVE THAT STUFF YOU TOOK, PLEASE?
WELL, SINCE YOU ASKED SO **NICELY**...
NO.
BUT I **WILL** TAKE YOU AS A **HOSTAGE.**
HONESTLY, I DON'T UNDERSTAND WHY SIDEKICKS AREN'T MORE **PROPERLY TRAINED** BEFORE THEY GO OUT WITH--
SPROING!
UH, MY LINE IS STILL--
I KNOW! **I KNOW!**
CRIK!
THWAP!

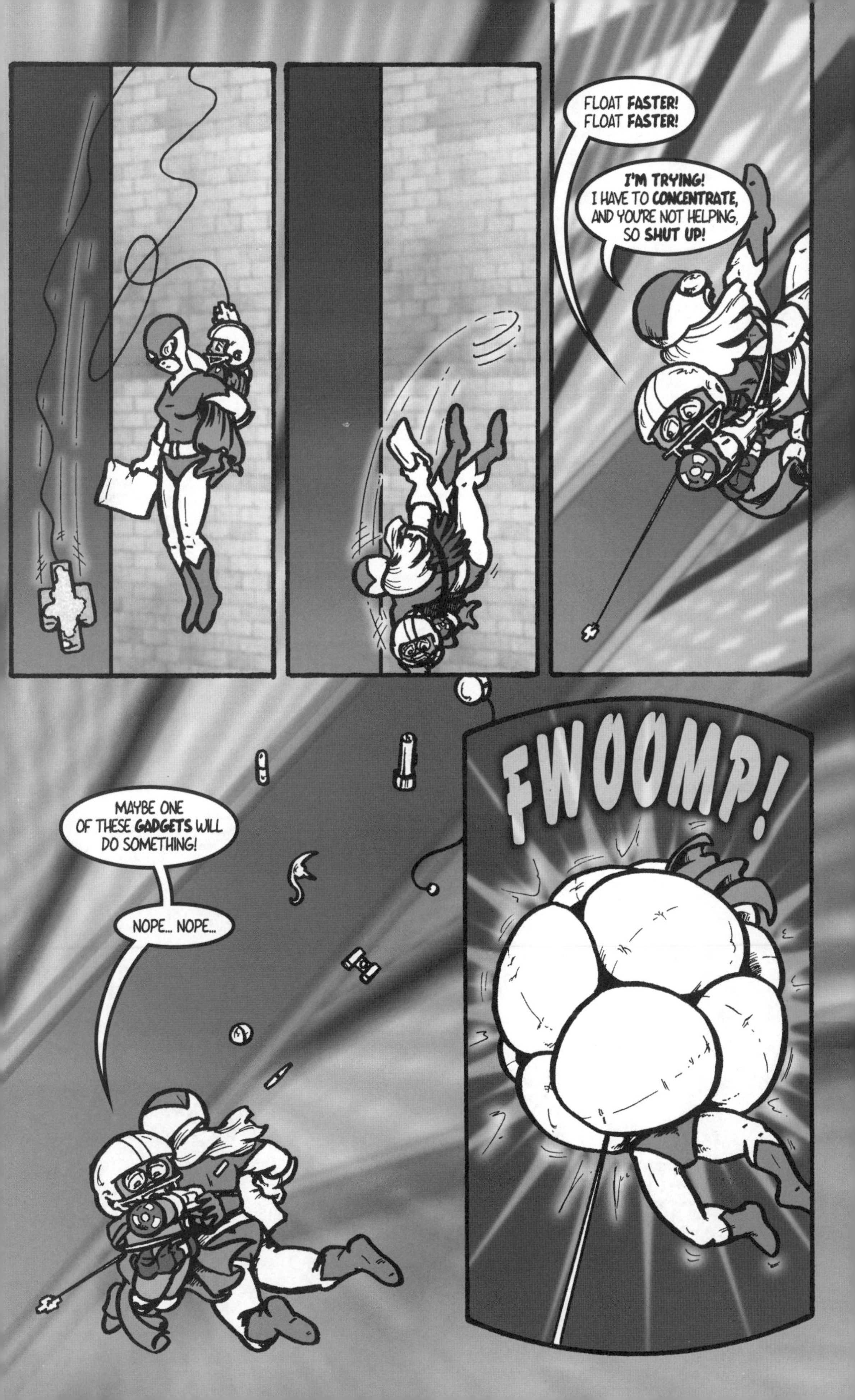
FLOAT **FASTER!** FLOAT **FASTER!**
I'M TRYING! I HAVE TO **CONCENTRATE,** AND YOU'RE NOT HELPING, SO **SHUT UP!**
MAYBE ONE OF THESE **GADGETS** WILL DO SOMETHING!
NOPE... NOPE...
FWOOMP!

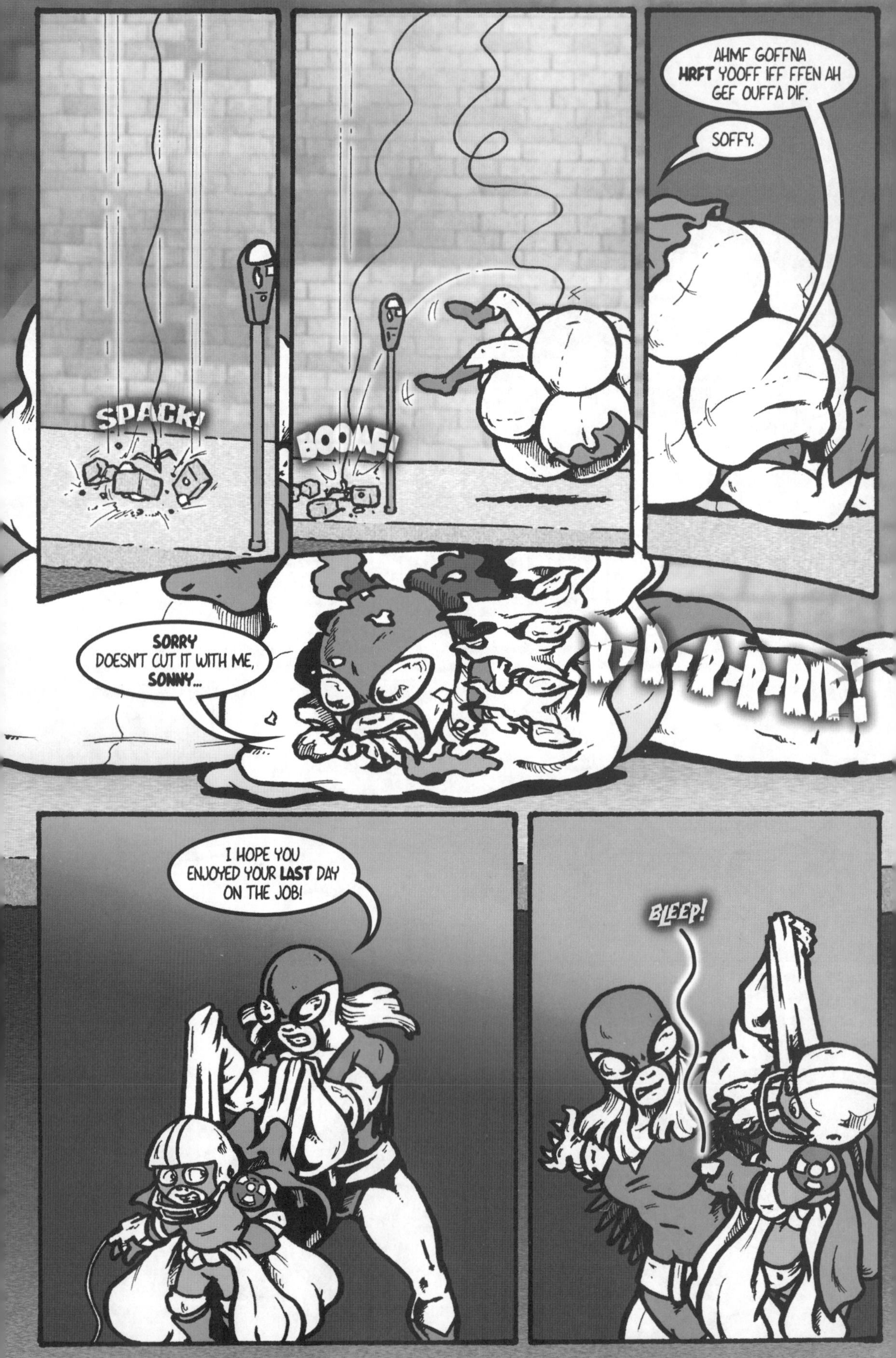
SPACK!
BOOMF!
AHMF GOFFNA HRFT YOOFF IFF FFEN AH GEF OUFFA DIF.
SOFFY.
SORRY DOESN'T CUT IT WITH ME, SONNY...
R-R-R-R-RIP!
I HOPE YOU ENJOYED YOUR LAST DAY ON THE JOB!
BLEEP!

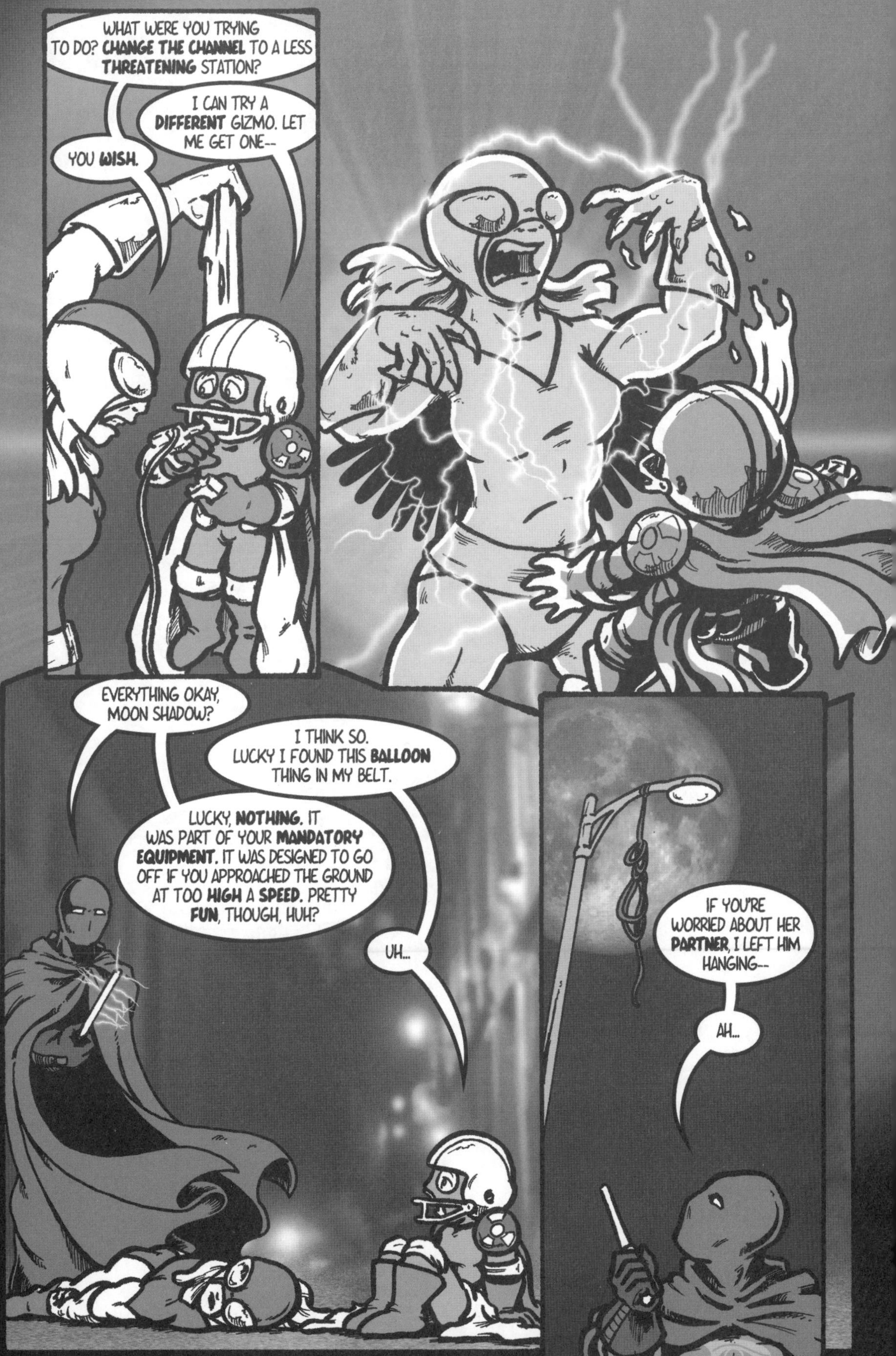
WHAT WERE YOU TRYING TO DO? CHANGE THE CHANNEL TO A LESS THREATENING STATION?
YOU WISH.
I CAN TRY A DIFFERENT GIZMO. LET ME GET ONE--
EVERYTHING OKAY, MOON SHADOW?
I THINK SO. LUCKY I FOUND THIS BALLOON THING IN MY BELT.
LUCKY, NOTHING. IT WAS PART OF YOUR MANDATORY EQUIPMENT. IT WAS DESIGNED TO GO OFF IF YOU APPROACHED THE GROUND AT TOO HIGH A SPEED. PRETTY FUN, THOUGH, HUH?
UH...
IF YOU'RE WORRIED ABOUT HER PARTNER, I LEFT HIM HANGING--
AH...

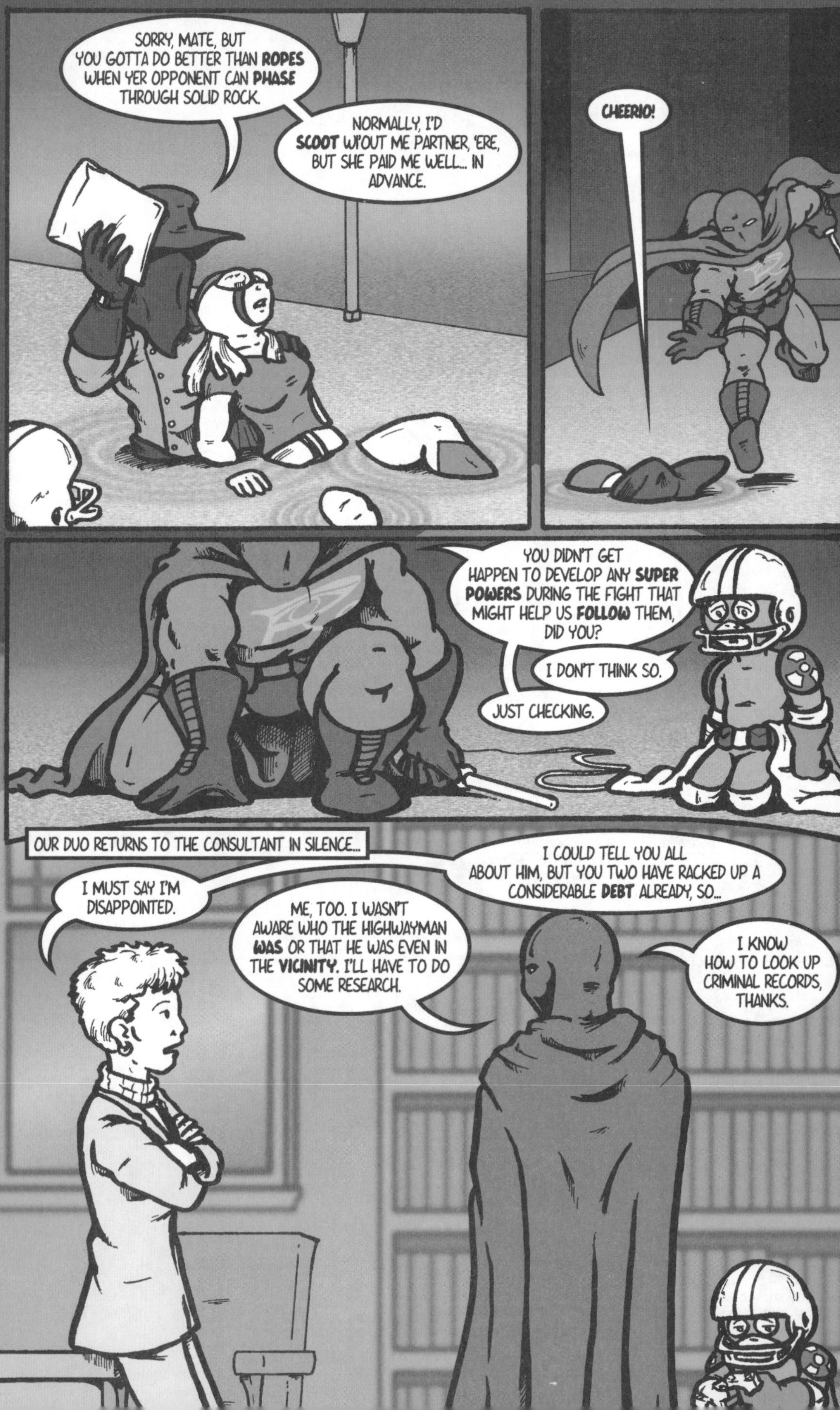
SORRY, MATE, BUT YOU GOTTA DO BETTER THAN ROPES WHEN YER OPPONENT CAN PHASE THROUGH SOLID ROCK.
NORMALLY, I'D SCOOT WI'OUT ME PARTNER, 'ERE, BUT SHE PAID ME WELL... IN ADVANCE.
CHEERIO!
YOU DIDN'T GET HAPPEN TO DEVELOP ANY SUPER POWERS DURING THE FIGHT THAT MIGHT HELP US FOLLOW THEM, DID YOU?
I DON'T THINK SO.
JUST CHECKING.
OUR DUO RETURNS TO THE CONSULTANT IN SILENCE...
I MUST SAY I'M DISAPPOINTED.
ME, TOO. I WASN'T AWARE WHO THE HIGHWAYMAN WAS OR THAT HE WAS EVEN IN THE VICINITY. I'LL HAVE TO DO SOME RESEARCH.
I COULD TELL YOU ALL ABOUT HIM, BUT YOU TWO HAVE RACKED UP A CONSIDERABLE DEBT ALREADY, SO...
I KNOW HOW TO LOOK UP CRIMINAL RECORDS, THANKS.

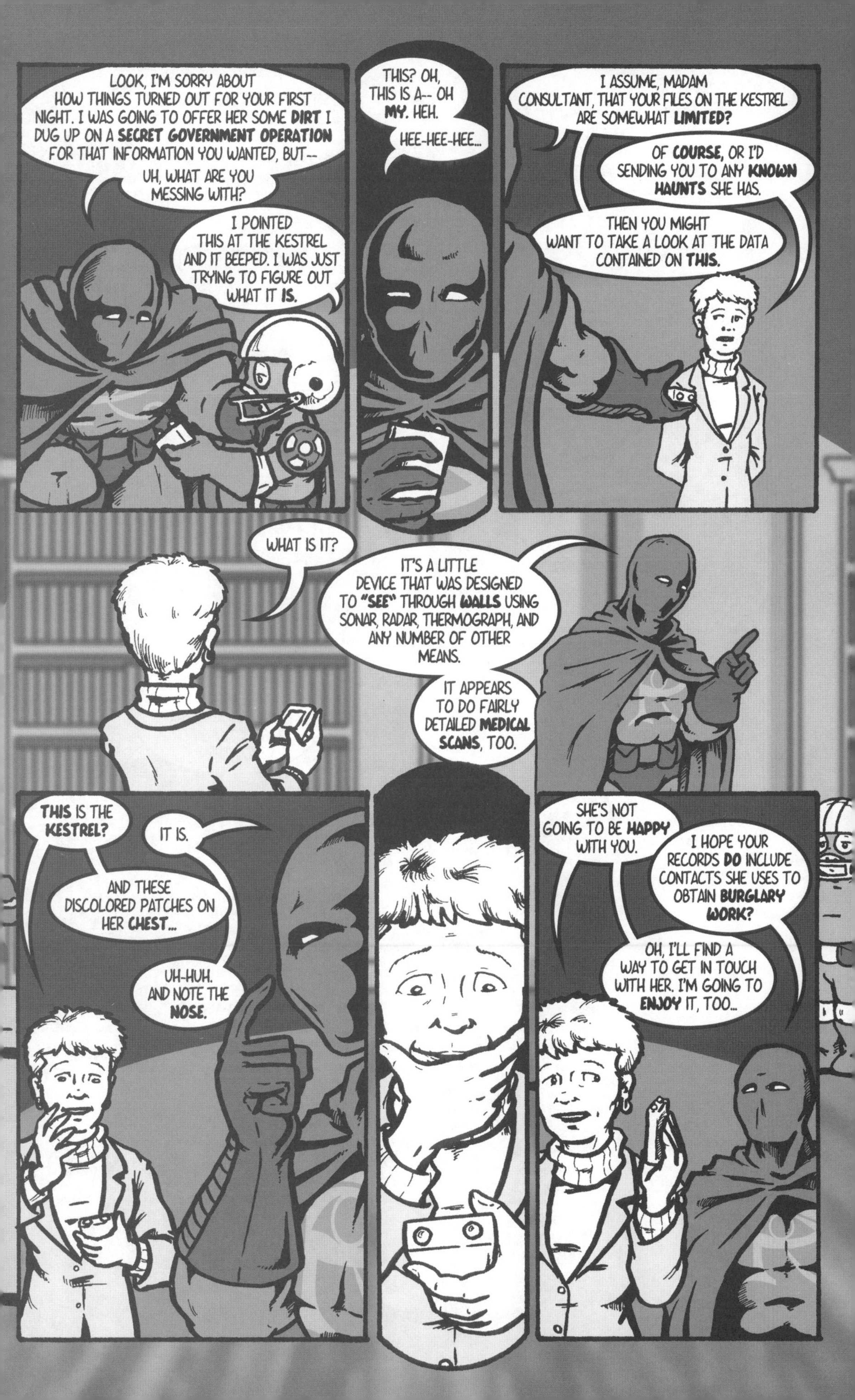

LOOK, I'M SORRY ABOUT HOW THINGS TURNED OUT FOR YOUR FIRST NIGHT. I WAS GOING TO OFFER HER SOME DIRT I DUG UP ON A SECRET GOVERNMENT OPERATION FOR THAT INFORMATION YOU WANTED, BUT--
UH, WHAT ARE YOU MESSING WITH?
I POINTED THIS AT THE KESTREL AND IT BEEPED. I WAS JUST TRYING TO FIGURE OUT WHAT IT IS.
THIS? OH, THIS IS A-- OH MY. HEH.
HEE-HEE-HEE...
I ASSUME, MADAM CONSULTANT, THAT YOUR FILES ON THE KESTREL ARE SOMEWHAT LIMITED?
OF COURSE, OR I'D SENDING YOU TO ANY KNOWN HAUNTS SHE HAS.
THEN YOU MIGHT WANT TO TAKE A LOOK AT THE DATA CONTAINED ON THIS.
WHAT IS IT?
IT'S A LITTLE DEVICE THAT WAS DESIGNED TO "SEE" THROUGH WALLS USING SONAR, RADAR, THERMOGRAPH, AND ANY NUMBER OF OTHER MEANS.
IT APPEARS TO DO FAIRLY DETAILED MEDICAL SCANS, TOO.
THIS IS THE KESTREL?
IT IS.
AND THESE DISCOLORED PATCHES ON HER CHEST...
UH-HUH. AND NOTE THE NOSE.
SHE'S NOT GOING TO BE HAPPY WITH YOU.
I HOPE YOUR RECORDS DO INCLUDE CONTACTS SHE USES TO OBTAIN BURGLARY WORK?
OH, I'LL FIND A WAY TO GET IN TOUCH WITH HER. I'M GOING TO ENJOY IT, TOO...

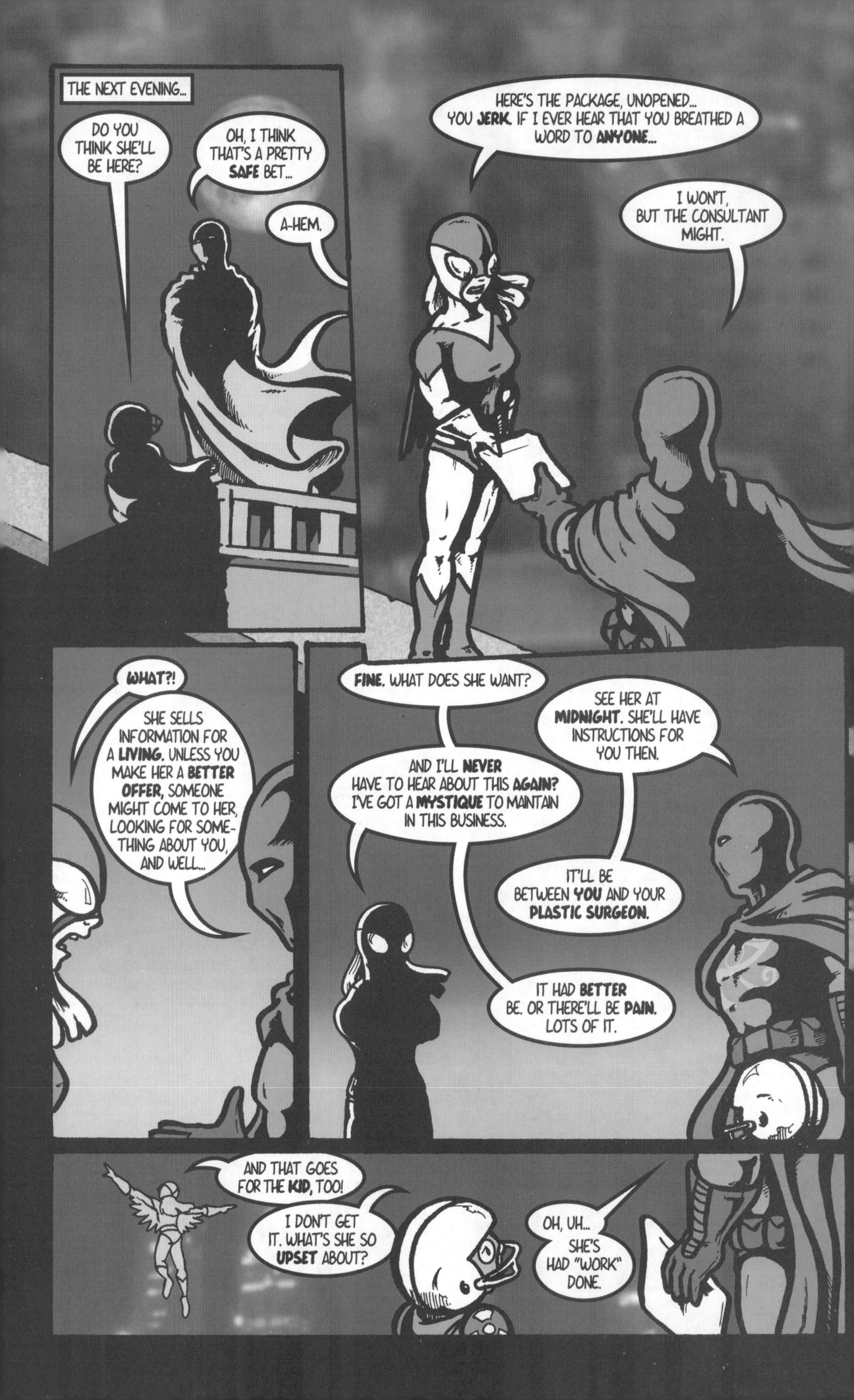
THE NEXT EVENING...
DO YOU THINK SHE'LL BE HERE?
OH, I THINK THAT'S A PRETTY SAFE BET...
A-HEM.
HERE'S THE PACKAGE, UNOPENED... YOU JERK. IF I EVER HEAR THAT YOU BREATHED A WORD TO ANYONE...
I WON'T, BUT THE CONSULTANT MIGHT.
WHAT?!
SHE SELLS INFORMATION FOR A LIVING. UNLESS YOU MAKE HER A BETTER OFFER, SOMEONE MIGHT COME TO HER, LOOKING FOR SOME-THING ABOUT YOU, AND WELL...
FINE. WHAT DOES SHE WANT?
SEE HER AT MIDNIGHT. SHE'LL HAVE INSTRUCTIONS FOR YOU THEN.
AND I'LL NEVER HAVE TO HEAR ABOUT THIS AGAIN? I'VE GOT A MYSTIQUE TO MAINTAIN IN THIS BUSINESS.
IT'LL BE BETWEEN YOU AND YOUR PLASTIC SURGEON.
IT HAD BETTER BE. OR THERE'LL BE PAIN. LOTS OF IT.
AND THAT GOES FOR THE KID, TOO!
I DON'T GET IT. WHAT'S SHE SO UPSET ABOUT?
OH, UH... SHE'S HAD "WORK" DONE.

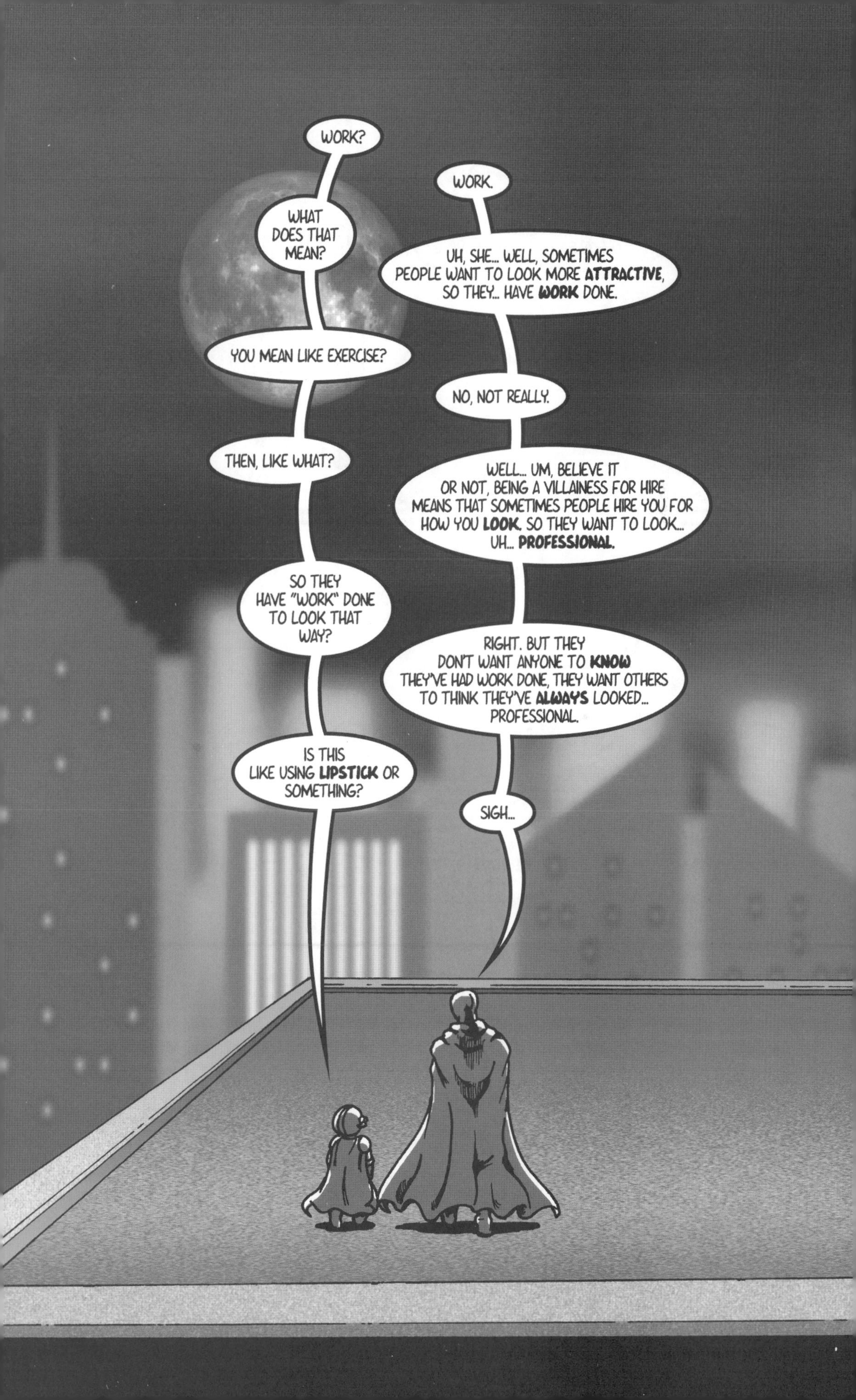
WORK?
WORK.
WHAT DOES THAT MEAN?
UH, SHE... WELL, SOMETIMES PEOPLE WANT TO LOOK MORE **ATTRACTIVE**, SO THEY... HAVE **WORK** DONE.
YOU MEAN LIKE EXERCISE?
NO, NOT REALLY.
THEN, LIKE WHAT?
WELL... UM, BELIEVE IT OR NOT, BEING A VILLAINESS FOR HIRE MEANS THAT SOMETIMES PEOPLE HIRE YOU FOR HOW YOU **LOOK**. SO THEY WANT TO LOOK... UH... **PROFESSIONAL.**
SO THEY HAVE "WORK" DONE TO LOOK THAT WAY?
RIGHT. BUT THEY DON'T WANT ANYONE TO **KNOW** THEY'VE HAD WORK DONE, THEY WANT OTHERS TO THINK THEY'VE **ALWAYS** LOOKED... PROFESSIONAL.
IS THIS LIKE USING **LIPSTICK** OR SOMETHING?
SIGH...

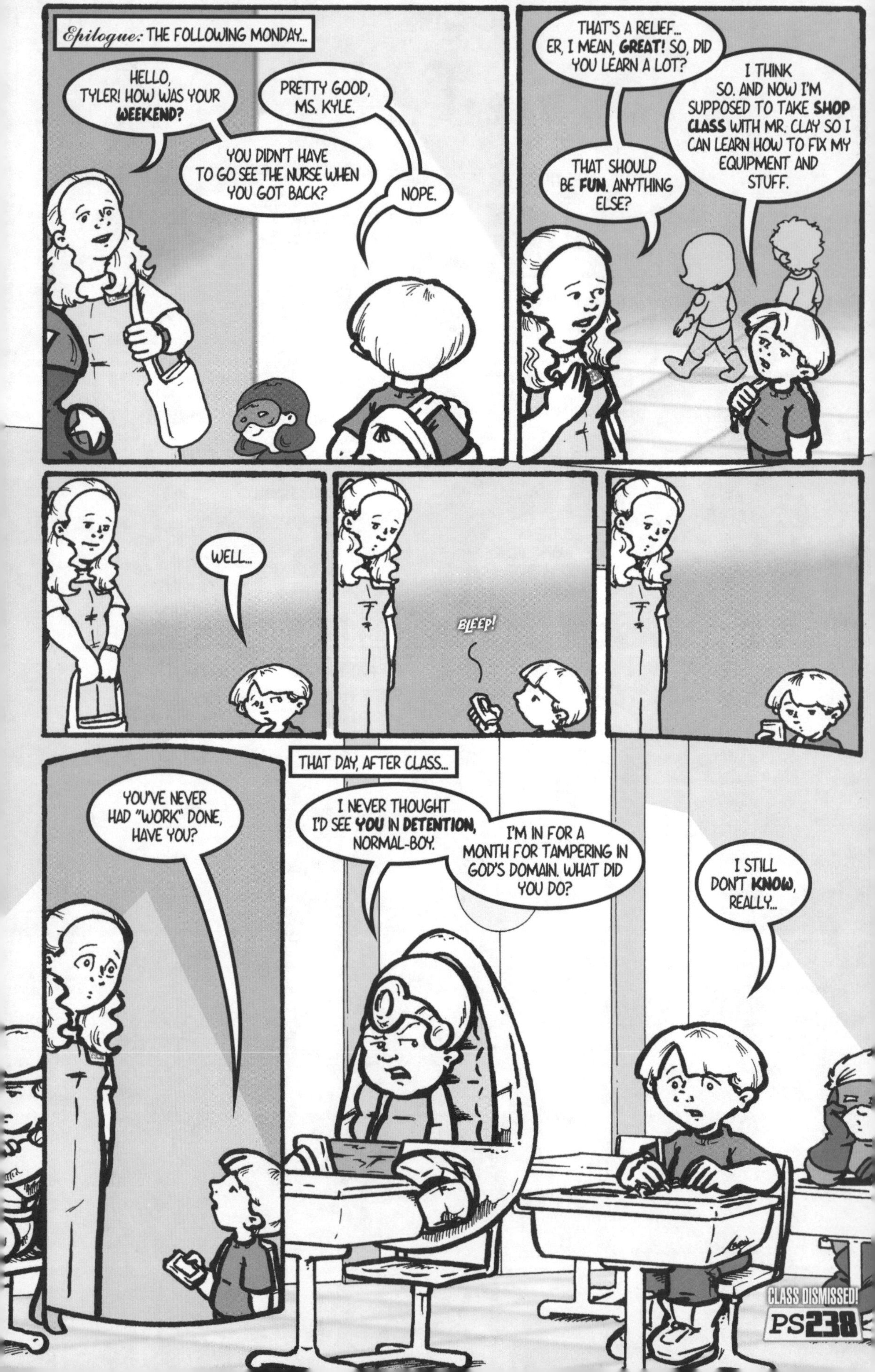
Epilogue: THE FOLLOWING MONDAY...
HELLO, TYLER! HOW WAS YOUR WEEKEND?
PRETTY GOOD, MS. KYLE.
YOU DIDN'T HAVE TO GO SEE THE NURSE WHEN YOU GOT BACK?
NOPE.
THAT'S A RELIEF... ER, I MEAN, GREAT! SO, DID YOU LEARN A LOT?
I THINK SO. AND NOW I'M SUPPOSED TO TAKE SHOP CLASS WITH MR. CLAY SO I CAN LEARN HOW TO FIX MY EQUIPMENT AND STUFF.
THAT SHOULD BE FUN. ANYTHING ELSE?
WELL...
BLEEP!
YOU'VE NEVER HAD "WORK" DONE, HAVE YOU?
THAT DAY, AFTER CLASS...
I NEVER THOUGHT I'D SEE YOU IN DETENTION, NORMAL-BOY.
I'M IN FOR A MONTH FOR TAMPERING IN GOD'S DOMAIN. WHAT DID YOU DO?
I STILL DON'T KNOW, REALLY...
CLASS DISMISSED!
PS238

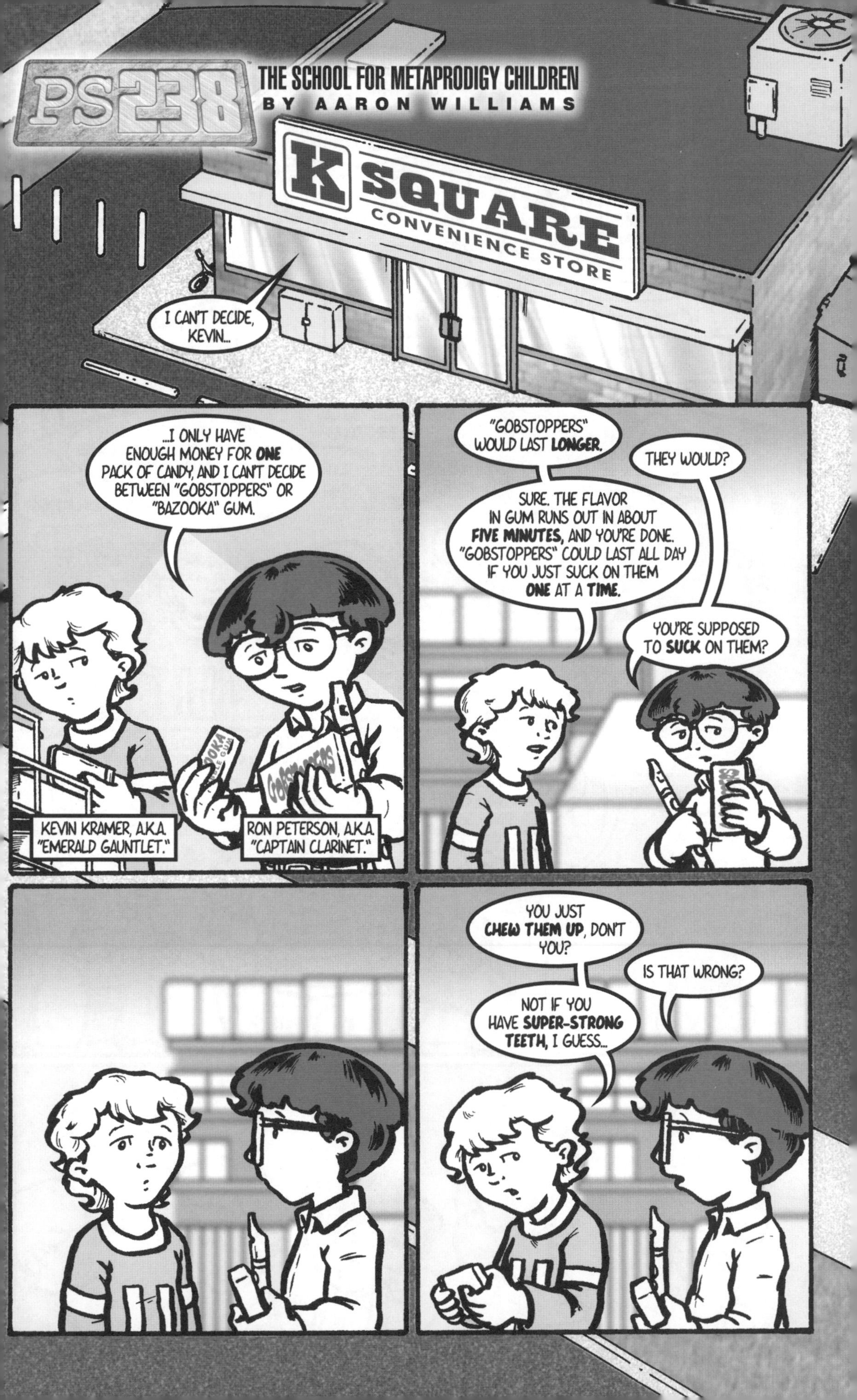
PS238
THE SCHOOL FOR METAPRODIGY CHILDREN
BY AARON WILLIAMS
K SQUARE CONVENIENCE STORE
I CAN'T DECIDE, KEVIN...
...I ONLY HAVE ENOUGH MONEY FOR ONE PACK OF CANDY, AND I CAN'T DECIDE BETWEEN "GOBSTOPPERS" OR "BAZOOKA" GUM.
KEVIN KRAMER, A.K.A. "EMERALD GAUNTLET."
RON PETERSON, A.K.A. "CAPTAIN CLARINET."
"GOBSTOPPERS" WOULD LAST LONGER.
THEY WOULD?
SURE. THE FLAVOR IN GUM RUNS OUT IN ABOUT FIVE MINUTES, AND YOU'RE DONE. "GOBSTOPPERS" COULD LAST ALL DAY IF YOU JUST SUCK ON THEM ONE AT A TIME.
YOU'RE SUPPOSED TO SUCK ON THEM?
YOU JUST CHEW THEM UP, DON'T YOU?
IS THAT WRONG?
NOT IF YOU HAVE SUPER-STRONG TEETH, I GUESS...

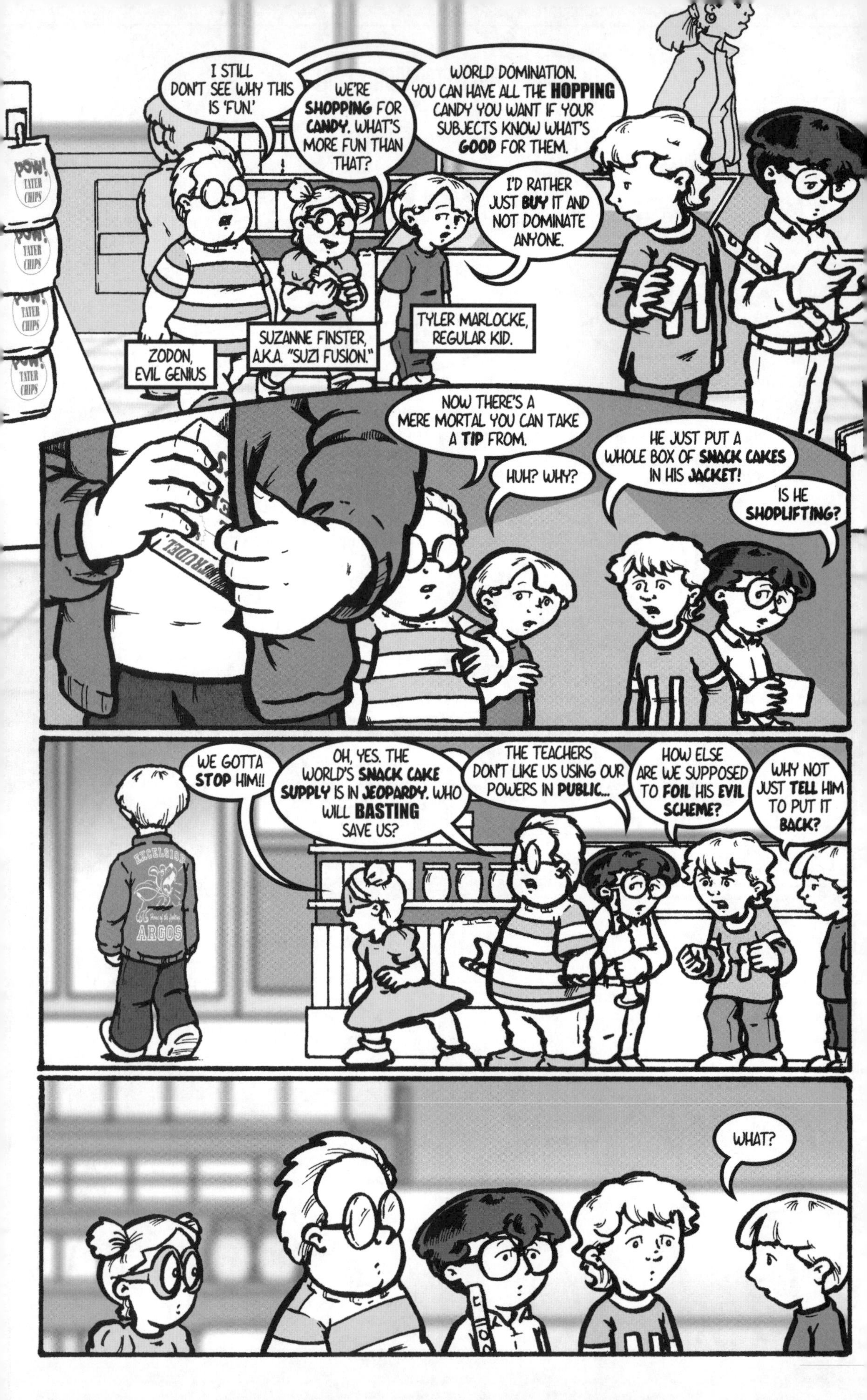

I STILL DON'T SEE WHY THIS IS 'FUN.'
WE'RE **SHOPPING** FOR **CANDY**. WHAT'S MORE FUN THAN THAT?
WORLD DOMINATION. YOU CAN HAVE ALL THE **HOPPING** CANDY YOU WANT IF YOUR SUBJECTS KNOW WHAT'S **GOOD** FOR THEM.
I'D RATHER JUST **BUY** IT AND NOT DOMINATE ANYONE.
ZODON, EVIL GENIUS
SUZANNE FINSTER, A.K.A. "SUZI FUSION."
TYLER MARLOCKE, REGULAR KID.
POW! TATER CHIPS
NOW THERE'S A MERE MORTAL YOU CAN TAKE A **TIP** FROM.
HUH? WHY?
HE JUST PUT A WHOLE BOX OF **SNACK CAKES** IN HIS **JACKET!**
IS HE **SHOPLIFTING?**
WE GOTTA **STOP** HIM!!
OH, YES. THE WORLD'S **SNACK CAKE SUPPLY** IS IN **JEOPARDY**. WHO WILL **BASTING** SAVE US?
THE TEACHERS DON'T LIKE US USING OUR POWERS IN **PUBLIC**...
HOW ELSE ARE WE SUPPOSED TO **FOIL** HIS **EVIL SCHEME?**
WHY NOT JUST **TELL** HIM TO PUT IT **BACK?**
EXCELSIOR ARGOS
WHAT?

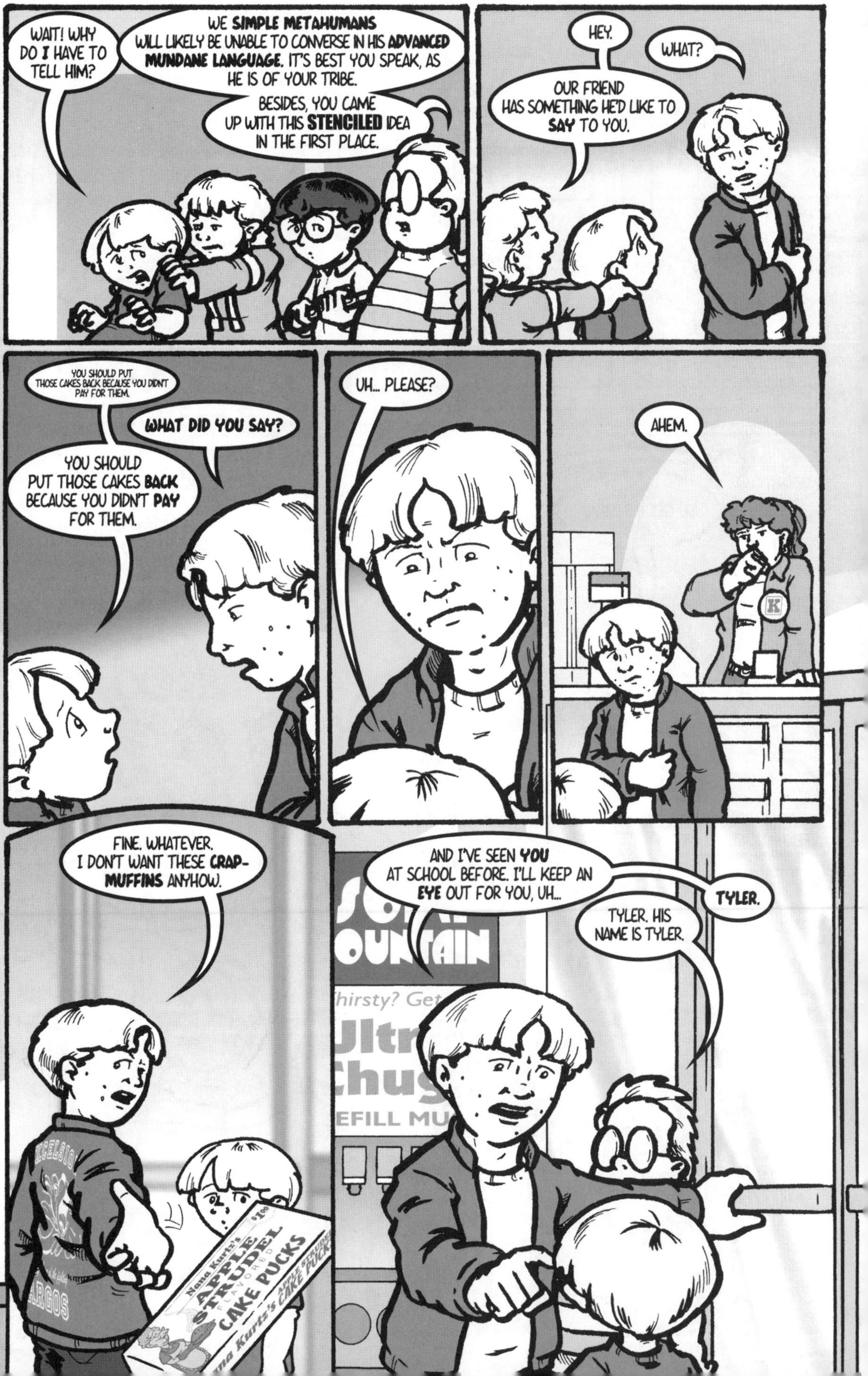
WAIT! WHY DO I HAVE TO TELL HIM?
WE SIMPLE METAHUMANS WILL LIKELY BE UNABLE TO CONVERSE IN HIS ADVANCED MUNDANE LANGUAGE. IT'S BEST YOU SPEAK, AS HE IS OF YOUR TRIBE.
BESIDES, YOU CAME UP WITH THIS STENCILED IDEA IN THE FIRST PLACE.
HEY.
WHAT?
OUR FRIEND HAS SOMETHING HE'D LIKE TO SAY TO YOU.
YOU SHOULD PUT THOSE CAKES BACK BECAUSE YOU DIDN'T PAY FOR THEM.
WHAT DID YOU SAY?
YOU SHOULD PUT THOSE CAKES BACK BECAUSE YOU DIDN'T PAY FOR THEM.
UH... PLEASE?
AHEM.
FINE. WHATEVER. I DON'T WANT THESE CRAP-MUFFINS ANYHOW.
AND I'VE SEEN YOU AT SCHOOL BEFORE. I'LL KEEP AN EYE OUT FOR YOU, UH...
TYLER.
TYLER. HIS NAME IS TYLER.
Thirsty? Get
REFILL MU
ARGOS
$1.00
Nana Kurtz's APPLE STRUDEL FLAVORED CAKE PUCKS
APPLE STRUDEL Nana Kurtz's CAKE PUCKS

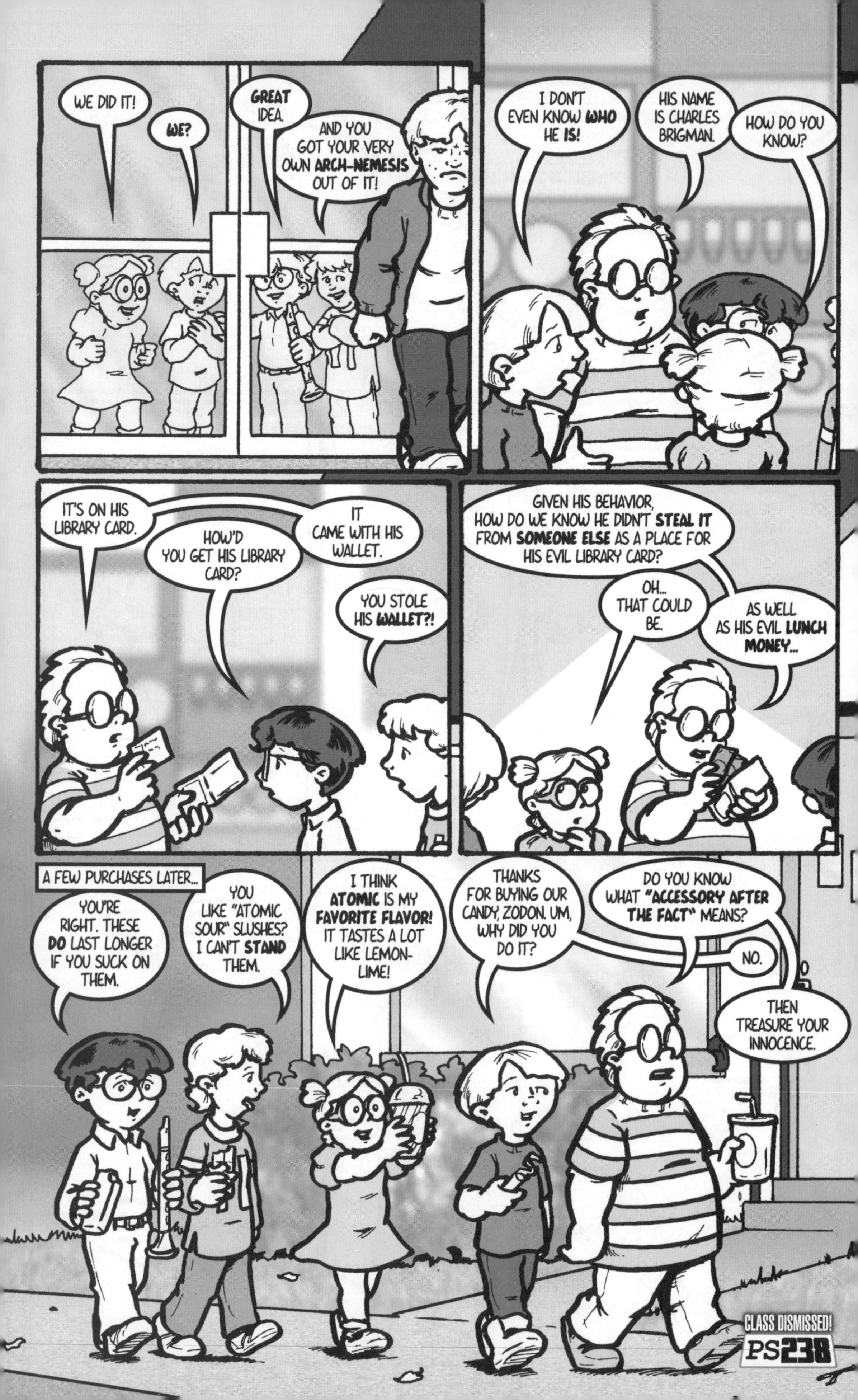
WE DID IT!
WE?
GREAT IDEA.
AND YOU GOT YOUR VERY OWN ARCH-NEMESIS OUT OF IT!
I DON'T EVEN KNOW WHO HE IS!
HIS NAME IS CHARLES BRIGMAN.
HOW DO YOU KNOW?
IT'S ON HIS LIBRARY CARD.
HOW'D YOU GET HIS LIBRARY CARD?
IT CAME WITH HIS WALLET.
YOU STOLE HIS WALLET?!
GIVEN HIS BEHAVIOR, HOW DO WE KNOW HE DIDN'T STEAL IT FROM SOMEONE ELSE AS A PLACE FOR HIS EVIL LIBRARY CARD?
OH... THAT COULD BE.
AS WELL AS HIS EVIL LUNCH MONEY...
A FEW PURCHASES LATER...
YOU'RE RIGHT. THESE DO LAST LONGER IF YOU SUCK ON THEM.
YOU LIKE "ATOMIC SOUR" SLUSHES? I CAN'T STAND THEM.
I THINK ATOMIC IS MY FAVORITE FLAVOR! IT TASTES A LOT LIKE LEMON-LIME!
THANKS FOR BUYING OUR CANDY, ZODON. UM, WHY DID YOU DO IT?
DO YOU KNOW WHAT "ACCESSORY AFTER THE FACT" MEANS?
NO.
THEN TREASURE YOUR INNOCENCE.
CLASS DISMISSED!
PS238

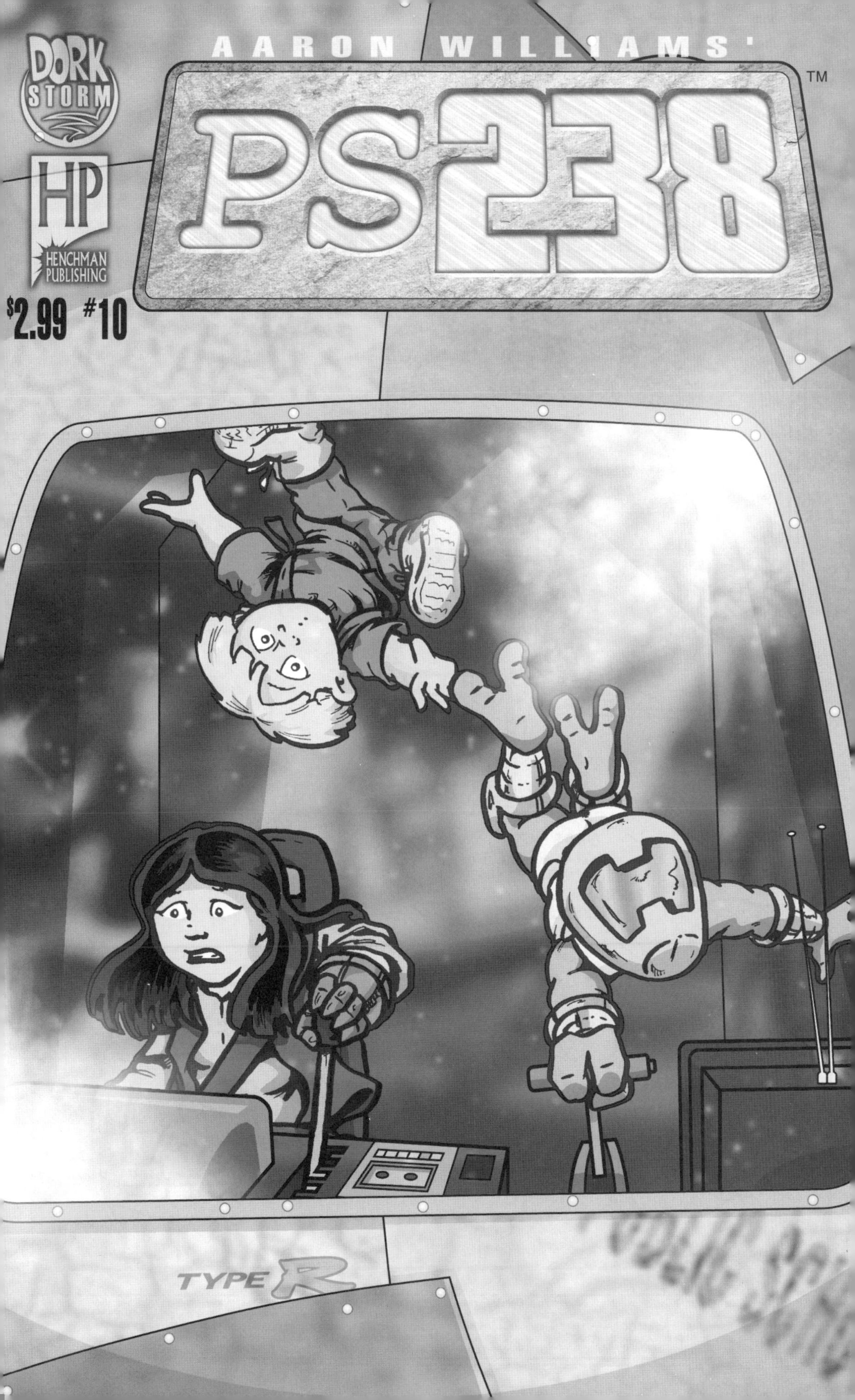

DORK STORM
HP
HENCHMAN PUBLISHING
$2.99 #10
AARON WILLIAMS'
PS238™
TYPE R

PS238 #10 by Aaron Williams, January 2005. Distributed by Dork Storm Press, published by Henchman Publishing, 5545 Holmes St, Kansas City, MO 64110. Fax: (608)255-1342. E-mail: aaron@ps238.com. Story and art ©2004 Aaron Williams. "The Revenant" is ©2005 Michael Stackpole. All rights reserved. No portion of this publication save for brief review excerpts may be reproduced without the express consent of the copyright holder. This is a work of fiction: any similarities to any actual persons or metahumans save for the purpose of satire is purely coincidental. ADVERTISING: sales@DorkStorm.com. SUBSCRIPTIONS: $26 per year. Please contact adventureretail2@qwest.net, or call (651) 488-2433 details. All letters to PS238 assumed intended for publication unless otherwise stated, and become the property of the copyright holder. [Theorizing] could, after all, be a step toward a newer and even sillier putty." -Roger L. Welsch. FIRST PRINTING, January 2005. PRINTED IN CANADA

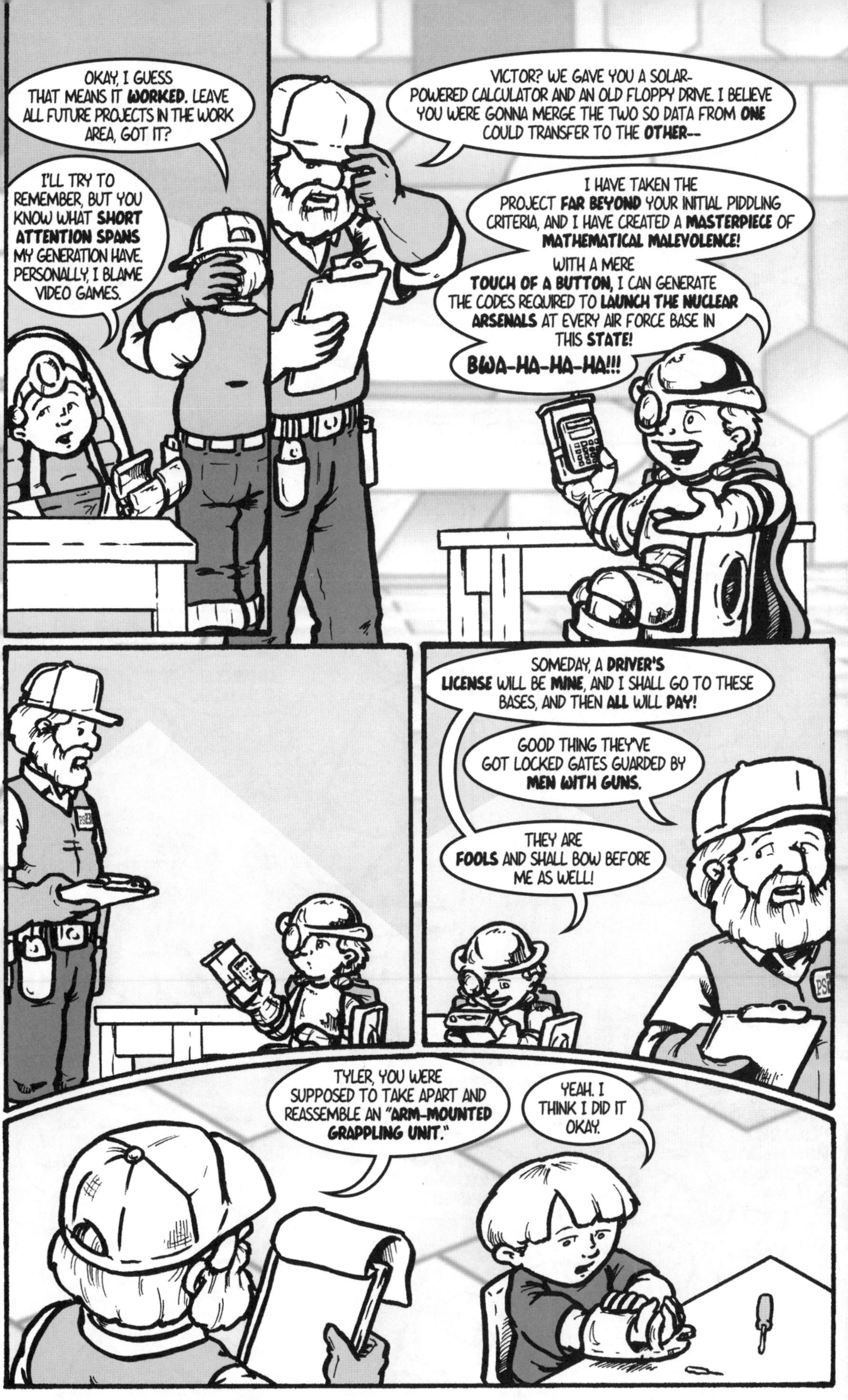
OKAY, I GUESS THAT MEANS IT **WORKED.** LEAVE ALL FUTURE PROJECTS IN THE WORK AREA, GOT IT?
I'LL TRY TO REMEMBER, BUT YOU KNOW WHAT **SHORT ATTENTION SPANS** MY GENERATION HAVE. PERSONALLY, I BLAME VIDEO GAMES.
VICTOR? WE GAVE YOU A SOLAR-POWERED CALCULATOR AND AN OLD FLOPPY DRIVE. I BELIEVE YOU WERE GONNA MERGE THE TWO SO DATA FROM **ONE** COULD TRANSFER TO THE **OTHER**--
I HAVE TAKEN THE PROJECT **FAR BEYOND** YOUR INITIAL PIDDLING CRITERIA, AND I HAVE CREATED A **MASTERPIECE** OF **MATHEMATICAL MALEVOLENCE!**
WITH A MERE **TOUCH OF A BUTTON,** I CAN GENERATE THE CODES REQUIRED TO **LAUNCH THE NUCLEAR ARSENALS** AT EVERY AIR FORCE BASE IN THIS **STATE!**
BWA-HA-HA-HA!!!
SOMEDAY, A **DRIVER'S LICENSE** WILL BE **MINE**, AND I SHALL GO TO THESE BASES, AND THEN **ALL** WILL **PAY!**
GOOD THING THEY'VE GOT LOCKED GATES GUARDED BY **MEN WITH GUNS.**
THEY ARE **FOOLS** AND SHALL BOW BEFORE ME AS WELL!
TYLER, YOU WERE SUPPOSED TO TAKE APART AND REASSEMBLE AN **"ARM-MOUNTED GRAPPLING UNIT."**
YEAH. I THINK I DID IT OKAY.

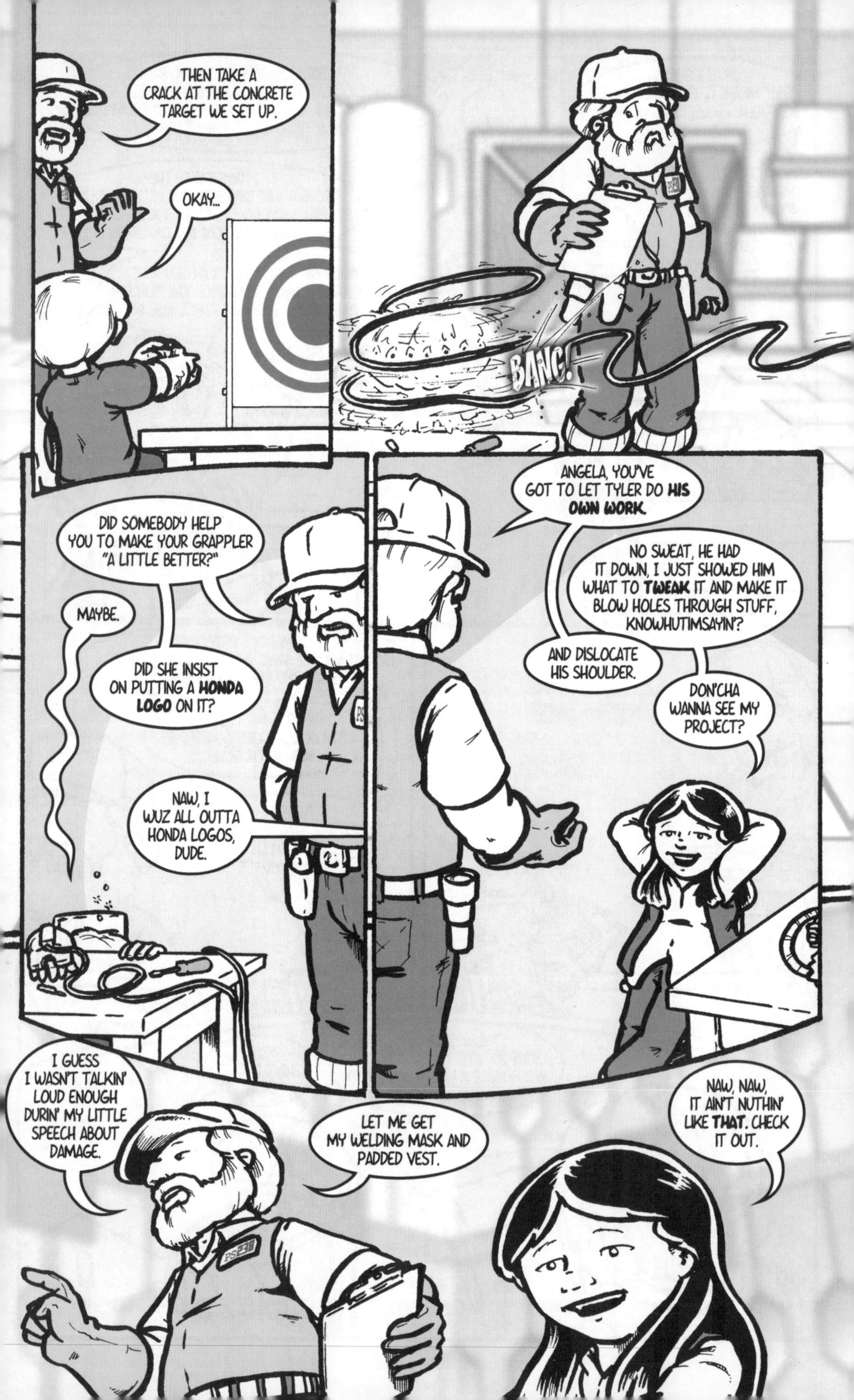
THEN TAKE A CRACK AT THE CONCRETE TARGET WE SET UP.
OKAY...
BANG!
DID SOMEBODY HELP YOU TO MAKE YOUR GRAPPLER "A LITTLE BETTER?"
MAYBE.
DID SHE INSIST ON PUTTING A HONDA LOGO ON IT?
NAW, I WUZ ALL OUTTA HONDA LOGOS, DUDE.
ANGELA, YOU'VE GOT TO LET TYLER DO HIS OWN WORK.
NO SWEAT, HE HAD IT DOWN, I JUST SHOWED HIM WHAT TO TWEAK IT AND MAKE IT BLOW HOLES THROUGH STUFF, KNOWHUTIMSAYIN'?
AND DISLOCATE HIS SHOULDER.
DON'CHA WANNA SEE MY PROJECT?
I GUESS I WASN'T TALKIN' LOUD ENOUGH DURIN' MY LITTLE SPEECH ABOUT DAMAGE.
LET ME GET MY WELDING MASK AND PADDED VEST.
NAW, NAW, IT AIN'T NUTHIN' LIKE THAT. CHECK IT OUT.

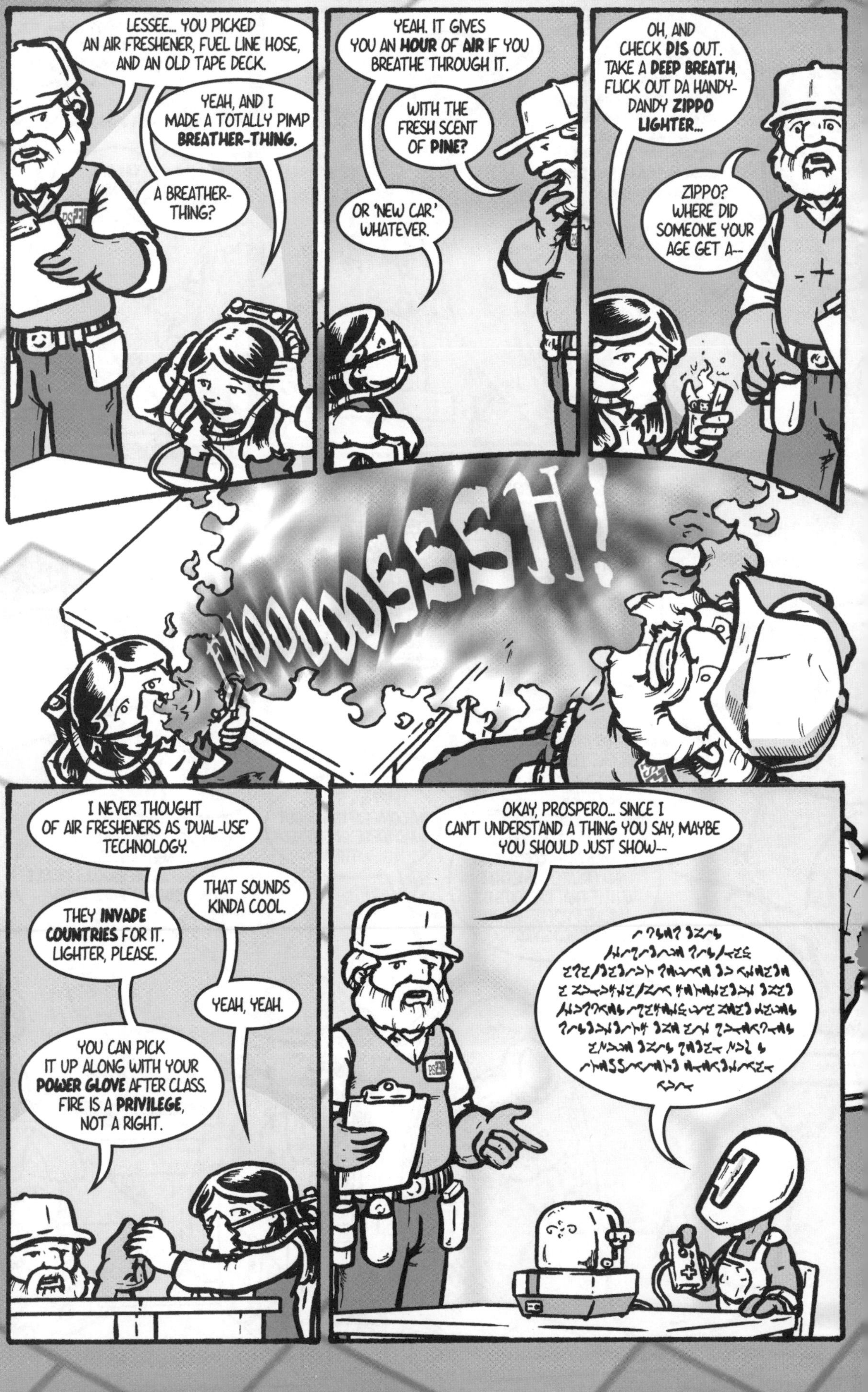
LESSEE... YOU PICKED AN AIR FRESHENER, FUEL LINE HOSE, AND AN OLD TAPE DECK.
YEAH, AND I MADE A TOTALLY PIMP **BREATHER-THING.**
A BREATHER-THING?
YEAH. IT GIVES YOU AN **HOUR** OF **AIR** IF YOU BREATHE THROUGH IT.
WITH THE FRESH SCENT OF **PINE?**
OR 'NEW CAR.' WHATEVER.
OH, AND CHECK **DIS** OUT. TAKE A **DEEP BREATH,** FLICK OUT DA HANDY-DANDY **ZIPPO LIGHTER...**
ZIPPO? WHERE DID SOMEONE YOUR AGE GET A--
FWOOOOOSSSH!
I NEVER THOUGHT OF AIR FRESHENERS AS 'DUAL-USE' TECHNOLOGY.
THAT SOUNDS KINDA COOL.
THEY **INVADE COUNTRIES** FOR IT. LIGHTER, PLEASE.
YEAH, YEAH.
YOU CAN PICK IT UP ALONG WITH YOUR **POWER GLOVE** AFTER CLASS. FIRE IS A **PRIVILEGE,** NOT A RIGHT.
OKAY, PROSPERO... SINCE I CAN'T UNDERSTAND A THING YOU SAY, MAYBE YOU SHOULD JUST SHOW--

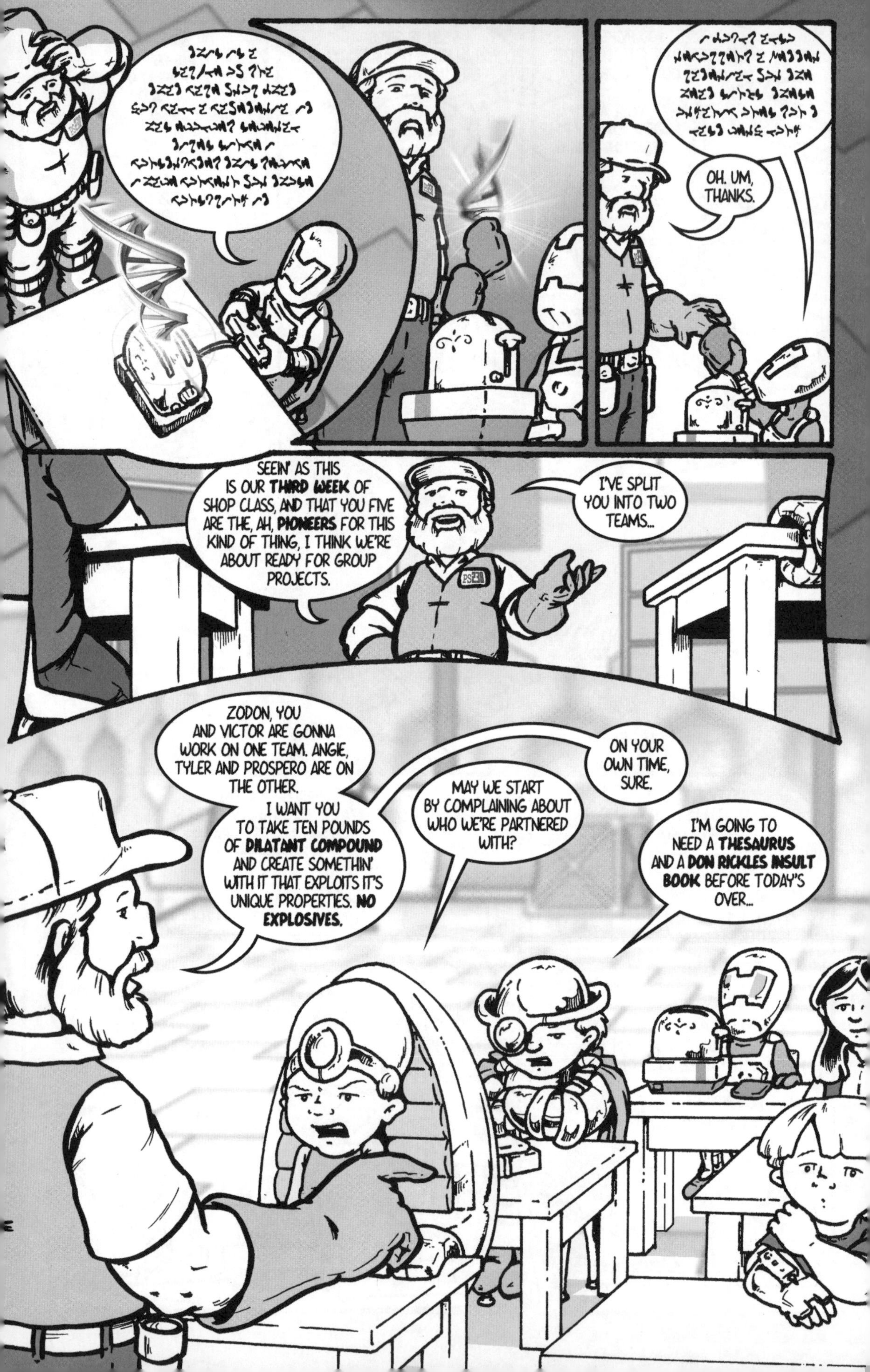
OH. UM, THANKS.
SEEIN' AS THIS IS OUR THIRD WEEK OF SHOP CLASS, AND THAT YOU FIVE ARE THE, AH, PIONEERS FOR THIS KIND OF THING, I THINK WE'RE ABOUT READY FOR GROUP PROJECTS.
I'VE SPLIT YOU INTO TWO TEAMS...
ZODON, YOU AND VICTOR ARE GONNA WORK ON ONE TEAM. ANGIE, TYLER AND PROSPERO ARE ON THE OTHER.
I WANT YOU TO TAKE TEN POUNDS OF DILATANT COMPOUND AND CREATE SOMETHIN' WITH IT THAT EXPLOITS IT'S UNIQUE PROPERTIES. NO EXPLOSIVES.
MAY WE START BY COMPLAINING ABOUT WHO WE'RE PARTNERED WITH?
ON YOUR OWN TIME, SURE.
I'M GOING TO NEED A THESAURUS AND A DON RICKLES INSULT BOOK BEFORE TODAY'S OVER...

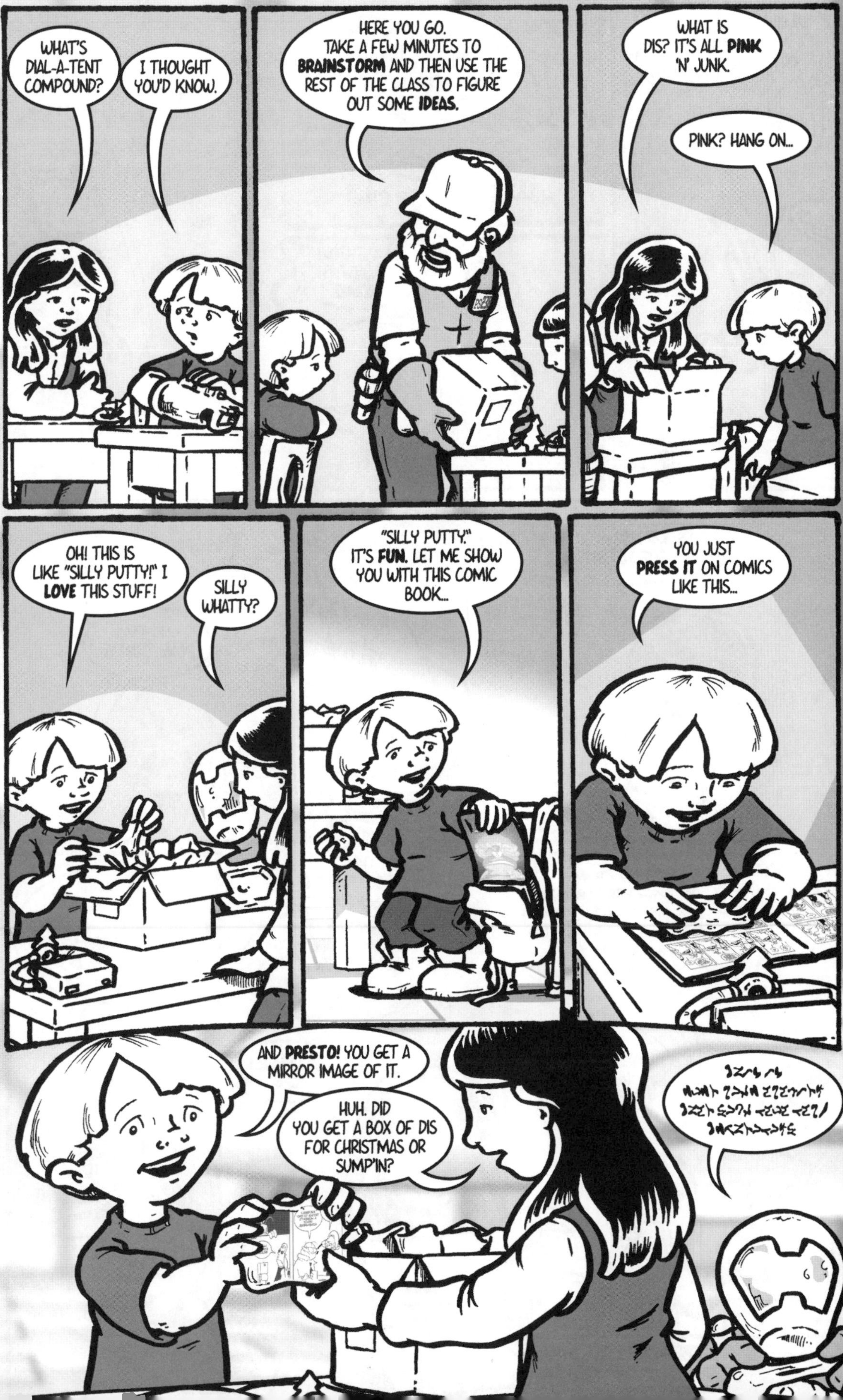
WHAT'S DIAL-A-TENT COMPOUND?
I THOUGHT YOU'D KNOW.
HERE YOU GO. TAKE A FEW MINUTES TO BRAINSTORM AND THEN USE THE REST OF THE CLASS TO FIGURE OUT SOME IDEAS.
WHAT IS DIS? IT'S ALL PINK 'N' JUNK.
PINK? HANG ON...
OH! THIS IS LIKE "SILLY PUTTY!" I LOVE THIS STUFF!
SILLY WHATTY?
"SILLY PUTTY." IT'S FUN. LET ME SHOW YOU WITH THIS COMIC BOOK...
YOU JUST PRESS IT ON COMICS LIKE THIS...
AND PRESTO! YOU GET A MIRROR IMAGE OF IT.
HUH. DID YOU GET A BOX OF DIS FOR CHRISTMAS OR SUMP'IN?

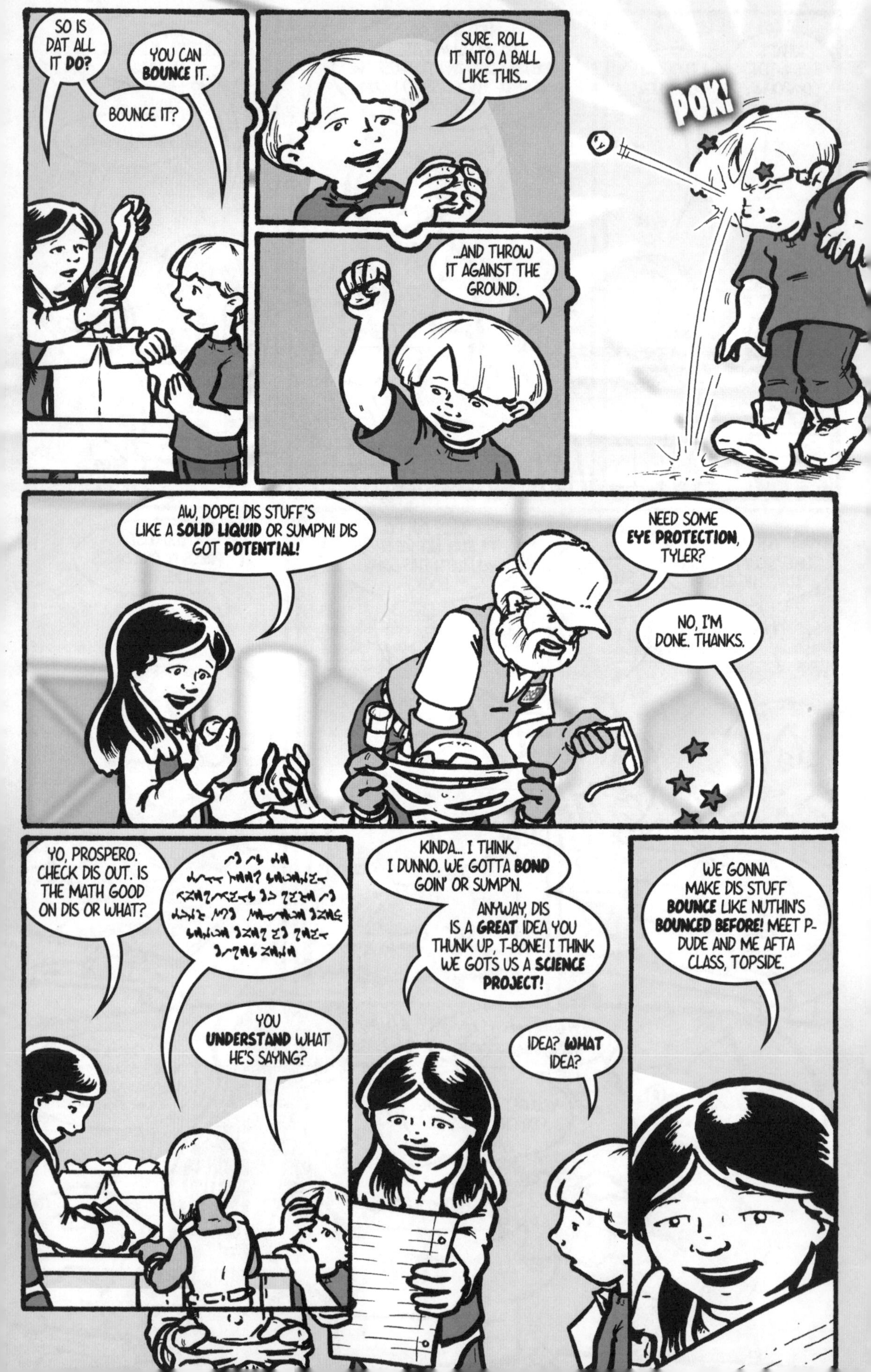
SO IS DAT ALL IT DO?
YOU CAN BOUNCE IT.
BOUNCE IT?
SURE. ROLL IT INTO A BALL LIKE THIS...
...AND THROW IT AGAINST THE GROUND.
POK!
AW, DOPE! DIS STUFF'S LIKE A SOLID LIQUID OR SUMP'N! DIS GOT POTENTIAL!
NEED SOME EYE PROTECTION, TYLER?
NO, I'M DONE. THANKS.
YO, PROSPERO. CHECK DIS OUT. IS THE MATH GOOD ON DIS OR WHAT?
YOU UNDERSTAND WHAT HE'S SAYING?
KINDA... I THINK. I DUNNO. WE GOTTA BOND GOIN' OR SUMP'N.
ANYWAY, DIS IS A GREAT IDEA YOU THUNK UP, T-BONE! I THINK WE GOTS US A SCIENCE PROJECT!
IDEA? WHAT IDEA?
WE GONNA MAKE DIS STUFF BOUNCE LIKE NUTHIN'S BOUNCED BEFORE! MEET P-DUDE AND ME AFTA CLASS, TOPSIDE.

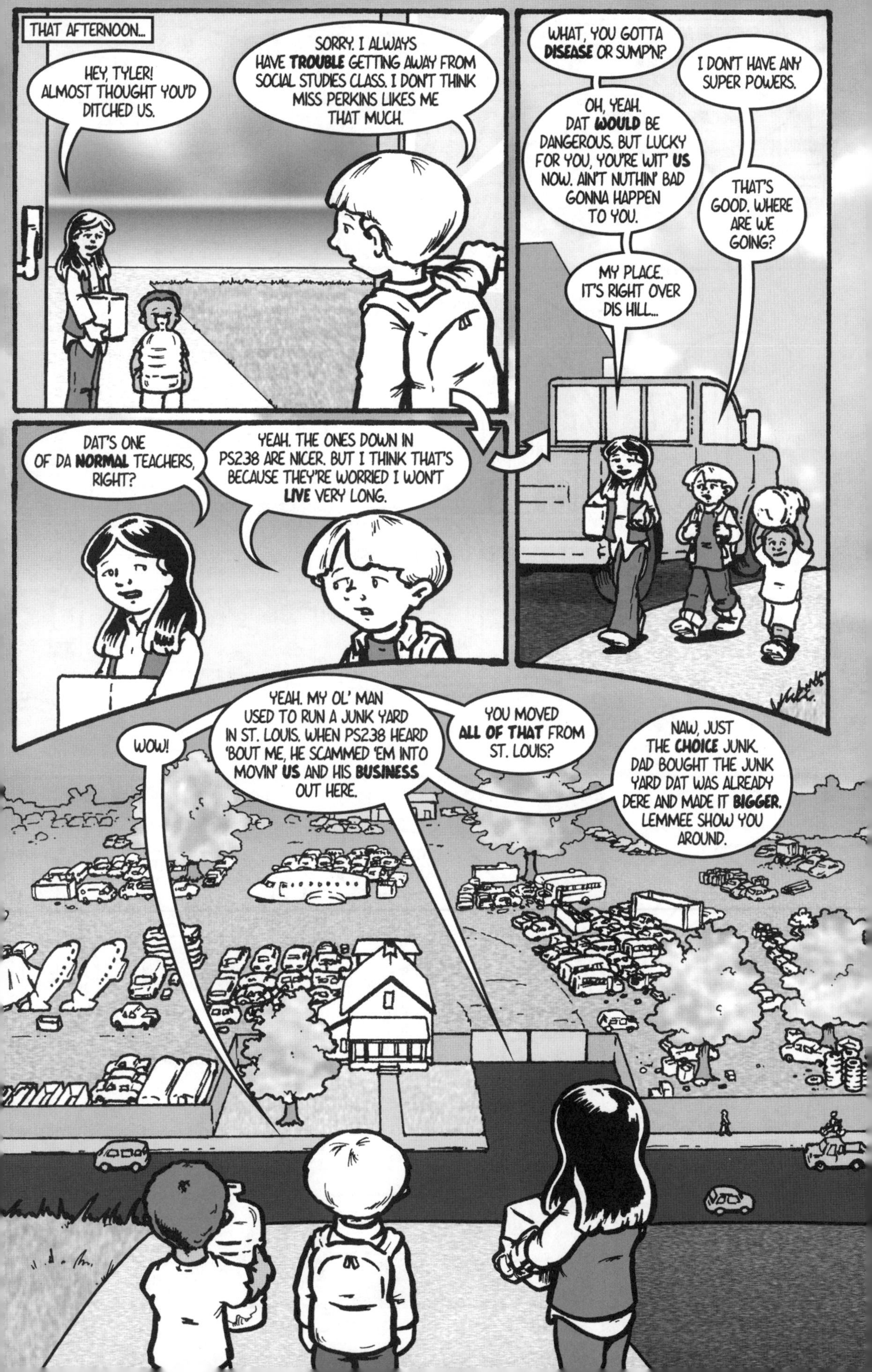
THAT AFTERNOON...
HEY, TYLER! ALMOST THOUGHT YOU'D DITCHED US.
SORRY. I ALWAYS HAVE TROUBLE GETTING AWAY FROM SOCIAL STUDIES CLASS. I DON'T THINK MISS PERKINS LIKES ME THAT MUCH.
DAT'S ONE OF DA NORMAL TEACHERS, RIGHT?
YEAH. THE ONES DOWN IN PS238 ARE NICER. BUT I THINK THAT'S BECAUSE THEY'RE WORRIED I WON'T LIVE VERY LONG.
WHAT, YOU GOTTA DISEASE OR SUMP'N?
I DON'T HAVE ANY SUPER POWERS.
OH, YEAH. DAT WOULD BE DANGEROUS. BUT LUCKY FOR YOU, YOU'RE WIT' US NOW. AIN'T NUTHIN' BAD GONNA HAPPEN TO YOU.
THAT'S GOOD. WHERE ARE WE GOING?
MY PLACE. IT'S RIGHT OVER DIS HILL...
WOW!
YEAH. MY OL' MAN USED TO RUN A JUNK YARD IN ST. LOUIS. WHEN PS238 HEARD 'BOUT ME, HE SCAMMED 'EM INTO MOVIN' US AND HIS BUSINESS OUT HERE.
YOU MOVED ALL OF THAT FROM ST. LOUIS?
NAW, JUST THE CHOICE JUNK. DAD BOUGHT THE JUNK YARD DAT WAS ALREADY DERE AND MADE IT BIGGER. LEMMEE SHOW YOU AROUND.

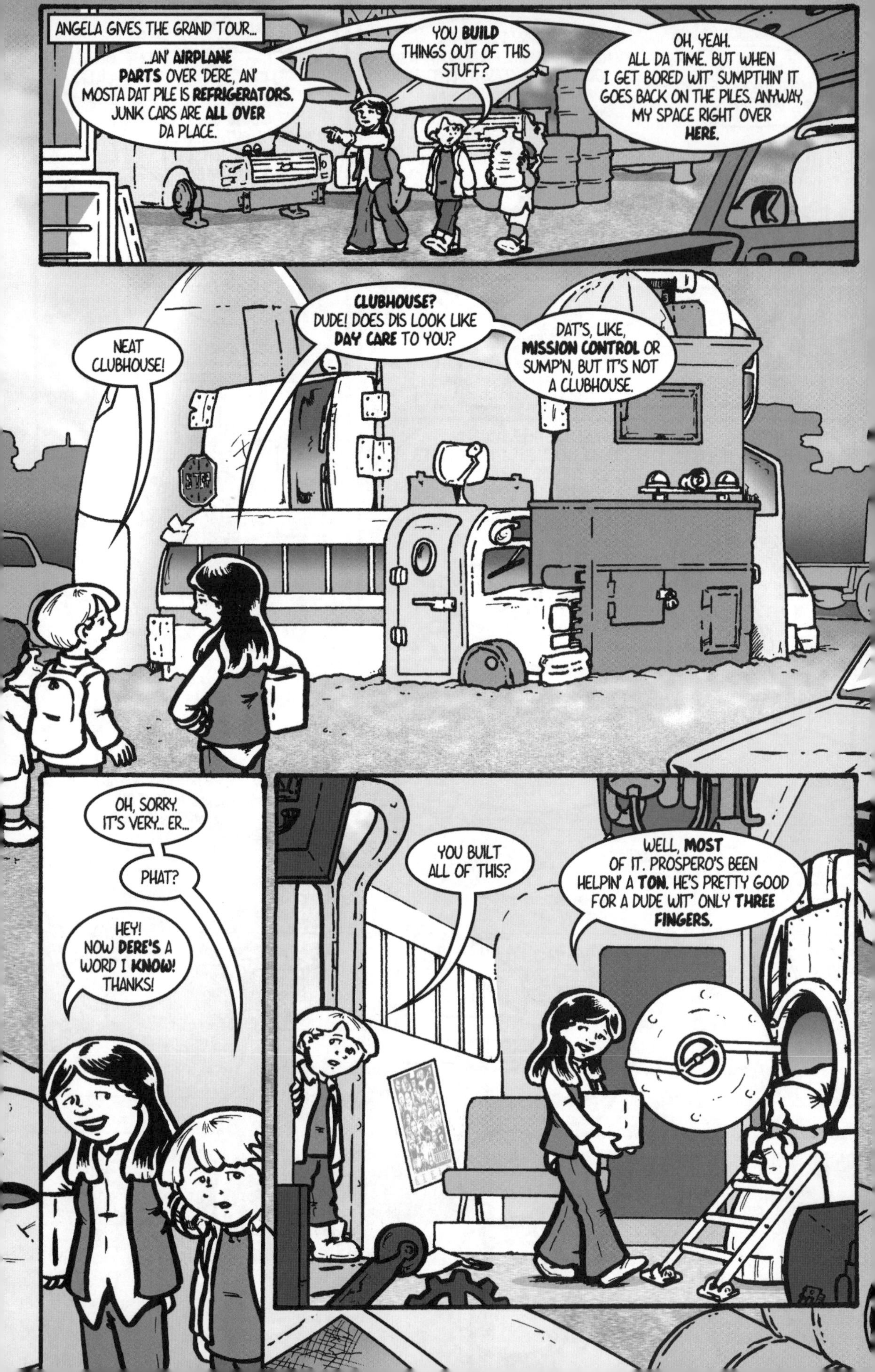
ANGELA GIVES THE GRAND TOUR...
...AN' AIRPLANE PARTS OVER 'DERE, AN' MOSTA DAT PILE IS REFRIGERATORS. JUNK CARS ARE ALL OVER DA PLACE.
YOU BUILD THINGS OUT OF THIS STUFF?
OH, YEAH. ALL DA TIME. BUT WHEN I GET BORED WIT' SUMPTHIN' IT GOES BACK ON THE PILES. ANYWAY, MY SPACE RIGHT OVER HERE.
NEAT CLUBHOUSE!
CLUBHOUSE? DUDE! DOES DIS LOOK LIKE DAY CARE TO YOU?
DAT'S, LIKE, MISSION CONTROL OR SUMP'N, BUT IT'S NOT A CLUBHOUSE.
OH, SORRY. IT'S VERY... ER...
PHAT?
HEY! NOW DERE'S A WORD I KNOW! THANKS!
YOU BUILT ALL OF THIS?
WELL, MOST OF IT. PROSPERO'S BEEN HELPIN' A TON. HE'S PRETTY GOOD FOR A DUDE WIT' ONLY THREE FINGERS.

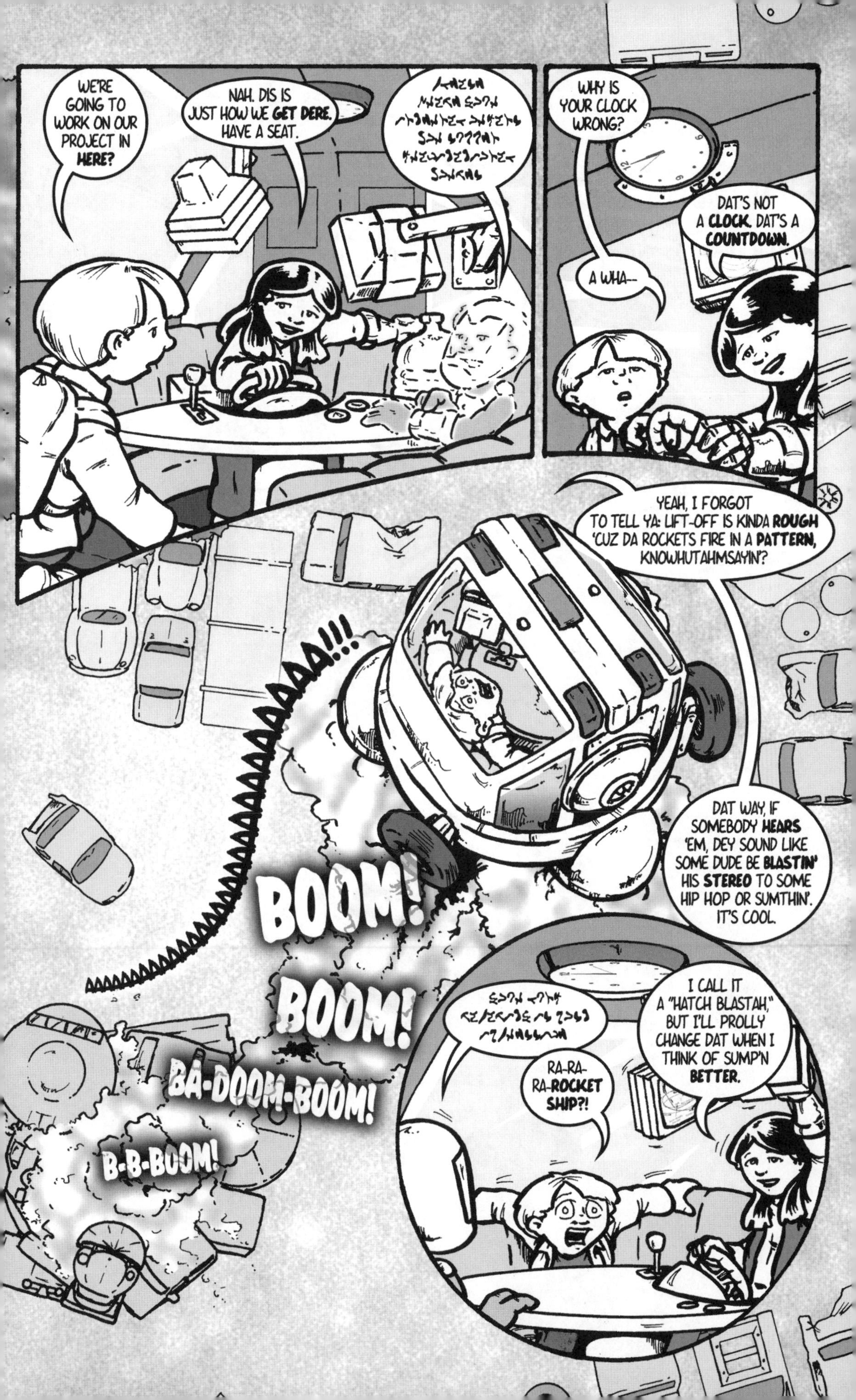
WE'RE GOING TO WORK ON OUR PROJECT IN HERE?
NAH. DIS IS JUST HOW WE GET DERE. HAVE A SEAT.
WHY IS YOUR CLOCK WRONG?
DAT'S NOT A CLOCK. DAT'S A COUNTDOWN.
A WHA--
YEAH, I FORGOT TO TELL YA: LIFT-OFF IS KINDA ROUGH 'CUZ DA ROCKETS FIRE IN A PATTERN, KNOWHUTAHMSAYIN'?
AAAAAAAAAAAAAAAAAAAAAAAAAAAAAAAAAAAA!!!
DAT WAY, IF SOMEBODY HEARS 'EM, DEY SOUND LIKE SOME DUDE BE BLASTIN' HIS STEREO TO SOME HIP HOP OR SUMTHIN'. IT'S COOL.
BOOM!
BOOM!
BA-DOOM-BOOM!
B-B-BOOM!
RA-RA-RA-ROCKET SHIP?!
I CALL IT A "HATCH BLASTAH," BUT I'LL PROLLY CHANGE DAT WHEN I THINK OF SUMP'N BETTER.

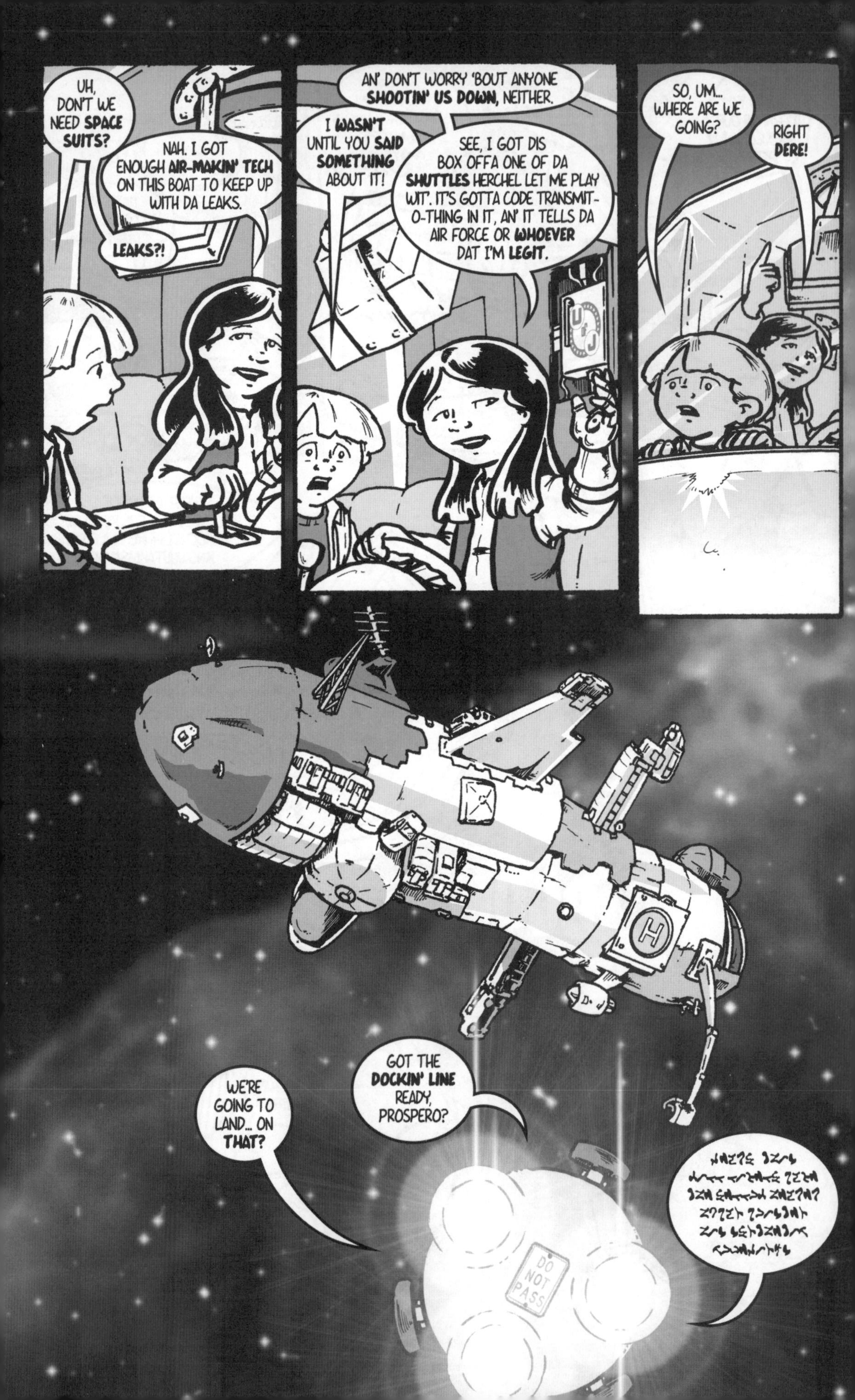
UH, DON'T WE NEED SPACE SUITS?
NAH. I GOT ENOUGH AIR-MAKIN' TECH ON THIS BOAT TO KEEP UP WITH DA LEAKS.
LEAKS?!
AN' DON'T WORRY 'BOUT ANYONE SHOOTIN' US DOWN, NEITHER.
I WASN'T UNTIL YOU SAID SOMETHING ABOUT IT!
SEE, I GOT DIS BOX OFFA ONE OF DA SHUTTLES HERCHEL LET ME PLAY WIT'. IT'S GOTTA CODE TRANSMIT-O-THING IN IT, AN' IT TELLS DA AIR FORCE OR WHOEVER DAT I'M LEGIT.
SO, UM... WHERE ARE WE GOING?
RIGHT DERE!
WE'RE GOING TO LAND... ON THAT?
GOT THE DOCKIN' LINE READY, PROSPERO?
DO NOT PASS

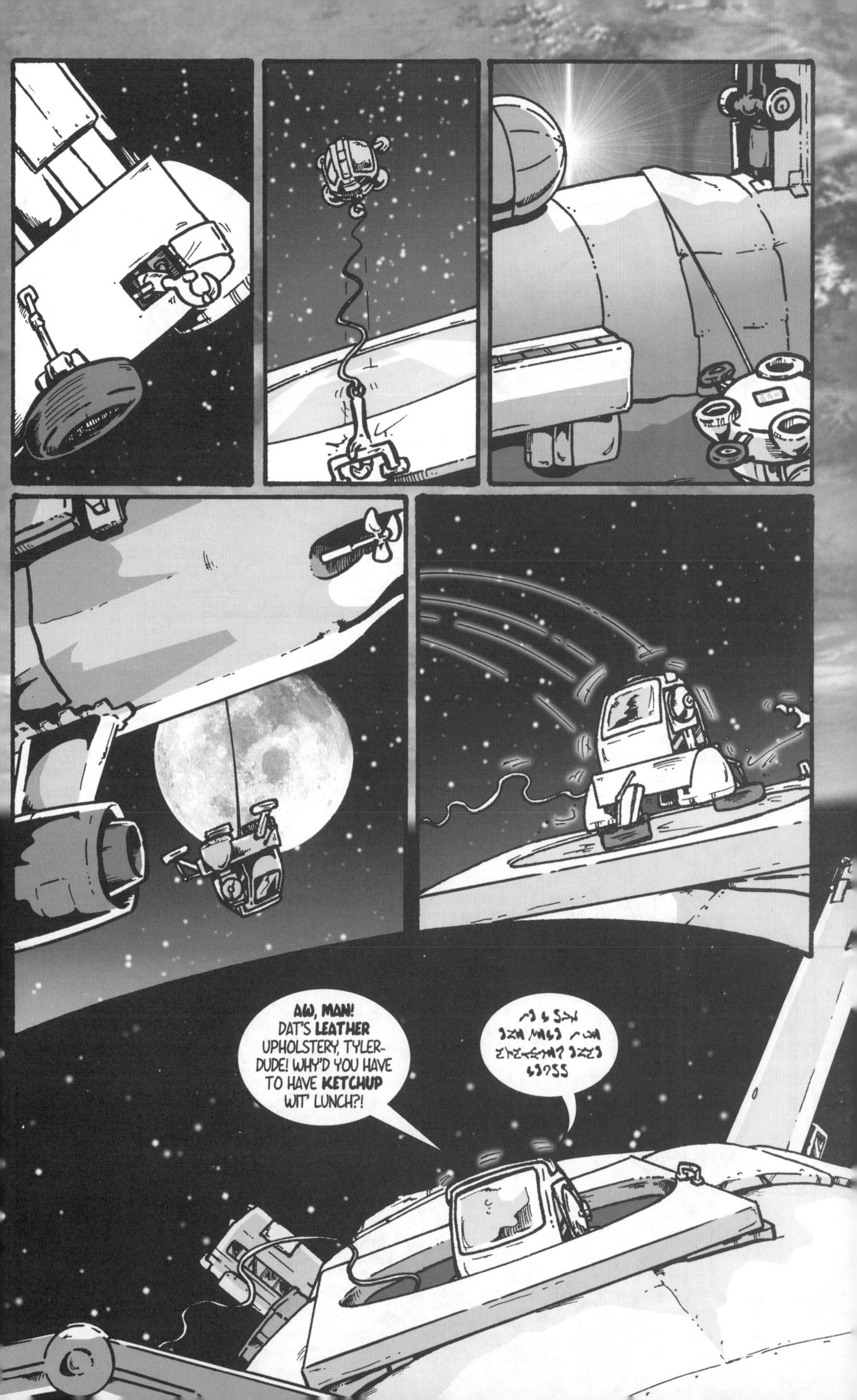
AW, MAN! DAT'S LEATHER UPHOLSTERY, TYLER-DUDE! WHY'D YOU HAVE TO HAVE KETCHUP WIT' LUNCH?!

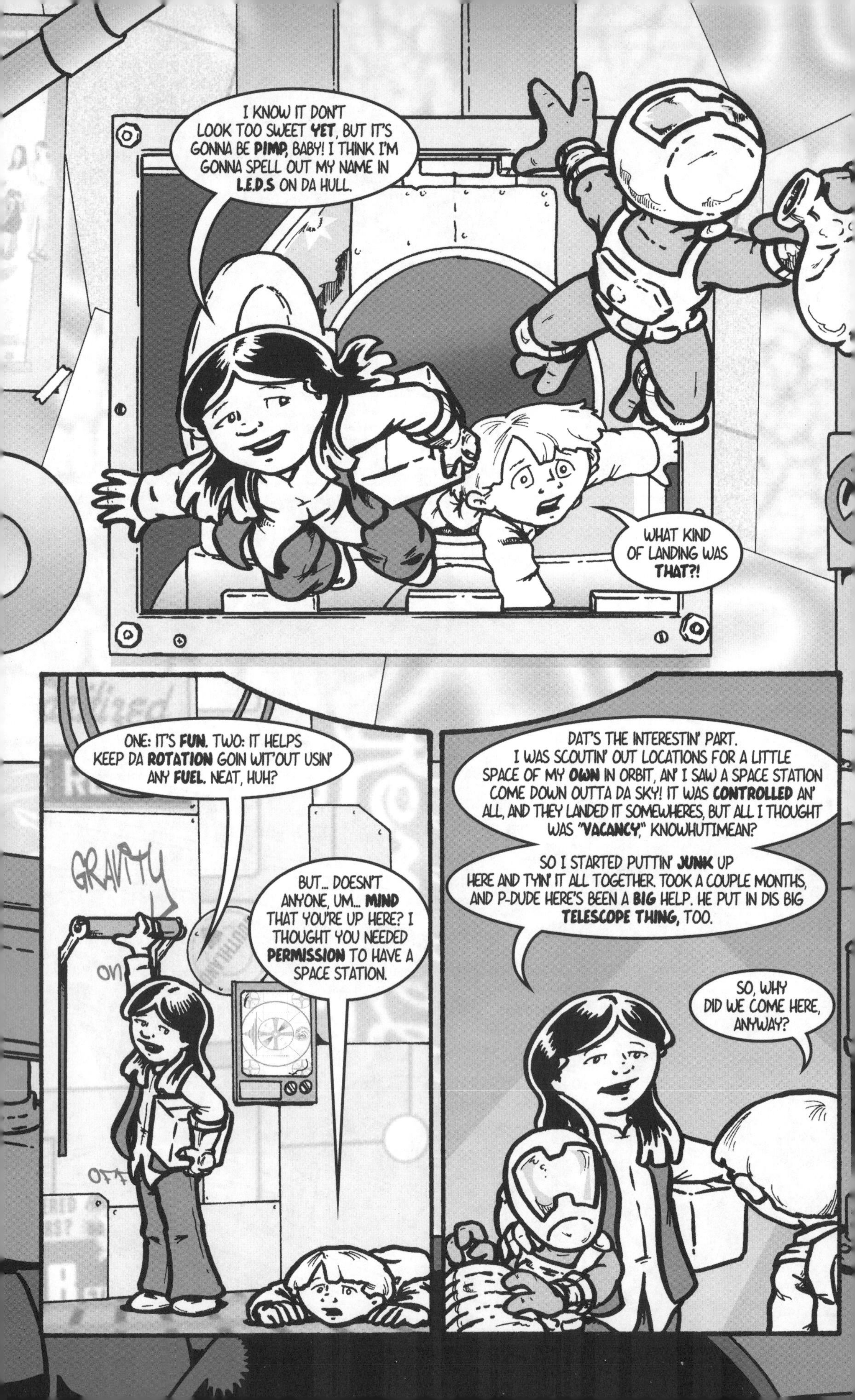

I KNOW IT DON'T LOOK TOO SWEET YET, BUT IT'S GONNA BE PIMP, BABY! I THINK I'M GONNA SPELL OUT MY NAME IN L.E.D.S ON DA HULL.
WHAT KIND OF LANDING WAS THAT?!
ONE: IT'S FUN. TWO: IT HELPS KEEP DA ROTATION GOIN WIT'OUT USIN' ANY FUEL. NEAT, HUH?
GRAVITY
ON
OFF
BUT... DOESN'T ANYONE, UM... MIND THAT YOU'RE UP HERE? I THOUGHT YOU NEEDED PERMISSION TO HAVE A SPACE STATION.
DAT'S THE INTERESTIN' PART. I WAS SCOUTIN' OUT LOCATIONS FOR A LITTLE SPACE OF MY OWN IN ORBIT, AN' I SAW A SPACE STATION COME DOWN OUTTA DA SKY! IT WAS CONTROLLED AN' ALL, AND THEY LANDED IT SOMEWHERES, BUT ALL I THOUGHT WAS "VACANCY," KNOWHUTIMEAN?
SO I STARTED PUTTIN' JUNK UP HERE AND TYIN' IT ALL TOGETHER. TOOK A COUPLE MONTHS, AND P-DUDE HERE'S BEEN A BIG HELP. HE PUT IN DIS BIG TELESCOPE THING, TOO.
SO, WHY DID WE COME HERE, ANYWAY?

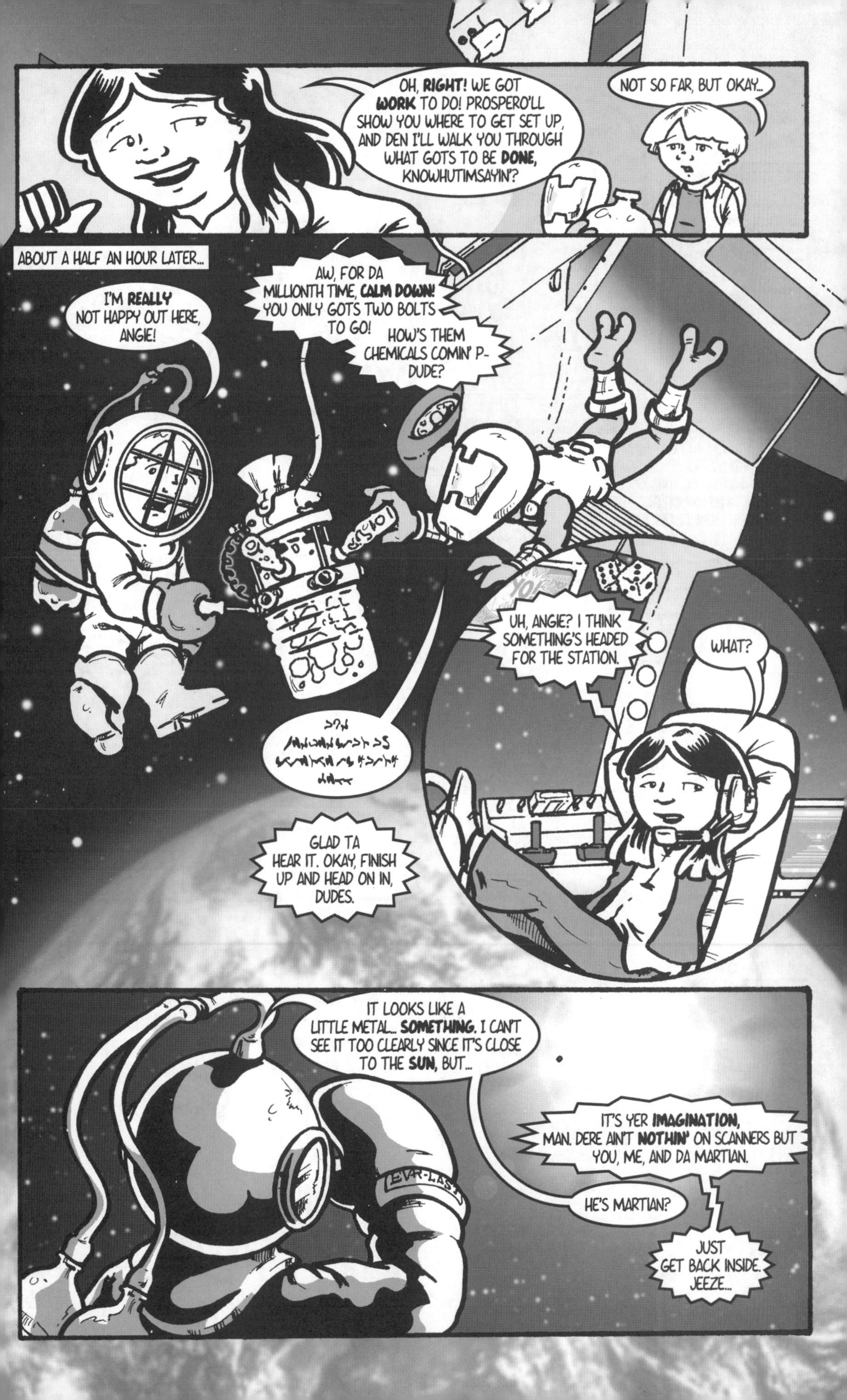
OH, RIGHT! WE GOT WORK TO DO! PROSPERO'LL SHOW YOU WHERE TO GET SET UP, AND DEN I'LL WALK YOU THROUGH WHAT GOTS TO BE DONE, KNOWHUTIMSAYIN'?
NOT SO FAR, BUT OKAY...
ABOUT A HALF AN HOUR LATER...
I'M REALLY NOT HAPPY OUT HERE, ANGIE!
AW, FOR DA MILLIONTH TIME, CALM DOWN! YOU ONLY GOTS TWO BOLTS TO GO!
HOW'S THEM CHEMICALS COMIN' P-DUDE?
UH, ANGIE? I THINK SOMETHING'S HEADED FOR THE STATION.
WHAT?
GLAD TA HEAR IT. OKAY, FINISH UP AND HEAD ON IN, DUDES.
IT LOOKS LIKE A LITTLE METAL... SOMETHING. I CAN'T SEE IT TOO CLEARLY SINCE IT'S CLOSE TO THE SUN, BUT...
IT'S YER IMAGINATION, MAN. DERE AIN'T NOTHIN' ON SCANNERS BUT YOU, ME, AND DA MARTIAN.
HE'S MARTIAN?
JUST GET BACK INSIDE. JEEZE...

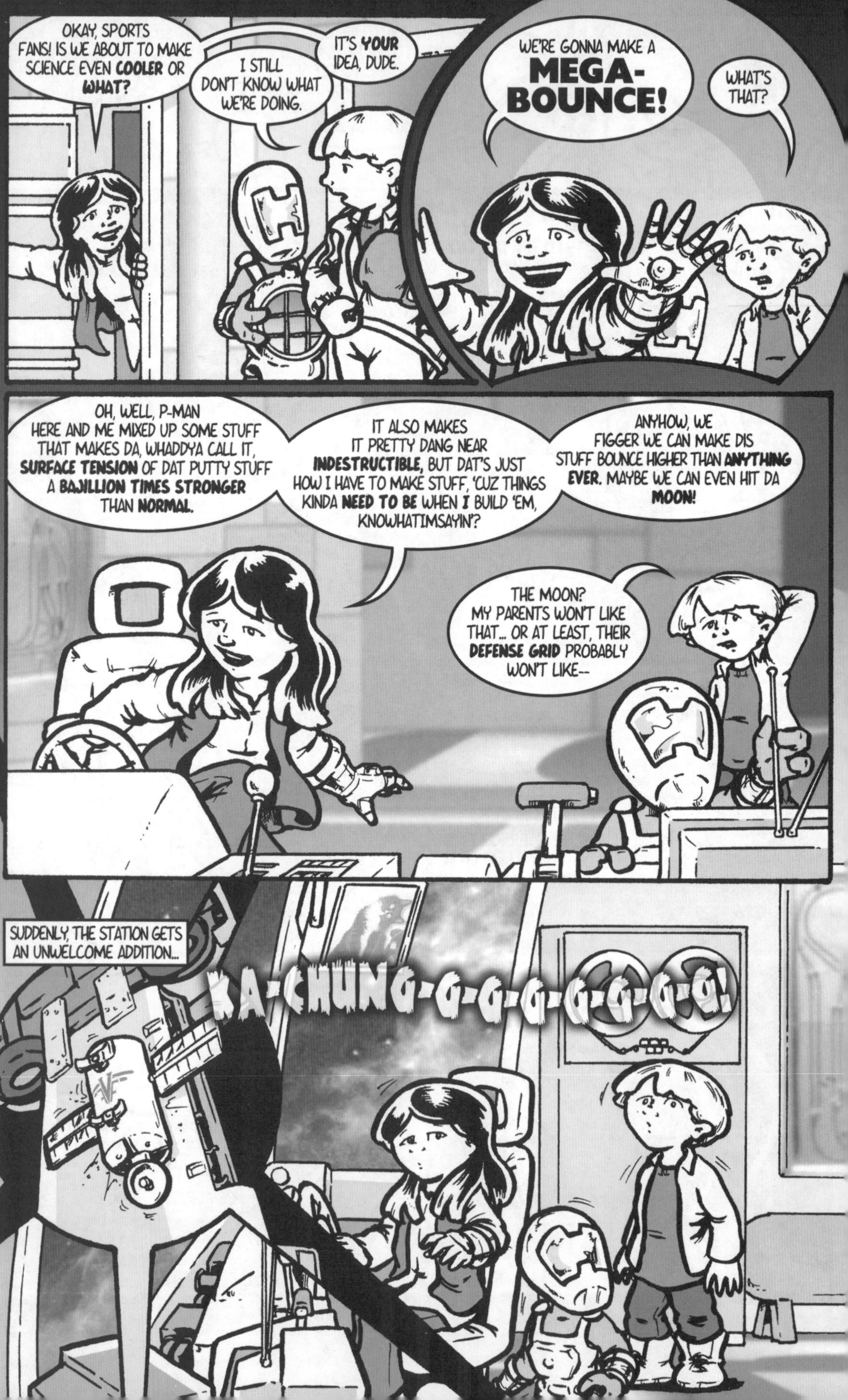

OKAY, SPORTS FANS! IS WE ABOUT TO MAKE SCIENCE EVEN COOLER OR WHAT?
I STILL DON'T KNOW WHAT WE'RE DOING.
IT'S YOUR IDEA, DUDE.
WE'RE GONNA MAKE A MEGA-BOUNCE!
WHAT'S THAT?
OH, WELL, P-MAN HERE AND ME MIXED UP SOME STUFF THAT MAKES DA, WHADDYA CALL IT, SURFACE TENSION OF DAT PUTTY STUFF A BAJILLION TIMES STRONGER THAN NORMAL.
IT ALSO MAKES IT PRETTY DANG NEAR INDESTRUCTIBLE, BUT DAT'S JUST HOW I HAVE TO MAKE STUFF, 'CUZ THINGS KINDA NEED TO BE WHEN I BUILD 'EM, KNOWHATIMSAYIN'?
ANYHOW, WE FIGGER WE CAN MAKE DIS STUFF BOUNCE HIGHER THAN ANYTHING EVER. MAYBE WE CAN EVEN HIT DA MOON!
THE MOON? MY PARENTS WON'T LIKE THAT... OR AT LEAST, THEIR DEFENSE GRID PROBABLY WON'T LIKE--
SUDDENLY, THE STATION GETS AN UNWELCOME ADDITION...
KA-CHUNG-G-G-G-G-G-G-G!

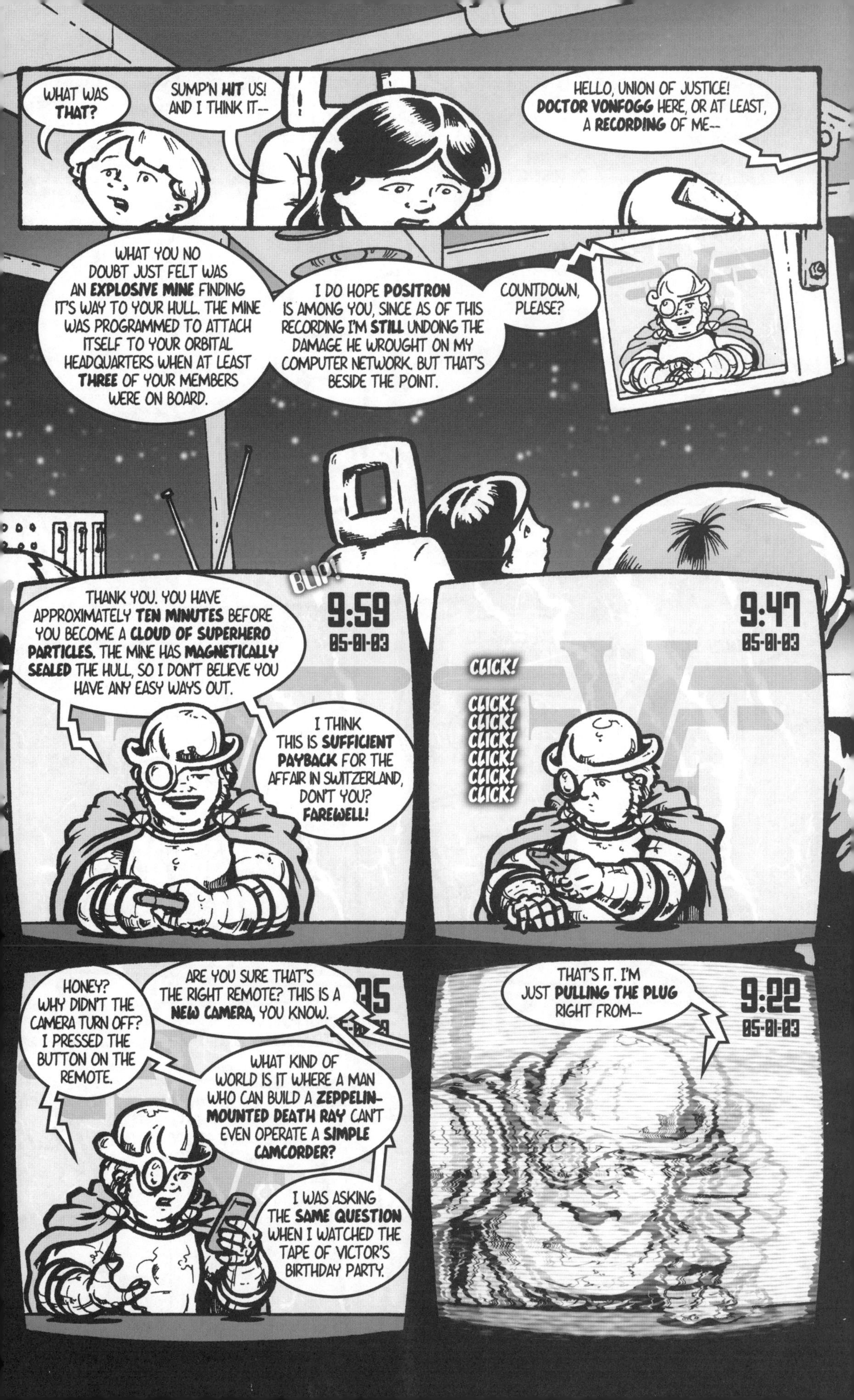
WHAT WAS THAT?
SUMP'N HIT US! AND I THINK IT--
HELLO, UNION OF JUSTICE! DOCTOR VONFOGG HERE, OR AT LEAST, A RECORDING OF ME--
WHAT YOU NO DOUBT JUST FELT WAS AN EXPLOSIVE MINE FINDING IT'S WAY TO YOUR HULL. THE MINE WAS PROGRAMMED TO ATTACH ITSELF TO YOUR ORBITAL HEADQUARTERS WHEN AT LEAST THREE OF YOUR MEMBERS WERE ON BOARD.
I DO HOPE POSITRON IS AMONG YOU, SINCE AS OF THIS RECORDING I'M STILL UNDOING THE DAMAGE HE WROUGHT ON MY COMPUTER NETWORK. BUT THAT'S BESIDE THE POINT.
COUNTDOWN, PLEASE?
BLIP!
9:59
05-01-03
THANK YOU. YOU HAVE APPROXIMATELY TEN MINUTES BEFORE YOU BECOME A CLOUD OF SUPERHERO PARTICLES. THE MINE HAS MAGNETICALLY SEALED THE HULL, SO I DON'T BELIEVE YOU HAVE ANY EASY WAYS OUT.
I THINK THIS IS SUFFICIENT PAYBACK FOR THE AFFAIR IN SWITZERLAND, DON'T YOU? FAREWELL!
9:47
05-01-03
CLICK!
CLICK! CLICK! CLICK! CLICK! CLICK! CLICK!
HONEY? WHY DIDN'T THE CAMERA TURN OFF? I PRESSED THE BUTTON ON THE REMOTE.
ARE YOU SURE THAT'S THE RIGHT REMOTE? THIS IS A NEW CAMERA, YOU KNOW.
WHAT KIND OF WORLD IS IT WHERE A MAN WHO CAN BUILD A ZEPPELIN-MOUNTED DEATH RAY CAN'T EVEN OPERATE A SIMPLE CAMCORDER?
I WAS ASKING THE SAME QUESTION WHEN I WATCHED THE TAPE OF VICTOR'S BIRTHDAY PARTY.
THAT'S IT. I'M JUST PULLING THE PLUG RIGHT FROM--
9:22
05-01-03

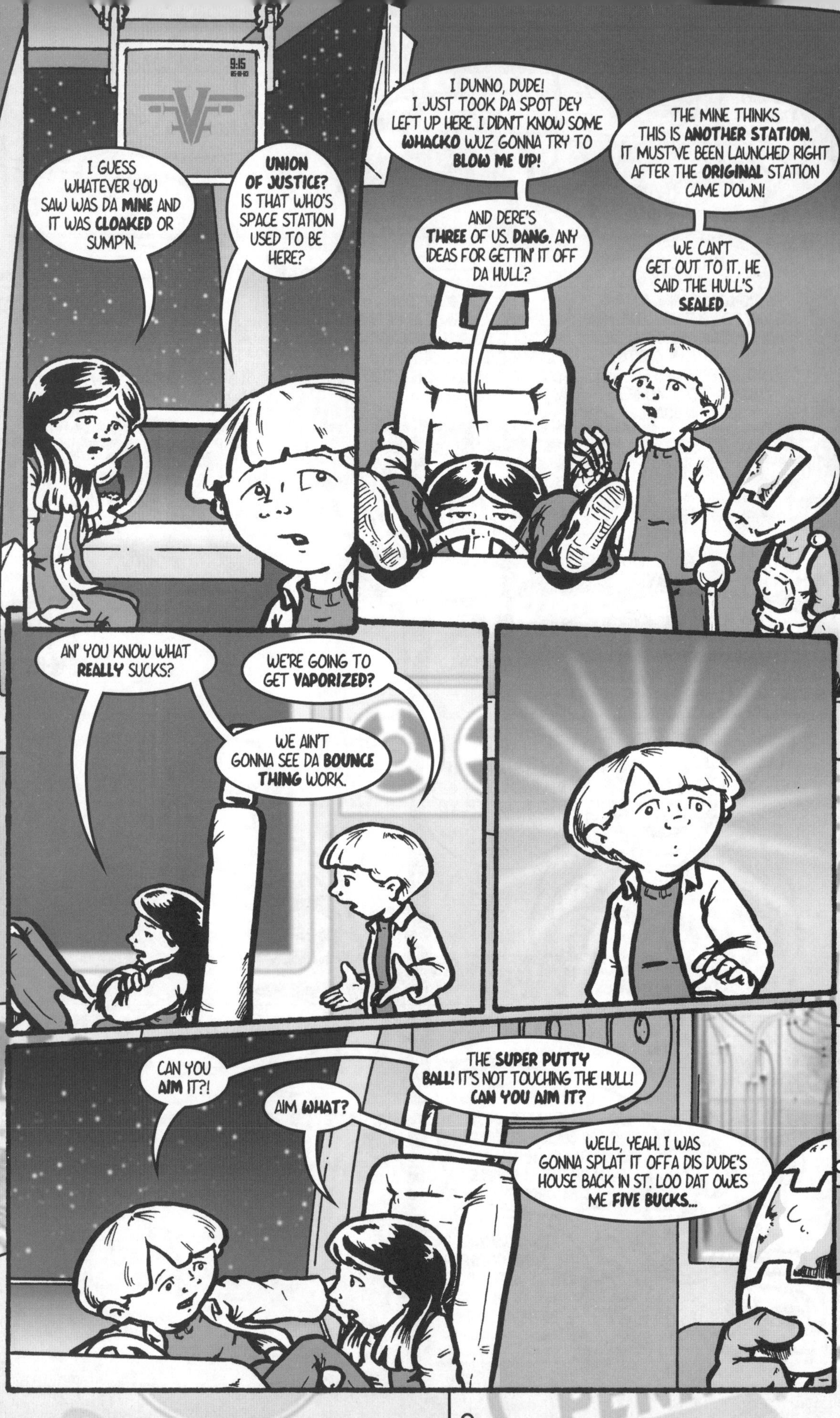
9:15
I GUESS WHATEVER YOU SAW WAS DA MINE AND IT WAS CLOAKED OR SUMP'N.
UNION OF JUSTICE? IS THAT WHO'S SPACE STATION USED TO BE HERE?
I DUNNO, DUDE! I JUST TOOK DA SPOT DEY LEFT UP HERE. I DIDN'T KNOW SOME WHACKO WUZ GONNA TRY TO BLOW ME UP!
AND DERE'S THREE OF US. DANG. ANY IDEAS FOR GETTIN' IT OFF DA HULL?
THE MINE THINKS THIS IS ANOTHER STATION. IT MUST'VE BEEN LAUNCHED RIGHT AFTER THE ORIGINAL STATION CAME DOWN!
WE CAN'T GET OUT TO IT. HE SAID THE HULL'S SEALED.
AN' YOU KNOW WHAT REALLY SUCKS?
WE'RE GOING TO GET VAPORIZED?
WE AIN'T GONNA SEE DA BOUNCE THING WORK.
CAN YOU AIM IT?!
THE SUPER PUTTY BALL! IT'S NOT TOUCHING THE HULL! CAN YOU AIM IT?
AIM WHAT?
WELL, YEAH. I WAS GONNA SPLAT IT OFFA DIS DUDE'S HOUSE BACK IN ST. LOO DAT OWES ME FIVE BUCKS...

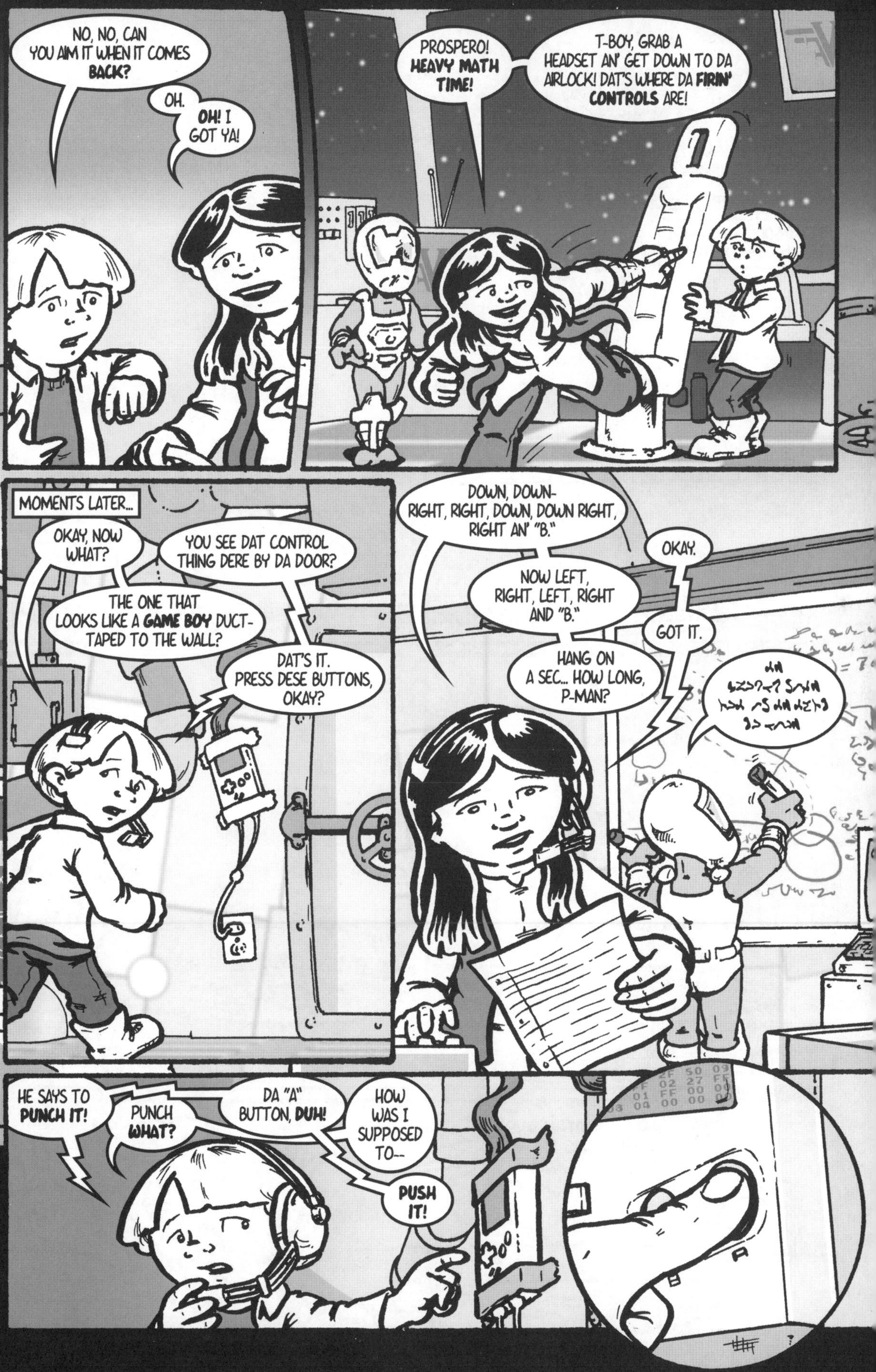
NO, NO, CAN YOU AIM IT WHEN IT COMES BACK?
OH.
OH! I GOT YA!
PROSPERO! HEAVY MATH TIME!
T-BOY, GRAB A HEADSET AN' GET DOWN TO DA AIRLOCK! DAT'S WHERE DA FIRIN' CONTROLS ARE!
MOMENTS LATER...
OKAY, NOW WHAT?
YOU SEE DAT CONTROL THING DERE BY DA DOOR?
THE ONE THAT LOOKS LIKE A GAME BOY DUCT-TAPED TO THE WALL?
DAT'S IT. PRESS DESE BUTTONS, OKAY?
DOWN, DOWN-RIGHT, RIGHT, DOWN, DOWN RIGHT, RIGHT AN' "B."
OKAY.
NOW LEFT, RIGHT, LEFT, RIGHT AND "B."
GOT IT.
HANG ON A SEC... HOW LONG, P-MAN?
HE SAYS TO PUNCH IT!
PUNCH WHAT?
DA "A" BUTTON, DUH!
HOW WAS I SUPPOSED TO--
PUSH IT!

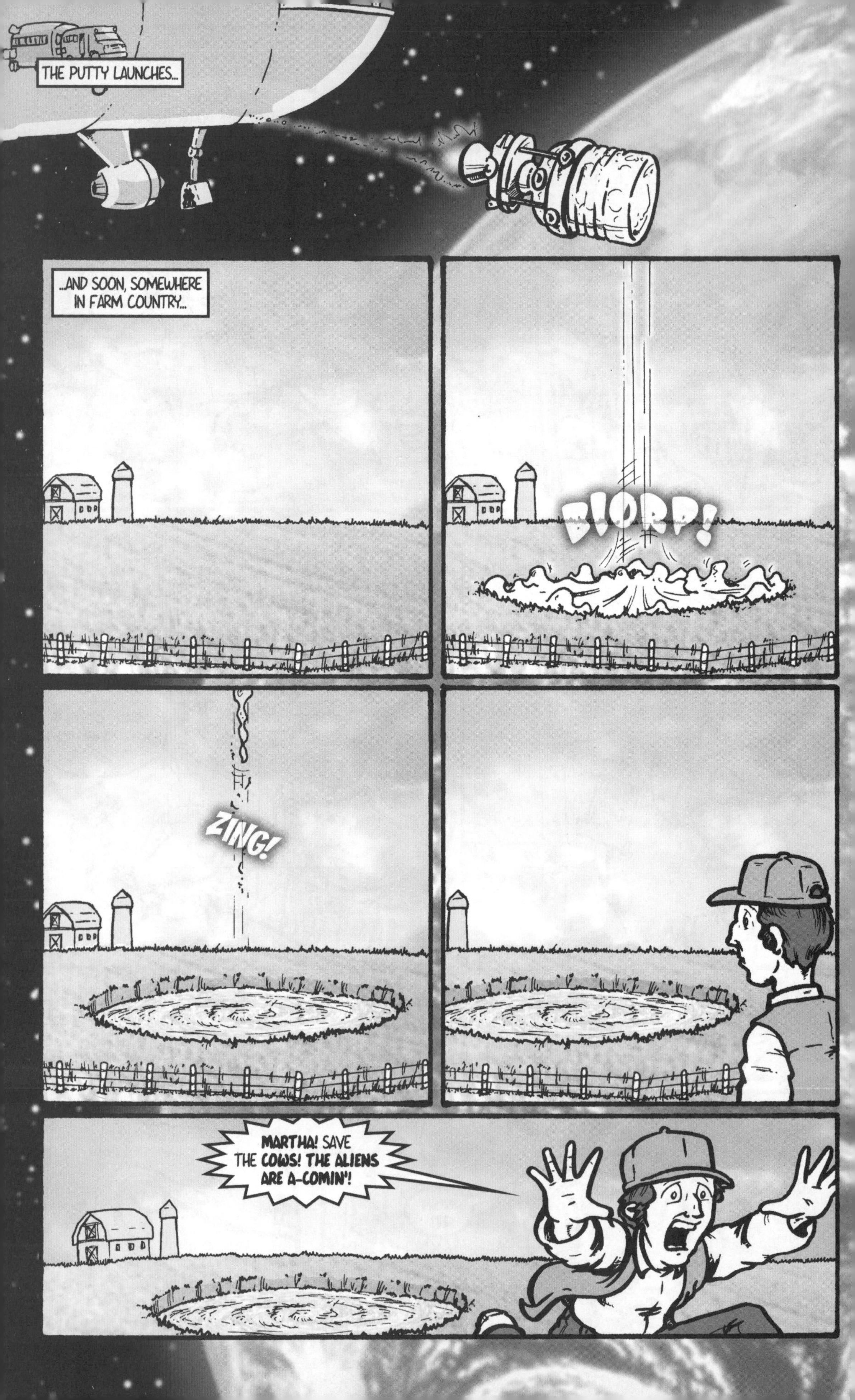
THE PUTTY LAUNCHES...
...AND SOON, SOMEWHERE IN FARM COUNTRY...
BLORP!
ZING!
MARTHA! SAVE THE COWS! THE ALIENS ARE A-COMIN'!

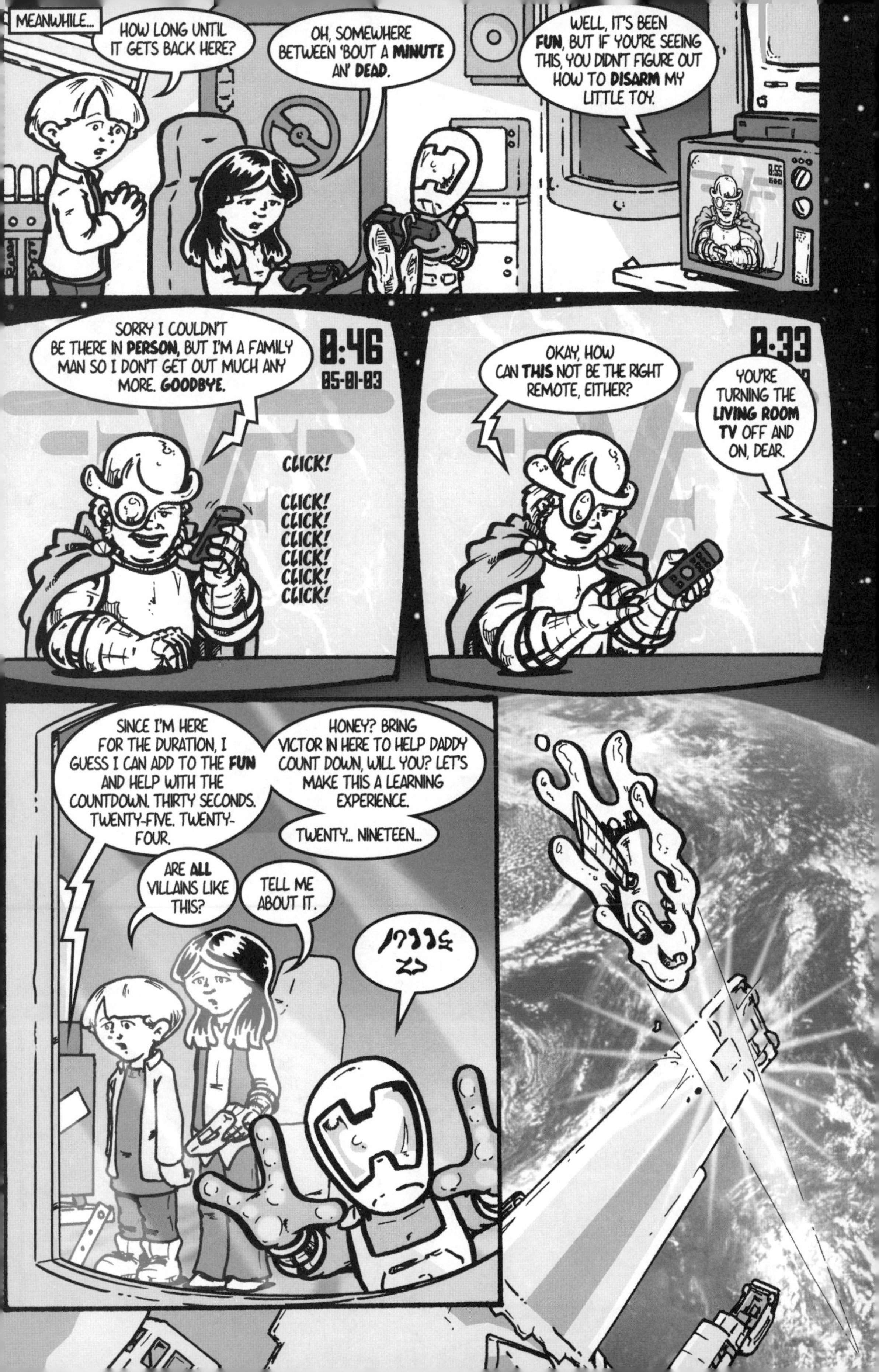
MEANWHILE...
HOW LONG UNTIL IT GETS BACK HERE?
OH, SOMEWHERE BETWEEN 'BOUT A **MINUTE** AN' **DEAD**.
WELL, IT'S BEEN **FUN**, BUT IF YOU'RE SEEING THIS, YOU DIDN'T FIGURE OUT HOW TO **DISARM** MY LITTLE TOY.
0:55
SORRY I COULDN'T BE THERE IN **PERSON**, BUT I'M A FAMILY MAN SO I DON'T GET OUT MUCH ANY MORE. **GOODBYE.**
0:46
05-01-03
CLICK!
CLICK! CLICK! CLICK! CLICK! CLICK! CLICK!
OKAY, HOW CAN **THIS** NOT BE THE RIGHT REMOTE, EITHER?
YOU'RE TURNING THE **LIVING ROOM TV** OFF AND ON, DEAR.
SINCE I'M HERE FOR THE DURATION, I GUESS I CAN ADD TO THE **FUN** AND HELP WITH THE COUNTDOWN. THIRTY SECONDS. TWENTY-FIVE. TWENTY-FOUR.
HONEY? BRING VICTOR IN HERE TO HELP DADDY COUNT DOWN, WILL YOU? LET'S MAKE THIS A LEARNING EXPERIENCE.
TWENTY... NINETEEN...
ARE **ALL** VILLAINS LIKE THIS?
TELL ME ABOUT IT.

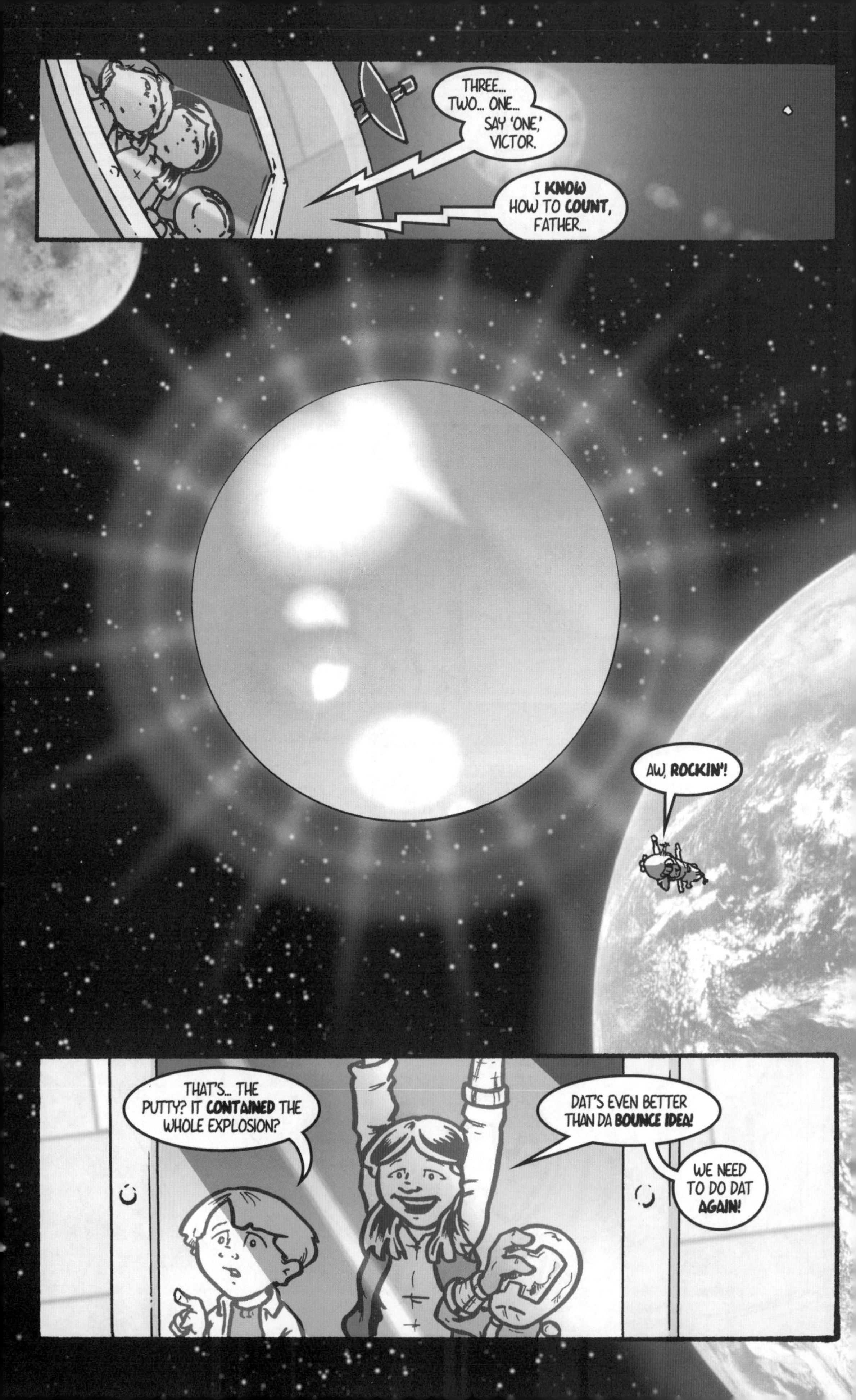
THREE... TWO... ONE... SAY 'ONE,' VICTOR.
I KNOW HOW TO COUNT, FATHER...
AW, ROCKIN'!
THAT'S... THE PUTTY? IT CONTAINED THE WHOLE EXPLOSION?
DAT'S EVEN BETTER THAN DA BOUNCE IDEA!
WE NEED TO DO DAT AGAIN!

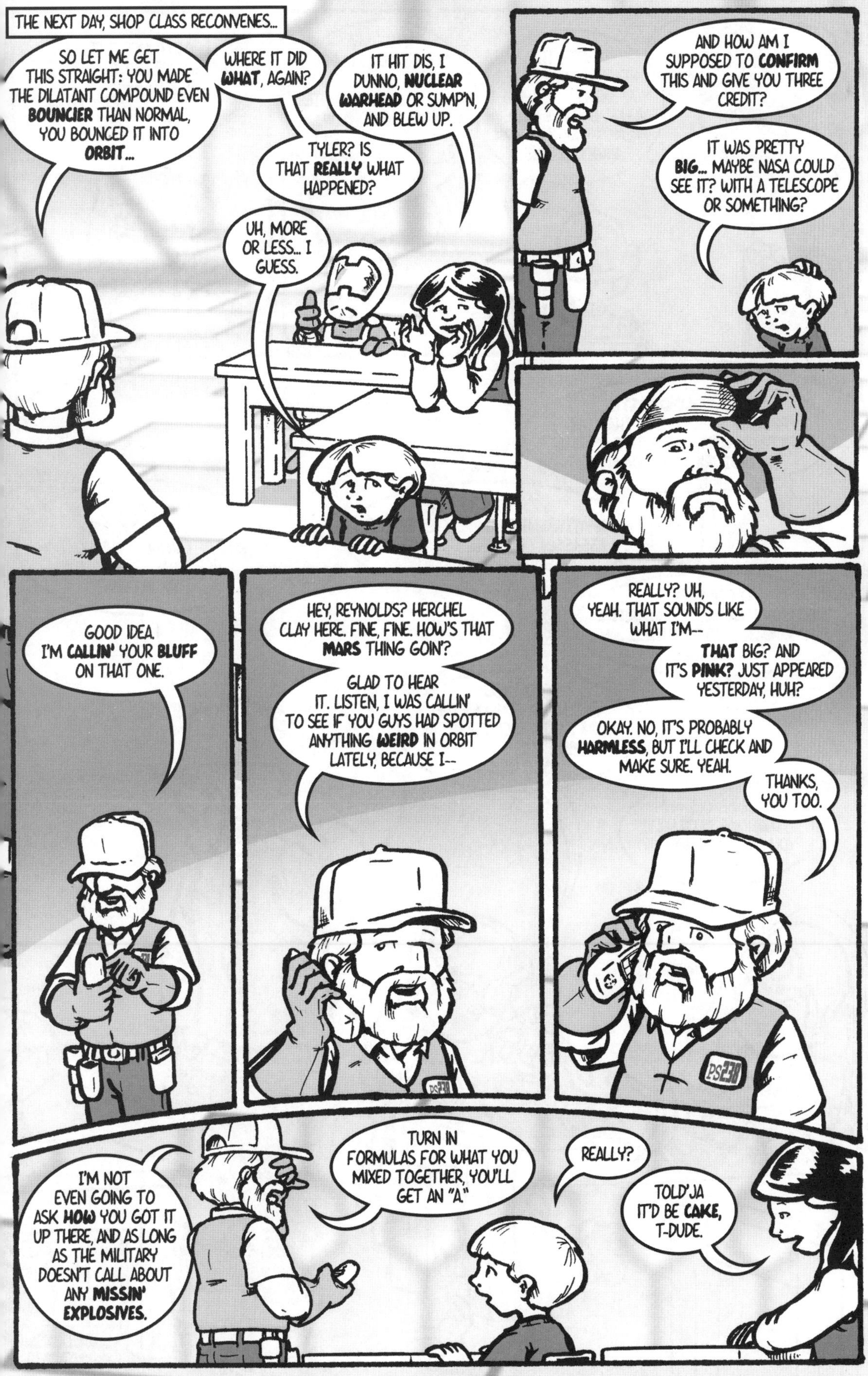

THE NEXT DAY, SHOP CLASS RECONVENES...
SO LET ME GET THIS STRAIGHT: YOU MADE THE DILATANT COMPOUND EVEN BOUNCIER THAN NORMAL, YOU BOUNCED IT INTO ORBIT...
WHERE IT DID WHAT, AGAIN?
IT HIT DIS, I DUNNO, NUCLEAR WARHEAD OR SUMP'N, AND BLEW UP.
TYLER? IS THAT REALLY WHAT HAPPENED?
UH, MORE OR LESS... I GUESS.
AND HOW AM I SUPPOSED TO CONFIRM THIS AND GIVE YOU THREE CREDIT?
IT WAS PRETTY BIG... MAYBE NASA COULD SEE IT? WITH A TELESCOPE OR SOMETHING?
GOOD IDEA. I'M CALLIN' YOUR BLUFF ON THAT ONE.
HEY, REYNOLDS? HERCHEL CLAY HERE. FINE, FINE. HOW'S THAT MARS THING GOIN'?
GLAD TO HEAR IT. LISTEN, I WAS CALLIN' TO SEE IF YOU GUYS HAD SPOTTED ANYTHING WEIRD IN ORBIT LATELY, BECAUSE I--
REALLY? UH, YEAH. THAT SOUNDS LIKE WHAT I'M--
THAT BIG? AND IT'S PINK? JUST APPEARED YESTERDAY, HUH?
OKAY. NO, IT'S PROBABLY HARMLESS, BUT I'LL CHECK AND MAKE SURE. YEAH.
THANKS, YOU TOO.
PS238
I'M NOT EVEN GOING TO ASK HOW YOU GOT IT UP THERE, AND AS LONG AS THE MILITARY DOESN'T CALL ABOUT ANY MISSIN' EXPLOSIVES.
TURN IN FORMULAS FOR WHAT YOU MIXED TOGETHER, YOU'LL GET AN "A."
REALLY?
TOLD'JA IT'D BE CAKE, T-DUDE.

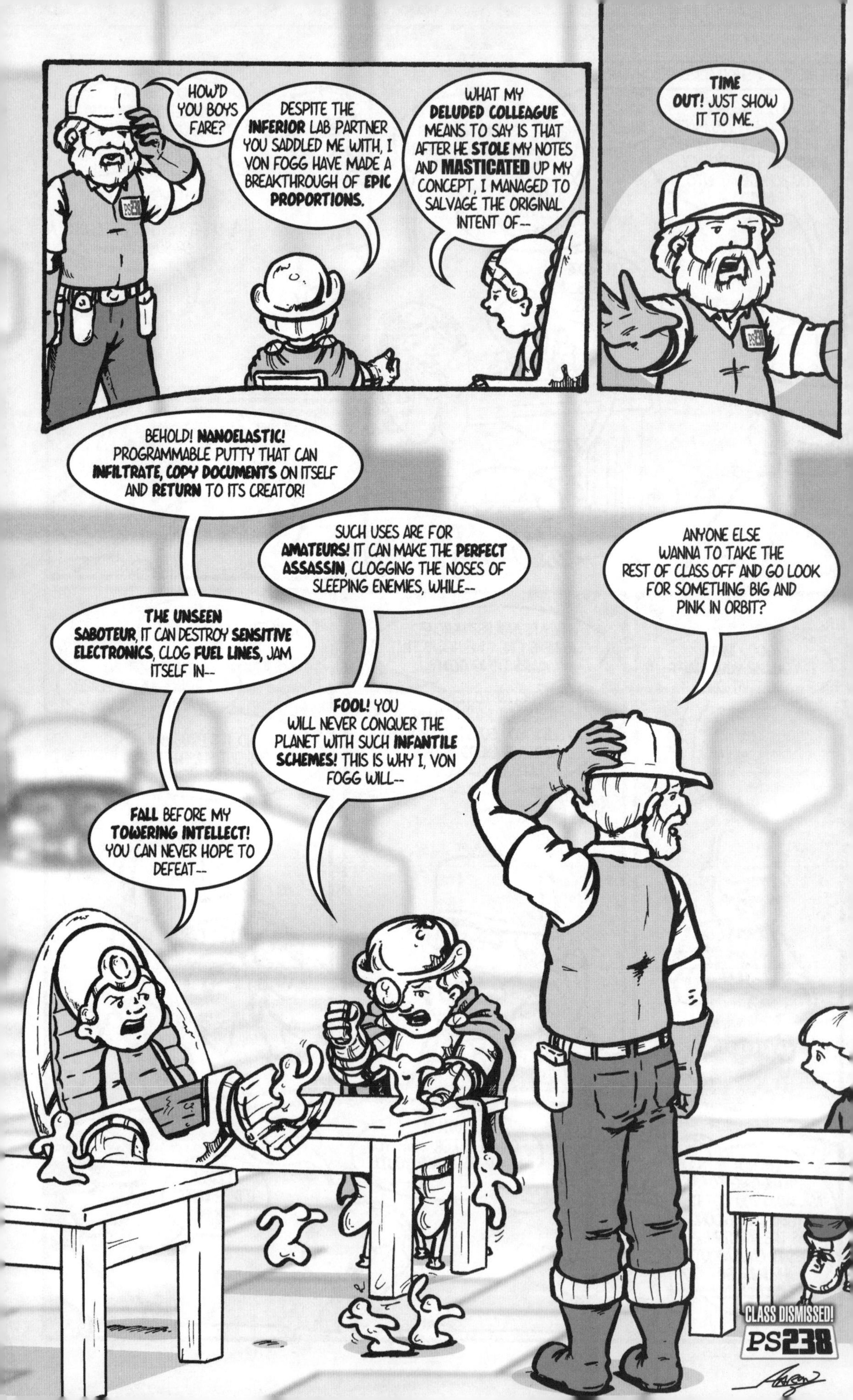
HOW'D YOU BOYS FARE?
DESPITE THE INFERIOR LAB PARTNER YOU SADDLED ME WITH, I VON FOGG HAVE MADE A BREAKTHROUGH OF EPIC PROPORTIONS.
WHAT MY DELUDED COLLEAGUE MEANS TO SAY IS THAT AFTER HE STOLE MY NOTES AND MASTICATED UP MY CONCEPT, I MANAGED TO SALVAGE THE ORIGINAL INTENT OF--
TIME OUT! JUST SHOW IT TO ME.
BEHOLD! NANOELASTIC! PROGRAMMABLE PUTTY THAT CAN INFILTRATE, COPY DOCUMENTS ON ITSELF AND RETURN TO ITS CREATOR!
SUCH USES ARE FOR AMATEURS! IT CAN MAKE THE PERFECT ASSASSIN, CLOGGING THE NOSES OF SLEEPING ENEMIES, WHILE--
THE UNSEEN SABOTEUR, IT CAN DESTROY SENSITIVE ELECTRONICS, CLOG FUEL LINES, JAM ITSELF IN--
FOOL! YOU WILL NEVER CONQUER THE PLANET WITH SUCH INFANTILE SCHEMES! THIS IS WHY I, VON FOGG WILL--
FALL BEFORE MY TOWERING INTELLECT! YOU CAN NEVER HOPE TO DEFEAT--
ANYONE ELSE WANNA TO TAKE THE REST OF CLASS OFF AND GO LOOK FOR SOMETHING BIG AND PINK IN ORBIT?
CLASS DISMISSED!
PS238

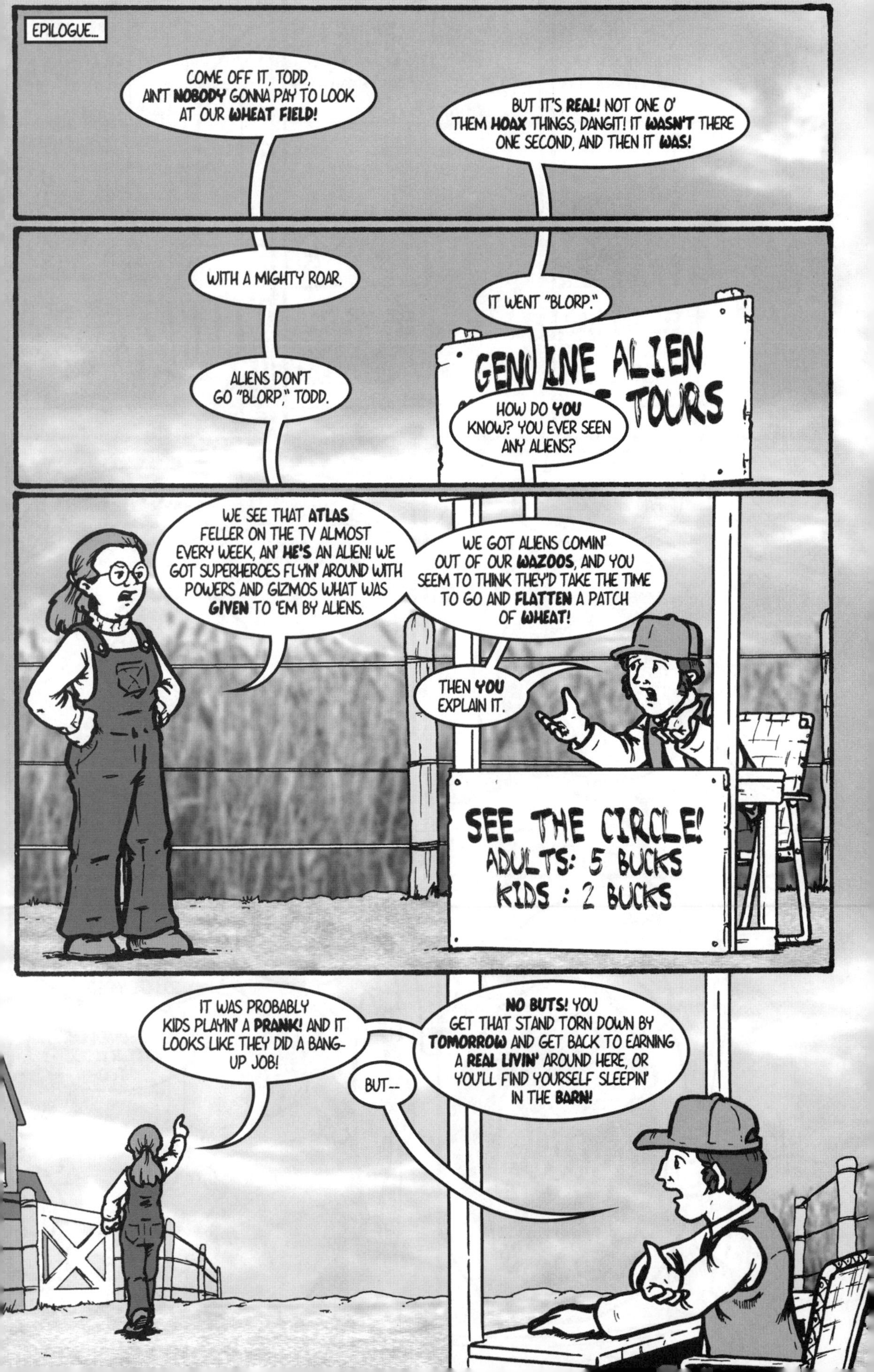
EPILOGUE...
COME OFF IT, TODD, AIN'T NOBODY GONNA PAY TO LOOK AT OUR WHEAT FIELD!
BUT IT'S REAL! NOT ONE O' THEM HOAX THINGS, DANGIT! IT WASN'T THERE ONE SECOND, AND THEN IT WAS!
WITH A MIGHTY ROAR.
IT WENT "BLORP."
ALIENS DON'T GO "BLORP," TODD.
GENUINE ALIEN
TOURS
HOW DO YOU KNOW? YOU EVER SEEN ANY ALIENS?
WE SEE THAT ATLAS FELLER ON THE TV ALMOST EVERY WEEK, AN' HE'S AN ALIEN! WE GOT SUPERHEROES FLYIN' AROUND WITH POWERS AND GIZMOS WHAT WAS GIVEN TO 'EM BY ALIENS.
WE GOT ALIENS COMIN' OUT OF OUR WAZOOS, AND YOU SEEM TO THINK THEY'D TAKE THE TIME TO GO AND FLATTEN A PATCH OF WHEAT!
THEN YOU EXPLAIN IT.
SEE THE CIRCLE!
ADULTS: 5 BUCKS
KIDS : 2 BUCKS
IT WAS PROBABLY KIDS PLAYIN' A PRANK! AND IT LOOKS LIKE THEY DID A BANG-UP JOB!
NO BUTS! YOU GET THAT STAND TORN DOWN BY TOMORROW AND GET BACK TO EARNING A REAL LIVIN' AROUND HERE, OR YOU'LL FIND YOURSELF SLEEPIN' IN THE BARN!
BUT--

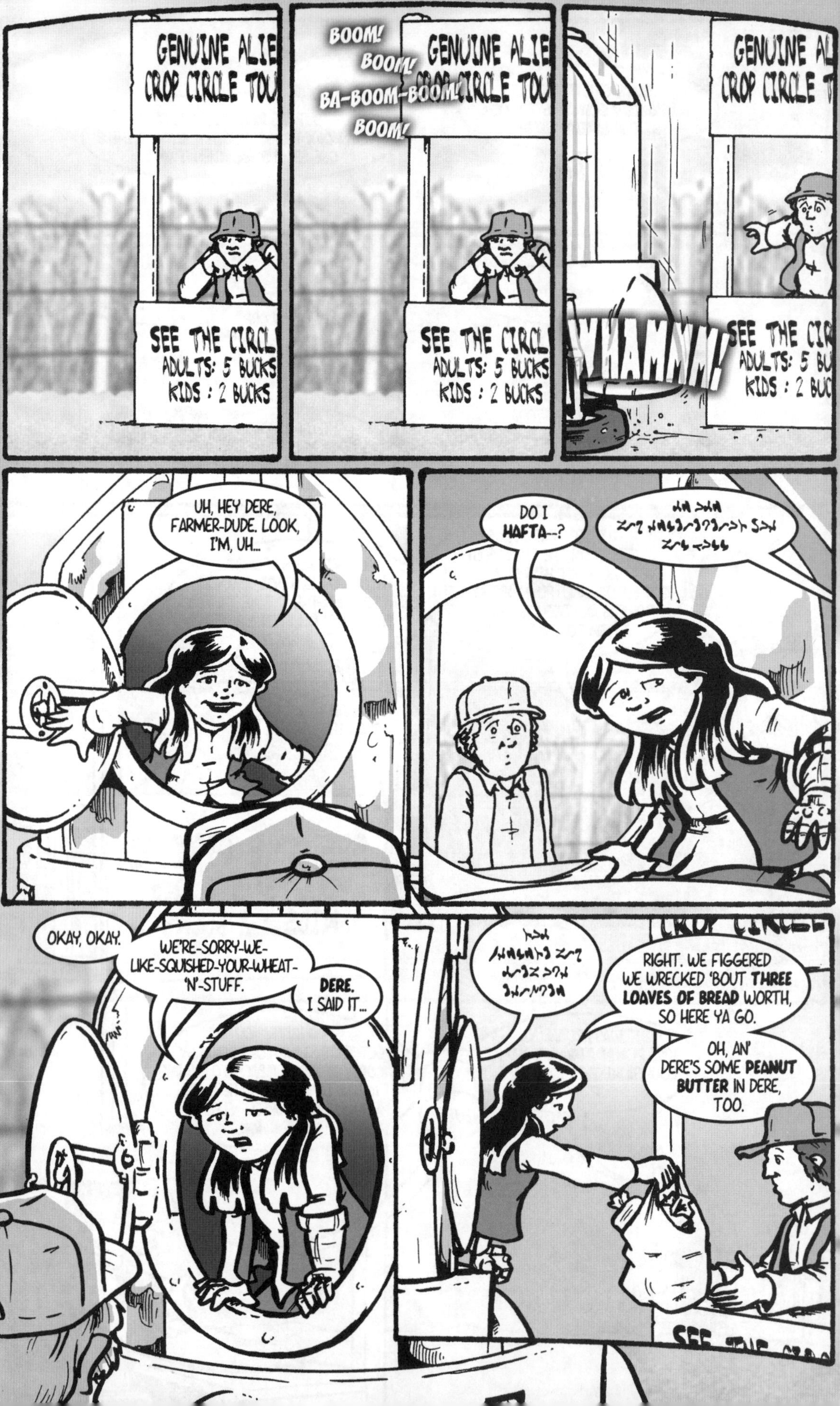
GENUINE ALIE
CROP CIRCLE TOU
SEE THE CIRCL
ADULTS: 5 BUCKS
KIDS : 2 BUCKS
BOOM!
BOOM!
BA-BOOM-BOOM!
BOOM!
GENUINE ALIE
CROP CIRCLE TOU
SEE THE CIRCL
ADULTS: 5 BUCKS
KIDS : 2 BUCKS
GENUINE AL
CROP CIRCLE T
WHAMMM!
SEE THE CIR
ADULTS: 5 BU
KIDS : 2 BUC
UH, HEY DERE, FARMER-DUDE. LOOK, I'M, UH...
DO I HAFTA--?
OKAY, OKAY.
WE'RE-SORRY-WE-LIKE-SQUISHED-YOUR-WHEAT-'N'-STUFF.
DERE. I SAID IT...
RIGHT. WE FIGGERED WE WRECKED 'BOUT THREE LOAVES OF BREAD WORTH, SO HERE YA GO.
OH, AN' DERE'S SOME PEANUT BUTTER IN DERE, TOO.

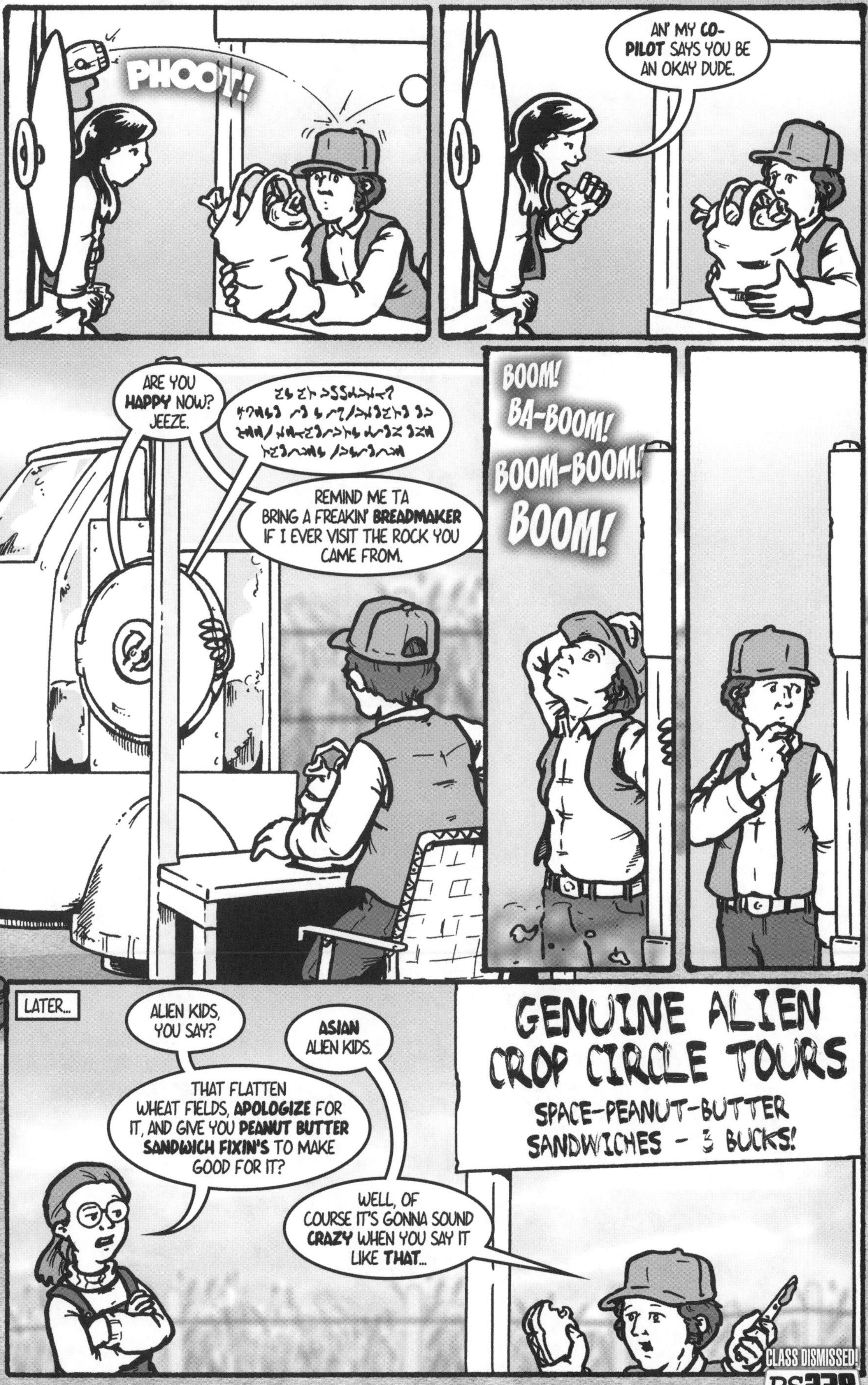
PHOOT!
AN' MY CO-PILOT SAYS YOU BE AN OKAY DUDE.
ARE YOU HAPPY NOW? JEEZE.
REMIND ME TA BRING A FREAKIN' BREADMAKER IF I EVER VISIT THE ROCK YOU CAME FROM.
BOOM!
BA-BOOM!
BOOM-BOOM!
BOOM!
LATER...
ALIEN KIDS, YOU SAY?
ASIAN ALIEN KIDS.
THAT FLATTEN WHEAT FIELDS, APOLOGIZE FOR IT, AND GIVE YOU PEANUT BUTTER SANDWICH FIXIN'S TO MAKE GOOD FOR IT?
WELL, OF COURSE IT'S GONNA SOUND CRAZY WHEN YOU SAY IT LIKE THAT...
GENUINE ALIEN CROP CIRCLE TOURS
SPACE-PEANUT-BUTTER SANDWICHES - 3 BUCKS!
CLASS DISMISSED!

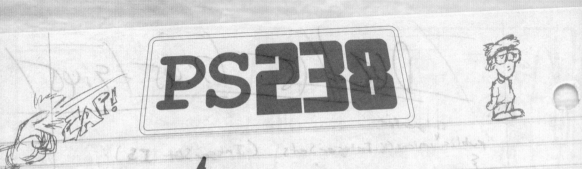

PS238

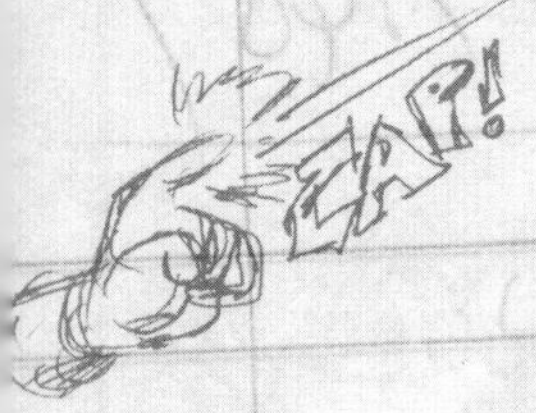
ZAP!

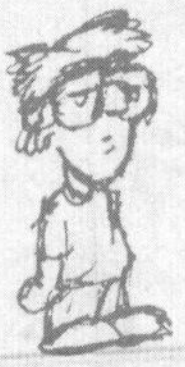

Notes from Class

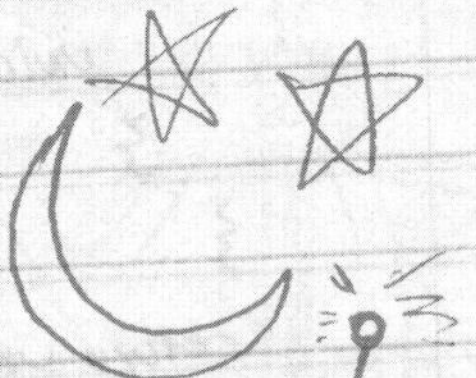

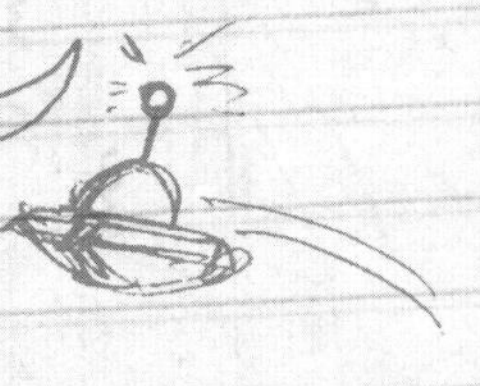

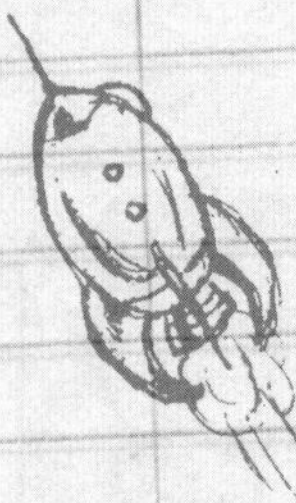

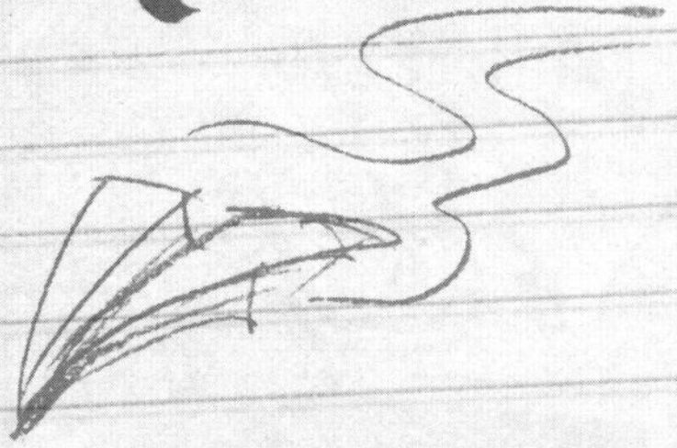

What follows are a few more short ps238 stories. The first gave us the title for this very volume, and the final tale appeared in a book printed for "Free Comic Book Day." "Fracas with the Flea" introduces a character I hope to spotlight in the future and gives us a clue that dire things may be in store for our super-students...

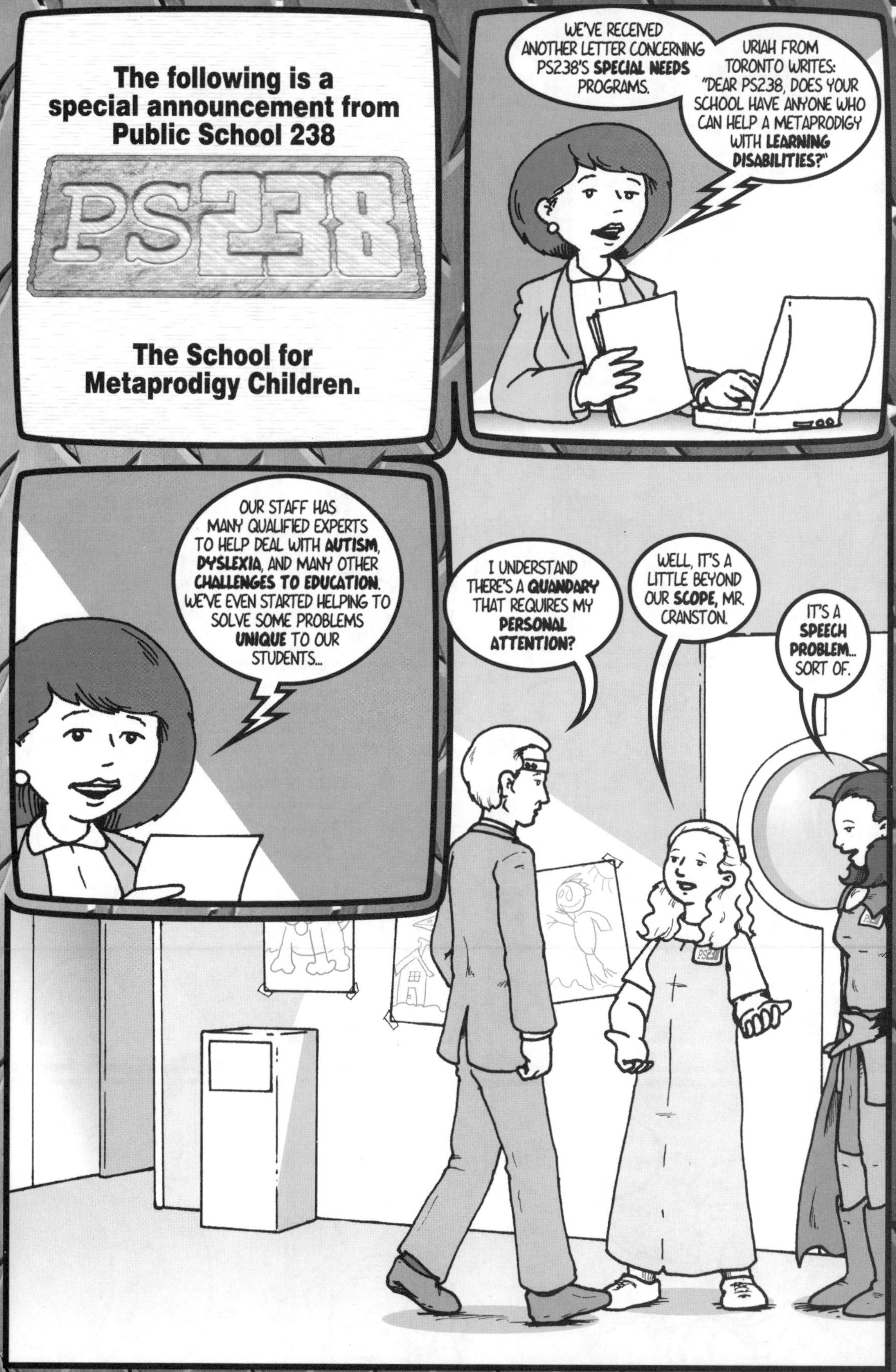
The following is a special announcement from Public School 238
PS238
The School for Metaprodigy Children.
WE'VE RECEIVED ANOTHER LETTER CONCERNING PS238'S SPECIAL NEEDS PROGRAMS.
URIAH FROM TORONTO WRITES: "DEAR PS238, DOES YOUR SCHOOL HAVE ANYONE WHO CAN HELP A METAPRODIGY WITH LEARNING DISABILITIES?"
OUR STAFF HAS MANY QUALIFIED EXPERTS TO HELP DEAL WITH AUTISM, DYSLEXIA, AND MANY OTHER CHALLENGES TO EDUCATION. WE'VE EVEN STARTED HELPING TO SOLVE SOME PROBLEMS UNIQUE TO OUR STUDENTS...
I UNDERSTAND THERE'S A QUANDARY THAT REQUIRES MY PERSONAL ATTENTION?
WELL, IT'S A LITTLE BEYOND OUR SCOPE, MR. CRANSTON.
IT'S A SPEECH PROBLEM... SORT OF.

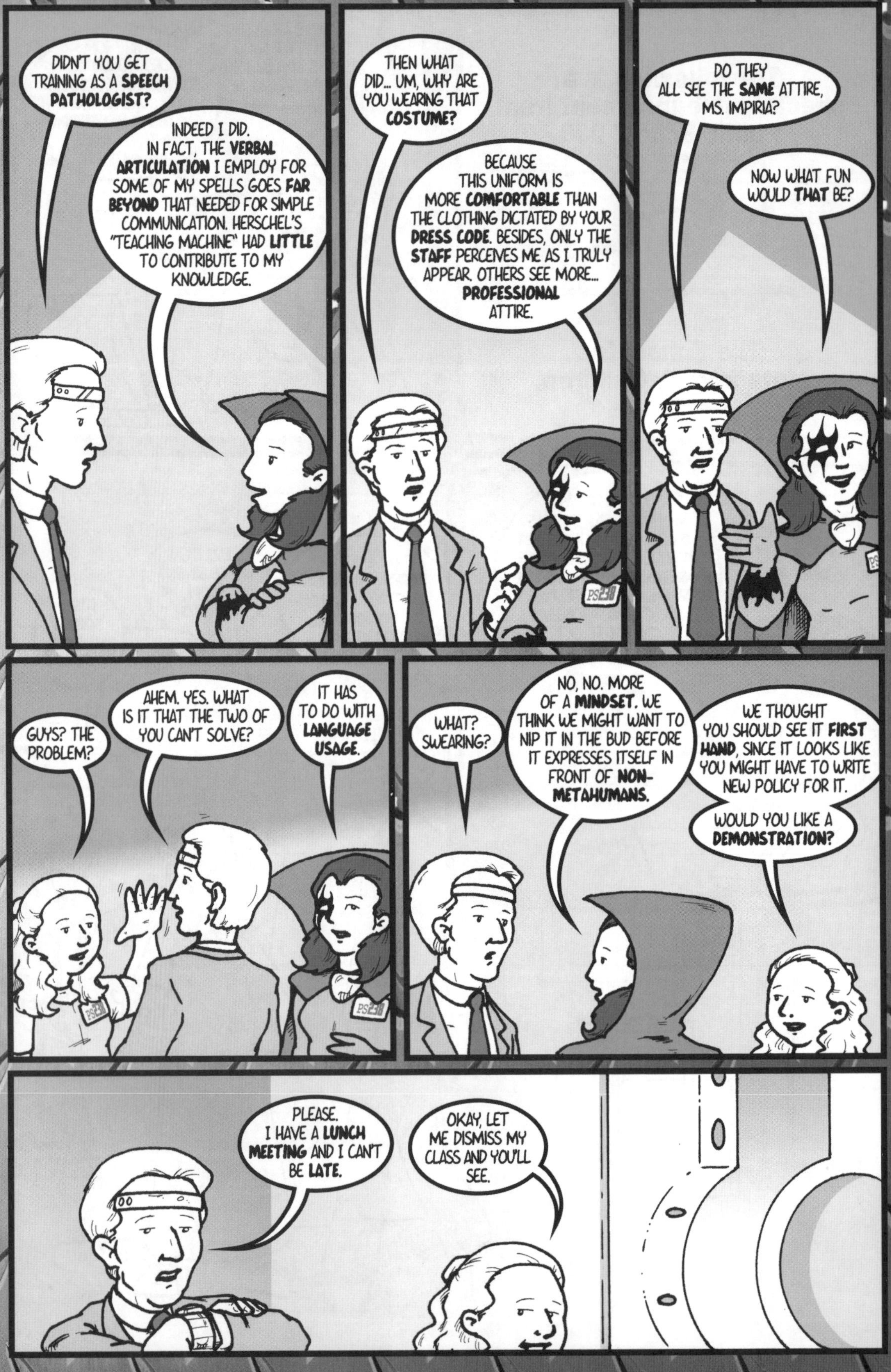
DIDN'T YOU GET TRAINING AS A SPEECH PATHOLOGIST?
INDEED I DID. IN FACT, THE VERBAL ARTICULATION I EMPLOY FOR SOME OF MY SPELLS GOES FAR BEYOND THAT NEEDED FOR SIMPLE COMMUNICATION. HERSCHEL'S "TEACHING MACHINE" HAD LITTLE TO CONTRIBUTE TO MY KNOWLEDGE.
THEN WHAT DID... UM, WHY ARE YOU WEARING THAT COSTUME?
BECAUSE THIS UNIFORM IS MORE COMFORTABLE THAN THE CLOTHING DICTATED BY YOUR DRESS CODE. BESIDES, ONLY THE STAFF PERCEIVES ME AS I TRULY APPEAR. OTHERS SEE MORE... PROFESSIONAL ATTIRE.
DO THEY ALL SEE THE SAME ATTIRE, MS. IMPIRIA?
NOW WHAT FUN WOULD THAT BE?
GUYS? THE PROBLEM?
AHEM. YES. WHAT IS IT THAT THE TWO OF YOU CAN'T SOLVE?
IT HAS TO DO WITH LANGUAGE USAGE.
WHAT? SWEARING?
NO, NO. MORE OF A MINDSET. WE THINK WE MIGHT WANT TO NIP IT IN THE BUD BEFORE IT EXPRESSES ITSELF IN FRONT OF NON-METAHUMANS.
WE THOUGHT YOU SHOULD SEE IT FIRST HAND, SINCE IT LOOKS LIKE YOU MIGHT HAVE TO WRITE NEW POLICY FOR IT.
WOULD YOU LIKE A DEMONSTRATION?
PLEASE. I HAVE A LUNCH MEETING AND I CAN'T BE LATE.
OKAY, LET ME DISMISS MY CLASS AND YOU'LL SEE.

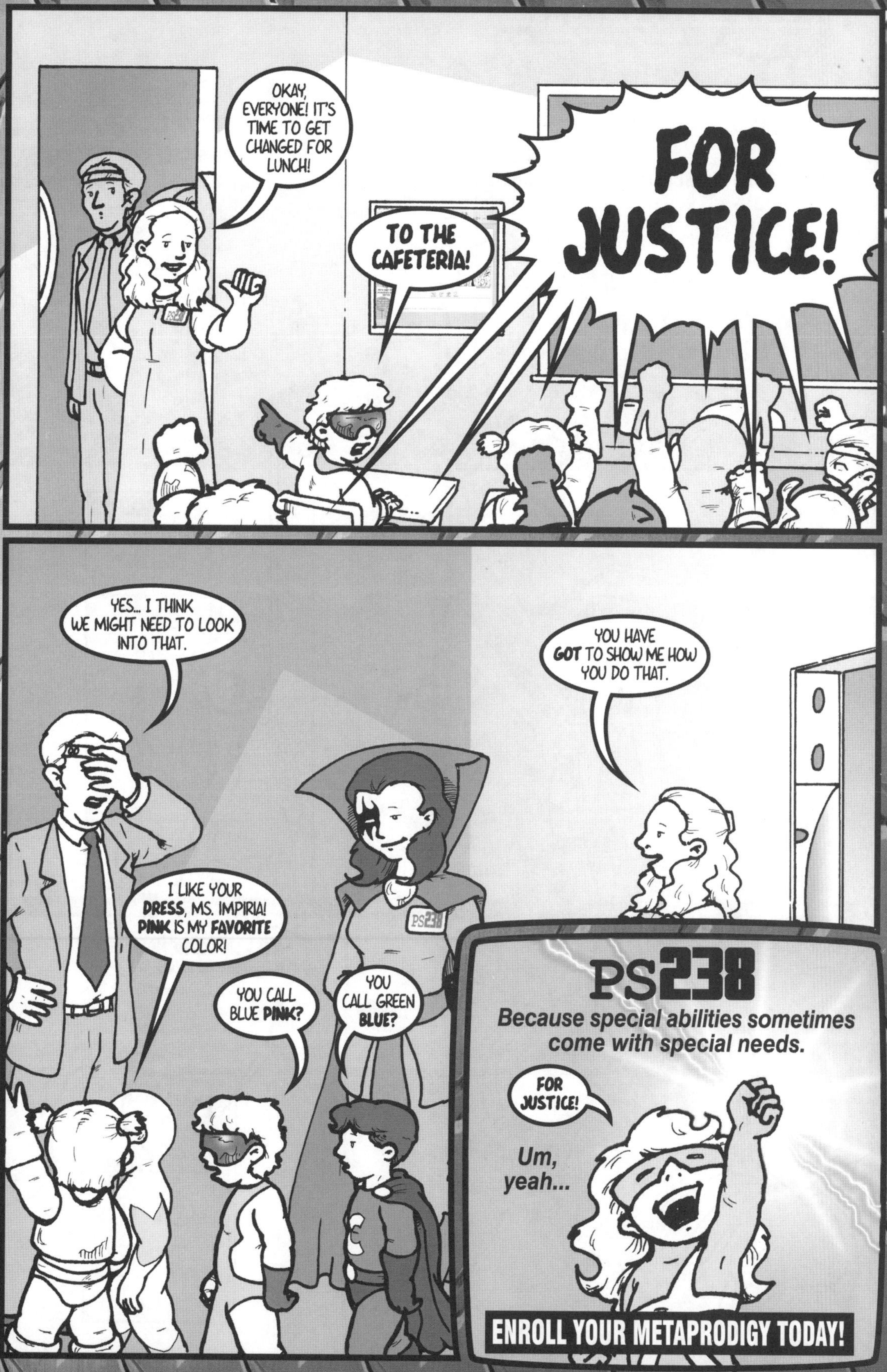
OKAY, EVERYONE! IT'S TIME TO GET CHANGED FOR LUNCH!
TO THE CAFETERIA!
FOR JUSTICE!
YES... I THINK WE MIGHT NEED TO LOOK INTO THAT.
YOU HAVE GOT TO SHOW ME HOW YOU DO THAT.
I LIKE YOUR DRESS, MS. IMPIRIA! PINK IS MY FAVORITE COLOR!
YOU CALL BLUE PINK?
YOU CALL GREEN BLUE?
PS238
Because special abilities sometimes come with special needs.
FOR JUSTICE!
Um, yeah...
ENROLL YOUR METAPRODIGY TODAY!

by Aaron Williams • www.nodwick.com

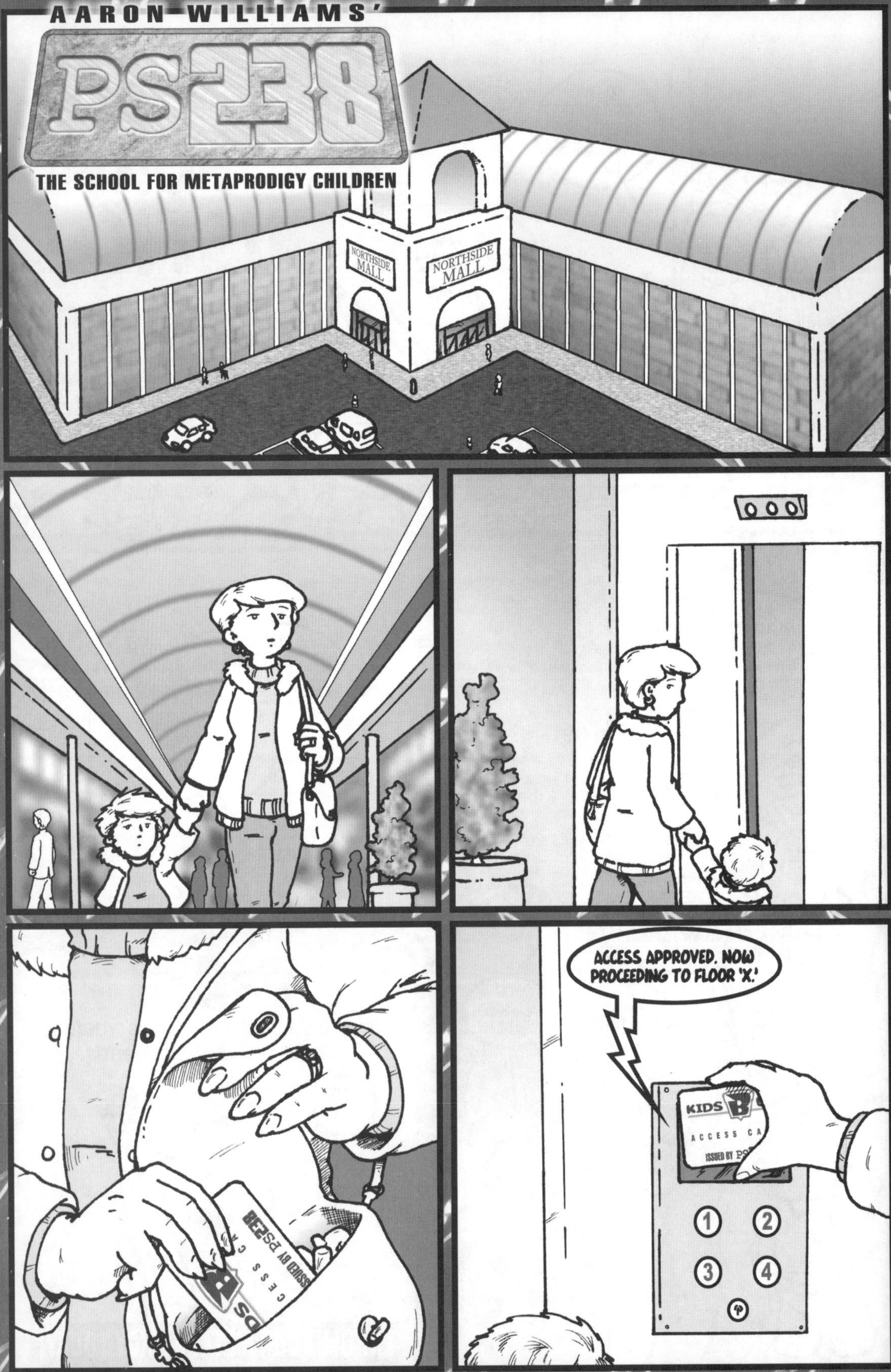
AARON WILLIAMS'
PS238
THE SCHOOL FOR METAPRODIGY CHILDREN
NORTHSIDE MALL
NORTHSIDE MALL
ACCESS APPROVED. NOW PROCEEDING TO FLOOR 'X.'
KIDS

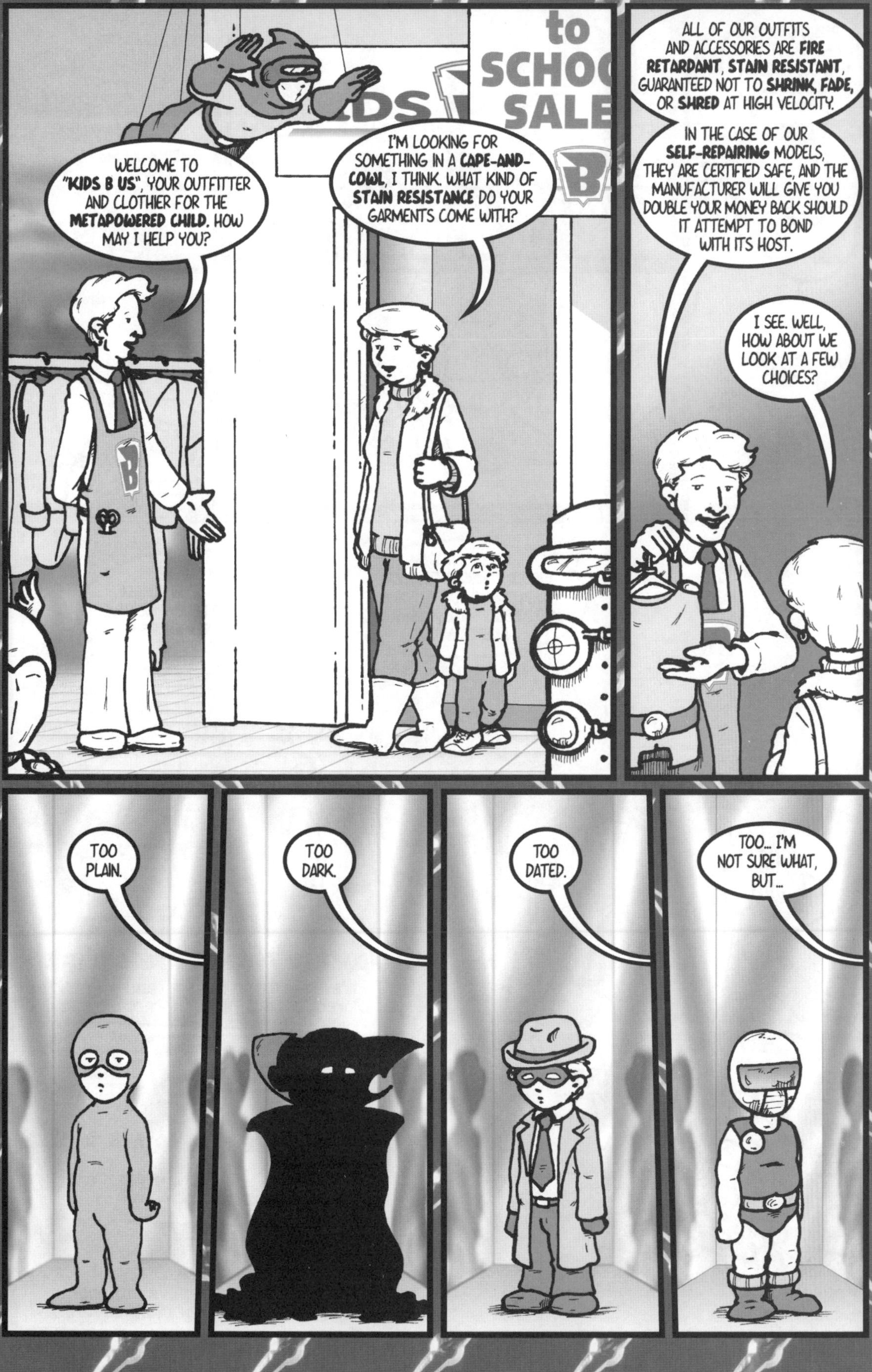
to SCHOO SALE
WELCOME TO "KIDS B US", YOUR OUTFITTER AND CLOTHIER FOR THE METAPOWERED CHILD. HOW MAY I HELP YOU?
I'M LOOKING FOR SOMETHING IN A CAPE-AND-COWL, I THINK. WHAT KIND OF STAIN RESISTANCE DO YOUR GARMENTS COME WITH?
ALL OF OUR OUTFITS AND ACCESSORIES ARE FIRE RETARDANT, STAIN RESISTANT, GUARANTEED NOT TO SHRINK, FADE, OR SHRED AT HIGH VELOCITY.
IN THE CASE OF OUR SELF-REPAIRING MODELS, THEY ARE CERTIFIED SAFE, AND THE MANUFACTURER WILL GIVE YOU DOUBLE YOUR MONEY BACK SHOULD IT ATTEMPT TO BOND WITH ITS HOST.
I SEE. WELL, HOW ABOUT WE LOOK AT A FEW CHOICES?
TOO PLAIN.
TOO DARK.
TOO DATED.
TOO... I'M NOT SURE WHAT, BUT...

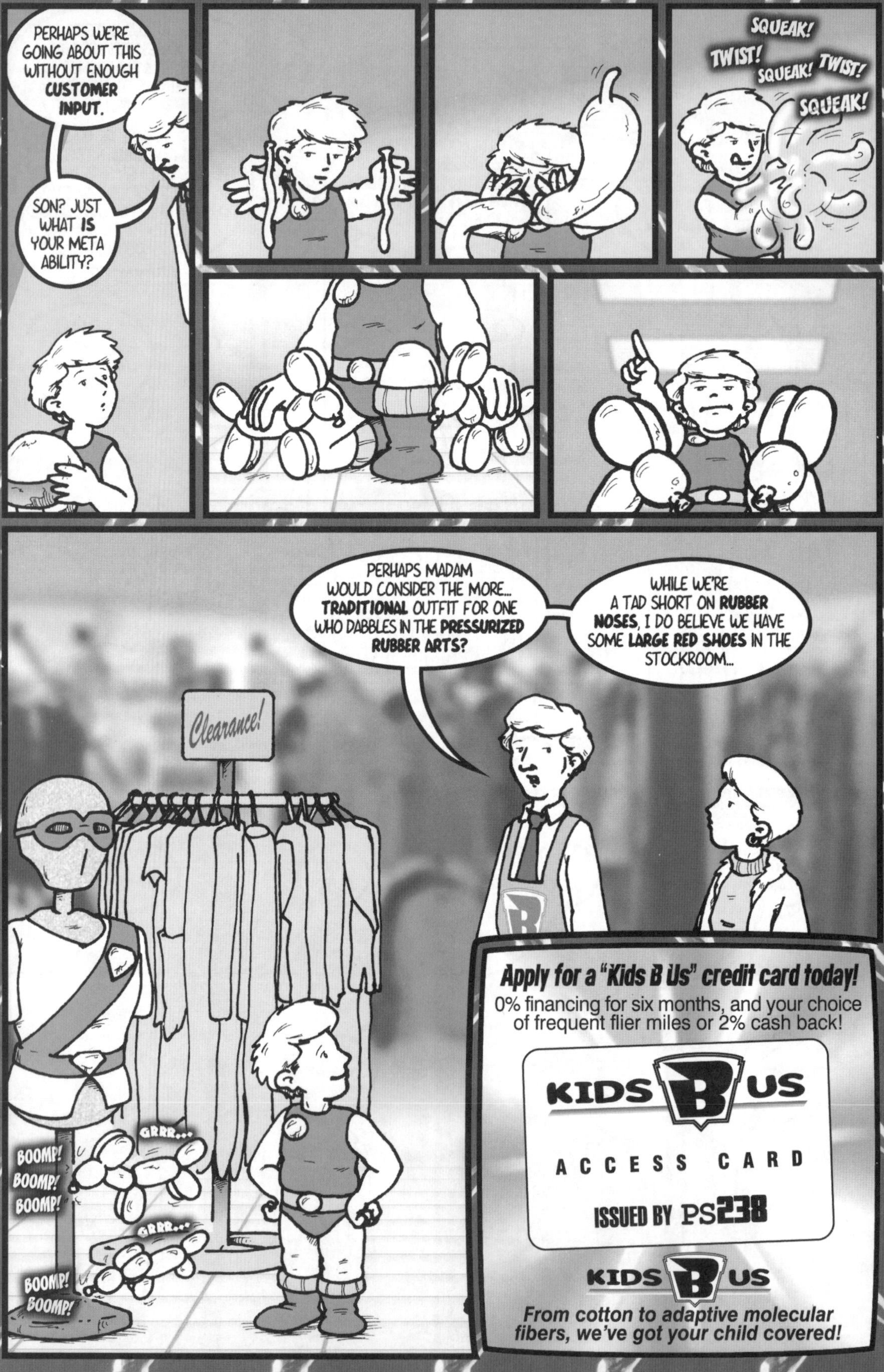
PERHAPS WE'RE GOING ABOUT THIS WITHOUT ENOUGH CUSTOMER INPUT.
SON? JUST WHAT IS YOUR META ABILITY?
SQUEAK!
TWIST!
SQUEAK!
TWIST!
SQUEAK!
PERHAPS MADAM WOULD CONSIDER THE MORE... TRADITIONAL OUTFIT FOR ONE WHO DABBLES IN THE PRESSURIZED RUBBER ARTS?
WHILE WE'RE A TAD SHORT ON RUBBER NOSES, I DO BELIEVE WE HAVE SOME LARGE RED SHOES IN THE STOCKROOM...
Clearance!
GRRR...
BOOMP! BOOMP! BOOMP!
GRRR...
BOOMP! BOOMP!
Apply for a "Kids B Us" credit card today!
0% financing for six months, and your choice of frequent flier miles or 2% cash back!
KIDS B US
ACCESS CARD
ISSUED BY PS238
KIDS B US
From cotton to adaptive molecular fibers, we've got your child covered!

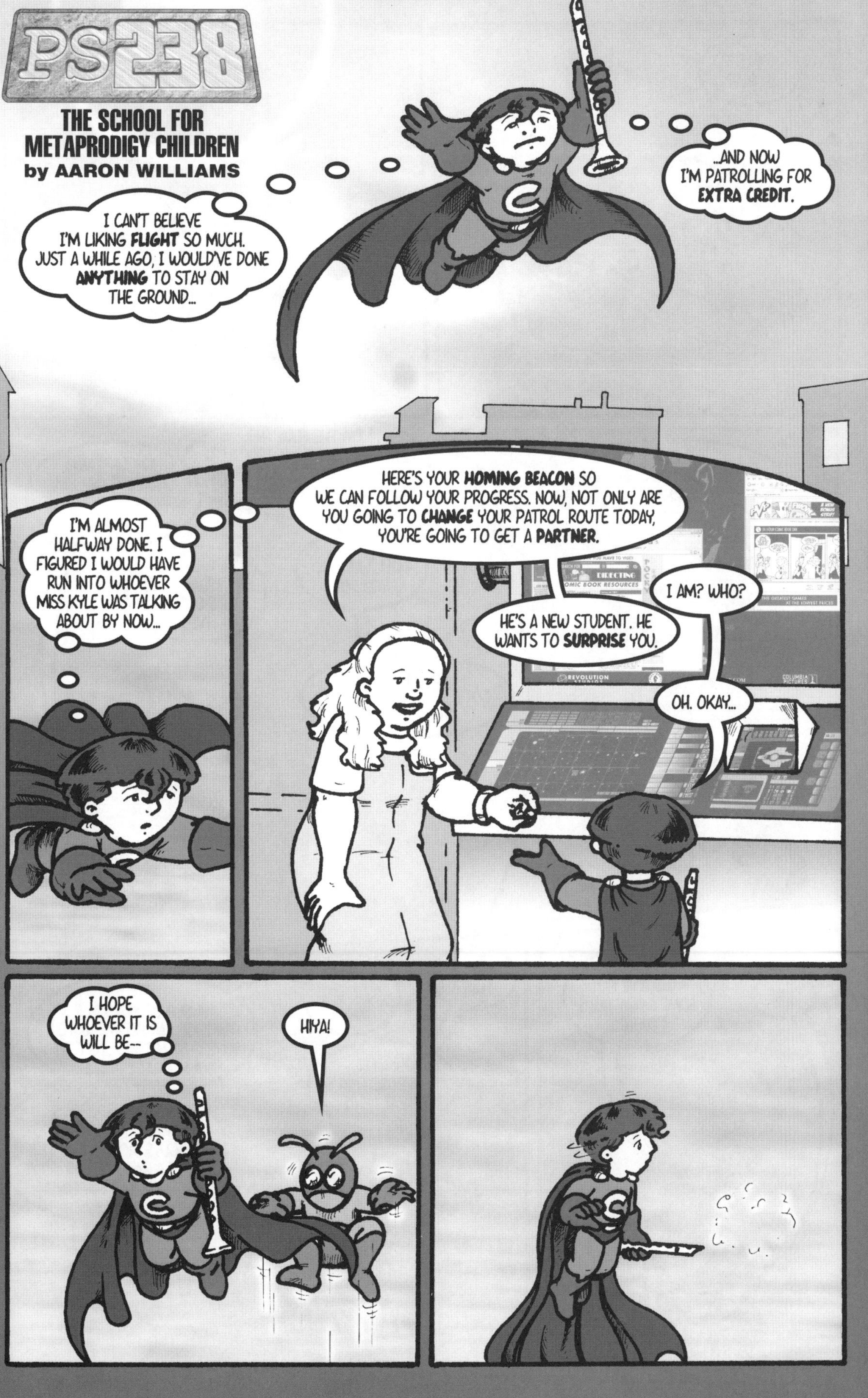
PS 238
THE SCHOOL FOR METAPRODIGY CHILDREN
by AARON WILLIAMS
I CAN'T BELIEVE I'M LIKING FLIGHT SO MUCH. JUST A WHILE AGO, I WOULD'VE DONE ANYTHING TO STAY ON THE GROUND...
...AND NOW I'M PATROLLING FOR EXTRA CREDIT.
I'M ALMOST HALFWAY DONE. I FIGURED I WOULD HAVE RUN INTO WHOEVER MISS KYLE WAS TALKING ABOUT BY NOW...
HERE'S YOUR HOMING BEACON SO WE CAN FOLLOW YOUR PROGRESS. NOW, NOT ONLY ARE YOU GOING TO CHANGE YOUR PATROL ROUTE TODAY, YOU'RE GOING TO GET A PARTNER.
I AM? WHO?
HE'S A NEW STUDENT. HE WANTS TO SURPRISE YOU.
OH. OKAY...
I HOPE WHOEVER IT IS WILL BE--
HIYA!

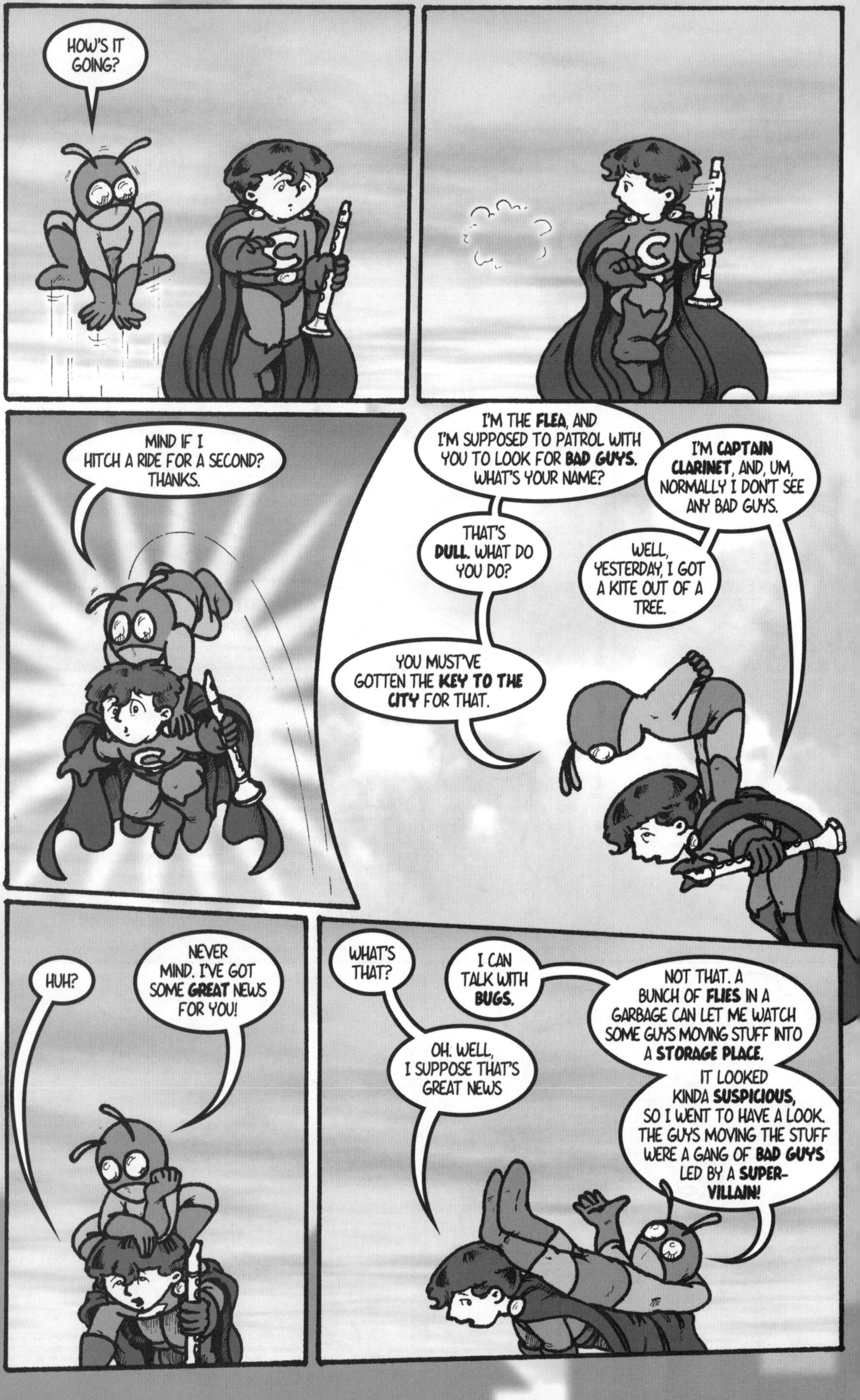
HOW'S IT GOING?
MIND IF I HITCH A RIDE FOR A SECOND? THANKS.
I'M THE FLEA, AND I'M SUPPOSED TO PATROL WITH YOU TO LOOK FOR BAD GUYS. WHAT'S YOUR NAME?
I'M CAPTAIN CLARINET, AND, UM, NORMALLY I DON'T SEE ANY BAD GUYS.
THAT'S DULL. WHAT DO YOU DO?
WELL, YESTERDAY, I GOT A KITE OUT OF A TREE.
YOU MUST'VE GOTTEN THE KEY TO THE CITY FOR THAT.
HUH?
NEVER MIND. I'VE GOT SOME GREAT NEWS FOR YOU!
WHAT'S THAT?
I CAN TALK WITH BUGS.
OH. WELL, I SUPPOSE THAT'S GREAT NEWS
NOT THAT. A BUNCH OF FLIES IN A GARBAGE CAN LET ME WATCH SOME GUYS MOVING STUFF INTO A STORAGE PLACE.
IT LOOKED KINDA SUSPICIOUS, SO I WENT TO HAVE A LOOK. THE GUYS MOVING THE STUFF WERE A GANG OF BAD GUYS LED BY A SUPER-VILLAIN!

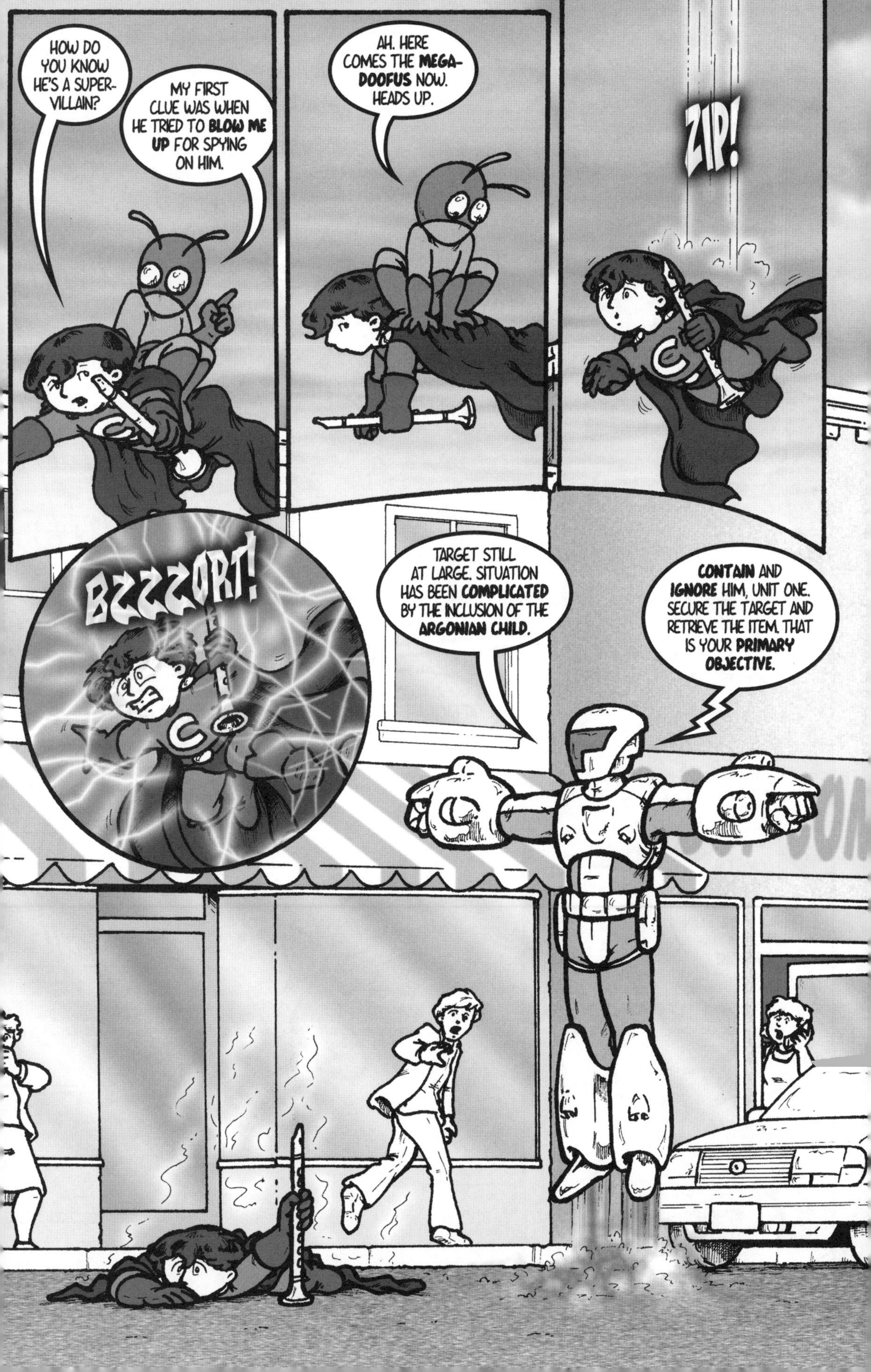
HOW DO YOU KNOW HE'S A SUPER-VILLAIN?
MY FIRST CLUE WAS WHEN HE TRIED TO **BLOW ME UP** FOR SPYING ON HIM.
AH. HERE COMES THE **MEGA-DOOFUS** NOW. HEADS UP.
ZIP!
BZZZORT!
TARGET STILL AT LARGE. SITUATION HAS BEEN **COMPLICATED** BY THE INCLUSION OF THE **ARGONIAN CHILD**.
CONTAIN AND **IGNORE** HIM, UNIT ONE. SECURE THE TARGET AND RETRIEVE THE ITEM. THAT IS YOUR **PRIMARY OBJECTIVE**.

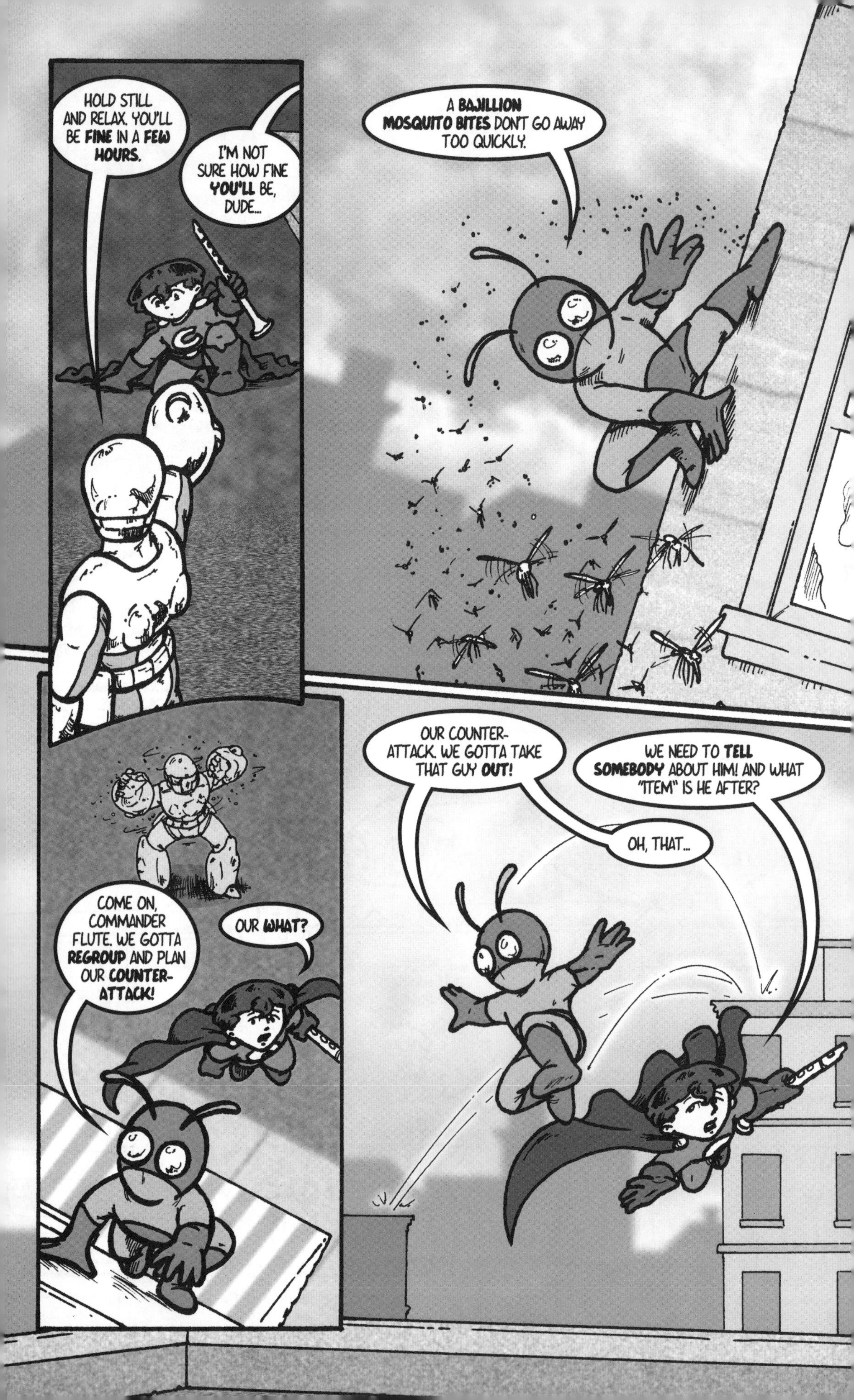

HOLD STILL AND RELAX. YOU'LL BE FINE IN A FEW HOURS.
I'M NOT SURE HOW FINE YOU'LL BE, DUDE...
A BAJILLION MOSQUITO BITES DON'T GO AWAY TOO QUICKLY.
COME ON, COMMANDER FLUTE. WE GOTTA REGROUP AND PLAN OUR COUNTER-ATTACK!
OUR WHAT?
OUR COUNTER-ATTACK. WE GOTTA TAKE THAT GUY OUT!
WE NEED TO TELL SOMEBODY ABOUT HIM! AND WHAT "ITEM" IS HE AFTER?
OH, THAT...

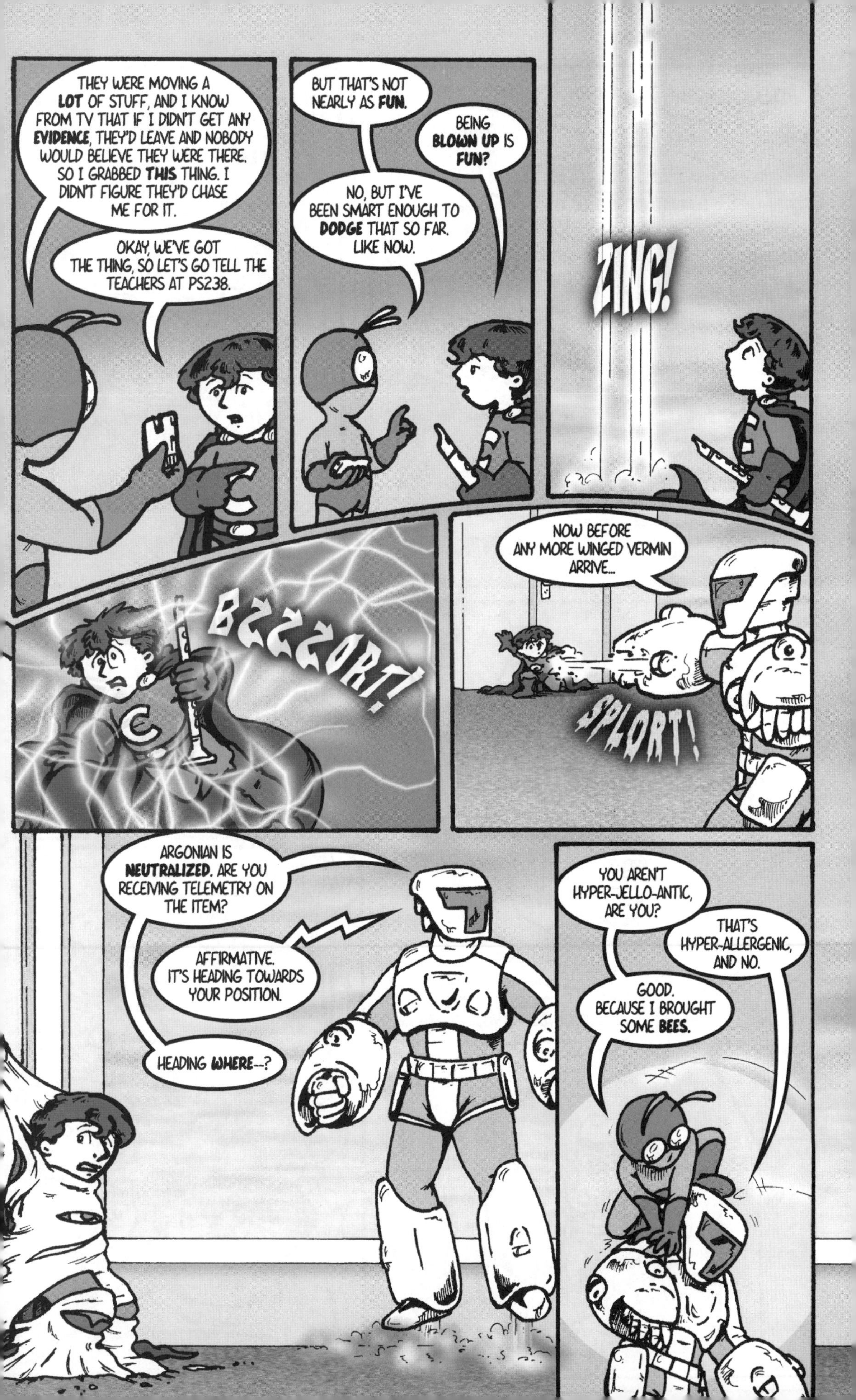
THEY WERE MOVING A LOT OF STUFF, AND I KNOW FROM TV THAT IF I DIDN'T GET ANY EVIDENCE, THEY'D LEAVE AND NOBODY WOULD BELIEVE THEY WERE THERE. SO I GRABBED THIS THING. I DIDN'T FIGURE THEY'D CHASE ME FOR IT.
OKAY, WE'VE GOT THE THING, SO LET'S GO TELL THE TEACHERS AT PS238.
BUT THAT'S NOT NEARLY AS FUN.
BEING BLOWN UP IS FUN?
NO, BUT I'VE BEEN SMART ENOUGH TO DODGE THAT SO FAR. LIKE NOW.
ZING!
BZZZORT!
NOW BEFORE ANY MORE WINGED VERMIN ARRIVE...
SPLORT!
ARGONIAN IS NEUTRALIZED. ARE YOU RECEIVING TELEMETRY ON THE ITEM?
AFFIRMATIVE. IT'S HEADING TOWARDS YOUR POSITION.
HEADING WHERE--?
YOU AREN'T HYPER-JELLO-ANTIC, ARE YOU?
THAT'S HYPER-ALLERGENIC, AND NO.
GOOD. BECAUSE I BROUGHT SOME BEES.

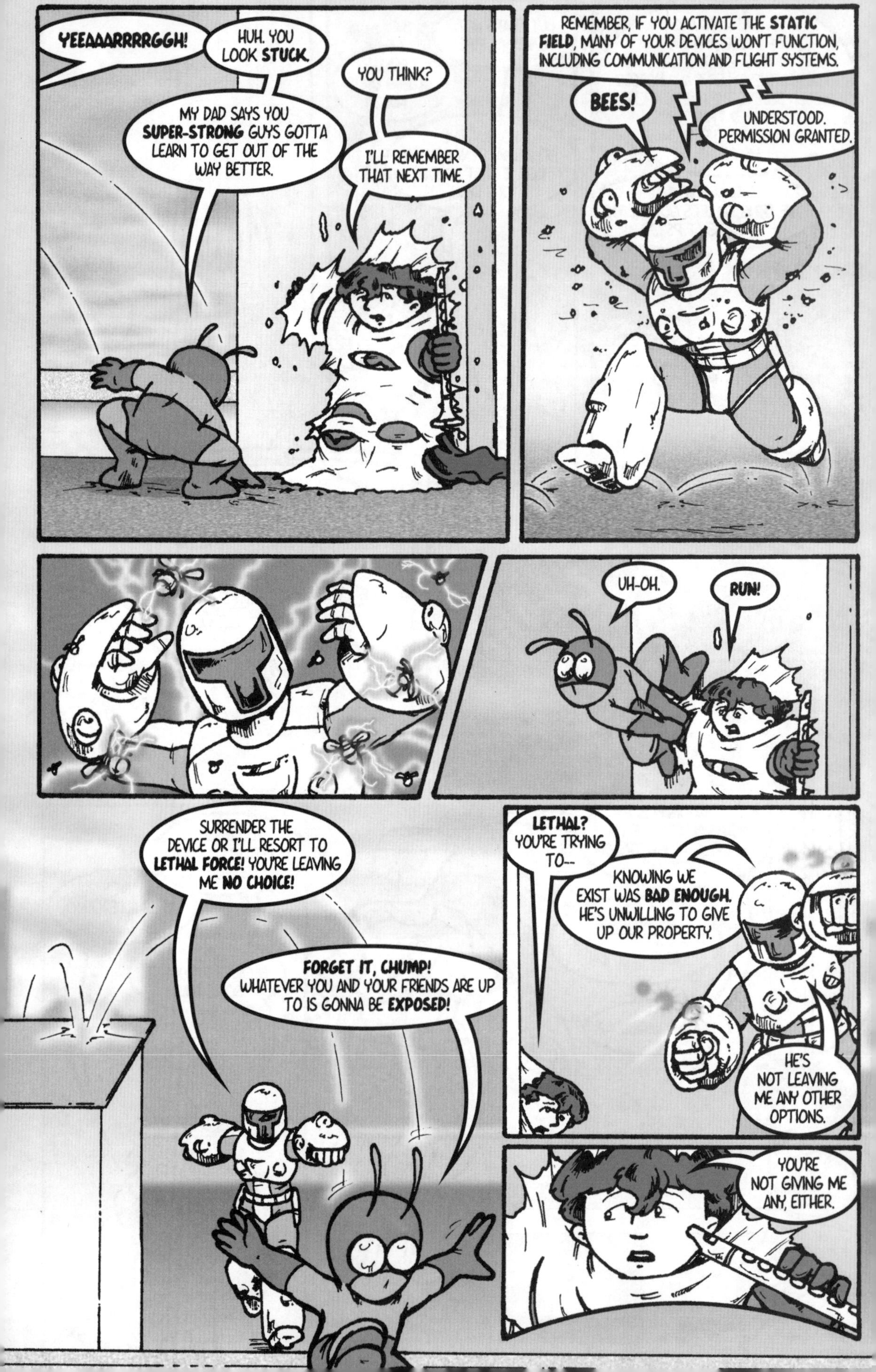
YEEAAARRRRGGH!
HUH. YOU LOOK STUCK.
YOU THINK?
MY DAD SAYS YOU SUPER-STRONG GUYS GOTTA LEARN TO GET OUT OF THE WAY BETTER.
I'LL REMEMBER THAT NEXT TIME.
REMEMBER, IF YOU ACTIVATE THE STATIC FIELD, MANY OF YOUR DEVICES WON'T FUNCTION, INCLUDING COMMUNICATION AND FLIGHT SYSTEMS.
BEES!
UNDERSTOOD. PERMISSION GRANTED.
UH-OH.
RUN!
SURRENDER THE DEVICE OR I'LL RESORT TO LETHAL FORCE! YOU'RE LEAVING ME NO CHOICE!
FORGET IT, CHUMP! WHATEVER YOU AND YOUR FRIENDS ARE UP TO IS GONNA BE EXPOSED!
LETHAL? YOU'RE TRYING TO--
KNOWING WE EXIST WAS BAD ENOUGH. HE'S UNWILLING TO GIVE UP OUR PROPERTY.
HE'S NOT LEAVING ME ANY OTHER OPTIONS.
YOU'RE NOT GIVING ME ANY, EITHER.

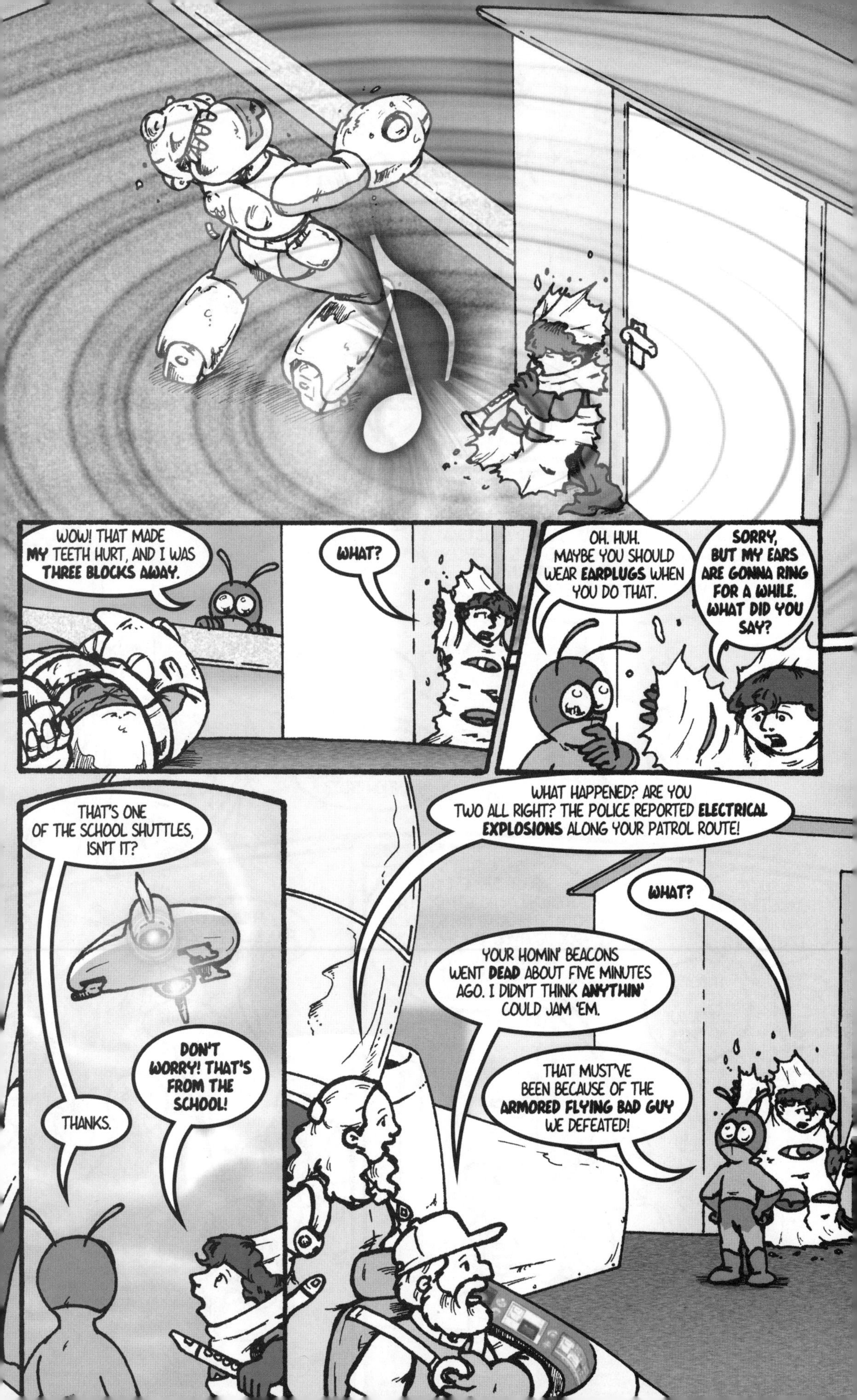
WOW! THAT MADE MY TEETH HURT, AND I WAS THREE BLOCKS AWAY.
WHAT?
OH. HUH. MAYBE YOU SHOULD WEAR EARPLUGS WHEN YOU DO THAT.
SORRY, BUT MY EARS ARE GONNA RING FOR A WHILE. WHAT DID YOU SAY?
THAT'S ONE OF THE SCHOOL SHUTTLES, ISN'T IT?
WHAT HAPPENED? ARE YOU TWO ALL RIGHT? THE POLICE REPORTED ELECTRICAL EXPLOSIONS ALONG YOUR PATROL ROUTE!
WHAT?
YOUR HOMIN' BEACONS WENT DEAD ABOUT FIVE MINUTES AGO. I DIDN'T THINK ANYTHIN' COULD JAM 'EM.
THAT MUST'VE BEEN BECAUSE OF THE ARMORED FLYING BAD GUY WE DEFEATED!
DON'T WORRY! THAT'S FROM THE SCHOOL!
THANKS.

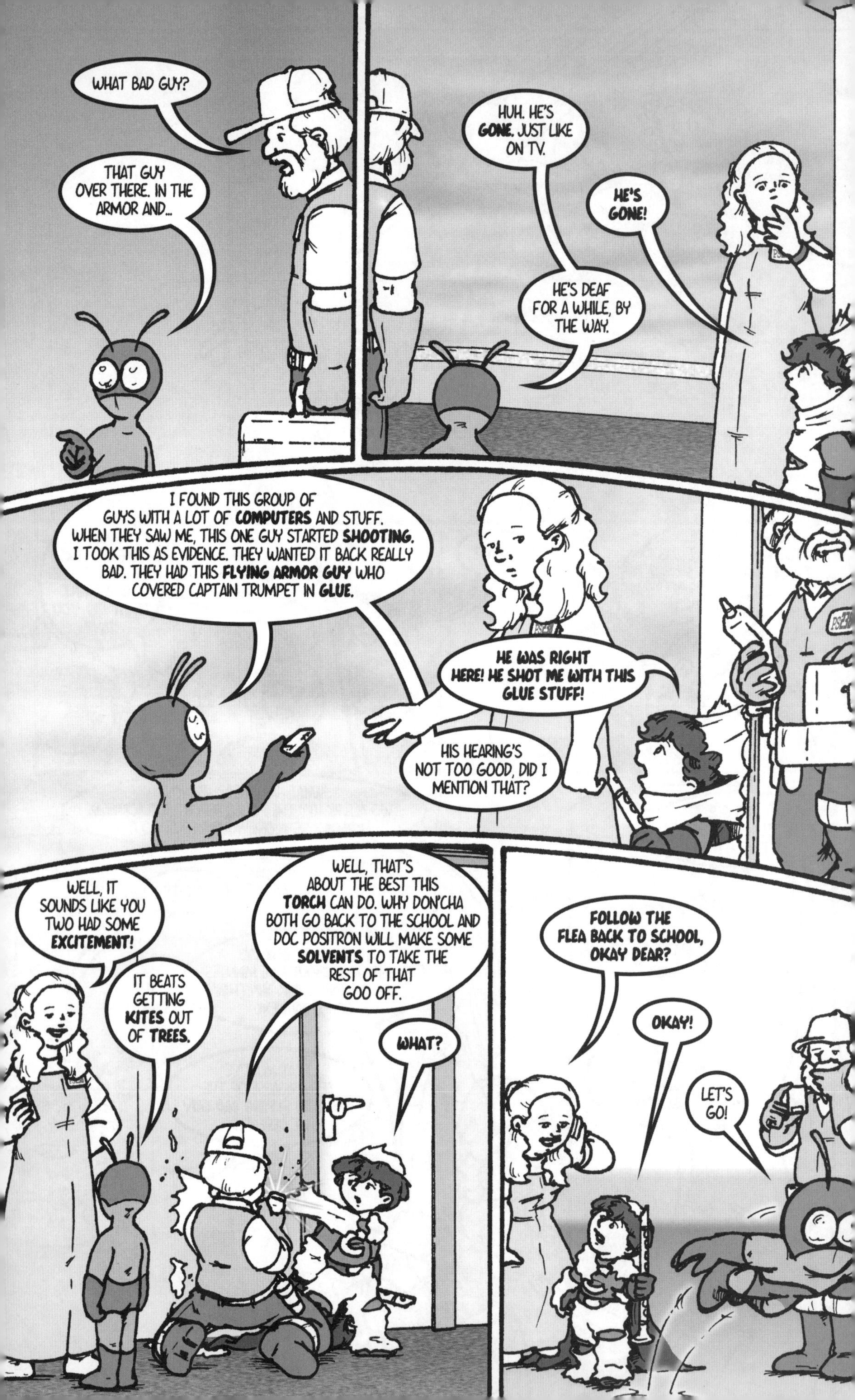
WHAT BAD GUY?
THAT GUY OVER THERE. IN THE ARMOR AND...
HUH. HE'S **GONE**. JUST LIKE ON TV.
HE'S GONE!
HE'S DEAF FOR A WHILE, BY THE WAY.
I FOUND THIS GROUP OF GUYS WITH A LOT OF **COMPUTERS** AND STUFF. WHEN THEY SAW ME, THIS ONE GUY STARTED **SHOOTING**. I TOOK THIS AS EVIDENCE. THEY WANTED IT BACK REALLY BAD. THEY HAD THIS **FLYING ARMOR GUY** WHO COVERED CAPTAIN TRUMPET IN **GLUE**.
HE WAS RIGHT HERE! HE SHOT ME WITH THIS GLUE STUFF!
HIS HEARING'S NOT TOO GOOD, DID I MENTION THAT?
WELL, IT SOUNDS LIKE YOU TWO HAD SOME **EXCITEMENT!**
IT BEATS GETTING **KITES** OUT OF **TREES**.
WELL, THAT'S ABOUT THE BEST THIS **TORCH** CAN DO. WHY DON'CHA BOTH GO BACK TO THE SCHOOL AND DOC POSITRON WILL MAKE SOME **SOLVENTS** TO TAKE THE REST OF THAT GOO OFF.
WHAT?
FOLLOW THE FLEA BACK TO SCHOOL, OKAY DEAR?
OKAY!
LET'S GO!

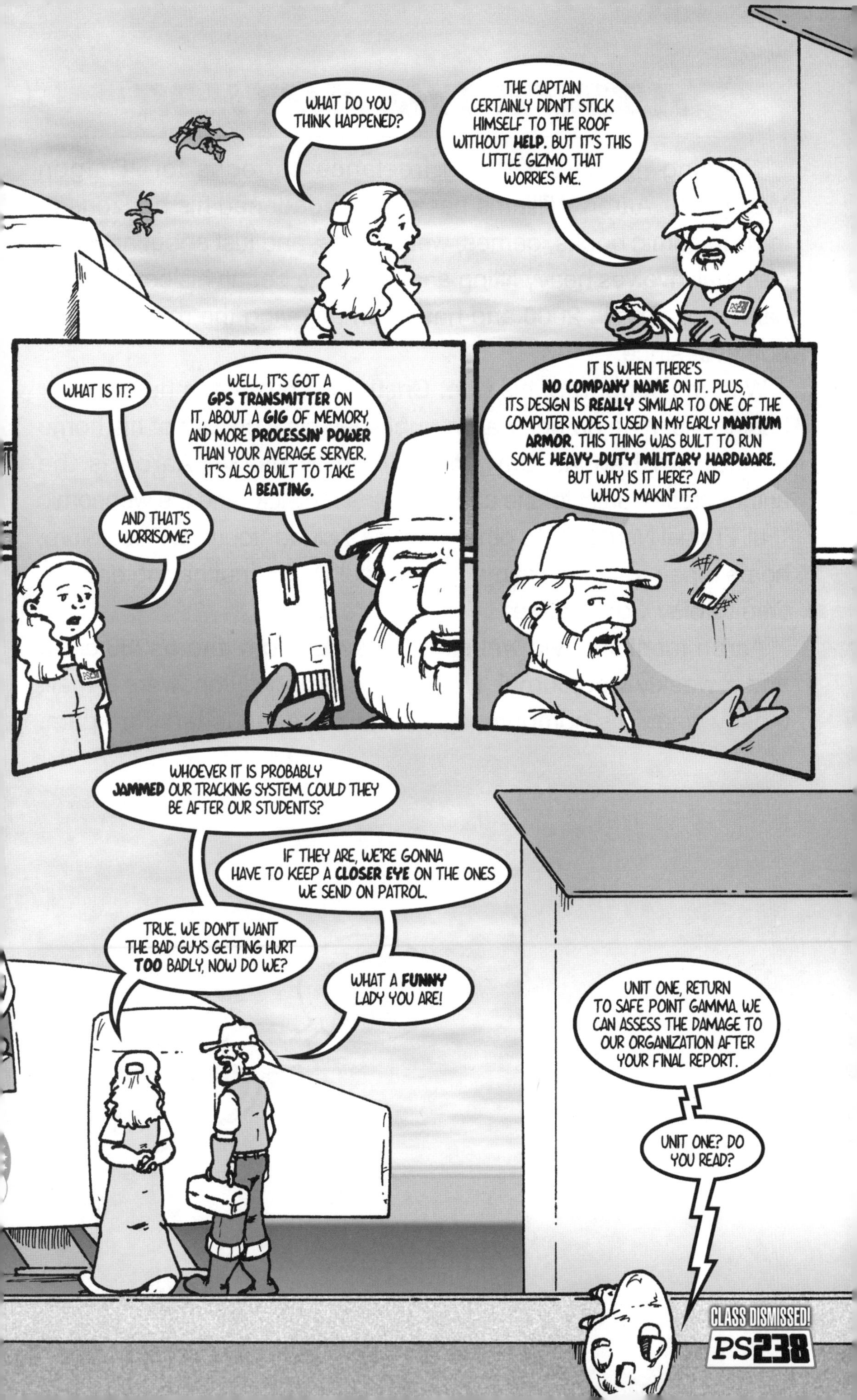
WHAT DO YOU THINK HAPPENED?
THE CAPTAIN CERTAINLY DIDN'T STICK HIMSELF TO THE ROOF WITHOUT HELP. BUT IT'S THIS LITTLE GIZMO THAT WORRIES ME.
WHAT IS IT?
WELL, IT'S GOT A GPS TRANSMITTER ON IT, ABOUT A GIG OF MEMORY, AND MORE PROCESSIN' POWER THAN YOUR AVERAGE SERVER. IT'S ALSO BUILT TO TAKE A BEATING.
AND THAT'S WORRISOME?
IT IS WHEN THERE'S NO COMPANY NAME ON IT. PLUS, ITS DESIGN IS REALLY SIMILAR TO ONE OF THE COMPUTER NODES I USED IN MY EARLY MANTIUM ARMOR. THIS THING WAS BUILT TO RUN SOME HEAVY-DUTY MILITARY HARDWARE. BUT WHY IS IT HERE? AND WHO'S MAKIN' IT?
WHOEVER IT IS PROBABLY JAMMED OUR TRACKING SYSTEM. COULD THEY BE AFTER OUR STUDENTS?
IF THEY ARE, WE'RE GONNA HAVE TO KEEP A CLOSER EYE ON THE ONES WE SEND ON PATROL.
TRUE. WE DON'T WANT THE BAD GUYS GETTING HURT TOO BADLY, NOW DO WE?
WHAT A FUNNY LADY YOU ARE!
UNIT ONE, RETURN TO SAFE POINT GAMMA. WE CAN ASSESS THE DAMAGE TO OUR ORGANIZATION AFTER YOUR FINAL REPORT.
UNIT ONE? DO YOU READ?
CLASS DISMISSED!
PS238

ABOUT THE AUTHOR

Starting his career doing freelance cartoons for "Dragon Magazine," Aaron Williams has since broadened his horizons to include comic books, games, webcomics, and just about anything else that involves heavy lifting and math. He began his comic book career full-time in 2000 and has been enjoying the roller coaster ride ever since.

With the support of his wife, Cristi, who has yet to hurt him for basing Ms. Kyle on her, Aaron publishes his work out of his home in midtown Kansas City. In addition to ps238, Aaron is the author/creator/artist for the comic book "Nodwick" and the webcomic "Full Frontal Nerdity." His other hobbies include "found art" sculpture, home repair (often the same hobby, really), and not having enough time to play video games.

Aaron mantains two websites (nodwick.com and ps238.com) and a weekly webjournal. He even occasionally answers e-mail, mostly when his computer fails to mistake fan letters for spam.

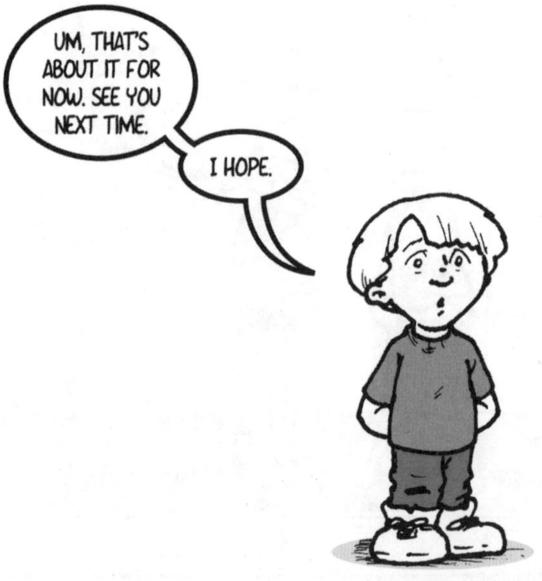
UM, THAT'S ABOUT IT FOR NOW. SEE YOU NEXT TIME.
I HOPE.